LIVERPOOL

Player by Player

LIVERPOOL

Player by Player

Ivan Ponting

Hamlyn

ACKNOWLEDGEMENTS

The author would like to thank the following: Pat, Rosie and Joe Ponting; Bob Bickerton; Andy Cowie, Matthew Impey and all at Colorsport; Steve Small; Steve Hale; Adrian Killen; The Barretts of Crosby; Ian Callaghan; Tommy Smith; Phil Thompson; David Johnson; Alan Kennedy; Roger Hunt; Barry Hugman; Jack Rollin; George Herringshaw; Les Gold; Julian Brown, Adam Ward and Trevor Davies.

The author is also grateful for permission to reproduce photographs. The vast majority are from Colorsport, with sizeable contributions from Steve Hale and Associated Sports Photography/Nigel French/George Herringshaw. There are also pictures from Stewart Kendall, Gary Talbot and LP Sports Service.

First published in Great Britain by
The Crowood Press in 1990

This revised and updated edition published in 1998 by Hamlyn an imprint of Reed Consumer Books Limited, Michelin House, 81 Fulham Road, London SW 3 6RB and Auckland, Melbourne, Singapore and Toronto.

ISBN 0600 54993 9

A CIP catalogue record for this book is available from the British Library

Printed and bound in Spain by Graphycem

INTRODUCTION

There is an essential joy and romance about football which cannot be diluted, even by the greed and the grimness, the creeping commercialism and the crass controversy which haunts the upper levels of the modern game. For instance, what could be more uplifting, in sporting terms, than the vivid emergence of young Michael Owen? To the fan in the stand, when Liverpool's prodigy makes mincemeat of a defence before depositing the ball in the net, nothing matters but the spontaneous beauty of the act, the glory of competition, the euphoria of victory. That's why footballers have always made such splendid heroes, why there is plenty for supporters to enjoy even when their team is not producing the results they would want, and why this particular soccer obsessive has put together *Liverpool Player By Player*.

Roy Evans' current team have their critics and it would be idle to deny there have been mutterings of discontent on Merseyside, where past triumphs have created perennially gigantic expectation. But patience is a virtue which the fans of other clubs, notably Manchester United, have had to acquire and, whatever else, the heroes have continued to flow from the Anfield production line.

Since the first edition of this book was published in 1990, when the Reds were the kings of all they surveyed, they have undergone turbulent changes. Back then they were reigning League Champions, having just captured their 10th crown in 15 years and their 18th overall; more significantly, they were so far ahead of the opposition in the business of gathering trophies that there might have been a case for calling in the Monopolies Commission. At their helm was Kenny Dalglish, one of the most able young managers the British game had ever known, and it seemed the future was unremittingly bright.

Then came the bombshell. Dalglish departed in confusingly dramatic circumstances, the machine spluttered alarmingly during the stormy tenure of Graeme Souness, Kenny's controversial successor, and suddenly a dynasty was under threat. Since then Roy Evans has come to the rescue, first restoring stability and then fuelling hopes of major advances in the second half of the nineties, hopes which have yet to be realised.

Of course, all this activity has thrown up a colourful cavalcade of new performers to add to those covered in the first edition. Thus such names as Fowler and McManaman, Redknapp and the aforementioned Owen, join those of Liddell and Hunt, Keegan and Dalglish and the rest, as I attempt to capture in words the essence of the 160 or so players who have served Anfield's cause since the dawn of the Shankly era in December 1959. Even since the third edition in 1997, fresh faces such as Riedle, Leonhardsen and Ince have appeared and are examined here, while others are looked at again in the light of new information. As a result, this expanded volume amounts to a complete catalogue of modern Reds.

My objective assessments have been put together after countless fascinating hours in the company of Liverpool legends such as Roger Hunt, Ian Callaghan, Tommy Smith, Phil Thompson, Alan Kennedy and David Johnson, and to them I am eternally grateful. Also I have been privileged to draw on the recollections of a lively cross-section of candid Kopites past and present, a vitally important ingredient as the book is intended not merely as a souvenir but as a realistic record, with room for a little sentiment here and there but essentially down-to-earth and honest.

Alongside the profiles, *Liverpool Player By Player* features a photograph of every man to represent the club in the Premiership, Football League, FA Cup, League Cup (in all its guises) and European competition since the above-mentioned starting point. Nobody is excluded, even if he appeared in only a few minutes of a single match, but for the handful of individuals whose contributions were so minor as to render detailed examination inappropriate, only brief statistical resumes of their careers appear alongside their pictures.

In general, I have tried to keep figures to a minimum, though I have included all the basic facts, such as games played (with substitute appearances in brackets), goals scored etc, at the end of each profile. The Liverpool figures refer to all matches (a breakdown for each competition begins on page 214) but under the heading of 'Other Clubs', the games and goals are in the League only. The dates in large type refer to the seasons in which the player appeared in the first team, not when he joined or left the club. Under 'Honours' I have included only those won as a Red, except in the case of international caps, the figures for which cover each man's complete career to date. All records are complete to 16 May 1998. Transfer fees mentioned are those favoured in the press as clubs do not always reveal official figures. Though the meat of the book consists of a roughly chronological look at players from 1959/60 to the present day, I have not ignored the years that went before, going back to the club's 19th-century beginnings and looking at every subsequent era.

Recent campaigns have been anti-climactic, yet Liverpool continue to field some of the most exciting footballers in the world, men with the capacity to restore the club to its former eminence. I hope I have managed to do justice to them in the pages of this book.

Ivan Ponting
Chewton Mendip,
August 1998

CONTENTS

THE EARLY YEARS 1892 - 1915

LEAGUE CHAMPIONS
1905/06

Back row (Left to right):

V CONNELL (trainer),

JOE HEWITT (03/04-09/10, forward, 164 games, 69 goals).

CHARLIE WILSON (97/98-04/05, wing-half, 90 games, 3 goals).

SAM HARDY (05/06-11/12, goalkeeper, 239 games, 0 goals).

MAURICE PARRY (00/01-08/09, right-half, 221 games, 3 goals).

NED DOIG (04/05-07/08, goalkeeper, 53 games, 0 goals).

BILLY DUNLOP (94/95-08/09, left-back, 358 games, 2 goals).

J HARDY (reserve who never played a senior match).

Middle row:

ROBBIE ROBINSON (03/04-11/12, inside-forward, 271 games, 65 goals).

JIMMY GORMAN (05/06-07/08, centre-half, 23 games, 1 goal).

DAVID MURRAY (04/05-05/06, full-back, 15 games, 0 goals).

JOHN HUGHES (03/04, wing-half, 32 games, 2 goals).

ALEX RAISBECK (98/99-08/09, centre half, 340 games, 21 goals).

JACK COX (97/98-08/09, winger, 360 games, 80 goals).

GEORGE FLEMING (01/02-05/06, utility, 83 games, 6 goals).

SAM RAYBOULD (99/00-06/07, centre-forward, 224 games, 127 goals).

ALF WEST (03/04-10/11, right-back, 140 games, 6 goals).

Front row:

ARTHUR GODDARD (01/02-13/14, outside-right, 415 games, 80 goals).

GEORGE LATHOM (02/03-07/08, half-back, 19 games, 0 goals).

JOHN CARLIN (02/03-06/07, inside-forward, 34 games, 8 goals).

ALEX RAISBECK

It's not easy to imagine now, but Liverpool FC did exist before the Shankly revolution. Somewhat bizarrely in view of subsequent rivalry, the club was formed as an offshoot of neighbouring Everton in 1892 and, with an almost exclusively Scottish side, topped the Second Division in 1893/94, their first Football League season.

However, after winning a 'test' match to establish their right to promotion, they could not hold their own in the top flight, being relegated straight away. A gradual advance was being made, though, and another promotion in 1896 – which owed much to the goals of Jimmy Ross – was consolidated, culminating in the Reds' first League Championship in 1900/01.

By then the most prominent performer was centre-half Alex Raisbeck, whose contribution remained remarkably consistent, in stark contrast to Liverpool's continued switchback progress through the early years of the century. There was relegation in 1904, followed immediately by a Second Division title triumph and another League Championship in 1905/06. Thus the Reds became the first club to win back-to-back Second and First Division crowns and but for FA Cup semi-final defeat at the hands of Everton, might have lifted the much-coveted double.

The new star was Sam Hardy, recognised as the finest goalkeeper in the land, who shone for seven seasons at Anfield before departing to win further fame with Aston Villa. In the seasons leading up to the Great War, Liverpool's League fortunes continued to fluctuate, but much more mildly than in earlier days and, apart from an FA Cup Final defeat by Burnley in 1914, there were no more major alarms or excursions before top-class soccer closed down for four years.

SAM HARDY

THE REDS IN 1914/15

(BELOW)

Back row *(left to right):*

TOM FAIRFOUL (13/14-14/15, right-half, 71 games, 0 goals).

HARRY LOVE (11/12-19/20, half-back. 135 games, 2 goals).

SAM SPEAKMAN (12/13-19/20, full-back, 26 games, 1 goal).

KENNY CAMPBELL (11/12-19/20, goalkeeper, 142 games, 0 goals).

BOB PURSELL (11/12-19/20, left-back, 112 games, 0 goals).

DON McKINLAY (09/10-28/29, left-back or left-half, 433 games, 34 goals).

BOB FERGUSON (12/13-14/15, half-back, 103 games, 3 goals).

Front row:

JACKIE SHELDON (13/14-20/21, outside-right, 147 games, 20 goals).

ARTHUR METCALFE (12/13-14/15, inside-forward, 63 games, 26 goals).

R McDOUGALL (13/14-14/15, outside-right, 8 games, 1 goal).

BILLY LACEY (11/12-23/24, utility, 257 games, 29 goals).

JIMMY NICHOL (13/14- 14/15, forward, 59 games, 14 goals).

Other notable players from the preWW1 era

GEORGE ALLAN (95/96-98/99, centre-forward, 97 games, 60 goals).

JIM BRADLEY (05/06-10/11, left-half, 184 games, 8 goals).

ARCHIE GOLDIE (95/96-99/00, full-back, 150 games, 1 goal).

BILL GOLDIE (97/98-02/03, left-half, 174 games, 6 goals).

ANDY McGUIGAN (00/01-01/02, inside-left, 35 games, 14 goals).

JACK PARKINSON (99/00-13/14, forward, 222 games 128 goals).

BILL PERKINS (98/99-02/03, goalkeeper, 116 games, 0 goals).

JACK ROBERTSON (00/01-01/02, right-back, 46 games, 1 goal).

TOM ROBINSON (97/98-01/02, winger, 141 games, 37 goals).

JIMMY ROSS (94/95-96/97, inside right, 85 games, 40 goals).

CHARLIE SATTERTHWAITE (99/00-01/02, inside-left, 46 games, 12 goals).

JOHN WALKER (97/98-01/02, inside-right, 133 games, 31 goals).

BETWEEN THE WARS 1919 - 1939

GORDON HODGSON

Liverpool began life after World War One in enterprising fashion, finishing fourth in the First Division in the two opening peacetime campaigns. That excitement proved a prelude to more concrete achievement, the Championship being secured convincingly in both 1921/22 and 1922/23, each time by six points.

The twin triumphs were built on a parsimonious defence in which long-serving 'keeper Elisha Scott, full-backs Eph Longworth and Don McKinlay and wing-half Tom Bromilow were outstanding, while the attack was served memorably by an almost bizarrely contrasting left-flank partnership. Inside-left Harry Chambers top-scored in both seasons, netting a total of 41 times, while winger Fred Hopkin managed to hit the target only once. Clearly, though, Fred's immaculate service to team-mates was a prime factor in the side's success. Thereafter Liverpool entered a lengthy period of League mediocrity, their final placings during the remainder of the 1920s and the '30s varying from 4th to 19th. Broadly speaking, it could be perceived as a steady decline which was especially irksome to Kopites when Everton, inspired by the prolific Dixie Dean, were ascendant. True, the Reds had a goal-scoring hero of their own in Gordon Hodgson, who held the club record until he was outstripped in the 1960s by Roger Hunt, but even he was overshadowed by Dean.

Between the wars there was no consolation to be found in the FA Cup, though the appointment of George Kay as the club's first full-time manager in 1935 spoke of ambition for the future. However, the fruits of his labour were not to be apparent until after World war Two.

LEAGUE CHAMPIONS 1922/23

Back row *(left to right):*

WALTER WADSWORTH (14/15-25/26, centre-half, 240 games, 8 goals).

V CONNELL (trainer)

JOCK McNAB (19/20-27/28, right-half, 221 games, 6 goals).

ELISHA SCOTT (12/13-33/34, goalkeeper, 467 games, 0 goals).

JIMMY WALSH (23/24-27/28, 76 games, 27 goals).

A DIRECTOR

TOM BROMILOW (19/20-29/30, left-half, 374 games, 11 goals).

Front row:

EPH LONGWORTH (10/11-27/28, full-back, 370 games, 0 goals).

CYRIL GILHESPY (21/22-24/25, outside-right, 19 games, 3 goals).

DICK FORSHAW (19/20-26/27, 287 games, 124 goals).

DON McKINLAY (09/10-28/29, left-back or left-half, 433 games, 34 goals).

HARRY CHAMBERS (19/20-27/28, forward, 338 games, 151 goals).

FRED HOPKIN (21/22-30/31, outside-left, 359 games, 11goals).

Other between-the-wars stars

TOM 'TINY' BRADSHAW 19/20-37/38, centre-half, 291 games, 4 goals).

MATT BUSBY (35/36-39/40, wing-half, 125 games, 3 goals).

ALF HANSON (32/33-37/38, outside-left, 177 games, 52 goals).

GORDON HODGSON (25/26-35/36, inside-forward, 378 games, 240 goals).

JIMMY 'PARSON' JACKSON (25/26-32/33), defender, 224 games, 2 goals).

DICK JOHNSON (19/20-24/25, centre-forward, 83 games, 30 goals).

TOMMY LUCAS (19/20-32/33, full-back, 366 games, 3 goals).

JIMMY McDOUGALL (28/29-37/38, left-half or inside-left, 357 games, 12 goals).

TOM MORRISON (27/28-34/35, right-half, 254 games,4 goals).

BERRY NIEUWENHUYS (33/34-46/47, outside-right, 260 games, 79 goals).

ARTHUR RILEY (25/26-36/37, goalkeeper, 338 games, 0 goals).

DANNY SHONE (21/22-25/26, forward, 81 games, 26 goals).

ELISHA SCOTT

JIMMY McDOUGALL

ALF HANSON

MATT BUSBY

BEFORE THE REVOLUTION

ALBERT STUBBINS

Once again, Liverpool FC emerged from years of earth-shaking conflict in fine fettle. Indeed, the first post-war season saw the Reds pip Manchester United - led by distinguished Anfield old-boy Matt Busby - for the League Championship, and in 1950 they reached Wembley, where they were beaten by Arsenal in the FA Cup Final.

That side boasted outstanding individuals such as Billy Liddell, Albert Stubbins and Jack Balmer and was a credit to manager George Kay, who was to retire through ill health in 1951.

He was replaced by Don Welsh, who introduced new blood to the side, but it was not enough to stop a gradual slide which culminated in relegation in 1953/54. Despite narrowly missing out on promotion in 1955/56 Don was dismissed and the job of putting Liverpool back among the elite was handed to the club's former skipper, Phil Taylor. He held the reins for three Second Division campaigns, finishing third, fourth and fourth again before bowing to the strain and stepping down in November 1959. Then came Shankly - and life at Anfield was never the same again.

Pictured on these two pages are the leading players in the years of mixed fortunes between 1946 and 1959. Turn over to begin meeting the men who, over subsequent decades, took part in the most remarkable success story in the history of English soccer.

FA CUP FINALISTS 1949-50

Back row *(left to right)*:

GEORGE KAY (manager)

PHIL TAYLOR (35/6-53/4, wing-half, 345 games, 34 goals).

RAY LAMBERT (45/6-55/6. full-back, 341 games, 2 goals).

CYRIL SIDLOW (46/7-50/1, goalkeeper, 165 games, 0 goals).

BOB PAISLEY (45/6-53/4, wing-half, 278 games, 13 goals).

EDDIE SPICER (45/6-53/4, full-back/wing-half, 168 games, 2 goals).

ALBERT SHELLEY (trainer)

Front row:

JIMMY PAYNE (48/9-55/6, winger, 245 games, 42 goals).

KEVIN BARON (45/6-53/4, inside-forward, 152 games, 33 goals).

CYRIL DONE (39/40-51/2, centre-forward, 109 games, 37 goals).

WILLIE FAGAN (37/8-51/2, forward, 185 games, 57 goals).

BILLY LIDDELL (45/6-60/1, forward, 537 games, 229 goals).

LAURIE HUGHES (45/6-57/8, centre-half, 326 games, 1 goal).

Top row *(left to right)*:

BILL JONES (46/7-53/4, utility player, 278 games, 17 goals).

JOHN EVANS (53/4-56/7, inside-forward, 106 games, 53 goals).

ROY SAUNDERS (52/3-58/9, wing-half, 144 games, 1 goal).

Centre row *(left to right)*:

GEOFF TWENTYMAN (53/4-59/60, left-half, 184 games, 19 goals).

BRIAN JACKSON (51/2-57/8, winger, 131 games, 12 goals).

BARRY WILKINSON (53/4-59/60, wing-half, 79 games, 0 goals).

Bottom row *(left to right)*:

TOMMY YOUNGER (56/7-58/9, goalkeeper, 127 games, 0 goals).

LOUIS BIMPSON (52/3-59/60, centre-forward, 100 games, 40 goals).

DOUG RUDHAM (54/5-59/60, goalkeeper, 66 games, 0 goals).

Left:
JACK BALMER (35/6-51/2, inside-forward, 313 games, 111 goals).

Far left:
ALBERT STUBBINS (46/7-52/3, centre-forward, 180 games, 83 goals).

DON WELSH

PHIL TAYLOR

JACK BALMER

BILLY LIDDELL

It is scarcely possible to exaggerate the stature of Billy Liddell in the history of Liverpool FC. As a footballer he thrilled the Anfield faithful; as a man he warmed their hearts; as a symbol of all that was fine in the field of sporting endeavour he was unmatchable.

For nearly 15 years the self-effacing Scottish winger cum centre-forward was the outstanding player for a club which experienced fleeting moments of glory but which, in general, was a frustrated hotbed of unfulfilled potential. Had he been born two, three or four decades later and played under Shankly or Paisley, Fagan or Dalglish, he would have been knee-deep in honours. As it was he had to be content with a solitary League Championship medal and the knowledge that not for nothing was the team he graced known as Liddellpool.

Billy signed on at Anfield as a promising flankman in 1939 and then saw the first six years of his career lost to the war. During the conflict he served as an RAF navigator but his soccer talents were not entirely redundant. He played almost 150 times for his new club in emergency competitions and served notice that here was something special.

In January 1946, with life gradually returning to something approaching normality, he made his official Liverpool debut five days short of his 24th birthday, scoring at Chester in the FA Cup. But it was in the following campaign that Billy Liddell really set sail on the course that was to earn him sporting immortality on Merseyside.

Playing 35 games as the Reds took the title, he revealed the pace and power which were to become his hallmarks. Billy was particularly dangerous running at defenders and cutting inside from the left wing, and although he found the net only seven times that season he effectively demonstrated the dashing style which was to make him one of Liverpool's most prolific goal-scorers.

As he grew in experience his influence on the team burgeoned. He was muscular and skilful, blessed with a sprinter's speed and a fearsome shot, good in the air and unfailingly courageous. He took the eye whether lining up on the left, the right or in the centre, a veritable one-man forward line. Sadly the side did not progress at the same rate and Billy - by now a Scotland regular whose international standing and durability were recognised by selection for Great Britain against the Rest of Europe in 1947 and 1955 - was in the unfortunate position of being a star in a team which plunged first to mid-table mediocrity and ultimately, in 1953/54, to relegation.

He reacted with characteristic determination and in his first four seasons in the lower grade notched 101 goals in 156 League matches - he was the Reds' leading scorer in eight out of nine seasons in the fifties - but it was not enough to secure promotion.

As his pace waned with age, he lost that stirring ability to run past defenders but compensated with a more mature passing game from a deep-lying position. The devotion of the supporters never wavered and when he returned at the age of 37 after one of several spells on the sidelines he scored two spectacular goals against Bristol City in August 1959. The acclaim was rapturous, and deservedly so.

But there was more to Billy than his athletic attributes. A chivalrous, loyal man who was not too proud to stud the boots for his team-mates when left out of the side in 1959, he was always ready to help youngsters and went on to become a youth worker, lay preacher and JP. If ever a footballer deserved to be called a hero, then it was Billy Liddell. He will be forever revered on Merseyside and beyond.

BORN: Dunfermline, 10.1.22. GAMES: 537. GOALS: 229.
HONOURS: League Championship 46/7. 28 Scotland caps (47-56).

1945/46 – 1960/61

For four seasons, as Liverpool knocked in vain on the door of the First Division, Dick White was the calm and valiant kingpin of a generally resolute defence.

The first link in the Reds' illustrious Scunthorpe connection, which was to lead the likes of Ray Clemence and Kevin Keegan to Anfield, Dick was a part-timer at the Old Showground when he was signed by 'Pool boss Don Welsh in November 1955 as a prospective long-term replacement for stalwart stopper Laurie Hughes.

The veteran responded with spirit to the challenge of youth and Dick was allowed only sporadic opportunities during his initial 18 months on Merseyside. He made the most of his time, though, helping his new club take the Central League title in his first full season, and when Laurie bowed finally to the inevitable, Dick appropriated the number-five shirt with relish, missing only two League matches between 1957/58 and 1960/61. He built a reputation as a dependable, unspectacular centre-half who was willing to assume responsibility and carry it well. As befitted a six-footer, he excelled in aerial combat but, as with so many of his ilk, distribution was not his strong point.

Dick rarely suffered a chasing but when pressurised - Tom Johnston of an excellent, underrated Leyton Orient side and Graham Moore of Cardiff City were two opponents of the late fifties who had the ability to stretch him - he stuck to his task with admirable tenacity.

Attack was never his forte and he scored only one goal in more than 200 Liverpool appearances, though he is remembered for one surging sortie which took him past three Orient defenders to lay on an injury-time winner for Roger Hunt in the FA Cup at Anfield in January 1960.

Dick's tenure in central defence ended, as did a spell as captain, with the advent of Ron Yeats in 1961/62, but he was both adaptable and quick enough to switch to right-back to win a Second Division title medal - two own-goals at Middlesbrough in the Reds' first defeat of the campaign provided a minor hiccup - before seeing out his career with Doncaster.

BORN: Scunthorpe, 18.8.31. GAMES: 216.
GOALS: 1. HONOURS: Second Division
Championship 61/2.

OTHER CLUBS: Scunthorpe United
50/1-55/6 (133, 11);

Doncaster Rovers 62/3-63/4 (82, 0).

DICK WHITE

1955/56 – 1961/62

JOHNNY WHEELER

1956/57 – 1961/62

The twin peaks of Johnny Wheeler's career were both behind him when he arrived at Anfield as one of the first signings of new Liverpool boss Phil Taylor in September 1956. Three years earlier the cultured right-half had played for Bolton Wanderers in the celebrated 'Matthews Final' at Wembley and in 1954 he had won his solitary England cap. But although Johnny's prime had gone he still had plenty to offer an Anfield outfit locked in perennial struggle to escape from the Second Division, and on joining his home-town club he gave immediate value for money.

Johnny, an adaptable performer who spent much of his first term with Liverpool as an inside-right playing behind his fellow forwards, was a graceful prompter, precise of pass, firm of tackle and never short of attacking ideas. He was not a heavy scorer but sometimes surprised goalkeepers with snap shots, one of his most memorable being a 20-yard drive past Harry Gregg in an FA Cup defeat by Manchester United in 1960. Port Vale, though, have best reason to remember his striking powers. With nine minutes remaining of a Second Division encounter at Anfield in November 1956 the score was 1-1. Enter Johnny with a hat-trick in five minutes to transform the game.

On the debit side, there were times when quickness of thought was not matched by fleetness of foot. If possession was lost, Johnny's recovery was not always rapid, which resulted in pressure on the defence, but more often his experience made him a joy to play alongside. He spent only one season, 1958/59, as captain – before the job passed to his cousin, Ronnie Moran – but he continued to exert a major influence, using his vast experience to nurse youngsters through their early matches.

In autumn 1959, aged 31, he was sidelined by injury and then suffered a spell of indifferent form. The end appeared to be nigh but he fought back with some fine displays under new boss Bill Shankly, eventually giving way to youth in the form of Gordon Milne. Johnny, a kind and humorous character who went on to be trainer and assistant manager of Bury, won no medals at Anfield but can look back on a job well done.

BORN: Liverpool, 26.7.28. GAMES: 177. GOALS: 23.

HONOURS: 1 England cap (54).

OTHER CLUBS: Tranmere Rovers 48/9-50/1 (101, 9); Bolton Wanderers 50/1-55/6 (189, 18).

ALAN ARNELL

1953/54 – 1960/61

The scoring rate of Alan Arnell would be enough to have many modern managers reaching feverishly for their chequebooks. But the big, rangy centre-forward, who averaged a fraction short of a goal every two games for Liverpool during the middle and late fifties, never established himself as a regular in the side.

Alan – who was blooded by the Reds as an amateur, perhaps a sign of desperation in the quest for talent to lift the club back into the top flight – had all the attributes expected of a typical front-line bustler of his era. He was strong, energetic and good in the air; his touch on the ball, while not delicate, was respectable and his distribution was adequate. During his most prolific campaigns, 1955/56 and 1956/57, he scored 23 times in 37 League outings yet failed to convince successive managers, Don Welsh and Phil Taylor, that Billy Liddell would be better employed on the wing than leading the line.

Some contemporary observers reckon Alan was short of aggression and lacked the necessary drive to elbow aside even the challenge of fellow striker Louis Bimpson – who had a similarly unsatisfying Anfield career despite contributing plenty of goals – let alone those of the altogether more accomplished Dave Hickson and Roger Hunt at the end of the decade.

Nevertheless Alan Arnell had his triumphs, notably a brave hat-trick after pulling a muscle early in the game at Huddersfield in 1956, before going on to maintain his strike-rate in the lower divisions.

BORN: Chichester, 25.11.33. GAMES: 75. GOALS: 35.

OTHER CLUBS: Tranmere Rovers 60/1–62/3 (68, 33); Halifax Town 63/4 (14, 6).

FRED MORRIS

Fred Morris was a tall, dashing right-winger whose neck-or-nothing style was beloved of supporters; he was a clean striker of the ball who scored some rousing goals; and he was a joker, his face usually split in a wide grin.

In short, Fred was a soccer character. Unfortunately, despite several stirring displays – a two-goal show against Leyton Orient at Anfield in November 1959 comes to mind – he didn't have enough class to make the grade with Liverpool.

Fred was signed from Mansfield Town by Phil Taylor in March 1958 for £7,000. He was then 28 and had perhaps spent too long in the lower reaches of the League to make a successful transition.

After missing the first two games of the following season he played 40 without a break, netting a dozen times in the process, a creditable achievement. He was injured early in 1959/60 and had just reclaimed his place when Bill Shankly moved in at Anfield. Fred played in the next match – a 4–0 drubbing by Cardiff City – and was never selected again.

BORN: Oswestry, 15.6.29. GAMES: 48. GOALS: 14.

OTHER CLUBS: Walsall 50/1–56/7 (210, 43);
Mansfield Town 56/7–57/8 (57, 17); Crewe Alexandra 60/1 (8, 1);
Gillingham 60/1 (10, 1); Chester 61/2 (29, 3).

1958/59 – 1959/60

BOBBY CAMPBELL

The end of season 1959/60 came too soon for Bobby Campbell. The constructive wing-half was enjoying his most effective run in the Liverpool side and although the arrival of Tommy Leishman and Gordon Milne made his future challenging, to say the least, there were some grounds for optimism.

As the Reds completed their League programme with a 3-0 home victory over Sunderland, Bobby was in his element. His neat, creative skills were beginning to mesh impressively with fellow providers Jimmy Melia and Johnny Wheeler and his tackling, never his strongest feature, was taking on a promising crispness. Sadly, his impetus was shattered by the summer recess and never regained. He made only one more senior appearance for Liverpool before joining Portsmouth.

The major flaws in Bobby's game were a marked lack of pace and, because he was at his best going forward, a tendency to be lured out of position. This was never better illustrated than against Cardiff City in December 1959 when, offered the chance to create a favourable early impression on new boss Bill Shankly, he was given the runaround by Derek Tapscott. Bobby went on to become a coach and manager with some success.

BORN: Liverpool, 23.4.37. GAMES: 14. GOALS: 1.

OTHER CLUBS: Portsmouth 61/2–65/6 (61, 2);
Aldershot: 66/7 (5, 0). MANAGER: Fulham 76-80, Portsmouth 82-84, Chelsea 88-91.

1959/60 – 1960/61

JOHN MOLYNEUX

John Molyneux might have been the prototype for the popular image of a fifties full-back. Tall and solidly constructed, he was far removed from the modern breed of overlapping defender, but when it came to doing his primary job - keeping out the opposition - there could be few complaints about his work during his seven years at Anfield.

Indeed, for six of those campaigns John was a first-team regular, performing with credit for three managers. Initially he served Don Welsh for nearly two seasons after arriving from Chester for £4,500, and then saw out the three-and-a-half year reign of Phil Taylor. But perhaps the greatest measure of his ability is that Bill Shankly was content for him to retain the right-back berth for 18 months as the decade closed.

John's primary attributes were his strength in the tackle and an instinct for danger which made goal-line clearances a much-appreciated speciality. His distribution was efficient and he formed a useful understanding with right-half Johnny Wheeler but he could be exposed for lack of pace, a defect he tended to disguise by a cautious approach. Fleet-footed wingmen such as Peter McParland of Aston Villa and Middlesbrough's Edwin Holliday sometimes posed problems, but on his day John could subdue the majority of Second Division speed merchants.

Getting forward was not one of his major concerns but he did allow himself the occasional flourish, one notable foray coming in an epic 4-4 draw at Villa Park in March 1960 when he scored one of his rare goals after combining, typically, with Wheeler.

John, a dedicated all-round sportsman, ultimately lost his place when Dick White moved to right-back in the Shankly reshuffle of 1961/62. He then returned to Chester for a second substantial spell.

BORN: Warrington, 3.2.31. GAMES: 249. GOALS: 3.

OTHER CLUBS: Chester 49/50-54/5 (178, 1) and 62/3-64/5 (67, 0).

1955/56 – 1961/62

JIMMY HARROWER

1957/58 – 1960/61

Jimmy Harrower was blessed with a treasure trove of natural ability; sadly, the Anfield career of the stocky Scottish inside-forward failed to do justice to his extravagant gifts.

When Phil Taylor persuaded Hibernian to part with the ball-playing under-23 international for £11,000 in January 1958, the Liverpool manager was optimistic that he had secured a man capable of scheming the Reds' return to the First Division. There were few apparent defects to Jimmy's game. His ball control was magnetic, his passing majestic; he possessed a savage, if sometimes wayward shot and he was strong with a low centre of gravity which made knocking him off the ball seem like removing a limpet from a rock.

The one superficial flaw was a lack of pace, for which it was reasonably reckoned his other talents would compensate. Several early displays confirmed his potential and one exhibition against Stoke in April 1958 had the Kop drooling as he stroked the ball around, giving full expression to his repertoire of delicate chips, lobs and dummies.

Unfortunately he could not attain consistency and often drifted through games making scant contribution, perhaps not benefiting from the presence of another play-maker, Jimmy Melia. The two frequently made pretty patterns together as they interchanged passes but this joint artistry frequently led nowhere in terms of team advantage.

An abrasive aspect to the Harrower game also surfaced. This sometimes provoked altercations, such as the petty series of clashes with Bristol City's Tom Casey which led to a booking in August 1959. More unwelcome was a certain cockiness which was entertaining when it took the form of saucy flicks and daring through-balls but unsavoury when it descended, on occasion, into petulance and the taunting of less skilful opponents.

As first Phil Taylor and then Bill Shankly explored every option in the push for promotion, Jimmy was tried on the wing and as a deep-lying centre-forward, a role in which he shone briefly. Eventually Shankly opted to look elsewhere for inspiration and sold his fellow Scot to Newcastle for £15,000. An unfulfilling Anfield sojourn was at an end.

BORN: Alva, Clackmannanshire, 18.8.35.
GAMES: 105. GOALS: 22.

OTHER CLUBS: Hibernian 55/6-57/8 (36, 12); Newcastle United 60/1-61/2 (5, 0); Falkirk 61/2-62/3; St Johnstone 63/4-64/5; Albion Rovers 64/5.

DAVE HICKSON

There have been some sensational Merseyside transfer tales in recent decades – those involving Alan Ball, Kevin Keegan and Ian Rush spring to mind – but none created a greater furore than the sale of Everton idol Dave Hickson to Liverpool in November 1959. When Dave crossed Stanley Park, which separates the two grounds, feelings ran so high that some Everton fans swore they would follow him and defect to the old enemy, while a contingent from the Kop pledged to make the opposite journey in protest at the £10,500 deal.

Dave – Phil Taylor's last signing before handing over to Bill Shankly – was a fiery, buccaneering centre-forward, a man obsessed with scoring goals, whose distinctive blond thatch had stood out like a beacon in the Blues' attack during two successful spells. The stage was thus set for a bold entrance and Dave obliged with a show that was pure theatre. He bagged both goals – one a glorious diving header – in a 2–1 win over Division Two pace-setters Aston Villa and exuded such charisma that the Anfield crowd cheered his every touch. Having transformed Liverpool's lacklustre season into one seething with possibilities, he consolidated with a run of dashing displays which yielded 21 goals in 27 games.

Big Dave had been coached by the legendary Dixie Dean, as his aerial work bore witness, but he actually boasted a respectable all-round game. One of his most lasting contributions to the Reds' cause was his part in the development of Roger Hunt, whom he gladly relieved of some of the scoring responsibility, and Roger still recalls him as one of the most effective partners he ever had. Dave continued to score freely in his second Anfield campaign, before the arrival of Ian St John made him surplus to requirements and he took his talents to fresh fields.

During his travels he was dubbed soccer's stormy petrel, a reference to assorted clashes with referees, but his only major offence in a Liverpool shirt was a sending-off for retaliation – he was a constant victim of provocation – against Sheffield United, after which he was cleared of deliberate violent conduct. A quiet man off the pitch, Dave Hickson deserves to be remembered as a footballer, not a fighter.

BORN: Ellesmere Port, 30.10.29. GAMES: 67. GOALS: 38.

OTHER CLUBS: Everton 51/2–55/6 (139, 63) and 57/8–59/60 (86, 32); Aston Villa 55/6 (12, 1); Huddersfield Town 55/6–56/7 (54, 28); Cambridge City; Bury 61/2 (8, 0); Tranmere Rovers 62/3–63/4 (45, 21).

1959/60 – 1960/61

ALAN A'COURT

In full flight, left-winger Alan A'Court was a stirring sight. When he hared for the byline and crossed the ball at full stretch, he was one of the most difficult customers to confront Second Division full-backs in the late fifties.

He wore a number-nine shirt for his Liverpool debut at Middlesbrough in February 1953 but his speed, directness and capacity to provide accurate centres marked him out as a natural wingman. Accordingly, with Billy Liddell usually occupying Alan's favoured left flank, the youngster drifted in and out of the side during his first two seasons in serious contention for a place, getting a chance only when the Scottish international switched wings or was selected at centre-forward.

Alan established himself during the Reds' first season following relegation to the Second Division and was a linchpin in the struggle for promotion which was to last for eight campaigns. He remained a regular for half of Liverpool's initial term back among the elite in 1962/63 before giving way temporarily to Kevin Lewis. His first-team ambitions were finally extinguished when the richly promising Peter Thompson was signed in August 1963. Alan could be expected to scrap for a place with Kevin but, at such a late stage in his career, there could be no contest with the brilliant Peter.

Never a heavy scorer, Alan nevertheless packed a strong shot and had a knack of finding the net when it mattered. Liverpool were on the threshold of promotion in March 1962 when they found themselves two down with ten minutes to go in the vital confrontation with fellow high-fliers Leyton Orient at Brisbane Road. In stepped the faithful A'Court with a brace of point-saving goals, neither as spectacular as his memorable strike against Chelsea in the FA Cup earlier that year, but of crucial importance.

By then Alan was perhaps beginning to go past his peak and it was easy to forget there had been a time when his left-flank fire, control and consistency had looked likely to win him a place in the game's higher echelons. He played five times for England, including three appearances in the 1958 World Cup Finals in Sweden, before becoming one of several players who lost out to the emerging Bobby Charlton - Bolton's Doug Holden and Edwin Holliday of Middlesbrough suffered a similar fate.

But failure to become an international star should not detract from Alan's achievements at Anfield before he left to see out his playing days at Tranmere and coach at Norwich, Chester, Crewe, Stoke and in Zambia. The teenager who caused a stir in his rugby-loving family by choosing soccer as his livelihood gave distinguished and loyal service to Liverpool. His deeds on the field spoke for themselves but he was also an inestimable asset to the club behind the scenes, keeping morale bubbling with his infectious humour and encouraging young players such as Ian Callaghan. Football would be the richer for more men like Alan A'Court.

BORN: Rainhill, Lancashire, 30.9.34. GAMES: 382. GOALS: 63.
HONOURS: Second Division Championship 61/2. 5 England caps (57-58).
OTHER CLUBS: Tranmere Rovers 64/5-65/6 (50, 11).

1952/53 – 1964/65

BERT SLATER

Bert Slater was fearless, agile and short. Unfortunately it was the last-mentioned characteristic which seemed to be constantly in the spotlight during his early days as Liverpool's number-one goalkeeper.

The modest, 5ft 8½in Scot arrived at Anfield as part of the transaction which took his predecessor, Tommy Younger, to Falkirk in the summer of 1959, and he made a chequered start with his new club. After performing heroics at Cardiff on his debut, Bert blundered once against Bristol City and then twice against Hull. He was replaced by Doug Rudham and returned to the side only when the South African was injured.

After several more alarming incidents, for which his lack of inches was usually blamed, Bert improved and eventually hit brilliant form. During the following term he was an ever-present and conceded only 27 goals in the first 29 games of the 1961/62 promotion campaign before surprisingly being axed - to the consternation of some team-mates - in favour of Jim Furnell. Throughout that fine run he displayed exceptional handling on the ground and missed little in the air, benefiting enormously from an instant understanding with the dominant new centre-half Ron Yeats.

There was clearly no future for Bert at Anfield and he returned to Scotland to prove his class in Dundee's progress to the 1963 European Cup semi-finals. In 1965 he headed south again to join Watford and defied Liverpool in an epic FA Cup draw two years later. When he moved into coaching he could look back on an accomplished career.

BORN: Musselburgh, Midlothian, 5.5.36.
GAMES: 111. GOALS: 0.

HONOURS: Second Division Championship 61/2.

OTHER CLUBS: Falkirk 53/4-58/9; Dundee 62/3-64/5; Watford 65/6-68/9 (134, 0).

1959/60 – 1961/62

TOMMY LEISHMAN

1959/60 – 1962/63

Long-striding, fierce-tackling Scot Tommy Leishman presented a menacing prospect when he arrived at Anfield in November 1959, just two weeks ahead of Bill Shankly. Gangly and gaunt, his dark features accentuated by a severe crew-cut, Tommy would have been a natural to play a trainee undertaker, if only he had been an actor! Instead he was destined for a relatively short, but effective tenure as Liverpool's left-half.

Tommy was signed from St Mirren, with whom he had won a Scottish Cup medal earlier that year, as a £9,000 replacement for Geoff Twentyman, whose role had not been satisfactorily filled since he had joined Ballymena United in the twilight of his career. A part-timer with the Saints, Tommy benefited from Shankly's more rigorous training methods and soon impressed with a promising display against Charlton at Anfield.

He was quick off the mark, good in the air and always eager for the ball, though his distribution lacked the imagination and precision that were the hallmarks of his eventual successor, Willie Stevenson. Nevertheless Tommy, a very left-sided performer, was a regular choice for two and a half seasons, including the 1961/62 promotion campaign in which his drive and enthusiasm were important assets.

He played 11 games on Liverpool's return to the top grade but lacked the class essential for a tilt at the Championship. When Shankly turned to Stevenson, Tommy returned north of the border to play well for Hibernian before becoming player-manager of Irish club Linfield.

BORN: Stenhousemuir, 3.9.37. GAMES: 119. GOALS: 7.

HONOURS: Second Division Championship 61/2.

OTHER CLUBS: St Mirren 57/8-59/60; Hibernian 62/3-64/5; Linfield, Northern Ireland, 65/6-67/8.

MANAGER: Linfield (65-68).

KEVIN LEWIS

1960/61 – 1962/63

The Anfield career of Kevin Lewis was a perplexing affair. Playing almost exclusively as a winger, he averaged better than a goal every two games and yet failed to find a niche as Bill Shankly built his great side of the mid-sixties. The lanky flankman was recruited from Sheffield United in 1960 when Billy Liddell was on the verge of retirement and Ian Callaghan was adjudged too inexperienced. Kevin immediately began justifying his £13,000 fee, netting on his debut at home to Leeds and going on to notch 19 goals in 32 games. He thus became top scorer in his first term at Anfield – no mean feat with the likes of Hunt and Hickson in the side.

During the promotion campaign that followed, sharpshooter Kevin remained prolific. He scored in half his 20 games but was displaced by Callaghan and wasn't offered another run until midway through 1962/63 in Division One. Among the elite, he netted regularly and often spectacularly, only to be rewarded by Peter Thompson's arrival. Not surprisingly, he departed – to Huddersfield – perhaps wondering what was needed to cement a Liverpool place.

A versatile performer – he scored two when standing in at centre-forward for the suspended Ian St John when the Reds clinched promotion against Southampton – he was quick, skilful and good in the air but was at times easily brushed off the ball and inclined to be unpredictable.

Despite an outwardly casual manner, Kevin was nervous before games and may not have been temperamentally suited to the big time. He was lost to the British game when, still only 25, he emigrated to South Africa.

BORN: Ellesmere Port, 19.9.40. GAMES: 81. GOALS: 44. HONOURS: Second Division Championship 61/2.

OTHER CLUBS: Sheffield United 57/8–59/60 (62, 23); Huddersfield Town 63/4–64/5 (45, 13); Port Elizabeth, South Africa.

JOHNNY MORRISSEY

Life was not easy for an aspiring young winger at Anfield as the fifties drew towards a close. If he somehow managed to sidestep the great Billy Liddell and long-established Alan A'Court, there were still the likes of Ian Callaghan, Kevin Lewis and Fred Morris to contend with.

Even so, the denizens of the Kop reckoned they saw something special when little Johnny Morrissey broke through to the fringe of the team. He showed hardness unusual in a wingman, allied his pluck with cunning, carried a ferocious shot and was blessed with all-round, natural talent. To confirm his place in their hearts, he hailed from the tough Scotland Road area of the city; in short, he was one of their own.'

Limited chances during an unexpectedly brief Liverpool career allowed him to display his abilities to only intermittent effect but he was clearly a player of potential and it shocked supporters when he moved – to Everton, of all clubs – for £10,000 in August 1962.

There were rumours of strife over the deal between the board and Bill Shankly, who was said to be keen to keep Johnny. Feelings among the fans ran higher still as he helped the Blues win the League Championship in his first season at Goodison Park before going on to give ten years' distinguished service to Harry Catterick's team.

BORN: Liverpool, 18.4.40. GAMES: 37. GOALS: 6.

OTHER CLUBS: Everton 62/3–71/2 (259, 43); Oldham Athletic 72/3 (6, 1).

1957/58 – 1960/61

JIM FURNELL

Liverpool rescued Jim Furnell from the nether regions of professional football – where he had performed creditably but hitherto anonymously for Burnley's reserve teams for more than half a decade – and plunged him straight into the hunt for promotion in February 1962.

The popular Bert Slater had been controversially dropped and Jim, who had been limited to two League outings with the Turf Moor club by the consistency of Adam Blacklaw, came in for the final 13 games of the campaign. He let no one down and the Reds duly made it to the First Division, where Bill Shankly initially kept faith with his £18,000 acquisition.

Though he rarely inspired the confidence of his defenders in the way his predecessor had, Jim held on to his place in the top flight until he broke his finger 13 games into the season, an injury which effectively signalled the end of his Anfield career. He was replaced by Tommy Lawrence, who proved to be an infinitely superior performer, and moved to Arsenal a year later. Jim enjoyed a creditable mid-sixties spell with the Gunners before going on to do well with Rotherham United and, particularly, Plymouth Argyle, for whom he played until he was 39.

BORN: Clitheroe, Lancashire, 23.11.37. GAMES: 28. GOALS: 0. HONOURS: Second Division Championship 61/2.

OTHER CLUBS: Burnley 59/60–60/1 (2, 0); Arsenal 63/4–67/8 (141, 0); Rotherham United 68/9–69/70 (76, 0); Plymouth Argyle 70/1–75/6 (183, 0).

1961/62 – 1963/64

JIMMY MELIA

Everything had gone Jimmy Melia's way in 1963, a year in which the creative inside-forward's subtle promptings had helped lift Liverpool into a Championship-challenging position by late December. He was the ideas man of a side well on the way to becoming one of Britain's best and, though just turned 26, had already played nearly 300 times for the Reds. Recently his advance had been recognised with two England caps and, with such a blend of quality and experience, Jimmy seemed to be hovering on the very edge of greatness.

The soccer fates, however, are nothing if not unpredictable. A minor ankle injury sidelined the prematurely balding schemer shortly before Christmas and Bill Shankly was forced to make a radical change to his line-up. There was no obvious replacement for Jimmy so the manager improvised, moving Ian St John into a deep-lying position to take some of the midfield responsibility and introducing Alf Arrowsmith to partner Roger Hunt up front. Ian and Alf revelled in their new roles and though Jimmy made a brief and unconvincing reappearance when he regained fitness, his Anfield days were done.

But this rather abrupt exit should not obscure the earlier achievements of a player of enviable natural skills, who had celebrated his debut with a goal against Nottingham Forest in December 1955 and in the following seasons established himself in a side perpetually pushing for promotion. The 1958/59 term, in which he netted 21 times, was a personally productive one, but his most impressive form was reserved for 1961/62 when, finally, the Reds left Division Two behind them.

At his best Jimmy Melia was one of the most constructive players Liverpool ever had, combining flair, industry and intelligence. He was the master of the penetrating through-pass and was adept at shielding the ball, though there were times when he retained possession too long and a delicate dribble might take him past the same opponent twice.

Such over-elaboration antagonised the Anfield fans, normally such an inspiration, and he was on the receiving end of some unreasonably barbed criticism. An occasional tendency to drift out of a match in which he had made a bright start also infuriated Kopites, who traditionally favoured players with a little more obvious fire about their games than Jimmy's more measured approach. The abuse was particularly scathing when he missed a penalty five minutes from time against Brighton at Anfield - with the visitors a goal up - in October 1959. As ever, he demonstrated commendable resilience in the face of adversity and had the satisfaction of nodding the equaliser seconds ahead of the final whistle.

The same fortitude saw Jimmy survive the disappointment of a short, unsuccessful stint with Wolves before giving admirable service to Southampton, whom he helped to reach the First Division in 1966. There was to follow a wandering managerial career, perhaps the sweetest moment of which was the unceremonious ejection of Liverpool from the FA Cup by his Brighton side on the way to Wembley in 1983.

BORN: Liverpool, 1.11.37. GAMES: 287. GOALS: 78.
HONOURS: League Championship 63/4. Second Division Championship 61/2.
2 England caps (63).

OTHER CLUBS: Wolverhampton Wanderers 63/4-64/5 (24, 4); Southampton 64/5-68/9 (139, 11); Aldershot 68/9-71/2 (135, 14); Crewe Alexandra 71/2 (4, 0).
MANAGER: Aldershot 69-72; Crewe Alexandra 72-74; Southport 75;
Brighton and Hove Albion 83; Belenenses, Portugal, 83-85;
Stockport County 86.

1955/56 – 1963/64

RONNIE MORAN

Ronnie Moran's inspired backroom work as Liverpool evolved into the dominant power in English football has tended to overshadow his playing career, a circumstance which does grave injustice to one of the Reds' sturdiest bulwarks throughout a testing period of their history and on to the dawn of the glory days.

A burly full-back with a penchant for dead-ball situations - his left foot was a devastating weapon from the penalty spot and at free kicks - Ronnie ranks high among Anfield's most enthusiastic and effective defenders down the years. Indeed, some shrewd contemporary observers maintain that he should have won more representative honours than a brace of appearances for the Football League.

Ronnie's ample build might have suggested a lack of pace but he covered ground with deceptive speed and was rarely caught out. Strong in the tackle and combative in the air, he was a reassuring sight when his side came under pressure and his presence was never more appreciated than at Eastville in December 1959 when a rampant Bristol Rovers threatened to rout the Reds. The visiting defence wobbled visibly with the notable exception of Ronnie, who made three goal-line clearances and numerous last-yard tackles as Liverpool went on to win with two breakaway goals - a victory due largely to their left-back.

In his early days Ronnie concentrated so avidly on his defensive skills that he was rarely found in attack, but confidence came with maturity and he grew more adventurous. Ipswich bore the brunt of one telling excursion at Anfield in 1959 when he surged upfield, found Fred Morris on the wing and ran on to nod Fred's centre down for Roger Hunt to net.

Ronnie had made his League debut for an indifferent Liverpool outfit at Derby in November 1952, but failed to claim a regular place during the two-year struggle against relegation which ended unsuccessfully in the spring of 1954. His break-through came half-way through the first, acclimatising term in the lower grade when he ousted Frank Lock. Thereafter he missed only six League outings in the following five campaigns and enjoyed a spell as skipper at the end of the decade as his team strained unremittingly to escape from Division Two.

Then 16 months of injury problems removed Ronnie from the action and, with promotion finally beckoning, he seemed likely to miss out on the triumph after striving for so long to achieve it. But he returned to fitness just in time to earn a richly deserved medal in 1961/62.

There was even better to come. In the Reds' second season back in the top flight they lifted the title and Ronnie capped his career by playing in 35 games on the way to the trophy. By now, though, he really was slowing down and in 1964/65 Chris Lawler came in at right-back, with Gerry Byrne switching to Ronnie's left-flank slot.

But one last bonus awaited the old campaigner before he turned his attention to coaching the club's youngsters. Byrne broke his collar-bone in the FA Cup Final against Leeds and Ronnie was called up to do battle in two European Cup semi-final encounters with mighty Inter Milan, giving a good account of himself against the brilliant Brazilian, Jair. It was a fitting end to the playing days of one of the most dedicated one-club men who ever drew breath.

BORN: Liverpool, 28.2.34. GAMES: 379. GOALS: 16.
HONOURS: League Championship 63/4. Second Division Championship 61/2.

1952/53 – 1964/65

GORDON MILNE

Gordon Milne was the first Shankly signing destined to play a role in Liverpool's triumphant march through the early and mid sixties. He arrived with none of the fanfares which greeted the subsequent entrances of Ian St John and Ron Yeats but in his own way he was as crucial a cog in the Anfield machine as his more famous team-mates.

A stocky and industrious right-half, Gordon was never a player to grab a game by the scruff of its neck and dominate it. He was the fetcher and carrier of the side, rather like a middle man in a relay race; the job he did was indispensable to the team effort but he was rarely the centre of attention when it was time to hand out the plaudits.

Gordon's approach was neat and unflashy, like the man himself. He was not a ferocious tackler, relying on anticipation to make interceptions before setting up attacks with admirably precise distribution. He was adept at brisk one-two manoeuvres, a style which complemented the often more ambitious, probing methods of Willie Stevenson on his left.

Some believed that for a man who popped up so often around the opposition's penalty box Gordon did not find the net regularly enough, but though his haul was admittedly on the meagre side, he had the knack of scoring vital goals. Match-winning efforts on the way to the 1965/66 title against fellow contenders Burnley, Leeds and Manchester United were typical.

Gordon was bought from Preston in August 1960 and Bill Shankly could be unusually certain that he was getting value for his £16,000. He had known the Lancashire lad from the cradle and watched him grow up - having been a Deepdale colleague of Gordon's father, Jimmy, during his playing days - and judged that he was acquiring a 'hardy little boy who would fight for the Liverpool cause'.

In fact, Milne Junior made an indifferent start with his new club. After being preferred to the experienced Johnny Wheeler for an early eight-game run, he was ousted by the veteran, who was enjoying something of an Indian summer. But Gordon fought back with spirit, as Shanks knew he would. By March 1962 he had regained his place and, growing in confidence all the time, was an ever-present in the Second Division title campaign that followed.

His performances had assumed a reassuring consistency and he won two Championship medals, but suffered the abiding disappointment of missing the 1965 FA Cup victory through an injury sustained in a 4-0 Good Friday defeat at Stamford Bridge. The only sad image of an otherwise glorious Wembley occasion was of a forlorn and soggy Milne, seated on the bench in his tracksuit in the pouring rain as the team of which he was normally such an integral part enjoyed one of its finest hours.

In 1967 Gordon was allowed to move up the coast to Blackpool although many supporters felt that, while his form had dipped, he still had plenty to offer. But Shankly had decided that his side, which was betraying slight hints of a relative slide, needed surgery and that, at 30, the dapper wing-half was needed no more. Gordon, after a brief sojourn at Bloomfield Road, went on to an enterprising career in management.

BORN: Preston, 29.3.37. GAMES: 277 (2). GOALS: 19.
HONOURS: League Championship 63/4, 65/6.
Second Division Championship 61/2.
14 England caps (63-64).
OTHER CLUBS: Preston North End 56/7-60/1 (81, 3); Blackpool
67/8-69/70 (64, 4). MANAGER: Wigan Athletic 70-72;
Coventry City 72-81, executive manager until 82;
Leicester City 82-86, general manager until 87; Besiktas, Turkey 87-95.

1960/61 – 1966/67

GERRY BYRNE

When Bill Shankly breezed into Anfield in December 1959, the career of full-back Gerry Byrne was going nowhere rather too quickly for comfort. After making only two first-team appearances in two seasons and performing but moderately for the reserves, the swarthy defender was on the transfer list and looked for all the world like a player who would loiter on the fringe of the big time for several years before drifting inevitably towards a lower grade of football.

The new boss, however, saw something that everyone else had evidently missed. He transformed Gerry from a Central League plodder into one of the most effective backs in the land - and although he couldn't have known it at the time he was breathing life into the future of a man who, one rainy day in May 1965, was destined to become one of the true heroes of Liverpool soccer history.

But even the most inspired manager needs a little help from fate and it came in the form of injuries to regular left-back Ronnie Moran. Gerry stepped in with a string of accomplished performances and, when Ronnie returned to first-team duty, continued his development by switching to right-back at the expense of Dick White.

He was an ever-present in the 1961/62 promotion campaign and became an automatic choice throughout the heady triumphs of the mid-sixties, reclaiming his left-sided role when Chris Lawler replaced the ageing Moran. Quiet and undemonstrative in both play and demeanour, Gerry brought a granite reliability to the Reds' defence. He wasn't over-endowed with pace but compensated by reading the game with cool assurance and with a tackle that was fearsome. Shankly was adamant that there wasn't a harder - or fairer - footballer in the game and, never a man prone to understatement, he described his protege's performance in the defeat of Belgian champions Anderlecht in late 1964 as 'the best full-back display Europe has ever seen'.

The match which clinched Gerry's place in Liverpool legend was the 1965 FA Cup Final against Leeds United in which he played for 117 minutes with a broken collar-bone, overcoming grinding pain and disguising his infirmity from Don Revie's men, who would certainly have taken advantage if they had recognised his plight. Not only did he subdue the lively Johnny Giles, he also laid on the Reds' first goal in extra time when he took a glorious pass from Willie Stevenson, reached the byline and swept over a cross for Roger Hunt to head home.

Having played a full part in taking two Championships as well as the Cup triumph, Gerry hurt a knee against Leicester City in August 1966 and was never quite the same dominant force again. When recurring knee trouble prompted premature retirement in 1969, leading to a spell as an Anfield coach, Shanks was again warm in his praise: 'When Gerry went, it took a big chunk out of Liverpool. Something special was missing.'

For a man who enjoyed so much success at club level, Gerry had little international joy. In the first of his two outings for England he endured a chasing from Scotland's Willie Henderson, and he lacked the class, perhaps, to mount a serious challenge to the immaculate Ray Wilson. Liverpool, though, knew his value - and it was immense.

BORN: Liverpool, 29.8.38. GAMES: 329 (1). GOALS: 3.
HONOURS: League Championship 63/4, 65/6.
Second Division Championship 61/2. FA Cup 64/5. 2 England caps (63-66).

1957/58 – 1968/69

ROGER HUNT

It was the night they dubbed him 'Sir Roger'. More than 60,000 people had sallied forth in torrential rain, forsaking the comforts of hearth and home to bid farewell to one of Liverpool's favourite sons. Never mind that he had left the club more than two years earlier; he would have a place in their hearts forever. It was the testimonial match for one of the all-time great goal-scorers and no one wanted to miss the party.

Those locked out on that emotional evening in April 1972, when Anfield's capacity stood at 56,000, were left to listen to the roars from within and reflect on the supreme importance of Roger Hunt to the Reds throughout the fabulously successful sixties - a decade in which his goals had been their staff of life.

Roger's rise was little less than meteoric after scoring on his debut - as a 21-year-old with only amateur football and five Central League games behind him - against Scunthorpe at Anfield in September 1959. He quickly secured a regular place, netting 21 times in 36 games. In 1961/62 his prolific partnership with Ian St John was born and Roger struck 41 times in 41 outings, including five hat-tricks, to play a crucial role in turning the Reds' promotion dream into reality. Division One didn't know what was about to hit it.

The next six years brought an avalanche of goals - 149 in a mere 229 League games, to be precise - and it's no coincidence that Liverpool won the Championship in Roger's two most prosperous campaigns. In fact in 1965/66, the season of their second title triumph, the Reds didn't lose a First Division match in which he scored.

But there was more to Roger Hunt and his value to Liverpool than mere statistics. The explosive shot, the sudden and destructive pace, the strength which made him so hard to dispossess and his phenomenal work-rate were all well known. Less appreciated, perhaps, were his accomplished but unflashy ball control, neat distribution, refusal to hide from the ball when things were not going his way and an agile soccer brain which might have made him effective in a deep-lying role.

Goal-getting, though, was his golden gift and he employed it to the full. Never afraid to miss, Roger scored spectacular goals and easy goals, those that he bludgeoned into the net, like the brutal volley that jolted Inter Milan in the 1965 European Cup semi-final at Anfield, and those that he caressed past the 'keeper, such as the subtle touch that deceived Manchester United's Alex Stepney at Old Trafford in 1968.

His England record - 18 goals in 34 games, which included only two defeats - was outstanding, though he never received due credit for that, perhaps because he replaced national hero Jimmy Greaves in the 1966 World Cup. That Roger was the least-lauded member of Alf Ramsey's team was the outrageous product of ignorance and bias, and it was scandalous that such a selfless player should be driven to end his England tenure voluntarily as a result of constant and often hysterical criticism.

Modest to a fault and even-tempered, Roger was a referee's dream. The only moment of controversy came in March 1969, when he was substituted in an FA Cup defeat by Leicester and hurled his shirt into the dugout in frustration - a wholly untypical incident. By then he had survived a post-World Cup dip in form to bounce back with a brief but bountiful liaison with Tony Hateley before his Liverpool days tailed off as Bill Shankly sought new faces to end a relatively lean period. In December 1969 the 31-year-old Roger moved to Bolton, the club he had supported as a boy, to close a career which had seen him shatter the Reds' scoring record and bring unprecedented glory to the club. The fans loved him for it; a knighthood was the least they could offer . . .

BORN: Glazebury, Lancashire, 20.7.38. GAMES: 484 (5). GOALS: 285.
HONOURS: League Championship 63/4, 65/6.
Second Division Championship 61/2. FA Cup 64/5. 34 England caps (62-69).

OTHER CLUBS: Bolton Wanderers 69/70-71/2 (76, 24).

1959/60 – 1969/70

IAN ST JOHN

Ian St John was the spark that lit a flame destined to burn triumphantly for the next three decades and beyond. When quizzed by his board about the wisdom of paying Motherwell £37,500 for the Scottish international centre-forward, Bill Shankly described him as the man the Reds couldn't afford *not* to buy, the most urgently needed component of his brave new team. The manager's judgement, as usual, was impeccable.

From the night of Ian's first appearance in a red shirt - a Liverpool Senior Cup Final against Everton at Goodison Park in August 1961- it was clear that he and his new club were made for each other. He moved with a jaunty swagger, 5ft 7½in of concentrated aggression topped by a pugnacious crew-cut - and he scored a hat-trick. His rapport with the fans was instant and complete; a folk hero was born.

The opening matches of the Division Two title campaign showed that Ian needed time to adjust but there was no doubting his quality. He was strong, cunning and courageous, devastating in the air for such a small man and adept at delicate flicks which did much to promote a fruitful scoring partnership with Roger Hunt. Ian notched 18 goals as the Reds went up, following that with 19 as a First Division new boy and 21 in 1963/64, on the way to the Championship.

That season saw a turning point which meant 'The Saint' would never score as heavily again but would contribute even more significantly to the eternal Anfield trophy quest. When schemer Jimmy Melia was injured, Shankly withdrew Ian into a deep-lying role in which he revealed his full potential for the first time. He became mastermind of the attack, feeding colleagues with possession and creating space for them to use it with his intelligent running. It didn't mean the goals dried up entirely - witness the jack-knife header which won the FA Cup against Leeds in 1965 - but simply that Ian's vision, mobility and all-round skills were employed to bring a new dimension to Liverpool's game.

Hunt continued to be prime beneficiary of his former front-running comrade's talents, as he acknowledged after scoring against Standard Liege in the European Cup Winners' Cup tie in December 1965. Ian had run half the length of the field, drawing defenders with him, before slipping the ball through for an unmarked Roger to net.

By the dawn of the seventies, with the Reds' first wave of Shankly-inspired honours behind them, Ian was into his thirties and his fitness had declined but, used sparingly, he remained capable of transforming a game with his subtle touch and slick, close passing. Rumanians Dynamo Bucharest were the victims in December 1970 when he was taken off the bench to turn a shaky 1-0 lead into a comfortable 3-0 margin by laying on two late goals in the European Fairs Cup.

Throughout his playing days 'The Saint' was no stranger to controversy. Often he was criticised for flashes of bad temper, such as the clash with Preston's Tony Singleton in March 1962 which led to a joint dismissal, but fire was an integral part of his make-up and, crucially, there never appeared to be malice aforethought.

On retirement he tried coaching and then management but didn't excel as many people thought he might and eventually became a TV personality. But in years to come it should not be as Jimmy Greaves' chat show sparring partner that he is recalled. In assessing his place in Liverpool's modern history, students of the Reds would do well to heed the wisdom of one Bill Shankly when he said: 'In the beginning was Ian St John . . .'

BORN: Motherwell, 7.6.38. GAMES: 418 (5). GOALS: 118.
HONOURS: League Championship 63/4, 65/6.
Second Division Championship 61/2. FA Cup 64/5. 21 Scotland caps (59-65).

OTHER CLUBS: Motherwell 57/8-60/1; Coventry City 71/2 (18, 3); Tranmere Rovers 72/3 (9, 1). MANAGER: Motherwell 73-74; Portsmouth 74-77.

1961/62 – 1970/71

WILLIE STEVENSON

Frustration with life in the shadow of Jim Baxter drove Willie Stevenson from his native Scotland to the other side of the world, but he was to find his true niche much closer to home. The lanky left-half – as slim as Jim and with a similarly cultured style – had won League and Cup medals with Glasgow Rangers before being ousted by the arrival at Ibrox of the gifted but mercurial Baxter. Unwilling to languish in the reserves, Willie elected adventurously to sample soccer in Australia and it was while he was on loan Down Under that Bill Shankly stepped in.

The Reds had made a lacklustre start to their first campaign after regaining Division One status and the manager recognised that more class and creativity were needed. Accordingly he secured Willie for £20,000 in October 1962, outbidding Preston North End in the process, and then displayed admirable patience as his countryman took time to adjust to the demands of the English game. Willie was obviously skilful but the pace of First Division life was too hectic for him and intolerant fans demanded the recall of Tommy Leishman. Shankly, as imperturbable as ever, kept faith with his new signing and was to reap rich rewards.

As Willie settled he began to exert a compelling influence. His biting tackle was the equal of Leishman's but the constructive side of his game was a class apart. A keenly intelligent tactician, he could change the emphasis of attack with a raking wing-to-wing pass or, more deadly still, drive a stiletto-thrust to the heart of the stoutest defence with the most crisp and piercing of through-balls.

He was seen at his best when winger Peter Thompson joined him on the left side of the Reds' 1963/64 Championship-winning team. Peter was an ideal partner, adept at making the oblique runs which made the most of Willie's subtle ability to judge the weight and angle of a pass, and together they formed a crowd-pleasing duo.

The full Stevenson repertoire never received a better showcase than the FA Cup Final against Leeds United in 1965 when most observers made him man of the match. He revelled in the sweeping width of Wembley, with its bowling-green surface made lusher than ever by heavy rain, and did more than anyone to put Don Revie's dour side to the sword. Willie it was who strolled imperiously past two opponents and freed Gerry Byrne on the left for the full-back to lay on the first goal for Roger Hunt.

As the decade progressed, the one-time Ranger – a dressing-room joker who did much to boost team morale – continued to turn in immaculate performances, missing only nine games in four seasons and playing a valuable part in a second title triumph in 1965/66. The campaign that followed was an anti-climax for Liverpool but Willie, as consistent as ever, did not seem in imminent danger of the axe. It materialised, however, in the shape of Emlyn Hughes and the 29-year-old schemer, finding himself out of the side with little prospect of a quick return, moved to Stoke City in December 1968.

Some fans were outraged, as they were over Gordon Milne's exit, at what they saw as premature dismissal of a loyal favourite, but Shankly was nothing if not decisive. Willie, who missed out on an international career due to abnormally hot competition from the likes of Dave Mackay and Jim Baxter, thus left the club with plenty still to offer and spent six more years in the League. He will be remembered at Anfield as an entertainer in the classic mould, a thoroughbred who contributed royally to some of the Reds' greatest triumphs.

BORN: Leith, 26.10.39. GAMES: 237 (1). GOALS: 17. HONOURS: League Championship 63/4, 65/6. FA Cup 64/5.

OTHER CLUBS: Glasgow Rangers 58/9-61/2 (73, 1); Stoke City 67/8-72/3 (94, 5); Tranmere Rovers 73/4 (20, 0).

1962/63 – 1967/68

ALF ARROWSMITH

Alf Arrowsmith was the shooting star who burst across the Anfield heavens to wreath himself in glory for four dazzling months before his brightness was abruptly and prematurely dimmed. He rose sensationally to prominence in the second half of 1963/64 when the Reds' midfield general, Jimmy Melia, was injured. Ian St John moved back to assume the play-making role and the exuberant Alf came in to form a dual spearhead with Roger Hunt.

He signalled his intentions with a four-goal blitz on Derby in the FA Cup and for the duration of the season the young Mancunian could do little wrong, finishing with 15 League goals in 20 games and a Championship medal. Playing with refreshing innocence and verve, he ran at defences with unnerving pace and strength, and often attempted the seemingly impossible with spectacular success. Several goals were thrashed home with savage power from acute angles, and a 12-yard back-heel which beat Chelsea at Stamford Bridge would have delighted Denis Law himself. Easier opportunities were sometimes spurned but a glittering future seemed to be in store.

It all went wrong that August in the Charity Shield clash with West Ham when Alf damaged a knee so badly that he was out of contention for the first half of 1964/65. Although he stayed at Anfield for another four years, he was dogged by injuries and never regained his impetus. A popular, down-to-earth lad, he went on to spells with Bury and Rochdale.

BORN: Manchester, 11.12.42. GAMES: 50 (4). GOALS: 24. HONOURS: League Championship 63/4.

OTHER CLUBS: Bury 68/9–69/70 (48, 11); Rochdale 70/1–71/2 (47, 14).

1961/62 – 1967/68

GORDON WALLACE

Pocket-sized Scottish inside-left Gordon Wallace hogged the limelight in television's first *Match of the Day* when he scored twice – including an 87th-minute winner – against Arsenal at Anfield in August 1964. But that is undoubtedly a distinction he would trade for a small fraction of the glory predicted for him when he broke through to the fringe of the first team in 1962/63. Perhaps it was a typical piece of Shankly psychology when the perceptive Liverpool boss described Gordon as the nearest thing to Tom Finney since the war, but Bill was sincere in his regard for the abilities of a player whose career was cursed by brittle bones.

Gordon, also at home on the wing, was quick and skilful with a mesmeric body-swerve and on his debut at West Brom he tantalised England full-back Don Howe. When he deputised for appendix victim Ian St John and scored twice in the 1964 Charity Shield encounter with West Ham, it was the start of a six-goals-in-eight-days burst – including his brace on TV and two more against Reykjavik in the Reds' first European game – which might have established him at the top level. But Gordon then suffered a barren spell in his only extended run before a cruel succession of injuries ended his Anfield ambitions and he joined Crewe.

BORN: Lanark, 13.6.44. GAMES: 20 (1). GOALS: 5.
OTHER CLUBS: Crewe Alexandra 67/8–71/2 (94, 20).

1962/63 – 1966/67

PHIL FERNS

No one can take away from Phil Ferns the achievement of winning a League Championship medal with Liverpool in 1963/64. He earned the honour by the sweat of his brow, making 18 appearances as Bill Shankly's squad was hit by injuries, without remotely suggesting that he had the necessary class to forge a career in the First Division.

He stood in for Willie Stevenson at left-half, his most comfortable position, for a run of four games early in the campaign, returning later to deputise first for Ronnie Moran and then for Gerry Byrne at full-back. His most memorable game during this spell was at Old Trafford in November 1963 when he subdued Bobby Charlton as his side recorded a vital 1–0 victory.

Phil, who was already 24 when he made his League debut at home to Manchester City in August 1962, was a rugged defender whose enthusiasm outstripped his ability. He was rather lacking in pace and ball skill but his versatility stood the Reds in good stead over three seasons. The emergence of younger players ended his usefulness at Anfield and he moved on, first to Bournemouth, for whom his son was later to play, and then to Mansfield.

BORN: Liverpool, 14.11.37. GAMES: 28. GOALS: 1.
HONOURS: League Championship 63/4.

OTHER CLUBS: Bournemouth 65/6 (46, 0);
Mansfield Town 66/7–67/8 (56, 1).

1962/63 – 1964/65

RON YEATS

'Take a walk around my centre-half, gentlemen.' The gleeful invitation came from master of banter Bill Shankly, introducing his mountainous new signing to assembled pressmen at Anfield in the summer of 1961. The colossus in question was, of course, Ron Yeats, who had just arrived from Dundee United to become a cornerstone of the Liverpool legend.

Shankly's admiration for the 6ft 2in Scot dated back to his days in charge of Huddersfield Town but the Yorkshire club didn't have the brass to prise Ron from Tannadice. Thus, after failing in a bid for Jack Charlton of Leeds, the Reds' boss willingly parted with the required £30,000 for a man he was confident would put the fear of God into the Sassenachs. Having already tempted Ian St John south of the border, he had the backbone of his first great side.

Ron - inevitably nicknamed 'Rowdy' after Clint Eastwood's TV cowboy of that era - was made skipper within five months of his arrival and exercised monumental influence as the team galloped to promotion in his first season. Division Two centre-forwards seemed to be swallowed up by his all-pervading presence and even Sunderland's free-scoring Brian Clough, rampant against most opponents, was rendered ineffective.

Elevation to the top flight served only to emphasise Ron's talents. His aerial ability was awesome, his tackling thunderous and his distribution sensibly simple. Some said he was slow on the turn but, as Shankly revelled in pointing out, not many attackers got past him to find out.

He led the Reds to two Championships and through a succession of stirring European adventures but reserved some of his most rousing personal performances for the victorious 1965 FA Cup campaign. In fact, it all nearly went wrong at West Brom in the third round when a whistler in the crowd gulled Ron into picking up the ball in his own penalty area. Justice was done when Bobby Cram missed the resultant spot kick.

In the fifth round at Bolton the Liverpool captain gave one of his bravest displays after pulling a muscle ten minutes into the match and going on to sub-due the potent airborne menace of Wyn 'The Leap' Davies. He garnered further glory by laying on Roger Hunt's winner in the quarter-final against Leicester and then comfortably snuffed out the threat of Leeds' Alan Peacock at Wembley.

As the sixties wore on the Yeats game, though still essentially rugged, acquired a little more polish and it was a rare adversary who could unsettle him. One who did was playing for Ajax on that infamous Amsterdam night in December 1966 when the Reds were eclipsed 5-1, but Ron was neither the first nor the last defender to be given a chasing by Johan Cruyff.

By the end of the decade Ron had turned 32 and was beginning to suffer back trouble but when he eventually yielded his place to Larry Lloyd he still had the motivation to contribute a valuable stint at left-back.

Equal in stature to his footballing record were his off-the-field merits as skipper. Although he was quietly spoken, his imposing personality made him an impressive mouthpiece for colleagues in dealings with management, and he was a commendable influence on younger players.

These admirable attributes remain in the club's service in his current position of chief scout but it is as an inspiring leader who never flagged that Ron Yeats will go down in Liverpool folklore; while 'Rowdy' stood firm there was always hope. He was, in the words of his mentor Bill Shankly, a fantastic man.

BORN: Aberdeen, 15.11.37. GAMES: 450 (1). GOALS: 15.
HONOURS: League Championship 63/4, 65/6.
Division Two Championship 61/2. FA Cup 64/5. 2 Scotland caps (65-66).

OTHER CLUBS: Dundee United; Tranmere Rovers 71/2-73/4 (97, 5).
MANAGER: Tranmere Rovers 72-75; Barrow 76.

1961/62 — 1970/71

TOMMY LAWRENCE

It's always a pity to waste a good nickname, especially one as colourful as 'The Flying Pig', coined affectionately and with no trace of an insult by the Kop to describe their solidly-built sixties goalkeeper Tommy Lawrence. But it was an alternative epithet, less vivid but more precise and with a little added subtlety, which most aptly summed up the vastly underrated Scottish international. Shrewd observers dubbed him 'the sweeper-keeper', a description which neatly captured his style and the way he fitted into the Liverpool system.

Tommy operated behind a back four which usually played square and which pushed upfield whenever possible. When it was breached by a penetrating pass or an opponent's run from a deep position it was imperative to have a last line of defence capable of reacting instantly to the danger. This job called for anticipation, bravery and talent - qualities which Tommy possessed in abundance. There wasn't another 'keeper of his era better acquainted with the bootlaces of First Division forwards; diving at feet was his speciality and when even the likes of Law and Greaves were through with only Tommy to beat it was never a formality

The Reds were served royally by an intuitive understanding between their custodian and the mammoth centre-half Ron Yeats, who generally dominated the penalty area with his aerial strength. It was rare to see the two countrymen going for the same ball and while Ron was dealing with crosses, his unflappable 'keeper would be ready to protect the net with reliable handling and amazing agility for a man of his bulk.

Although Tommy was very much an under-praised stalwart throughout Liverpool's sixties triumphs, Bill Shankly was well aware of his value. He knew there were matches which his team won, apparently convincingly, but in which the scorelines were wholly misleading - thanks largely to the exploits of the undemonstrative Lawrence. One such was a 4-1 home win against Blackpool in the victorious 1965/66 Championship campaign. Alan Ball was rampant and threatened to overturn the title aspirants as he repeatedly sliced opened their defence with incisive service to Graham Oates and Ray Charnley. But the 'keeper was inspired, frustrating the Tangerines with a courageous and skilful display which enabled his side at first to survive and then to take both points.

By then Tommy was an experienced performer, having been first called to senior duty for the newly-promoted Reds - after five years at Anfield - when Jim Furnell was injured in October 1962. He impressed instantly, cementing his place with a run of impeccable form and earning an early cap for Scotland against Eire in June 1963.

The following season brought a Championship medal and Tommy climaxed an accomplished first full term by brilliantly saving a George Eastham penalty, the turning point in the 5-0 thrashing of Arsenal which clinched the title. He built on this early success, earning a much-deserved reputation for consistency, and it was a double mystery that his international recall should have been delayed for six years and then been limited to a mere two games when it finally arrived.

He remained Liverpool's first-choice goalkeeper until February 1970 - missing only five League games in eight seasons - when, in company with Ian St John and Ron Yeats, he finally gave way to the challenge of youth, having kept his successor waiting for two and a half years. The ultimate tribute to Tommy Lawrence is the identity of that young man who was made to wait so patiently - a certain Ray Clemence.

BORN: Dailly, Ayrshire, 14.5.40. GAMES: 387. GOALS: 0.
HONOURS: League Championship 63/4, 65/6. FA Cup 64/5. 3
Scotland caps (63-69).

OTHER CLUBS: Tranmere Rovers 71/2-73/4 (80, 0).

1962/63 – 1970/71

GEOFF STRONG

It is one of football's ironies that Geoff Strong wanted to leave Arsenal because Gunners boss Billy Wright switched the goal-scoring inside-forward to a wing-half role. Yet when he settled at Anfield he found himself, at one time or another, in virtually every outfield position and rarely had a shirt to call his own.

Geoff had averaged more than a goal every two games during his Highbury spell and it seemed likely that Bill Shankly would use him as a striker alongside Roger Hunt in place of the seriously injured Alf Arrowsmith. But the £40,000 newcomer took time to adjust to the Reds' rigorous training regime and by the time he was fully fit the side had a formidably stable look about it.

But neither player nor manager was dismayed. Shankly was adamant that he had bought the Geordie for his all-round talent, not for any specific task, and Geoff proceeded to become one of the most effective utility players the British game has known. Indeed, as well as proving the most versatile man at the club, he also showed that he was one of the most talented. His midfield performances were notable for their skill and vision; at the back he was cool and resourceful; in the front line he demonstrated an instinct for goals backed by a savage shot.

Geoff's first major assignment on joining Liverpool was born out of heartbreak for Gordon Milne when the right-half suffered an injury which put him out of the FA Cup Final against Leeds. In stepped the player who was to become Anfield's master-of-all-trades, to be handed the critical job of neutralising the threat of Don Revie's midfield general Bobby Collins. So well did he fare that Collins had but minor impact and Geoff had time to test Gary Sprake with several stinging drives on his way to a winner's medal.

During the Championship campaign that followed, the ex-Gunner firmly established himself as the Reds' chameleon. At various times he stood in for Thompson, Stevenson, Lawler, Milne and Hunt; the only man whose position he did not cover was goalkeeper Tommy Lawrence, though if the green jersey had become vacant Geoff could doubtless have distinguished himself in it.

His finest hours that term came with two winning goals on the way to the final of the European Cup Winners' Cup, which Liverpool lost to Borussia Dortmund at Hampden Park. The first was a 25-yard thunderbolt off the underside of the crossbar against Juventus in the preliminary round; the second, scored despite a crippling knee injury, was a semi-final header past Celtic's Ronnie Simpson. Such heroics didn't go unnoticed by the Kopites, who chanted Geoff's name until he hobbled off the bench to take his bow when the title was clinched against Chelsea.

Over the next four years, as the manager began to experiment with his side, Geoff was an integral part of the set-up. In his final two seasons on Merseyside his wanderings were largely halted, with an accomplished tenure at left-back. If he had a particular forte, however, it was perhaps as sweeper, a role denied him by the eminence of Tommy Smith. But it was for the diversity of his talents that he was most missed when, at the age of 33, he moved to Coventry City. Geoff Strong didn't leave one gap – he left ten.

BORN: Newcastle, 19.9.37. GAMES: 193 (5). GOALS: 32.
HONOURS: League Championship 65/6. FA Cup 64/5.

OTHER CLUBS: Arsenal 60/1–64/5 (125, 69); Coventry City 70/1–71/2 (33, 0).

1964/65 – 1969/70

ALAN BANKS

BOBBY THOMSON

ALAN JONES

ALAN BANKS 1958/59—1960/61

Centre-forward. BORN: Liverpool, 5.10.38. GAMES: 8. GOALS: 6.
OTHER CLUBS: Cambridge City; Exeter City 63/4–65/6 (85, 43)
and 67/8–72/3 (173, 58); Plymouth Argyle 66/7–67/8 (19, 5).

ALAN JONES 1959/60—1962/63

Full-back. BORN: Flint, 6.1.40. GAMES: 5, GOALS: 0.
OTHER CLUBS: Brentford 63/4–69/70 (249, 2).

BOBBY THOMSON 1962/63—1963/64

Full-back. BORN: Menstrie, Clackmannanshire, 21.11.39.
GAMES: 7. GOALS: 0. OTHER CLUBS: Partick Thistle;
Luton Town 65/6–66/7 (74, 0).

PHIL CHISNALL 1964/65—1965/66

Forward. BORN: Manchester, 27.10.42. GAMES: 8. GOALS: 2.
OTHER CLUBS: Manchester United 61/2–63/4 (35, 8);
Southend United 67/8–70/1 (142, 28); Stockport County 71/2 (30, 2).

BILLY MOLYNEUX 1964/65

Goalkeeper. BORN: Liverpool, 10.1.44. GAMES: 1. GOALS: 0.
OTHER CLUBS: Oldham Athletic 68/9 (8, 0).

PHIL CHISNALL

BILLY MOLYNEUX

ALAN HIGNETT

TOM LOWRY

JOHN OGSTON

JOHN SEALEY

ALAN HIGNETT 1964/65

Full-back. BORN: Liverpool, 1.11.46. GAMES: 1. GOALS: 0.
OTHER CLUBS: Chester 66/7 (6, 0).

TOM LOWRY 1964/65

Full-back. BORN: Liverpool, 26.8.45. GAMES: 1. GOALS: 0.
OTHER CLUBS: Crewe Alexandra 66/7–77/8 (436, 2).

JOHN OGSTON 1966/67

Goalkeeper. BORN: Aberdeen, 15.1.39. GAMES: 1. GOALS: 0.
OTHER CLUBS: Aberdeen; Doncaster Rovers 68/9–70/1 (70, 0).

JOHN SEALEY 1964/65

Forward. BORN: Wallasey, 27.12.45. GAMES: 1. GOALS: 1.
OTHER CLUBS: Chester 66/7–67/8 (4, 0).

DAVID WILSON 1966/67

Winger. BORN: Nelson, 24.12.42. GAMES: 0 (1).
GOALS: 0. OTHER CLUBS: Preston North End 60/1–66/7
(170, 31) and 68/9–73/4 (111, 10); Bradford City
on loan 71/2 (5, 0); Southport *on loan* 73/4 (2, 0).

DAVID WILSON

PETER THOMPSON

When a sprightly, if rather distant Championship challenge withered in April 1963 - the Reds' first spring in the top flight for nine years - Bill Shankly made a momentous decision. He earmarked Peter Thompson as the one crucial ingredient missing from his title-winning recipe and signed the Preston winger, in the face of opposition from Juventus, Everton and Wolves, for a club record fee of £40,000. A year later Bill's mission was accomplished and the new man had played a thrilling part in the first of many triumphs before his Anfield days were done.

Peter Thompson was a soccer sorcerer, a pleaser of crowds and a teaser of full-backs. On his day he brought to the game a dancer's grace and the daring of a matador, but when the Muse was not with him he was prone to over-elaboration and could be the most frustrating man afield. Unlike certain other gifted players, however, he offered no hint of the prima donna and he was never afraid of hard graft.

Despite being right-footed, Peter came into the side on the left flank where Alan A'Court and Kevin Lewis had both been judged deficient during the previous campaign. He made an eye-catching debut at Ewood Park, running at the Blackburn defenders, making them twist and turn in their efforts to stay with their elusive quarry and rendering an offside trap too perilous to contemplate. As autumn turned to winter and the points piled up, Peter and Ian Callaghan, whose more direct approach was in marked contrast to Thompson's jinking and swaying, became the most formidable wing pairing in British club football.

The former Deepdale man's impact at Anfield could hardly have been greater, though there were those who said he should have scored more goals and that his final pass too often went astray. The fact was that his fierce shot *could* be a wayward weapon but his crosses, while not always matching the brilliance of his approach play, were as reliable as those of most contemporaries. There was also a theory that Peter should switch to the right to encourage him to reach the byline and cross with his favoured foot instead of being forced infield as he was on the left, but such a scheme took no account of the excellent Callaghan.

The nitpickers were predictably notable by their silence when Peter capped his first, richly rewarding term as a Red with his most devastating display to date. He scored twice and turned the Arsenal defence inside out as Liverpool made certain of the title, drubbing the Gunners 5-0 in front of an ecstatic Kop.

Peter's progress continued as Shankly's men lifted the FA Cup in 1965. His personal highlight was waltzing past John Hollins and Marvin Hinton to grab the first goal in the semi-final against Chelsea with a fearsome left-foot drive between Peter Bonetti and his near post. A second Championship medal soon followed but the nearest Peter came to further Cup success was in 1971 when he came on as substitute to breathe life into a hitherto dull final which Arsenal won to clinch the Double. By then he was plagued by knee trouble and after a lot of time on the treatment table he moved to Bolton in November 1973. Surprisingly in view of past injuries, he was able to put in four spirited years before retiring.

One perennial gripe of Liverpool fans was Peter's banishment for long periods to the international wilderness. After starring in Brazil in 1964 his appearances were cruelly curtailed by Alf Ramsey's decision to do without wingers, though he did represent his country as late as 1970. But in the final analysis it is in a red shirt that Peter Thompson will be remembered - and as an entertainer, one of the finest of his time.

BORN: Carlisle, 27.11.42. GAMES: 404 (8). GOALS: 54.
HONOURS: League Championship 63/4, 65/6. FA Cup 64/5.
16 England caps (64-70).

OTHER CLUBS: Preston North End 60/1-62/3 (121, 20);
Bolton Wanderers 73/4-77/8 (117, 2).

1963/64 — 1971/72

TONY HATELEY

When Tony Hateley opened his Liverpool scoring account with a rousing hat-trick against Newcastle on the second Saturday of 1967/68, Anfield was the place to be. The stadium was bulging with nearly 52,000 people, the air was heady with the scent of triumphs to come and the 'H Bombers' – Roger Hunt also scored two in the 6–0 victory – had signalled their arrival as partners to be feared with a show of ruthless efficiency.

Bill Shankly, alarmed by a barren campaign after three seasons of glory, had paid Chelsea £96,000 for Tony in the belief that the towering centre-forward would hit the target with sufficient regularity to arrest any slide before it gained momentum. But despite such a euphoric start – somewhat marred by a Hateley own-goal in a defeat at Highbury two days later – and the new signing's commendable strike-rate of a goal every two games, the expensive remedy was doomed to failure.

The problem was that Tony, a majestic header of the ball who needed constant aerial fodder to function, was utterly alien to Liverpool's style. That didn't bother Roger, who fed avidly off his knock-downs and enjoyed unaccustomed freedom as markers homed in on the big man, but the other players were used to a varied build-up along the ground. Understandably, after years of more subtle methods, they struggled to adjust to the tactic of repeatedly slinging high balls into the penalty area. Thus, when that approach was non-productive – as it often was against top-class defenders – the Reds were left with few options because Tony was too clumsy to employ a passing game. Lacking the control to hold the ball and the precision to lay it off, he was the rock on which many of Liverpool's attacks broke down.

Despite these shortcomings, Tony had his moments. Twice he netted three times in League matches, and went one better in an FA Cup replay against Walsall to finish the season with 24 goals. No one could accuse him of not doing *his* job, even if he failed to fit the team pattern, but it was no surprise when he was replaced – by Alun Evans – early in the following campaign and joined Coventry for £80,000. Through no fault of his own, an 'H Bomber' had backfired.

BORN: Derby, 13.6.41. GAMES: 56. GOALS: 28.

OTHER CLUBS: Notts County 58/9–62/3 (131, 77) and 70/1–71/2 (57, 32); Aston Villa 63/4–66/7 (127, 68); Chelsea 66/7 (27, 6); Coventry City 68/9 (17, 4); Birmingham City 69/70–70/1 (28, 6); Oldham Athletic 73/4 (5, 1).

1967/68 – 1968/69

BOBBY GRAHAM

When Bobby Graham struck a hat-trick as a 19-year-old debutant against Aston Villa at Anfield in September 1964, the skilful Scot seemed to have the perfect platform on which to build a successful Liverpool career. In retrospect his explosive start more closely resembled a curse. Though Bill Shankly was far too wise to be carried away on the strength of one performance, the expectations of the fans were elevated to the heavens, and the inexperienced Bobby was not equal to them. Although he scored in the next match he then suffered a dozen blank games and, often bedevilled by injuries, dropped out of serious contention for the next four seasons as other strikers held sway.

But Bobby's chance came again - and this time he was ready. At the start of 1969/70 - with Hunt and St John nearing the end of their illustrious Anfield days, Hateley long gone and Evans injured - a more mature Graham was pitched into a side very much in a state of flux. Now he looked a different player to the boyish performer of half a decade earlier, adding new-found determination and confidence to his old virtues of pace and control.

That term Bobby was an ever-present, scoring 13 goals in a moderate campaign by Reds' standards, and there were even whispers of an international call. But ten games into the following season the Graham bandwagon, now moving so smoothly, came to an abrupt halt when he broke his ankle against Chelsea at Anfield. He didn't start another match for five months, by which time John Toshack was on the scene. When Kevin Keegan appeared in 1971/72 Bobby was effectively crowded out and, bowing to the inevitable, he joined Coventry City for £70,000.

A short spell at Highfield Road and an even briefer loan period with Tranmere preceded a move to his native Motherwell, for whom he excelled for four years and earned rich praise. Even then he was not finished, spending another four seasons at Hamilton until retirement at the age of 36. At Liverpool Bobby was an unfortunate footballer, struck down at his peak. How well he deserved his belated recognition north of the border.

BORN: Motherwell, 22.11.44. GAMES: 123 (8). GOALS: 42.

OTHER CLUBS: Coventry City 71/2-72/3 (19, 3);
Tranmere Rovers on loan 72/3 (10, 3); Motherwell 73/4-76/7 (132, 37);
Hamilton Academical 77/8-80/81 (118, 42).

1964/65 – 1971/72

ALUN EVANS

If ever a young player seemed set for greatness it was perky, flaxen-haired Alun Evans in the autumn of 1968. Bill Shankly had just made him the first £100,000 teenager in British soccer and he had started his stint as Liverpool centre-forward with two richly promising displays crowned by three goals. But four years later, Anfield dream in tatters and potential unfulfilled, the golden boy had gone.

It might all have been so different. Alun started as a 17-year-old prodigy with Wolves and impressed mightily during his brief Molineux interlude. He gave one particularly precocious performance against Liverpool, having the temerity to rattle Ron Yeats and score a goal in the process. The Reds' boss was not a man to ignore such talent and when Alun became available Bill made sure that Anfield was his destination.

He was bought as a long-term replacement for Tony Hateley and provided a stark contrast to his rather one-dimensional predecessor, bravery being the one quality they shared. Alun was quick and skilful, full of cute tricks and sudden changes of direction that threw defenders into disarray. The mop-topped newcomer quickly unveiled his effervescent armoury, scoring after ten minutes of his debut at home to Leicester and then netting two at Molineux in a 6–0 thrashing of his former employers.

Perhaps predictably, the young man's learning curve became more gradual and he managed only four more goals that season. The following campaign was one of total frustration, with injuries and a night-club incident – in which his face was badly scarred – sidelining him for long periods, but he returned to something like top form in 1970/71. Despite a cartilage operation, the result of playing on a bone-hard pitch in Bucharest, Alun scored ten League goals in 21 games and lit up Anfield with a brilliant hat-trick against Bayern Munich in the European Fairs Cup.

Fitness again eluded him in 1971/72, a term which brought but one highlight, a breathtaking half-volleyed goal in a Cup Winners' Cup defeat by Bayern. By then, though, he was in the shadow of Messrs Keegan and Toshack and took the road back to the Midlands, where a new start with Aston Villa was to add little joy to an unlucky, unsatisfying career.

BORN: Bewdley, Worcestershire, 30.4.49. GAMES: 104 (6). GOALS: 33.

OTHER CLUBS: Wolverhampton Wanderers 67/8–68/9 (21, 4);
Aston Villa 72/3–73/4 (62, 11); Walsall 75/6–77/8 (87, 7); Hellas FC, Melbourne.

1968/69 – 1971/72

IAN ROSS

Any player who could subdue Franz Beckenbauer and Alan Ball and yet – unlike so many man-to-man markers – use the ball constructively when given the chance, would be guaranteed a first-team place at most clubs. Sadly for Ian Ross, it was not the case at Liverpool.

Ian, who eventually assumed the role of utility man vacated by Geoff Strong, made his debut as a substitute in January 1967. In the next two campaigns he stood in briefly for Smith, Byrne and Yeats at the back, impressing with reliability and skill, before Bill Shankly began to employ his tenacious qualities to shackle specific opponents. Ian did an effective job on Ball, then at his peak, when the Reds won 3–0 at Goodison in December 1969, but his finest achievement was the eclipse of 'Kaiser Franz' in a European Fairs Cup encounter with Bayern Munich in March 1971. He even found time to score Liverpool's only goal of the game as they reached the semi-final.

Ian enjoyed his longest unbroken run in 1971/72, wearing five different numbers during his spell of 20 games, before joining Aston Villa, for whom he performed with distinction alongside big centre-half Chris Nicholl. His success away from the hot competition of Anfield was well deserved.

BORN: Glasgow, 26.11.47. GAMES: 59 (9). GOALS: 4.

OTHER CLUBS: Aston Villa 71/2–75/6 (175, 3); Notts County *on loan* 76/7 (4, 1); Northampton Town *on loan* 76/7 (2, 0); Peterborough United 76/7–78/9 (112, 1); Wolverhampton Wanderers 79/80–81/2 (0, 0); Hereford United 82/3 (15, 0).

1966/67 – 1971/72

DOUG LIVERMORE

Doug Livermore was a neat, workmanlike midfielder who simply didn't come up to the standard demanded at Anfield. He was handed the prompting role vacated by Ian St John when the Scot was axed after the Reds' shock FA Cup quarter-final exit at Watford in February 1970 and enjoyed a 13-match run to the end of the season as Bill Shankly set about reshaping his ageing team. His displays revealed strength, honesty and some skill but he lacked pace and, most crucially, the inspiration for such an onerous task.

After that sequence Doug, who had made his debut as a substitute for Tony Hateley at Upton Park in April 1968, was never to start another League game for Liverpool and joined Norwich in November 1970 for £22,000. Carrow Road saw the best years of his playing career as he helped the Canaries gain promotion to Division One in his first full campaign in East Anglia.

Doug, who later saw service with Bournemouth, Cardiff and Chester, went on to become a respected coach and worked with the Welsh national team. After a spell in charge at Tottenham, in 1994 he returned to his spiritual home of Anfield to assist his old team-mate, Roy Evans.

BORN: Liverpool, 27.12.47. GAMES: 14 (3). GOALS: 0.
OTHER CLUBS: Norwich City 70/1–74/5 (114, 4); Bournemouth *on loan* 74/5 (10, 0); Cardiff City 75/6–77/8 (88, 5); Chester 77/8–78/9 (71, 6). MANAGER: Tottenham Hotspur 92-93.

1967/68 – 1970/71

PETER WALL

Peter Wall was a cultured defender who once seemed likely to succeed Gerry Byrne as Liverpool's long-term left-back. He arrived from Wrexham in October 1966 as the junior partner in a £26,000 full-back package which included Stuart Mason. But while Stuart was destined never to make a first-team appearance before returning to the Racecourse Ground, Peter made promising progress.

He made his debut at home to Burnley in March 1968, soon after Gerry had suffered the injury which was to end his career prematurely. Then, after makeshift stints by Tommy Smith and Ian Ross, Peter settled in for the remaining eight games of that season and the first 13 of the next. He revealed poise, skill and a calm assurance under pressure which perhaps veered too close to being casual for Bill Shankly's peace of mind, and Geoff Strong was handed the number three shirt for the duration of the campaign.

Peter, who perhaps needed a shade more drive for a top-rank career, resurfaced for a nine-match spell half-way through 1969/70 but didn't become established and joined Crystal Palace for £35,000. At Selhurst Park he found his niche and served the Eagles well for eight years.

BORN: Westbury, Wiltshire, 13.9.44. GAMES: 42. GOALS: 0.

OTHER CLUBS: Shrewsbury Town 63/4–64/5 (18, 0); Wrexham 65/6–66/7 (22, 1); Crystal Palace 70/1–77/8 (177, 3); Orient *on loan* 72/3 (10, 0).

1967/68 – 1969/70

ROY EVANS

The football career of Roy Evans stands as an inspiring example to any young professional with not quite enough ability to make it as a player at the top level. Roy was a skilful left-back who made his League debut against Sheffield Wednesday at Anfield in March 1970 as Geoff Strong's tenure was coming to an end and before Alec Lindsay became established. He was comfortable on the ball, passed well with his left foot and possessed boundless enthusiasm, but lacked the necessary pace to make the position his own.

Roy hung on as a reliable stand-by for four frustrating seasons but looked destined for soccer oblivion until manager Bob Paisley stepped in with the offer of a job coaching the reserves. Still only 25, Roy must have been tempted to turn it down in favour of seeking a playing career elsewhere but perhaps felt, deep down, that Bob was being realistic.

Accordingly, he accepted the opportunity and worked hard to make the most of it, leading his charges to the Central League championship at his first three attempts and going on to repeat his success regularly in the eighties. Before long, Roy was being mentioned as a possible Liverpool manager of the future ...

BORN: Bootle, 4.10.48. GAMES: 11. GOALS: 0.
MANAGER: Liverpool 94–

1969/70 – 1973/74

CHRIS LAWLER

Chris Lawler was hardly an eye-catching performer, seeming to saunter through games with all the apparent urgency of a man out walking his dog. There was no swagger, no tricks, no histrionics, but in time opponents came to realise - often ruefully, as they retrieved the ball from their net - that they ignored Liverpool's faithful right-back at their peril.

Not that his defensive capabilities weren't respected from the outset. It was obvious from early apearances deputising for centre-half Ron Yeats that the callow but composed Chris had all the qualities of a future back-four stalwart. No, what crept only gradually into the consciousness of opposing teams was an almost uncanny ability to ghost in behind his forwards and snatch goals when no threat seemed imminent. Presumably it was the result of instinctive anticipation, though sometimes it seemed like second sight.

The odd thing was that, unlike many defenders who pride themselves on finding the net, Chris was not a dead-ball specialist, never took penalties and did not possess a particularly powerful shot. Yet he can point to a career record of 61 goals, including ten in 1969/70 when he was the Reds' second-highest scorer and 11 in European competitions, which saw some of his most famous efforts. His most prolific continental campaign was that of the 1965/66 Cup Winners' Cup, in which he scored in three successive ties, starting with a deft header against Juventus before striking twice against Standard Liege and once against Honved.

Back in the First Division, Everton were twice the victims of the Lawler goal habit, both times at Anfield. In November 1970 Chris capped a stirring Liverpool comeback from a 2-0 deficit with a late winner and the following season scored with an overhead kick to complete a 4-0 rout.

Priceless though these attacking diversions were, Chris never allowed them to distract him from his primary responsibilities at the back. In fact, he fulfilled them so well that he missed only one League game between October 1965 and November 1973 - and that was when he was rested before the 1971 FA Cup Final. He first came to prominence in the 1963 semi-final, slotting into the middle of a reshuffled defence alongside Yeats, and then earned widespread praise when he stood in for the skipper in three Easter victories during the title run-in a year later.

In 1964/65, when the ageing Ronnie Moran stepped down and Gerry Byrne switched to the left flank, Chris was handed the regular right-back berth. The slim, upright youngster took his chance with aplomb, underlining his progress by stifling the talents of speedy Leeds winger Albert Johanneson at Wembley and claiming a Cup-winner's medal. Calm, skilful and good in the air, Chris became a fixture and assisted in two Championship triumphs before a knee injury sustained at Loftus Road ended his proud record of consistency, effectively sidelining him for the rest of 1973/74. Despite a handful of appearances the following term he was never the same again and - after a move to Manchester City was called off by Liverpool at the last minute - he joined Portsmouth, later returning to Anfield for a coaching stint.

Chris's England outings were limited to four; there might have been more had he possessed a little extra pace. Some would point to competition from Keith Newton and Paul Madeley but Kopites would have none of it. For them the man they called 'The Silent Knight' - a reference to his quiet, modest nature - was simply the best right-back in the business.

BORN: Liverpool, 20.10.43. GAMES: 546. GOALS: 61. HONOURS: UEFA Cup 72/3. League Championship 65/6, 72/3. FA Cup 64/5.
4 England caps (71).
OTHER CLUBS: Portsmouth 75/6-76/7 (36, 1); Stockport County 77/8 (36, 3).

1962/63 – 1975/76

LARRY LLOYD

When strapping centre-half Larry Lloyd limped out of the Anfield action in early 1974, few observers could have guessed that the England international had played his last game for Liverpool. The thigh injury which had ended his interest in the encounter with Norwich City didn't seem serious and he was confidently expected to make a quick return.

It was never to be. The smaller but more skilful Phil Thompson was slotted in alongside Emlyn Hughes, bringing a continental style to the Reds' central defence, and the partnership prospered so fruitfully that Big Larry, an ever-present in the League Championship and UEFA Cup triumphs of the previous campaign, found himself discarded for good.

Bill Shankly bought the towering West Countryman, a dominant stopper in the Ron Yeats mould, from Bristol Rovers for £50,000 in April 1969. He saw him as the eventual successor to his vaunted colossus and so it proved. Larry made his entrance for a two-match spell when Ron was injured early in 1969/70, but it was not until the last six games of the campaign, when Shankly was breaking up his beloved sixties side, that the new man took his place on merit – and kept it until that fateful thigh strain changed the course of his career.

Larry confidently assumed the burden of replacing a Liverpool legend and, as his experience grew, he showed there was more to his game than the obvious asset of aerial power. Though lacking pace, he was capable of using the ball well, especially with his left foot, and was exceptionally active in urging on his colleagues. His huge physical presence in opposition penalty boxes brought Larry disappointingly few goals but he did make one vital strike, heading what was to prove the winner against Borussia Moenchengladbach in the 1972/73 UEFA Cup Final

Despite being out of the side already, Larry was devastated at missing the 1974 FA Cup Final and accepted a £225,000 move to Coventry three months later. He didn't settle there and Brian Clough got a bargain when he signed him for £60,000 in 1976. With Nottingham Forest, Larry played a leading role in League Championship and European Cup glories and, for one match, won back his England place. A rare resurrection was complete.

BORN: Bristol, 6.10.48. GAMES: 217. GOALS: 5.
HONOURS: UEFA Cup 72/3. League Championship 72/3.
4 England caps (71-80).

OTHER CLUBS: Bristol Rovers 68/9 (43, 1);
Coventry City 74/5-76/7 (50, 5); Nottingham Forest 76/7-80/1 (148, 6);
Wigan Athletic 80/1-82/3 (52, 2).
MANAGER: Wigan Athletic 81-83; Notts County 83-84.

1969/70 – 1973/74

EMLYN HUGHES

A new adjective should have been invented for Emlyn Hughes; nothing in the dictionary adequately captures the essence of a man possessed by an almost demonic fervour for football in general and Liverpool in particular. Enthusiastic, energetic, ebullient - they've all been used and deserve to be discarded. Ask his old Anfield team-mates and they'll tell you that mere words could never do justice to the man who led them to some of their most memorable triumphs.

Emlyn's arrival in February 1967 marked the beginning of the end of an era. Bill Shankly was making his first, tentative moves to dismantle his great sixties side and the bubbly Barrow boy, who made a handful of appearances at left-back in place of the injured Gerry Byrne before permanently replacing left-half Willie Stevenson for 1967/68, was the first newcomer to claim a regular place.

Shanks' admiration of the rookie Hughes began one spring day in 1966 when he watched the 18-year-old - who was to become, in the lurid language of the Reds' boss, 'one of the major signings of all time' - make his debut for Blackpool. Bill was so impressed that he made a £25,000 offer straight after the game but had to wait ten months before securing his quarry for £65,000.

Having moved to Merseyside, Emlyn wasted no time in making an impact. In his first game, at home to Stoke City, he dominated Potters' play-maker George Eastham and four matches later he earned a famous nickname. From the day he felled Newcastle forward Albert Bennett with a rugby tackle - nothing malicious, more an example of youthful impetuosity - Hughes was branded 'Crazy Horse', a label that was his for keeps.

Not that such eccentric acts were needed to draw attention to such a promising player, for whom Leeds were soon willing to offer Peter Lorimer in part-exchange. Built like a dreadnought and with strength to match, long-striding Emlyn rampaged around the football grounds of England like a frisky rhino. If subtlety was lacking in his early approach, and if he did occasionally commit himself to rash tackles, his vast potential was always evident. Left-sided but good with both feet, strong in the air and boisterously inspirational, Emlyn became known for his dynamic surges into enemy territory. Southampton were on the receiving end at Anfield in April 1971 when he broke up an attack in front of his own goal, played the ball wide and steamed up the centre of the pitch. Arriving with uncheckable impetus on the edge of the Saints' box, he cracked a first-time shot into the net. Irresistible!

In 1973/74 Emlyn replaced Tommy Smith as captain and moved into the centre of defence, forming an enterprising partnership with Phil Thompson. By this time his play had matured, his approach calmer and more reliant on anticipation than the buccaneering tactics of old. Though not as popular a skipper with team-mates as Smith or Yeats, Emlyn was a motivator supreme, leading by example and unflagging in his zest. In five seasons in charge he held aloft two European Cups, one UEFA Cup, two League Championship trophies and one FA Cup. At such moments his all-embracing grin - so familiar since his emergence as a TV person - was an emblem of Anfield ascendancy although, always one to wear his heart on his sleeve, he could also radiate utter dejection more thoroughly than most. None who saw him drag himself up Wembley's 39 steps to accept an FA Cup loser's medal in 1977 will forget his despair.

Emlyn - who won more England caps as a Red than anyone else - was an emotional performer and a magnificent one. When he moved to Molyneux it was no surprise that he helped Wolves to League Cup glory. Somehow, though, that grin looked out of place above an old-gold shirt . . .

BORN: Barrow, 28.8.47. GAMES: 657. GOALS: 48.
HONOURS: European Cup 76/7, 77/8. UEFA Cup 72/3, 75/6. League
Championship 72/3, 75/6, 76/7, 78/9. FA Cup 73/4. 62 England caps (69-80).

OTHER CLUBS: Blackpool 65/6-66/7 (28, 0); Wolverhampton Wanderers 79/80-
80/1 (58, 2); Rotherham United 81/2-82/3 (56, 6); Hull City 82/3 (9, 0);
Mansfield Town 83/4 (0, 0); Swansea City 83/4 (7, 0).
MANAGER: Rotherham United 81-83.

1966/67 – 1978/79

RAY CLEMENCE

Ray Clemence was possibly the most important factor in Liverpool's continued success throughout the seventies. That assessment came from Bill Shankly, the man who paid Scunthorpe United £18,000 for the 19-year-old goalkeeper in June 1967 and then saw him rise to become one of the best - maybe, at his peak, the very best - in the world.

When Ray arrived at Anfield, Bill hinted that a first-team spot was there for the taking. But the canny Reds boss was either under-valuing the ability of 'keeper-in-residence Tommy Lawrence, which was not likely, or indulging in kidology to spur the new boy to greater efforts, which was. In the event Ray had to wait two and a half seasons to claim a place. By then, having tuned his talents to an irresistible pitch of readiness at the elbow of his helpful predecessor, he was itching to prove himself.

His early games were played behind giant, aerially-dominant centre-halves - first Ron Yeats, then Larry Lloyd - and initially Ray impressed with safe handling, sharp reflexes and a knack of getting down quickly to low shots. But as his confidence grew in subsequent seasons it was clear that he was a truly outstanding all-rounder; apart from a weakness in goal-kicking - on which he worked until it came up to scratch - there were no perceptible flaws. Ray combined a keen positional sense with shrewd anticipation, instinctively knowing when to leave his line and when to stay on it. This made for an unflashy technique but Shankly knew that acrobatics were a poor substitute for clean sheets and blessed the day he'd rescued Ray from Third Division obscurity.

Another immense Clemence virtue, so vital to the 'keeper of a team such as Liverpool which spent long periods in their opponents' halves, was concentration, and Ray possessed it in abundance. He could spend lengthy chunks of a match marooned behind one of the world's most niggardly defences without getting a touch of the ball and it's a measure of his greatness that he could respond so magnificently when the need arose. Indeed, but for the positive approach of this compulsive shouter and organiser - which demanded involvement and sometimes made him more sweeper than 'keeper - he might have spent his Anfield years as the loneliest man in English football!

Statistical proof of Ray's excellence is plentiful. In his first full term, which ended with a brilliant display in the FA Cup Final defeat by Arsenal, he conceded only 22 goals in his 41 games to help his defence equal the First Division record of 24 in a season. The achievement was destined to be eclipsed, however, as Ray let in a miserly 16 in 1978/79. But it's saves rather than cold figures which live on in the memories of Reds fans, with penalty stops being particularly vivid. One in a goalless away leg against Dynamo Dresden on the way to winning the 1975/76 UEFA Cup, when he dived full-length to reach a firm, low shot, was a real heart-stopper.

Clem, a dedicated trainer who relished scoring in five-a-sides and dubbed himself 'The White Pele', ended his 'Pool days on a surprising note in August 1981. Still at the peak of his powers, he announced the need for a new challenge and joined Spurs, for whom he made more than 250 senior appearances. It's hard to see, though, what he hoped to find in the way of motivation at White Hart Lane that was missing at Anfield.

Running parallel to his club exploits was an illustrious international career throughout which he vied for the England jersey with Peter Shilton. The debate about who was the better will rage forever; suffice it to say that Kopites, like Ray's new fans at White Hart lane, were a touch peeved with England manager Bobby Robson's final verdict.

BORN: Skegness, 5.8.48. GAMES: 656. GOALS: 0. HONOURS: European Cup 76/7, 77/8, 80/1. UEFA Cup 72/3, 75/6. League Championship 72/3, 75/6, 76/7, 78/9, 79/80. FA Cup 73/4. League Cup 80/1. 61 England caps (72-83).

OTHER CLUBS: Scunthorpe United 65/6-66/7 (48, 0); Tottenham Hotspur 81/2-87/8 (240, 0). MANAGER: Barnet 94-96.

1968/69 – 1980/81

STEVE HEIGHWAY

When Steve Heighway burst irreverently on to a decidedly staid First Division scene in October 1970, it was like a fresh breeze sweeping through a musty boot-room. With Alf Ramsey still in and wingers largely out - the likes of George Best and Eddie Gray were gilt-edged exceptions - the cobwebs were gathering thick and fast. The established order needed a kick up the backside and Steve, an innocent abroad in the tough, serious world of professional football, delivered it in his own gloriously unorthodox style.

He arrived from non-League Skelmersdale to bring pace and width to the Liverpool attack - Steve was a winger despite wearing the number-nine shirt - and it was soon clear that Bill Shankly had not burdened him with contemporary Division One protocol. Instead of laying the ball off and running for a return pass in the accepted fashion, Steve had the audacity to take players on, and it confounded them. Knees high and elbows pumping, he ran at defenders and went past them - again and again. Sometimes the Reds' raw flyer seemed to overstep himself and an opponent would be odds-on to rob him; but Steve, basin haircut bobbing and moustache bristling, would often find an extra spurt of speed, stick out a toe and skip away with the ball. His raking stride made it hard for defenders to recover and his ability to cross accurately at full tilt gave a thrilling new dimension to the Liverpool front line.

Shankly had resisted the challenge of other top clubs to sign the athletic amateur but it was when Steve was safely installed at Anfield that the manager pulled his master stroke. It would have been easy to dismiss the young Irishman's dashing approach as fine for the Cheshire County League but altogether too naive for the big time. Shanks, though, was too wise for that; having spotted something special he was *not* going to allow it to be coached into oblivion.

Steve, who won his first Eire cap the night after making his Liverpool debut, quickly turned heads with two-footed talents which enabled him to cut inside opponents or nip past them on the outside. No one who saw him rescue an apparently lost cause in the Merseyside derby at Anfield in November 1970 had the slightest doubt about his pedigree. Everton were two up and coasting when Steve broke free to score from an acute angle; then he slipped past two defenders to make John Toshack's equaliser with a cross from the left wing. The Reds went on to win with a goal from Chris Lawler but it was Heighway who had turned the tide. He capped his first, exhilarating campaign - in which he had only rarely frustrated by over-elaboration - with a near-post shot which deceived Arsenal 'keeper Bob Wilson and gave Liverpool a short-lived lead in the FA Cup Final.

In the early years of his career 'Big Bamber' - a university graduate, as was Brian 'Little Bamber' Hall - seemed jaded at times but Shankly, that motivator supreme, was always able to supply the remedy and the arrival of another star, Kevin Keegan, removed much of the pressure. By the mid seventies Steve, while less spectacular than in the past, had become an enviably consistent performer and spent much of his time in deep positions prompting the Keegan-Toshack tandem. His touchline breaks, however, continued to be a potent attacking option and one such sortie set up the first goal for Terry McDermott in the 1977 European Cup Final.

At the end of the decade Steve, in his thirties and faced with stiff competition for a place, crossed the Atlantic to end his playing days before returning to Anfield to coach youngsters. At the time it was felt that if he brought half as much flair to his new task as he had· once displayed on the world's football fields, then Liverpool could look forward to a sparkling future. Recent evidence, in terms of young men rising excitingly through the ranks, has been impressive, indeed.

BORN: Dublin, 25.11.47. GAMES: 444 (23). GOALS: 76.
HONOURS: European Cup 76/7, 77/8. UEFA Cup 72/3, 75/6.
League Championship 72/3, 75/6, 76/7, 78/9. FA Cup 73/4.
34 Republic of Ireland caps (70-81).

OTHER CLUBS: Minnesota Kicks, USA, 81.

1970/71 – 1980/81

BRIAN HALL

Brian Hall was the man who made an art form out of being unobtrusive - but let none doubt the value to Liverpool of this perpetually busy and consistent footballer throughout the first half of the seventies.

The diminutive Glaswegian claimed a regular place when Ian Callaghan suffered cartilage trouble in autumn 1970. Brian, whose previous League experience had been limited to substitute appearances, slotted neatly into the team on the right side of midfield, foraging energetically for the ball and passing it on with a minimum of fuss.

Bill Shankly was so pleased with the way the skilful, slightly round-shouldered deputy fitted into the team pattern that when Ian was fit again he returned in a central position, allowing Brian to continue in the wide role. The newcomer kept his place for the rest of the season, making light of a slight deficiency in pace, and saw the Reds through to Wembley when he adroitly hooked home an Alun Evans cross to beat Everton in the FA Cup semi-final at Old Trafford. Arsenal won the final but the future beckoned promisingly.

The following term proved to be one of consolidation for Brian, despite several spells out of the side, as Shanks' task of replacing his first great team neared completion. Honours came in 1972/73 with triumph in the UEFA Cup and a Championship medal, though Brian was ousted for much of that campaign and the one that followed by the newly arrived Peter Cormack. He fought back to play in the victorious FA Cup Final against Newcastle in 1974 and then enjoyed his most active season in 1974/75, missing only seven League games. After that his first-team aspirations withered with the advent of Jimmy Case and he departed for Plymouth, then Burnley.

On retirement as a player, Brian - a graduate who rejoiced in the nickname of 'Little Bamber', standing four inches shorter than 'Big Bamber' Heighway - became a teacher, then returned to Liverpool as a Football In The Community officer.

He will go down as an untiring worker who didn't have that vital turn of speed which might have lifted him to a higher plane. But in the final analysis there'll be no complaints from Anfield about the days in a red shirt of the loyal, dependable and, yes, talented Brian Hall.

BORN: Glasgow, 22.1.46. GAMES: 196 (24). GOALS: 21.
HONOURS: UEFA Cup 72/3. League Championship 72/3. FA Cup 73/4.

OTHER CLUBS: Plymouth Argyle 76/7-77/8 (51, 16);
Burnley 77/8-79/80 (43, 3).

1968/69 – 1975/76

ALEC LINDSAY

Alec Lindsay was a man with a golden gift. Sadly, apart from three glorious seasons when he was arguably the best left-back in the land, he failed to make the most of it.

The talent in question was for passing, accurately and over long distances, with his left foot. To the casual observer that might not seem such a spectacular blessing but to anyone who has watched generations of defenders hoofing high balls hopefully in the general direction of their forwards it was an asset to be cherished.

Alec cost Liverpool £67,000 when he arrived from his home-town club of Bury in March 1969 and, like so many newcomers to Anfield from the lower divisions, went straight into the Central League 'finishing school'. He had been a wing-half with the Shakers and some respected judges were so impressed with his ball skills that they saw him developing along the lines of fellow Gigg Lane graduate Colin Bell.

After taking longer than many to settle with the Reds - Alec was not a 'natural' trainer - he made his debut and several more unremarkable appearances in midfield before switching to the left-back berth he was destined to grace so stylishly. He created a good impression with two spells in 1970/71, making the position his own in the following campaign when he forged one of the most profitable Anfield partnerships of the seventies. Much is heard of the Keegan-Toshack link but equally valuable, in a less obvious way, was Kevin's understanding with the resourceful blond defender. Alec's long, raking passes to his front-men, often bent teasingly around helpless opponents, were made for Kevin, who was adept at bringing them under instant control before creating his own brand of mayhem. The full-back seemed to sense where his nippy target was going to run, playing the ball into space intelligently and with perfect weight, and the tactic had a major influence in the Reds' UEFA Cup and League Championship double in 1972/73.

Come the 1974 FA Cup Final against Newcastle and Alec was still in tremendous form. He was under-employed at the back, courtesy of the Magpies' feeble attacking efforts, but was prominent on the overlap as the Reds surged forward. It was from one such foray that he made the crispest strike of his life, driving a ferocious cross-shot past 'keeper Iam McFaul, only to have his joy cut short by an offside whistle.

Such a minor disappointment did nothing to sour an accomplished season and when Joe Mercer, England's caretaker manager, drafted him into the national side that summer the career of Alec Lindsay was at its zenith with, it seemed, only cloudless horizons ahead. True, he had never been the quickest player and perhaps lacked the stamina for the midfield role which might have made more of his creative leanings, but he tackled well, read the game shrewdly and had found a productive niche.

Unfortunately, disillusionment was not far away. Alec's form faded badly in 1975 and he was replaced, first by Phil Neal and then by Joey Jones. For two years he strove in vain to regain his spot before taking that trusty left foot, briefly, to Stoke and the United States. The unhappy epitaph on the playing days of Alec Lindsay must be that many men of inferior ability managed to achieve much more.

BORN: Bury, 27.2.48. GAMES: 244 (2). GOALS: 18.
HONOURS: UEFA Cup 72/3. League Championship 72/3. FA Cup 73/4.
4 England caps (74).

OTHER CLUBS: Bury 64/5-68/9 (126, 14); Stoke City 77/8 (20, 3); Oakland, USA.

1969/70 – 1976/77

JOHN TOSHACK

John Toshack was the thinking man's version of that oft-maligned breed, the big, brave striker. While many of that ilk are strictly one-dimensional, ready to batter defences into submission or perish in the attempt, John ultimately offered - after much hard work - a more varied range of attacking possibilities. Of course, he had a distinct advantage over fellow members of the centre-forwards' union in that he was blessed for most of his Liverpool career with the presence of Kevin Keegan. The diverse talents of the towering Welshman and his nippy, opportunist partner combined to give the Reds many of their finest hours.

John, aged 21 and already an established international, was signed for £110,000 from Cardiff in November 1970 and quickly endeared himself to the Kop in the surest possible way - by dumping Everton on the seat of their pants. In one of the most rousing Merseyside derbies of modern times, John helped to erase a two-goal deficit, climbing high above the Blues' Brian Labone to head the equaliser, before nodding down Alec Lindsay's cross for Chris Lawler to clinch an emotional victory.

Such exploits were clearly a recipe for deification by the fans, but John's immediate progress did not match his dynamic start. His last 18 games of the season, including the FA Cup Final defeat by Arsenal, failed to produce a goal and it was apparent that, though he was always a power in the air, other aspects of his game were in need of serious attention. To his credit John applied himself well and - boosted by Kevin's breakthrough - gradually acquired more all-round skills, of which accurate distribution was the most notable. He used his newly-widened scope intelligently and often to devastating effect, laying on a steady stream of chances with subtle flicks to his effervescent accomplice and creating space by astute running off the ball.

But while this improvement enabled John to play an important role in winning six major trophies, his road to glory was rarely smooth. For most of his Anfield tenure he was dogged by a nagging thigh injury - only once did he exceed 30 League games in a campaign - and was engaged in perennial battle to defend his place. At various times he faced challenges from Graham, Evans, Whitham, Boersma, Waddle, Kennedy, Fairclough and Johnson, seeing off all but the latter two. In fact, his shirt returned to him so often that eventually he called it Lassie!

Despite sometimes dropping John, both Bill Shankly and Bob Paisley - who once agreed to sell him to Leicester only for the £160,000 deal to founder on a failed medical - liked him on duty for European encounters, in which he gave some of his finest performances. One of the most unexpected came in the 1972/73 UEFA Cup Final first leg at home to Borussia Moenchengladbach, for which Tosh had been omitted. The match was abandoned because of heavy rain but Shanks had spotted that the Germans were vulnerable in the air. Accordingly the six-foot target man was recalled for the rescheduled game and laid on two goals for Kevin.

John's most prolific term, though, was 1975/76 when he found the net 23 times, including three hat-tricks, on the way to a League title and UEFA Cup double. Thereafter fitness problems and hotter-than-ever competition for places preceded a move, as player-boss, to Swansea where phenomenal success put him on a management trail which was to take him all the way to Real Madrid. His stature as one of the greatest names in Welsh soccer history was confirmed.

BORN: Cardiff, 22.3.49. GAMES: 236 (9). GOALS: 95.
HONOURS: UEFA Cup 72/3, 75/6. League Championship 72/3, 75/6, 76/7.
FA Cup 73/4. 40 Wales caps (69-80). OTHER CLUBS: Cardiff City 65/6-70/1
(162, 75); Swansea City 77/8-83/4 (63, 24).
MANAGER: Swansea City 78-84; Sporting Lisbon, Portugal 84-85;
Real Sociedad 85-89; Real Madrid 89-90; Real Sociedad;
Deportivo La Coruna, all Spain; Besiktas, Turkey.

1970/71 – 1977/78

PHIL BOERSMA

Throughout his seven seasons on the fringe of the Liverpool team, Phil Boersma always seemed to be fighting a losing battle. A speedy utility forward with plenty of skill, he occasionally came agonisingly close to bridging the gap between Central League and First Division, but perpetually failed to convince first Bill Shankly and then Bob Paisley that he was any more than a handy man to have about the squad.

Phil first came into the reckoning on his 20th birthday in September 1969 when he was brought on as a substitute for Alun Evans during a League Cup defeat at Manchester City. Several League outings followed, but at a time of team transition and strong opposition for forward places, the curly-haired youngster failed to establish himself. He then made patchy progress over the next two campaigns, but in 1972/73 seemed on the verge of a breakthrough, playing 31 times and scoring 13 goals in all competitions to claim League Championship and UEFA Cup medals.

He might have spoilt his encouraging work and precipitated a premature end to his Liverpool days when he walked out on Shanks on FA Cup Final day 1974. Phil was outraged that after he had been substitute in previous rounds, Chris Lawler was given the job at Wembley. The manager understood his player's disappointment and the differences were patched up, but he continued to find himself on the edge of the action. Despite several settled runs, including one of 18 League matches in 1974/75, Phil remained Anfield's 'nearly man' and, pushed yet lower in the pecking order by the emergence of David Fairclough, finally relinquished his hopes of a long-term future with the Reds in December 1975 when he joined Middlesbrough for £72,000.

Liverpool had lost a player of some verve, as anyone who saw his spirited dash into the box to make a late winner for Kevin Keegan against Southampton at Anfield in March 1973 would confirm. But Phil's form was fitful and he wasn't helped by carping from over-critical fans, even if he was a split-second slower in reacting to opportunities than some of his international colleagues.

Subsequently, he fared no better in the lower divisions and after injury forced early retirement he took up coaching and physiotherapy. Phil returned to the Reds in 1991 as the right-hand man of Graeme Souness, his second Anfield sojourn proving rather less memorable than his first.

BORN: Liverpool, 24.9.49. GAMES: 98 (21). GOALS: 29.
HONOURS: League Championship 72/3. UEFA Cup 72/3.

OTHER CLUBS: Wrexham on loan 69/70 (5, 0);
Middlesbrough 75/6-76/7 (47, 3); Luton Town 77/8-78/9 (36, 8);
Swansea City 78/9 (18, 1).

1969/70 – 1975/76

JACK WHITHAM

Too much time on the treatment table robbed Jack Whitham of his chance to build a career at Anfield – and deprived Liverpool of a possible long-term successor to Roger Hunt. Jack was a strong, all-action centre-forward who was signed from Sheffield Wednesday for £57,000 in April 1970, four months after Roger's departure. At Hillsborough he had averaged only a little under a goal every two games but, alas, there was a catch. Jack had never started more than 18 games in a season thanks to a soul-destroying injury record; whenever he struck a patch of good form he was invariably sidelined before he could realise his potential.

He made his Reds debut as a stand-in for Bobby Graham in a goalless draw against Newcastle United at St James' Park early in 1970/71 but was offered only limited opportunities for the rest of that campaign. His first settled run came half-way through the following season and he responded with five goals in eight games, including a powerfully-struck hat-trick in a 3–2 Anfield defeat of Derby.

This sequence ended – inevitably – with fitness problems. After a two-game absence he returned to score the only goal in a victory at Huddersfield in February 1972 before he was struck down again. Although Jack, who was particularly prone to muscle strains, was to remain at Anfield for another two years before joining Cardiff City, he was never to play another first-team game for Liverpool. His bad luck continued wherever he went and he eventually gave up football to run a pub.

BORN: Burnley, 8.12.46. GAMES: 16. GOALS: 7.

OTHER CLUBS: Sheffield Wednesday 66/7–69/70 (63, 27); Cardiff City 73/4–74/5 (14, 3); Reading 75/6 (19, 3).

1970/71 – 1971/72

JOHN McLAUGHLIN

ALAN WADDLE

There was a time when Bill Shankly thought the slim, almost frail figure of schemer John McLaughlin would loom large in the seventies as one of the foundations of his second successful side. Sadly Shanks' optimism proved groundless as John's career withered and died in the harsh, hectic reality of First Division life.

His chance came during a period of transition for the Reds at the turn of the decade. The old order, so masterly in the sixties, was now being swept away and places were there for the taking. John was drafted in for the last match of 1969/70, a defeat at Stamford Bridge, and was then given 33 games in the following League campaign to establish himself.

He took the role of midfield creator and occasionally looked the part, coolly employing his deft touch on the ball and ability to judge the weight of a pass to good advantage. But pace and stamina were lacking, too often leaving John apparently out of his depth and struggling to have any effect on proceedings. Having failed to make the most of his lengthy settled run, he faded away as new players came into contention for his place. Eventually, after a brief spell on loan at Portsmouth, a serious knee injury put him out of the game.

BORN: Liverpool, 25.2.52. GAMES: 53 (2). GOALS: 3.

OTHER CLUBS: Portsmouth *on loan* 75/6 (5, 0).

The Liverpool career of gangling centre-forward Alan Waddle was a brief, unremarkable interlude enlivened by one moment of pure, unadulterated glory. It came after 68 goalless minutes of a Merseyside derby largely dominated by Everton at Goodison Park in December 1973. Ian Callaghan broke free on the flank and put in a speculative cross which Alan toe-poked at full stretch past stranded 'keeper David Lawson to win the match. It was the 6ft 3in striker's only goal in 22 appearances for the Reds – all made either deputising for John Toshack or as substitute – before he set off on a decade of travels which took him to six other League clubs.

Alan, a cousin of England winger Chris Waddle, never showed the necessary class to merit a prolonged stay at Anfield but he at least bowed out of the big time in an important match. He was called to the colours when Steve Heighway was injured in the 1977 European Cup semi-final second leg against FC Zurich at Anfield, but had little chance to impress and five months later was on his way to Leicester City for £45,000. His most productive spell came as a Toshack recruit at Swansea, whom he helped to rise from the Third Division to the First.

BORN: Wallsend, 9.6.54. GAMES: 16 (6). GOALS: 1.

OTHER CLUBS: Halifax Town 71/2–72/3 (39, 4);
Leicester City 77/8 (11, 1); Swansea City 78/9–80/1 (90, 34);
Newport County 80/1–81/2 (27, 8); Mansfield Town 82/3 (14, 4);
Hartlepool United 83/4 (12, 2); Peterborough United 83/4–84/5
(36, 12); Hartlepool United 84/5 (4, 0);
Swansea City 84/5–85/6 (40, 10).

1969/70 – 1974/75

1973/74 – 1976/77

IAN CALLAGHAN

If ever one player embodied the multitude of qualities which built Liverpool into one of the world's greatest clubs then, undeniably, Ian Callaghan was that man. From the day he made his debut as a teenager against Bristol Rovers at Anfield in April 1960 - receiving an ovation from team-mates, opponents, the crowd, even the referee! - until his departure for Swansea nearly two decades later, he was, without ever being a star in the accepted sense, a shining example of everything a top footballer should be.

Ian's career divides neatly into two halves. He spent the sixties as an orthodox right-winger, one of the best in the country, before converting into a chugging dynamo in central midfield, a role which was to win him a belated international recall at the age of 35.

He made his bow as a diminutive professional of six weeks' standing with only four Central League games behind him. A man-size shirt hung loosely on his wiry frame but there was no suggestion of a little boy lost when he started to play. In that first match he revealed confidence, bags of natural ability and a precious instinct which told him when to hold the ball and when to release it. A golden future awaited but Bill Shankly was wary of prematurely pitching his gifted rookie into the maelstrom of League football. A season and a half passed before he was awarded a regular berth and then he helped to win long-coveted promotion.

Ian's game blossomed in the First Division. He formed a potent partnership with left-flank trickster Peter Thompson and the honours flowed. While Peter was more devious, Ian was fast and direct, making it his business to reach the byline and feed Roger Hunt and Ian St John with a diet of crosses which did much to nourish the Reds' goal tally.

Never a heavy scorer himself, Ian did contribute several memorable strikes. Particularly satisfying was an acute-angled sidefoot from a well-rehearsed free-kick routine involving Hunt and Willie Stevenson that stunned Inter Milan in the 1965 European Cup semi-final at Anfield, though more spectacular was a 30-yarder which sunk Everton in autumn 1963 as Shankly's men headed for their first Championship.

The watershed in the Callaghan career came in 1970/71. Liverpool were experiencing an indifferent patch but their reliable right-winger was playing as well as ever until a cartilage operation sidelined him for four months. In his absence newcomer Brian Hall prospered and there were fears that Ian's days in a red shirt were numbered. Such qualms were not shared by the manager, who doubted neither his man's resilience, nor his capacity to adapt, and simply handed him a new job in midfield.

Ian responded by missing only four games in the subsequent five seasons, during which he was awarded the MBE, was voted Footballer of the Year and played a major part in placing untold strain on the Anfield trophy cabinet. His intelligence and enthusiasm, precise passing and limitless stamina were never seen to better effect and that return to the England side - he had been axed when Alf Ramsey abandoned wingers in 1966 - was a fitting reward. The cascade of tributes which followed genuinely puzzled the modest Cally, who felt his game had remained at the same consistent level throughout his years with the Reds.

When it was time to move on he could look back on an exemplary record. He had been the one common denominator in three fine teams, played more games than anyone in the club's history, never been cautioned by a referee and set a towering example of loyalty, dedication and skill. Ian Callaghan created a formidable standard; if others can meet it they will be great men indeed.

BORN: Liverpool, 10.4.42. GAMES: 843 (5). GOALS: 69.
HONOURS: European Cup 76/7. UEFA Cup 72/3, 75/6.
League Championship 63/4, 65/6, 72/3, 75/6, 76/7.
Second Division Championship 61/2. FA Cup 64/5, 73/4.
4 England caps (66-77).

OTHER CLUBS: Swansea City 78/9-79/80 (76, 1); Cork Hibernian;
Soudifjord, Norway; Crewe Alexandra 81/2 (15, 0).

1959/60 — 1977/78

PETER CORMACK

Peter Cormack was one of the most naturally talented Reds of the mid-seventies; sometimes surprising, invariably subtle, he was a pleasure to watch. Unlike so many midfielders, he was ready to risk losing possession to make a penetrating forward pass, often changing the pattern of play with a single touch. Bill Shankly had been an admirer of the talented Scot since he was capped as a teenage winger with Hibernian but it was in the more central, constructive role Peter adopted for Nottingham Forest that the Liverpool boss saw him making the greatest impact.

After paying £110,000 to prise him away from the City Ground in the summer of 1972, Shanks introduced Peter to his Championship-chasing side at the expense of the more prosaic Brian Hall, and revelled in his success. The new man quickly showed his mettle with incisive displays in which he employed his extensive repertoire of deft skills to full advantage and demonstrated that, for all his slight build, he was no shirker in the tackle. Despite standing only 5ft 8in, he was also good in the air - thanks to instinctive timing of the Ian St John variety - as Everton found out to their cost when he ghosted in at the near post to head the only goal of the October 1972 derby at Anfield.

Peter found a particularly able collaborator in Kevin Keegan, the quick-witted pair often dazzling opponents with their lightning one-two exchanges, and soon after the all-Mersey clash Birmingham fell victim to their tricks in front of the Kop. The Cormack-Keegan tandem seemed to skate over the greasy, rain-soaked surface, inspiring a thrilling 4-3 win after being a goal down at the interval.

Despite his undeniable artistic attributes, however, there were times when the Cormack contribution could be peripheral, his abilities submerged in the hurly-burly of the game, and there were those who championed the more consistent merits of the worthy Hall. But Shankly was convinced of Peter's values and he shared in League, FA Cup and UEFA Cup glory before a combination of cartilage trouble and the advance of other midfielders precipitated a November 1976 move to Bristol City. For three years he entertained fitfully at Ashton Gate before heading for Hibs and home.

BORN: Edinburgh, 17.7.46. GAMES: 168 (9). GOALS: 26.
HONOURS: UEFA Cup 72/3. League Championship 72/3, 75/6.
FA Cup 73/4. 9 Scotland caps.

OTHER CLUBS: Hibernian 62/3-69/70; Nottingham Forest 69/70-71/2 (74, 15); Bristol City 76/7-79/80 (67, 15); Hibernian 79/80-80/1.
MANAGER: Partick Thistle 80-84; Anartosi, Cyprus.

1972/73 – 1975/76

STEVE PEPLOW 1969/70

Forward. BORN: Liverpool, 8.1.49. GAMES: 3. GOALS: 0.
OTHER CLUBS: Swindon Town 70/1–72/3 (40, 11);
Nottingham Forest 73/4 (3, 0); Mansfield Town *on loan* 73/4 (4, 3);
Tranmere Rovers 73/4–80/1 (248, 44).

CHRIS FAGAN 1970/71

Full-back. BORN: Manchester, 5.6.50. GAMES: 1. GOALS: 0.
OTHER CLUBS: Tranmere Rovers 71/2–74/5 (84, 2).

STEVE ARNOLD 1970/71

Midfielder/Defender. BORN: Crewe, 5.1.51. GAMES: 1.
GOALS: 0. OTHER CLUBS: Crewe Alexandra 68/9–70/1 (15, 0);
Southport *on loan* 71/2 (16, 3); Torquay United *on loan*
72/3 (3, 1); Rochdale 73/4 (40, 1).

FRANK LANE 1972/73

Goalkeeper. BORN: Wallasey, 20.7.48. GAMES: 2. GOALS: 0.
OTHER CLUBS: Tranmere Rovers 69/70–71/2 (76, 0);
Notts County 75/6 (2, 0).

TREVOR STORTON 1972/73—1973/74

Midfielder/Defender. BORN: Keighley, 26.11.49.
GAMES: 11 (1). GOALS: 0. OTHER CLUBS:
Tranmere Rovers 67/8–71/2 (118, 9); Chester 74/5–83/4 (396, 17).

DEREK BROWNBILL 1973/74

Forward. BORN: Liverpool, 4.2.54. GAMES: 1. GOALS: 0.
OTHER CLUBS: Port Vale 74/5–77/8 (92, 13);
Wigan Athletic 78/9–79/80 (48, 8).

MAX THOMPSON 1973/74—1975/76

Defender. BORN: Liverpool, 31.2.56. GAMES: 1 (1).
GOALS: 0. OTHER CLUBS: Blackpool 77/8–80/1 (99, 6);
Swansea City 81/2–82/3 (26, 2); Bournemouth 83/4 (9, 0);
Port Vale *on loan* 83/4 (2, 0).

DAVE RYLANDS 1973/74

Defender. BORN: Liverpool, 7.3.53. GAMES: 1. GOALS: 0.
OTHER CLUBS: Hereford United 74/5–75/6 (22, 0);
Newport County *on loan* 74/5 (3, 1); Hartlepool United
on loan 75/6 (11, 0); Halifax Town 76/7 (5, 0).

BRIAN KETTLE 1975/76—1976/77

Full-back. BORN: Prescot, 22.4.56. GAMES: 4. GOALS: 0.
OTHER CLUBS: Houston, USA; Wigan Athletic 80/1 (14, 1).

CHRIS FAGAN

STEVE ARNOLD

FRANK LANE

DEREK BROWNBILL

TREVOR STORTON

STEVE PEPLOW

BRIAN KETTLE

DAVE RYLANDS

MAX THOMPSON

KEVIN KEEGAN

Kevin Keegan is one of the pivotal figures in Liverpool history and despite a dozen years of unprecedented, Dalglish-inspired dominance, he remains the biggest star the Reds have ever had. That's not to say he was the greatest footballer - such a claim would be contentious indeed - but for sheer charisma and public prominence there had been no one like him in the British game since the prime of George Best.

His initial impact after arriving from Scunthorpe for £35,000 in the spring of 1971 - 'robbery with violence' was how Bill Shankly later described the deal - was overwhelming. Kevin hit Anfield like a miniature tornado; he turned the hallowed training procedures upside down with an all-consuming urge to be first at everything, excelled on a pre-season tour of Scandinavia and, having been converted swiftly from deep-lying winger to striker, found himself in the team for the First Division opener against Nottingham Forest. He scored after seven minutes, ran amok like a demented jack-in-the-box for the rest of the match and generally served notice that Shanks had finally found the elusive special additive needed to inspire his rebuilt side.

Kevin proved quickly that his grand entrance was no fluke with a series of galvanising performances which caught the imagination of media and fans alike. He was a darting, irrepressible imp of a player, scampering to all corners of his opponents' territory and not loth to forage for the ball in his own half. Quick, brave and apparently inexhaustible, he possessed a sureness of touch with both feet which enabled him to trick defenders in tight spaces and, even at 5ft 8in, carried a potent aerial threat. Kevin's most precious assets, though, were a nimble brain - a delicately drifted European Cup goal against St Etienne in 1977 was a vivid example of improvisation at speed - and almost fiendish determination, a quality greatly admired by Shanks and which did much to forge a deep bond between the two men.

Kevin, whose front-line understanding with John Toshack appeared to border on telepathy at times, was instrumental in many of the Reds' most stirring mid-seventies triumphs. Personal highlights included his two-goal show in the 1974 FA Cup Final against Newcastle and, three years later, that scintillating swansong when he ran Bertie Vogts and Borussia Moenchengladbach ragged as Liverpool won the European Cup for the first time.

Sadly, but perhaps inevitably, there was bitterness on Merseyside when Kevin announced his decision to take his talents to Europe. Having been honest enough to give a full season's notice of his intention, he endured, with commendable dignity, the cooling of the Kop's ardour and perfidious jibes about his so-called greed. It even became fashionable to question his stature in the game and there were constant, slighting references to a 'manufactured' footballer, one who had reached the top by application rather than natural talent.

How short were the memories of such mealy-mouthed critics, and how blindly they lashed out at a man who had given no more than half a dozen below-par performances in as many years at Anfield, had captained England and was to go on to become European Footballer of the Year twice. Wherever he went thereafter, including Southampton and Newcastle (whom he was destined to transform as their manager in the nineties), he gave princely value for money. A Pele or a Maradona he was not, but in his own way Kevin Keegan *was* one of the greats.

BORN: Doncaster, 14.2.51. GAMES: 321. GOALS: 100.
HONOURS: European Cup 76/7. UEFA Cup 72/3, 75/6. League Championship 72/3, 75/6, 76/7. FA Cup 73/4. 63 England caps (72-82).

OTHER CLUBS: Scunthorpe United 68/9-70/1 (124, 18); SV Hamburg 77/8-79/80; Southampton 80/1-81/2 (68, 37); Newcastle United 82/3-83/4 (78, 48).
MANAGER: Newcastle United 92-97; Fulham as chief operating officer 97-.

1971/72 – 1976/77

RAY KENNEDY

Ray Kennedy was a rare bird, a deceptively talented individual whose inimitable contribution to one of Liverpool's most imperious sides made a nonsense of any attempt to pigeon-hole him. Glib descriptions of a powerful midfielder - which he became at Anfield after years as a successful striker with Arsenal - failed dismally to do justice to his full, subtle range of distinctive abilities.

When Bill Shankly signed Ray for £180,000 in the summer of 1974 - his last act as the Reds' boss - he was rescuing a slightly overweight centre-forward, still eight days short of his 23rd birthday, who had seemingly lost his way after playing a crucial part in the Gunners' League and FA Cup double of 1970/71. The newcomer found himself in at the dawn of the Paisley era and, despite an irritating injury which kept him out of the season's first four League games, impressed Bob enough to oust John Toshack from his front-running role. There followed a sequence of 24 games in which Ray managed ten goals, but then he lost his place as the Welshman was recalled in a bid to find a winning blend.

The turning point, however, was not far away. Towards the end of the campaign Paisley began experimenting with the former Highbury man in a deep-lying position behind the Keegan-Toshack spearhead - and liked what he saw. By November 1975 Ray was installed on the left of midfield where he was to help Liverpool lift ten major honours in six years of almost uninterrupted triumph.

His value to the team was incalculable, his footballing qualities legion, and if he didn't quite catch the eye like a Souness or a McDermott, Ray had much to offer the connoisseur. Still not the most athletic of figures - though more streamlined than on his arrival - he had a delicate touch for such a big man; he was adept at shielding the ball, a legacy of his days as a striker, and his distribution was intelligent, swift and decisive. Like all top players who are short of pace, Ray read the game well and often changed the emphasis of an attack with a sweeping crossfield pass, but perhaps his deadliest attribute was a knack of lurking unobtrusively on the left flank before making a late run into the box to finish off a move at the far post.

In important matches, he habitually spent the early minutes lying deeper than usual, doing a containing job before allowing his attacking flair to blossom as the game wore on, and opponents fell victim to a false sense of security. This tendency was especially marked in European encounters, in which the England international contributed some of his most vital strikes. An 83rd-minute away goal to upset Bayern Munich in the 1981 European Cup semi-final and a fierce second-half volley to turn the tide against Bruges when the Belgians were two up in the 1976 UEFA Cup Final are just a couple that remain sharp in the memory.

Ultimately squeezed out of the side by the youthful challenge of Ronnie Whelan in December 1982, Ray joined John Toshack's colony of former Reds at Swansea for only £20,000 less than his purchase price. A brief stint at Hartlepool preceded a spell as a publican and a coaching appointment at Sunderland before it was revealed that he had Parkinson's disease, which he has battled with characteristic courage. Shanks, as usual, encapsulated the essence of a footballer better than most when he said of Ray: 'He played in no-man's land in a world of his own but he gave the team balance. He had style and he reminded me of Matt Busby. Ray Kennedy was some player.'

BORN: Seaton Delaval, Northumberland, 28.7.51. GAMES: 381 (3). GOALS: 72.
HONOURS: European Cup 76/7, 77/8, 80/1. UEFA Cup 75/6. League
Championship 75/6, 76/7, 78/9, 79/80, 81/2. League Cup 80/1.
17 England caps (76-80).
OTHER CLUBS: Arsenal 69/70-73/4 (158, 53); Swansea City 81/2-83/4 (42, 2);
Hartlepool United 83/4 (23, 3).

1974/75 – 1981/82

TOMMY SMITH

If the spirit of the Anfield Reds ever took on human form it would probably tackle like a two-legged ton of bricks, bark orders in broadest Scouse and answer to the name of Tommy Smith. Here was a man, born in the shadow of his beloved ground, who served Liverpool for 18 years and grew to be the very personification of his club. He will go down in folklore as one of the hardest men the game has known - and he was - but to write him off as a mere destroyer is a mistake. Oh yes, Tommy could play a bit, too.

He made his debut at home to Birmingham in May 1963 as a deputy for injured right-half Gordon Milne, but it was in an Anfield encounter with Anderlecht in November the next year that he made his first major impact. Wearing a number-ten shirt, he operated as an extra defender, confusing the Belgians as Liverpool won comfortably. Instantly Tommy became an integral part of Bill Shankly's first great side, initially combative in midfield before moving into central defence where he could more easily make light of a comparative lack of pace. 'Think of yourself as Ron Yeats' right leg,' Shanks told him, and he developed into a trusty buttress of Division One's most formidable rearguard.

Tommy, a rumoured transfer target of Manchester United in his reserve days, was a confident, aggressive ball-winner whose distribution could rarely be faulted. His game, which always boasted more skill than he was given credit for, matured rapidly as he contributed vigorously to the 1965 Wembley victory over Leeds and the ensuing Championship campaign.

As the influence of better-known players waned with age, Tommy's authority grew ever more marked and he was the obvious choice to succeed Yeats as captain in March 1970. Taking over a team in the throes of transformation, he was an inspiration, constantly driving his team-mates to greater efforts - not shrinking from the task even if personally off form - and standing up for their rights in off-the-field dealings. Tommy relished the responsibility and in 1970/71 he delivered some of the finest performances of his life, being pipped as Footballer of the Year by Frank McLintock and winning his sole England cap.

That season he led Liverpool to the FA Cup Final, which was lost to Arsenal, before going on to a then unique double of the Championship and the UEFA Cup in 1972/73. His days as skipper were numbered, though, and he lost the job to Emlyn Hughes following a confrontation with Bill Shankly over being dropped in November 1973. After nearly joining Stoke, Tommy returned to the side at right-back in place of the sidelined Chris Lawler and helped to ensure a steady flow of trophies until, troubled by knee problems and with the team prospering in his absence, he announced in early 1977 that retirement was imminent.

How an injury to Phil Thompson changed all that! The old warhorse found himself back in central defensive harness to win a title medal, face Manchester United in the FA Cup Final and, most stirring of all, head the goal against Borussia Moenchengladbach in Rome that effectively won Liverpool their first European Cup. Fired anew with ambition, Tommy stayed for another term and would have played in a second European Cup Final if he hadn't dropped a pick-axe on his foot.

The Reds offered him a one-year contract while John Toshack came up with a better deal at Swansea, which he accepted. Tommy, who was to make a brief Anfield return as a coach, left in the knowledge that no one had ever fought more fiercely in the Liverpool cause. As one ex-opponent, himself no six-stone weakling, put it: 'There's a lot of very hard men - and then there's Tommy Smith!'

BORN: Liverpool, 5.4.45. GAMES: 632 (1). GOALS: 48. HONOURS: European Cup 76/7. UEFA Cup 72/3, 75/6. League Championship 65/6, 72/3, 75/6, 76/7. FA Cup 64/5, 73/4. 1 England cap (71).

OTHER CLUBS: Swansea City 78/9 (36, 2).

1962/63 – 1977/78

PHIL NEAL

Phil Neal will take his place in soccer history as the man who combined two of the game's most priceless commodities - success and consistency - to a hitherto unknown degree. In the nine seasons between 1975/76 and 1983/84 it took Liverpool 538 games to win 16 major honours; Phil was absent from the starting line-up just four times. His haul of medals is rivalled only by that of Alan Hansen, who missed more matches through injury and needed a little longer - without actually dragging his feet! - to assemble his collection.

A large slice of the credit for Phil's phenomenal record must go to Bob Paisley, who made the full-back his first signing when he handed Northampton Town a cheque for £66,000 in October 1974. It wasn't a case of plucking a teenage prodigy from the League's lower reaches as, despite the occasional flicker of interest from bigger clubs, Phil's six years of endeavour for the Cobblers had hardly secured him a national reputation. In Fourth Division circles, however, he was known for his consistency . . .

After joining the Reds it wasn't long before he was given a first-team chance - as deputy left-back for the injured Alec Lindsay in a goalless derby at Goodison Park - and then came a short stint standing in for Tommy Smith on the right. Phil's calm, assured performances were enough to convince Bob of his ability and he became a fixture in the side. For 18 months he alternated between the two full-back roles before settling on the right, partnering first Joey Jones and then, more enduringly, Alan Kennedy as Liverpool continued to gratify English football's most gargantuan appetite for trophies.

Phil's attributes, though immeasurably valuable to his team's cause, were of the unspectacular variety. He was not a fearsome tackler, preferring to jockey an attacker into a corner before perhaps nudging the ball away or forcing a rash pass. An intelligent positional player, he was masterful at denying space to wingers who often had the edge on him for pace but who rarely gave him a chasing - Leeds' Eddie Gray was one man who did so occasionally - and he was strong enough in the air to be an emergency centre-half.

Excellent though Phil's defensive work was, the constructive side of his game was even more outstanding. His distribution was immaculate, whether playing the ball in neat triangles with his midfielders or finding the front-men with long, fluent passes down the inside-right channel, and he was adept at stealing forward to deliver crisp crosses. The majority of his goals came from spot-kicks - his most famous sealed the 1977 European Cup Final victory over Borussia Moenchengladbach - but there were also several vital run-of-play strikes, the most notable being the prod which set Joe Fagan's side on the way to triumph in another European Cup Final, against Roma in 1984.

Dependable under pressure and an on-field talker who was constantly cajoling colleagues to greater efforts, Phil was well suited to succeed Graeme Souness as skipper for 1984/85 and carried the responsibility impressively. At 33, however, he was never going to be a long-term leader and half-way through the following term he left to become player-manager of Bolton Wanderers. The achievements of Phil Neal, the most-capped England right-back of all time, will stand forever as a monument to dedication, fitness and not a little skill.

BORN: Irchester, Northamptonshire, 29.2.51. GAMES: 633 (2). GOALS: 60.
HONOURS: European Cup 76/7, 77/8, 80/1, 83/4. UEFA Cup 75/6. League
Championship 75/6, 76/7, 78/9, 79/80, 81/2, 82/3, 83/4. League Cup 80/1. 81/2, 82/3,
83/4. 50 England caps (76-83).

OTHER CLUBS: Northampton Town 68/9-74/5 (186, 29); Bolton Wanderers 85/6-88/9
(64, 3). MANAGER: Bolton Wanderers 85-92; Coventry City 93-95; Cardiff City 96;
Manchester City as caretaker 96.

1974/75 – 1985/86

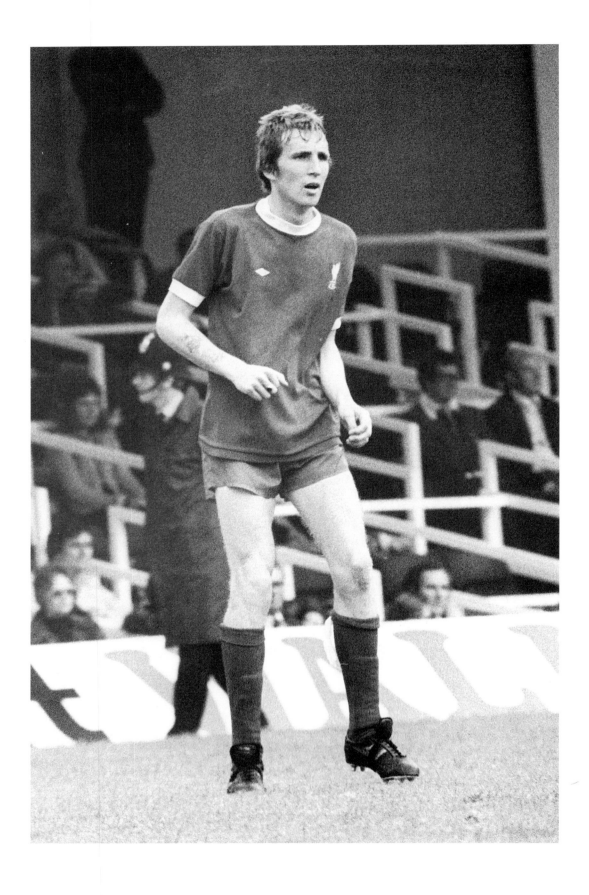

JOEY JONES

Who ate the Frogs' legs, made the Swiss roll and topped the lot by munching Gladbach? Why, none other than Joey Jones, of course, that tattooed tiger of a left-back taken to the hearts of Kopites like few of their heroes before or since. Joey, as proud to wear the red of Liverpool as that of his beloved Wales, enjoyed an affectionate rapport with the fans who loved his zealous approach, and they coined the colourful catchphrase to immortalise his spirited displays against the French, Swiss and West German champions on the way to lifting the 1977 European Cup.

Joey moved to Anfield from Wrexham for £110,000 in July 1975 to replace out-of-form Alec Lindsay, but early displays indicated too many rough edges for the top flight. Phil Neal switched to left-back, Tommy Smith came in on the right and Joey was out. That disappointment, however, was merely a prelude to his finest season; 1976/77 saw him claim a regular place in the side which took Europe's top prize, retained the Championship and narrowly lost the FA Cup Final to Manchester United.

Throughout that glorious campaign Joey played as though his life depended on it. Possessed with boundless enthusiasm, he was strong in the air and formidable in the tackle, though there was occasionally a tendency to commit himself to reckless challenges. But there were more serious weaknesses; his distribution was often wayward and offered a sorry comparison to the silky skills of Lindsay, and his reading of the game was at times rudimentary. Thus it was no real surprise when Joey lost his place during the following term as Bob Paisley shuffled the Reds' defence to accommodate the increasingly impressive Alan Hansen.

In September 1978 Jones returned to Wrexham for a paltry £20,000 but his days in the big time were not yet over. John Neal, his former boss at the Racecourse Ground, took him to Chelsea where he was doted on by the Shed as he had once been adored by the Kop, and Joey helped the Londoners win promotion to the First Division.

Next came a brief spell at Huddersfield, during which he overhauled Ivor Allchurch to become his country's most-capped player, an honour he retained for several years until his total of 72 was overtaken in turn by Peter Nicholas. Finally, and fittingly, Joey put in a third stint with his first club; this time the doughty Welsh warrior was home for good.

BORN: Llandudno, 4.3.55. GAMES: 97. GOALS: 3.
HONOURS: European Cup 76/7. League Championship 75/6, 76/7.
72 Wales caps (76-86).

OTHER CLUBS: Wrexham 72/3-74/5 (98, 2) and 78/9-82/3 (146, 6);
Chelsea 82/3-84/5 (78, 2); Huddersfield Town 85/6-86/7 (68, 3);
Wrexham 87/8-91/2 (132, 11).

1975/76– 1977/78

JIMMY CASE

It's a rare player who reaches his peak *after* leaving Liverpool but Jimmy Case was, after all, no ordinary performer. He bade farewell to the Reds at the age of 27, gave three and a half years' commendable but hardly remarkable service to Brighton, and then bloomed luxuriantly for Southampton in the play-maker's role denied to him at Anfield by the majesty of Graeme Souness. Was he allowed to leave Merseyside too soon or was the change as good as a rest? The question will always hang over the Case career, but should not be allowed to detract from six seasons of stirring achievements under Bob Paisley.

Jimmy, a £500 capture from non-League South Liverpool, made his debut at Anfield against Queen's Park Rangers in April 1975 in an attacking role wide on the right, but it was not until seven months later that his explosive talents earned a settled run in the team at the expense of midfielder Brian Hall. He marked his new stature with a rousing hat-trick at home to Slask Wroclaw of Poland in the UEFA Cup and then, having also scored against Dynamo Dresden in the quarter-final, exerted a crucial influence on the home leg of the final against FC Bruges. He had been omitted from the starting line-up in favour of David Fairclough but, with the Reds two down, was called on as substitute for John Toshack and immediately galvanised the side into three-goal retaliation. Rampaging ferociously down the right flank, Jimmy unsettled the hitherto calm Belgian defence, creating several clear-cut chances and chipping in with the equaliser himself.

Liverpool's vibrant, baby-faced rookie finished his first senior campaign with title and UEFA Cup medals and was clearly a prospect of prodigious potential. His value was twofold: in attack his pace, thrust and howitzer-style shooting offered a savage threat, while in deeper positions his lusty tackling, crisp distribution and general full-blooded vitality were a productive combination. Yet despite such an inpressive array of assets, Jimmy's place in the side during the treble-hunting campaign which followed was not a formality. Until the spring of 1977, when he slotted in on the right of Terry McDermott, the two had fought a well-matched battle for the number-eight shirt. Come the run-in, Jimmy was on his mettle, playing an enterprising part in the League and European Cup triumphs and winning plaudits as the Reds' best player in the FA Cup Final against Manchester United. Though a Wembley loser, he had the consolation of scoring the game's finest goal, swivelling on the 18-yard line to beat Alex Stepney with a sweetly-struck half-volley.

Over the next three seasons his name was seldom missing from Liverpool's team-sheet and with Souness, McDermott and Ray Kennedy formed one of the world's most effective - and attractive - midfield units. But in 1980/81 Jimmy was ousted by the industrious Sammy Lee and spent most of his time on the substitute's bench, clearly an unacceptable situation for a 27-year-old of his calibre.

With no likelihood of a swift recall he was sold to Brighton for £350,000 and, in his second season with the Seagulls, had the huge satisfaction of returning to Anfield to score the goal which knocked his former team-mates out of the FA Cup. When, aged 30, he moved to the Dell for a token £25,000, Jimmy's career looked to be petering out; half a decade and some 200 League matches later he was playing better than ever, maturity having revealed unsuspected depths of craft and insight. As his manager at the time, Chris Nicholl, put it: 'If the game is a language, then Jimmy is undoubtedly a professor.'

Even then he wasn't ready to retire, the Case history encompassing five more clubs until 1995, when a little matter of a suspected broken neck convinced him to step aside. A few days later Jimmy, his fears of serious injury laid to rest, put aside the temptation of a playing comeback but returned to the game for a demanding stint as boss of troubled Brighton,

BORN: Liverpool, 18.5.54. GAMES: 236 (25). GOALS: 45. HONOURS: European Cup 76/7, 77/8, 80/1. UEFA Cup 75/6. League Championship 75/6, 76/7, 78/9, 79/80. League Cup: 80/1. OTHER CLUBS: Brighton and Hove Albion 81/2-84/5 (127, 10); Southampton 84/5-90/1 (215, 10); Bournemouth 91/2 (40, 1); Halifax Town 92/3 (21, 2); Wrexham 92/3 (4, 0); Darlington 93/4 (1, 0); Brighton 93/4-95/6 (32, 0). MANAGER: Brighton 95-96.

1974/75 — 1980/81

TERRY McDERMOTT

There were suspicions during Terry McDermott's early days at Anfield that he was destined to be a £170,000 misfit; he became instead a creative inspiration in one of the Reds' most exhilarating combinations. At his irresistible best he was the free spirit in a beautifully balanced midfield quartet led by anchor man Graeme Souness with Jimmy Case on the right flank and Ray Kennedy on the left. Terry's roving commission gave full rein to a potent cocktail of vision and stamina which prised open many of the world's tightest defences.

It was not always thus. Bob Paisley signed the Liverpool-born schemer from Newcastle in November 1974 after he had impressed against his home-town club in that year's FA Cup Final. Terry went straight into the side but failed to settle as the new manager experimented in an attempt to emulate the success of the Shankly era. When the trophies started rolling in, largely without Terry's assistance - Bob's Reds won the Championship and UEFA Cup in 1975/76 - it seemed likely that he would be written off as a mistake, albeit an expensive one, and unloaded.

But Paisley kept faith with the wiry ex-Magpie and when, in the following campaign, Liverpool were pushing for a squad-sapping treble, Terry began to blossom. After vying for a place with Case - whose stern tackling he could never remotely emulate - for most of the season, he became established in the spring and played a memorable part in a tumultuous run-in which saw the title and the European Cup end up at Anfield but the FA Cup slip away to Old Trafford. He was especially dangerous when running from deep positions and was adept at arriving late in the penalty area where his finishing, by turns powerful and subtle, could be deadly. Terry's most valuable goal that term - and of his career, come to that - was the opener against Borussia Moenchengladbach in Rome where the Reds lifted Europe's top prize so gloriously. He ghosted, typically, down the inside-right channel to take a pass from Steve Heighway before clinically curling the ball past the German 'keeper. A month earlier there had been an even more mouth-watering piece of opportunism when Terry had spotted Everton's David Lawson off his line and chipped an exquisite goal in the FA Cup semi-final at Maine Road.

But the McDermott zenith was not reached until the arrival of Souness in 1978. The Scot's all-pervading influence on central midfield gave the newly-capped England international the liberty he needed to express his talents fully. A natural athlete, Terry made runs to all corners of the pitch, often acting as a decoy and creating space for colleagues to exploit, and when he did gain possession his instinctive control and incisive passing ability usually made the most of it.

He remained in his pomp for three years - in 1980 he was the first man to win awards from the football writers and his fellow players in the same season - and two incidents against Spurs during this period emphasise his dual value, as team man and individual. In September 1978 at Anfield he started and finished a flowing end-to-end move that capped a 7-0 annihilation, and 18 months later at White Hart Lane he decided an FA Cup quarter-final with a spontaneous flighted shot from near the corner flag.

Despite winning title and Milk Cup medals in 1981/82, Terry seemed to lose impetus and returned to Tyneside to help Kevin Keegan effect a Newcastle revival. That particular renaissance proved to be of the short-term variety, but when the two men were reunited at St James' Park a decade later - with Terry as assistant to manager Kevin - they transformed the Magpies into one of the most entertaining and dynamic sides of the nineties.

BORN: Kirkby, Liverpool, 8.12.51. GAMES: 310 (12). GOALS: 75.
HONOURS: European Cup 76/7, 77/8, 80/1. League Championship 76/7, 78/9, 79/80, 81/2. League Cup 80/1, 81/2.
25 England caps (77-82).

OTHER CLUBS: Bury 69/70-72/3 (90, 8); Newcastle United 72/3-74/5 (56, 6) and 82/3-83/4 (74, 12); Cork City 84/5; Apoel, Cyprus.

1974/75 – 1982/83

DAVID FAIRCLOUGH

It was not a palatable circumstance for a young, ambitious striker to stomach, but David Fairclough was invariably at his most effective in a number-12 shirt. He loathed the much-touted 'Supersub' tag, feeling it implied an inability to create a major impact over 90 minutes. Sadly for David, that was the truth.

He caused his first sensation when his goals in the spring of 1976 turned the title race in Liverpool's favour. Coming on as substitute he won the points against Burnley, Everton (after 88 minutes) and Stoke at Anfield as well as netting in games which he actually started at Carrow Road and Maine Road. Media and supporters were ecstatic; if he could cause so much havoc at the tail-end of matches, they reasoned, what on earth could he do if he was there at the kick-off?

David, also known as the 'Bionic Carrot' in reference to his flaming hair and blistering pace, elevated his reputation to yet dizzier heights a year later when he notched what was arguably the most important goal in his club's history to that date. Near the end of the European Cup quarter-final at Anfield, St Etienne held the advantage of an away goal; the Reds had to score or perish and on came David for John Toshack. Six minutes from time he received a pass on the left from Ray Kennedy, dribbled past three defenders and slipped the ball under the advancing 'keeper. He was practically canonised on Merseyside and Bob Paisley named him in his starting line-up with increasing frequency.

Though 1977/78 was his most successful season to date – his European Cup Final appearance was a personal highlight – it became disturbingly obvious that David was fractionally short of the all-round quality demanded at the top club level. He did have an unorthodox knack of going past opponents, often stumbling clumsily and getting rebounds from their legs, and continued to snatch the odd important goal. But his overall form was patchy and over a full 90 minutes he tended to drift out of the action, seeming to lack both stamina and concentration.

As new players arrived at Anfield, David slipped out of contention, though he remained a paradox to the last – one minute displaying a gloriously unexpected touch, the next fluffing a simple pass. After leaving the Reds he failed to settle elsewhere and will go down as a man of whom the public, beguiled by heavily edited TV highlights, expected too much.

BORN: Liverpool, 5.1.57. GAMES: 88 (62). GOALS: 52.
HONOURS: European Cup 77/8. UEFA Cup 75/6.
League Championship 75/6, 76/7, 79/80.

OTHER CLUBS: Toronto Blizzard, Canada 82; Lucerne, Switzerland 83/4-84/5;
Norwich City 84/5 (2, 0); Oldham Athletic 85/6 (17, 1);
Beveren SK, Belgium, 86/7-88/9; Tranmere Rovers 89/90 (14, 1);
Wigan Athletic 90/1 (7, 1).

1975/76 – 1982/83

DAVID JOHNSON

Reputations count for nothing at Anfield, as England centre-forward David Johnson discovered when he left Ipswich Town in August 1976 to become Liverpool's first £200,000 signing. During his initial two frustrating seasons with the Reds, neither international stature nor mammoth price tag was enough to guarantee him a regular place in the team. Not that David, a chirpy, down-to-earth character, expected any favours; with characteristic grit he fought back to justify fully Bob Paisley's original faith, helping to assemble a prodigious collection of silverware and, for good measure, winning five further caps.

Merseyside-born David checked in at Anfield, where he had once cheered his boyhood idols Roger Hunt and Ian St John, nine years after starting his career as an apprentice at Goodison Park. In fact, his delay in donning the red shirt would have been drastically reduced if either of Bill Shankly's bids to sign him in the early seventies had paid off, but first Everton's Harry Catterick - who was adamant that no player of his would join the Blues' greatest rivals - and then Ipswich boss Bobby Robson rebuffed all overtures.

Having got their man at the third attempt, Liverpool pitched him straight into first-team action. There seemed no reason why David would not be a hit; he was quick, skilful and unselfish, and his courageous approach - utterly refusing to be intimidated by the most physical of opponents - was guaranteed to endear him instantly to the Kop. But the manager was blessed with a large and gifted squad and, in the course of his permutations, David was often the man to be left out. Not helped by a succession of niggling injuries, he managed only glimpses of his best form and, although he collected a title medal and figured in the Wembley defeat by Manchester United, he missed out on European Cup glory.

In 1977/78, with Keegan gone and Toshack soon to depart, it was hoped that a link with newcomer Kenny Dalglish would give the Johnson career renewed impetus, but David Fairclough was often chosen to play alongside the Scot and it was not until the spring that the ex-Ipswich striker began to look like his old self. Then came bitter disappointment - with the European Cup campaign reaching a climax David strained knee ligaments and was sidelined for the rest of the season. After beating FC Bruges in the final, sympathetic team-mates - who knew him as 'Doc' because his kitbag contained a remedy for most ailments - procured him a special medal from FIFA, but it was an unfulfilled, if typically determined David Johnson who prepared for 1978/79.

At last, however, his luck had changed. Given the luxury of two settled stints in harness, he now struck up a prosperous partnership with Kenny which was to form the spearhead of one of the great Liverpool sides. After his lacklustre interlude, David was a revelation; his sharp control, work-rate and knack of taking up good positions brought him 37 goals in 63 starts over two League campaigns and his comeback was fittingly crowned when he netted twice against Aston Villa at Anfield in May 1980 to seal a second successive Championship.

His scoring rate diminished in the following term and when a young fellow called Ian Rush came along, David returned to his first club for £100,000. As the first man to score a derby winner for both Everton and Liverpool he occupies a unique place in Merseyside folklore. But Anfield saw more of his prime than Goodison and it is as a Red - a title he wore with such pride - that Johnno will be best remembered.

BORN: Liverpool, 23.10.51. GAMES: 174 (30). GOALS: 78.
HONOURS: European Cup 80/1.
League Championship 76/7, 78/9, 79/80, 81/2. 8
England caps (75-80).
OTHER CLUBS: Everton 70/1-72/3 (50, 11); Ipswich Town 72/3-75/6 (137, 35); Everton 82/3-83/4 (40, 4); Barnsley on loan 83/4 (4, 1); Manchester City 83/4 (6, 1); Tulsa Roughnecks, USA, 84; Preston North End 84/5 (24, 3).

1976/77 – 1981/82

SAMMY LEE

Scouser Sammy Lee was the chunky bundle of energy whose skill and enthusiasm cut short the Reds career of Jimmy Case in its prime - only for his own Liverpool days to end in a similarly premature fashion. Sammy made his League debut as a substitute against Leicester City at Anfield in April 1978, scoring in a 3-2 victory, but was then stranded on the fringe of the side for the next two years. With such formidable opposition for a place - if Case seemed hard to dislodge it was hardly conceivable that he would oust Souness or McDermott - his future seemed cloudy. Youngsters in that situation often fail to make the breakthrough, but Sammy was made of stern stuff and in 1980/81 he displaced Jimmy on the right side of midfield.

A buzzing support player and relentless marker, he quickly endeared himself to the fans with his never-say-die approach - on the Kop they reckoned the young Lee had the Liver Bird engraved on his heart - and became a fixture in the team that won three successive Championships, two European Cups and four League/Milk Cups. In some respects Sammy's play was reminiscent of Ian Callaghan's; he was a smooth passer, read the game well and had the ability to go past an opponent, though he lacked Cally's acceleration. His tackling, however, was fiercer than that of the great Anfield clubman and often he provided cover when full-back Phil Neal ventured forward. One of Sammy's most valuable defensive contributions came against Roma in the 1984 European Cup Final as the Reds withstood periods of pressure before going on to win on penalties.

At the opposite end of the pitch his strike-rate was disappointing, especially as he possessed a strong shot - as demonstrated with a goal from a powerful free-kick on his England debut against Greece - and the fine touch to deliver the most tantalising of chips. But finding the net had never been his priority, and at the outset of 1984/85 Sammy Lee seemed set for many more seasons at the top; he was only 25, at the peak of his powers and an established international.

Sadly, it wasn't to be. Fitness problems and a loss of form conspired to shatter his confidence and, faced with the exuberant challenge of Craig Johnston, he faded out of contention. In August 1986 he left his beloved Merseyside for Queen's Park Rangers, but failed to settle and a year later headed for the sun with Osasuna of Spain. He performed creditably in the Spanish League, but in January 1990 he returned to England and signed for Southampton, where he linked up again with Jimmy Case.

After making little impact either at The Dell or Bolton's Burnden Park, the final port of call in his playing career, Sammy answered the summons from Graeme Souness to take over from Phil Thompson as Liverpool's reserve-team coach. Back where he had been happiest, the likeable Lee flourished in his new role, surviving the fall of Souness and fitting seamlessly into the Roy Evans regime.

BORN: Liverpool, 7.2.59. GAMES: 279 (7). GOALS: 19.
HONOURS: European Cup 80/1, 83/4. League Championship 81/2, 82/3, 83/4, 85/6. League Cup 80/1, 81/2, 82/3, 83/4. 14 England caps (82-84).

OTHER CLUBS: Queen's Park Rangers 86/7 (30, 0); Osasuna, Spain; Southampton 89/90 (2, 0); Bolton Wanderers 90/1 (4,0).

1977/78 – 1985/86

GRAEME SOUNESS

There can hardly have been a more all-pervading influence in the middle of a football field than that of Graeme Souness; in his pomp he was the emperor of Anfield, a dead-eyed dictator of all that came his way. He was one of the few British players of the eighties to merit world-class status, but perhaps the greatest tribute to the lethal Souness combination of the devastatingly skilful and the crunchingly physical is that when he left for Italy in 1984 he was actually *missed*. When the likes of Kevin Keegan and Ian Rush moved on, and even when Kenny Dalglish forsook the red shirt for the manager's tracksuit, Liverpool merely shuffled the pack, changed gear and carried on with the business of winning trophies; the Scottish international play-maker's departure, however, left a void which took a full season to fill.

Few would have predicted such an illustrious career for the 17-year-old rookie when, after signing for Spurs as an outstanding schoolboy, he failed to settle in the south and left for Middlesbrough without making the White Hart Lane first-team. At Ayrsome Park he began to realise his potential and looked every inch a star of the future just waiting for a wider stage. That stage, of course, was Anfield and immediately after Bob Paisley signed him in January 1978 for £352,000 - then a record deal between Football League clubs - Graeme began to hint at the riches to come. In his Reds debut at West Bromwich he scarcely misplaced a pass and settled quickly to become the hub of a midfield which already contained McDermott, Case and Kennedy.

Graeme's first taste of glory with his new club came four months after his arrival, when his incisive through-ball created the winner for Dalglish in the European Cup Final against FC Bruges. In the campaigns which followed, his dominance mushroomed as he orchestrated some of the most compelling football ever served up by a Liverpool side, spearing passes to all corners of the pitch and tackling with an implacable ferocity which at times bordered on the brutal. Tottenham felt the Souness bite in March 1982 when he came on as substitute - he was returning after a back injury - with the Reds two goals down in a match dominated thus far by the strength of Graham Roberts and company. The abrasive number 12 soon made his mark, and the final score was 2-2. Graeme supplemented his creative and ball-winning talents with occasional displays of potent finishing, none more emphatic than the thunderous volley which screamed past Paddy Roche into the Manchester United net at Anfield in February 1978, though his swivelling drive which beat Everton in the 1984 Milk Cup Final replay was more valuable.

Was Graeme the complete player? Well, he lacked pace, though the side's pattern of play rendered the defect irrelevant, and for a man standing only an inch short of 6ft he was poor in the air. But such a trifle paled into nothingness compared with his overall contribution which, after a wretched team showing at home to Manchester City on Boxing Day 1981, increased still further when he replaced Phil Thompson as captain. In his 29 months in charge Graeme led Liverpool to three successive League titles and League/Milk Cups and one European Cup to become the most successful skipper in the club's history, forcibly demanding - and usually getting - the highest standards. In June 1984 he made a £650,000 move to Italy, where his brand of play was appreciated avidly, and he prospered there for two years before returning to Britain to have an even more significant effect on Rangers than he had exerted on Liverpool. 'Suey' - a man held more in awe than affection by most fans - was once again stamping his authority on one of football's greatest institutions, though turbulent times awaited. In due course, there would be a second coming at Anfield which would prove as traumatic as his first had been triumphant. More of that later; for now, it would be monstrously unjust if Graeme Souness's managerial imperfections were allowed to obscure his sheer majesty as a footballer.

BORN: Edinburgh, 6.5.53. GAMES: 350 (2). GOALS: 56.
HONOURS: European Cup 77/8, 80/1, 83/4. League Championship 78/9, 79/80, 81/2, 82/3, 83/4. League Cup 80/1, 81/2, 82/3, 83/4. 54 Scotland caps (74-86).

OTHER CLUBS: Middlesbrough 72/3-77/8 (176, 22); Sampdoria, Italy, 84/5-85/6; Rangers 86/7-89/90 (50, 3). MANAGER: Rangers 86-91; Liverpool 91-94; Galatasaray, Turkey, 95-96; Southampton 96-97; Torino, Italy, 97; Benfica, Portugal, 97-.

1977/78 – 1983/84

ALAN HANSEN

Alan Hansen is not a flamboyant man. If he were, if his football had exuded fire instead of ice, and he had greeted triumph with a swagger rather than his customary unassuming shrug, he would have received a more generous measure of the public acclaim which was his inalienable due as the outstanding British defender of the eighties. But no matter if his immaculate skills rarely earned the tabloid headlines. Alan can be content that no one in the game - with the mysterious exception of successive Scottish team managers - undervalued his colossal contribution to 13 seasons of almost uninterrupted Anfield glory as he ploughed his elegant furrow at the heart of the Reds defence.

The £100,000 signing of the tall, spindly centre-back from Partick Thistle in May 1977 was arguably Bob Paisley's most canny excursion into the transfer market. In the subsequent campaign, a handful of appearances deputising for the injured Phil Thompson made it amply clear that the pale, dark-haired youngster was an inspired long-term investment, even if the characteristic calm that was later to be hailed as one of his supreme assets set off tremors of apprehension on the Kop. Fans not familiar with the Hansen trademark of unflappability under pressure would gape as an apparently casual Alan would dribble his way out of the most perilous situation. Occasionally he would be caught in possession but, his confidence increasing as he replaced Emlyn Hughes as Thompson's regular partner in 1978/79, such errors grew so infrequent as to become collectors' items.

As a new decade dawned, Alan matured into a well-nigh matchless performer, his cool approach so much a speciality that if he found touch it was construed as wild panic! An instinctive ability to read the game provided the platform for his more obvious skills and offset a distinct lack of pace which was shown up only rarely - Gary Lineker *did* manage it in the first half of the 1986 FA Cup Final.

Having won the ball, probably by an intelligent interception, Alan invariably made the time and space to use it effectively, usually laying it off with the utmost precision. Rarely was a defender blessed with silkier distribution - the chipped pass which tore open the Manchester United defence and enabled Steve McMahon to set up a John Aldridge goal at Old Trafford in November 1987 would have done credit to any play-maker. Alternatively he would embark on one of those imperious sallies deep into opposition territory, with all the magisterial dignity of a ship in full sail, offering his side an extra attacking dimension.

Of course, the more mundane tasks were not beyond Alan. He was efficient in both the air and the tackle, though his economical, unobtrusive style meant that seldom did he seem stretched; certainly, it was unusual for him to land on his backside. An even temperament - Joe Jordan, in the 1979 FA Cup semi-final, was one of the few men to rattle him - made him an ideal choice to replace Phil Neal as captain in October 1985 and his leadership played a vital part in that season's League/FA Cup double.

Throughout an Anfield career which saw Alan thrive in successive partnerships with Thompson, Mark Lawrenson, Gary Gillespie and Glenn Hysen and brought him 16 major honours, he often suffered knee trouble, but it was not until 1988/89 that he endured a lengthy lay-off.

After his retirement, aged 35 in 1990, there were persistent rumours linking him with the Liverpool managerial seat vacated so dramatically by his friend, Kenny Dalglish. But he had witnessed at first hand the personal sacrifices demanded by the job, and he opted instead for a quieter life as a BBC soccer pundit. As cool and decisive in the studio as once he had been on the field, Alan Hansen became more of a household name by talking amiably about the game than ever he did by playing it so majestically.

BORN: Alloa, 13.6.55. GAMES: 604 (4). GOALS: 13.
HONOURS: European Cup 77/8, 80/1, 83/4. League Championship 78/9, 79/80, 81/2, 82/3, 83/4, 85/6, 87/8, 89/90. FA Cup 85/6, 88/9.
League Cup 80/1, 82/3, 83/4.
26 Scotland caps (79-87).

OTHER CLUBS: Partick Thistle 73/4-76/7 (86, 6).

1977/78 - 1989/90

RICHARD MONEY

When Liverpool paid Fulham £300,000 for England B and under-21 international Richard Money and promptly installed him in the reserves, it was no surprise to seasoned Anfield-watchers. It seemed inevitable that the Reds had signed up another promising youngster who would serve his time in the Central League before emerging a top-grade performer as the likes of Ray Clemence, Larry Lloyd and Alan Hansen had done before him. Sadly for Richard, the system is not infallible.

In his first term as a Red he made reasonable progress, twice deputising in the centre of defence – his favoured position – for Alan Hansen and even managing, briefly, to oust Alan Kennedy at left-back. A classy operator who was good in the air and comfortable on the ball, Richard hinted at a big-match temperament with sound displays in the successful second legs of two semi-finals – away to Bayern Munich in the European Cup and at home to Manchester City in the League Cup.

But Alan's resurgence in form and the arrival in August 1981 of Mark Lawrenson effectively closed the first-team door, and Richard joined Luton for £100,000. He never fulfilled his early potential and eventually returned to his first club, Scunthorpe, before becoming a coach.

BORN: Lowestoft, 13.10.55. GAMES: 15 (2). GOALS: 0.

OTHER CLUBS: Scunthorpe United 73/4–77/8 (173, 4); Fulham 77/8–79/80 (106, 3); Derby County *on loan* 81/2 (5, 0); Luton Town 81/2–82/3 (44, 1); Portsmouth 83/4–85/6 (17, 0); Scunthorpe United 85/6–88/9 (100, 0).

1980/81

HOWARD GAYLE

According to the Kop, Howard Gayle was the quickest thing on two legs - and Bayern Munich would certainly not disagree. The West Germans fell victim to the young winger's blistering speed in the second leg of the 1981 European Cup semi-final when he was brought on as substitute for the injured Kenny Dalglish. The Reds, hunting an away goal to reach the final (eventually supplied by Ray Kennedy), sent on Howard to run at the Bayern defenders and his pace had them floundering. Ultimately they were reduced to fouling him and when the enthusiastic rookie showed signs of retaliating he, in turn, was replaced by Jimmy Case.

It had been a performance of raw promise but the strongly-built Merseysider could not live up to it. Skilful and possessing a strong shot, Howard excelled in the Central League where he spent four fruitful seasons, but perhaps did not have the temperament for the big time. He was also unfortunate in that Liverpool at that time operated a four-man midfield which left little scope for a winger.

After various loan spells, Howard joined Birmingham City for £75,000 in January 1983 and won England under-21 recognition during an often impressive First Division stay at St Andrews. Further travels brought limited success before he seemed to settle with Blackburn Rovers. Late in his career, he had achieved a degree of consistency at last.

BORN: Liverpool, 18.5.58. GAMES: 3 (2). GOALS: 1.

OTHER CLUBS: Fulham on loan 79/80 (14, 0); Newcastle United on loan 82/3 (8, 2); Birmingham City 82/3–83/4 (46, 9); Sunderland 84/5–85/6 (48, 4); Dallas Sidekicks, USA, 86; Stoke City 86/7 (6, 2); Blackburn Rovers 87/8–91/2 (116, 29); Halifax Town 92/3 (5, 0).

1980/81

AVI COHEN

Avi Cohen was a back-four player of poise and class who had all the ability needed to make the grade with Liverpool but didn't stay long enough to do so. He stepped off the plane from Tel Aviv in May 1979 with a reputation as Israel's best all-round performer yet, at a cost of £200,000, he represented a sizeable gamble. Four months later in his first senior outing – replacing injured midfielder Ray Kennedy at Leeds – his peripheral showing proved he had plenty to learn about English football.

After six months of Reds-style training, Avi reappeared at left-back as deputy for Alan Kennedy and managed to score at both ends against Aston Villa at Anfield in the game that clinched the Championship. The second goal, the one that beat the visiting 'keeper, sent the Kop into paroxysms of delight and seemingly signalled the birth of a new hero.

Avi, as popular with team-mates as he was with the fans, complemented smooth distribution and shrewd anticipation with strength in the air and courage in the tackle, though he was a little short of pace. In 1980/81 he enjoyed an early run which threatened to evict Alan from the side but then, perhaps yearning for sunshine, he returned to Tel Aviv. Six years later he braved another British winter to be briefly reunited with former Liverpool team-mate Graeme Souness at Glasgow Rangers.

BORN: Cairo, 14.11.56. GAMES: 20 (3). GOALS: 1.
HONOURS: Israel caps.

OTHER CLUBS: Macabbi, Tel Aviv (twice); Glasgow Rangers.

1979/80 – 1980/81

COLIN IRWIN

Central defender Colin Irwin suffered two unhappy endings in a brief soccer career: hot competition brought his Liverpool days to a frustrating close and then, when he was making the most of a new start at Swansea, he was cruelly forced by injury into early retirement.

Colin had been an Anfield professional for nearly five years before making his debut in August 1979 at home to West Bromwich Albion. He gave a tidy display alongside Phil Thompson and that season made 14 appearances, deputising in turn for Alan Hansen and left-back Alan Kennedy.

It was a valuable grounding for his big chance in 1980/81 when knocks to Hansen and Thompson gave him an unbroken run of 17 League matches, with bonuses of a Wembley trip for the drawn League Cup Final against West Ham and a place in the away clash with Bayern Munich which put the Reds in the European Cup Final. Strong but never quite commanding, Colin again did a steady job without revealing the class to merit a first-team future, and when John Toshack's £340,000 offer to take him to Vetch Field coincided with the arrival of Mark Lawrenson, he was allowed to leave. He captained the Swans to sixth position in the First Division before bowing out, a sad casualty of soccer misfortune.

BORN: Liverpool, 9.2.57. GAMES: 40 (4). GOALS: 3.
OTHER CLUBS: Swansea City 81/2–83/4 (48, 0).

1979/80 – 1980/81

KENNY DALGLISH

There were Bobby Charlton and Jimmy Greaves, Denis Law and George Best; to list the absolute cream of British forwards over the last three decades is not an arduous task. But now the playing career of Kenny Dalglish is over and his achievements can be seen in true perspective, it is fitting that the name of the Scottish master be added to that exalted company. His exploits for Celtic alone would fill a book but it was the sublime gifts he displayed for Liverpool that lifted him on to the very highest plane. Kenny was one of those rare performers who brought true beauty to sport, his football at once exhilarating and aesthetic; some of his goals were acts of artistic creation and those who saw him at his peak were privileged indeed.

He arrived at Anfield from Parkhead in August 1977 for £440,000, then a record fee between British clubs, and inherited the number-seven shirt from Kevin Keegan. After a quiet start against Manchester United in the Charity Shield, he marked his League debut with a goal at Middlesbrough and soon it became apparent that the Reds had made an inspired investment. Kenny's first Anfield term yielded 30 goals in 59 matches but that represented only the most obvious aspect of his value; such was his prodigious natural ability that he gave a new dimension to the team.

Endowed with magnetic control and a deadly instinct for releasing the ball with nigh-perfect precision and timing, he brought the best out of team-mates, often creating for them precious extra seconds in which to capitalise on his skills. The Dalglish genius - yes, he *was* that good - was most eye-catching in crowded penalty areas. Wriggling like some muscular eel, he would feint one way, turn another and squeeze a vicious shot or exquisitely weighted pass through the narrowest of gaps.

Never a sprinter of Lineker-type velocity, Kenny's primary speed was of thought and he actually turned what would have been a defect in a lesser player - his lack of heading prowess - to his advantage. When faced with hulking defenders he would not waste time on ineffectual aerial challenges, instead looking to where the ball might drop, often as not arriving in exactly the right spot with almost uncanny anticipation. Crucially, too, Kenny had a tough streak. Solidly built with a low centre of gravity, he tackled with his whole body-weight and was strong enough to take most of the knocks which inevitably came his way, as his appearance record - he was ever-present in five of his first six League campaigns - reveals eloquently.

But rich and varied though Kenny's all-round talents were, it was his goals, so often the product of sheer virtuosity, that evoked the most wonder and created countless immortal memories: the subtle, Greaves-like dink to end the deadlock against FC Bruges in the 1978 European Cup Final; the delicate chip and curling, top-corner drive past poor Paul Cooper of Ipswich in two late-seventies League encounters; the 1981 League Cup Final winner, a delicious volley on the turn against West Ham; and the Stamford Bridge strike which secured the 1985/86 Championship, when Kenny took a Jim Beglin pass on his chest and, with characteristic calm, clipped the ball imperiously past Tony Godden. Golden moments all, though any Liverpool fan could recall another dozen equally thrilling and timeless examples of Dalglish magic.

In 1985 Kenny, the only Scot to win 100 caps, took over as the Reds' boss and by decade's end, before his enigmatic departure from Anfield, his managerial achievements were rivalling his playing triumphs. However, they could never outshine the on-the-field glory of the man who could justly be called the greatest footballer in Liverpool's history.

BORN: Glasgow, 4.3.51. GAMES: 481 (15). GOALS: 168. HONOURS: European Cup 77/8, 80/1, 83/4. League Championship 78/9, 79/80, 81/2, 82/3, 83/4, 85/6. FA Cup: 85/6. League Cup: 80/1, 81/2, 82/3, 83/4. 102 Scotland caps (71-87).

OTHER CLUBS: Celtic 68/9-76/7 (204, 112). MANAGER: Liverpool 85-91; Blackburn Rovers 91-95; Newcastle United 97-.

1977/78 – 1989/90

ALAN KENNEDY

Alan Kennedy was the buccaneering Wearsider who solved Liverpool's nagging left-back problem at the end of the seventies and went on to earn Anfield immortality by scoring the goals which won two European Cups - even if one of them, as he still emphasises with typical modesty, was in a penalty shoot-out.

Bob Paisley turned to Alan, one of the few Newcastle players to impress against the Reds in the 1974 FA Cup Final, in August 1978 after deciding to replace the worthy but unpolished Joey Jones. The fee of £330,000 was considered a massive outlay for a full-back but, at 26, Alan was in his prime and there was every reason to believe that his game would benefit from playing alongside top-class performers.

Unlike a number of other expensive Liverpool investments, the newcomer became an instant first-team regular, catching the eye with a scorching turn of speed which amply compensated for a sporadic tendency to commit himself to challenges in forward positions. He could be beaten on the half-way line but recover to win the ball before his opponent, believing Alan to be trailing safely in his wake, could reach the Reds' penalty area. His adventurous streak - characterised by surging left-flank runs which often took him past defenders and occasionally culminated in stinging strikes on goal - combined with an uncompromising tackle and endless enthusiasm to endear him to Kopites, who affectionately dubbed him 'Barney Rubble'.

At first Alan was slightly disconcerted by the need to adapt to the Liverpool method of building attacks from the back. At St James' Park he had been accustomed to slinging long balls forward for Malcolm Macdonald and John Tudor; now he was expected to play it short to Ray Kennedy, Terry McDermott or Kenny Dalglish. His distribution, initially a little erratic, improved with experience and he eventually became especially adept at one-two combinations with Kenny.

Overall, the former Magpie clearly vindicated Paisley's decision to buy him, playing a spirited part in the Championship triumphs of his first two campaigns, and when his character was put to the test in 1980/81 it was not found wanting. He had struck an inconsistent patch of form and the manager experimented with both Richard Money and Avi Cohen, but Alan - though troubled by injuries - fought back to regain his place in time for the European Cup Final against Real Madrid, a game that was to bring the most memorable moment of his Reds career. With nine minutes left and the score tied at 0-0, Alan received a throw-in from Ray Kennedy on the left and moved into the Spaniards' half. Unmolested by a defence which presumably expected a cross, the enterprising left-back cut in to arrow the ball over the 'keeper's shoulder for the winner.

As if inspired by that supreme moment, Alan took on new stature. He came under pressure on the arrival of Mark Lawrenson but again re-established himself to take three more (consecutive) title medals, being ever-present in 1982/83 and 1983/84. Then came his decisive penalty in the 1984 European Cup sudden-death defeat of Roma and a belated England call-up - he had dropped out with injury when picked nine years earlier. When finally ousted by Jim Beglin in the autumn of 1985, Alan joined Sunderland, his home-town club, for £100,000. He could walk out of Anfield with head held high, secure in the knowledge of a job well done.

BORN: Sunderland, 31.8.54. GAMES: 347 (2). GOALS: 21. HONOURS: European Cup 80/1, 83/4. League Championship 78/9, 79/80, 81/2, 82/3, 83/4. League Cup 80/1, 81/2, 82/3, 83/4. 2 England caps (84).

OTHER CLUBS: Newcastle United 72/3-77/8 (158, 9); Sunderland 85/6-86/7 (54, 2); Hartlepool United 87/8 (5, 0); Beerschot, Belgium, 87/8; Wigan Athletic 87/8 (22, 0); Wrexham 89/90-90/1 (16, 0).

1978/79 – 1985/86

PHIL THOMPSON

The wiry, almost scrawny frame of Phil Thompson was a source of much amusement to Bill Shankly. But the Reds' wisecracking boss knew an outstanding player when he saw one and his quips about 'the matchstick man with sparrow's legs' masked a profound respect and admiration for the former Kopite who lived for Liverpool. To be honest, Phil's spindly appearance hardly tied in with the popular image of a top footballer but, as most forwards of his era would testify, there wasn't a more awkward central defender to be found in the First Division - and precious few with more skill.

Originally a midfielder, Phil made his debut as a substitute at Old Trafford in April 1972 and went on to squeeze in just enough appearances in assorted positions to qualify for a Championship medal in the following season. He impressed with precise passing and improbably fierce tackling but was often found wanting for pace, and it became clear that his prospects in his chosen role were strictly limited. Shankly, however, had spotted a rich vein of potential and when centre-half Larry Lloyd was injured in February 1974 it was to Phil that the manager turned to partner Emlyn Hughes in the middle of his back four.

The enthusiastic Scouser was a natural in his new role. Though not as aerially dominant as his predecessor, he was an exquisite reader of the game who brought a new dimension to the Reds' defence. Whereas in the days of Yeats and Lloyd towering headers were often the preferred option for clearances, Phil was more likely to play his way out of trouble in European style, retaining possession and setting up attacks with his neat distribution.

One of the first to experience his cool, ruthless efficiency was Newcastle United's garrulous centre-forward Malcolm Macdonald, who had trumpeted imprudently to the world how he was going to bring Liverpool to their knees at Wembley in 1974. In the event it was Malcolm who partook of humble pie as Phil blotted him out of what proved to be the most one-sided FA Cup Final for years.

The Hughes-Thompson combination grew steadily in authority, remaining at the heart of the Reds' rearguard as the trophies piled up throughout the second half of the seventies. Ultimately, it was broken in 1978/79 when Emlyn relinquished his place to Alan Hansen and the captaincy went to Phil, who proved an inspiring and highly vocal motivator. The new pairing prospered with the Scot's sophisticated, often adventurous style dovetailing comfortably with his skipper's more simple but equally effective approach. When Liverpool were pouring forward en masse it was invariably Phil who held his position at the back, ready to deal with breakaway threats, and few British defenders were more accomplished in one-on-one encounters.

Liverpool's success did not abate during his spell in charge and he led his side to two League titles and 1981 European Cup victory over Real Madrid, making up for missing the 1977 final through injury, before Graeme Souness took the reins in 1981/82. Phil, who had a short stint as England skipper during a distinguished international career, went on to win two more Championship medals and retained his Reds place until injuries and the excellence of Mark Lawrenson accelerated his demise. After 18 months with Sheffield United he returned to Anfield as a coach, and there were those who reckoned one of Liverpool's most loyal sons was a realistic candidate to manage the club at some future stage. Sadly for Phil, sitting boss Graeme Souness had other ideas, dismissing his former team-mate in 1992.

BORN: Liverpool, 21.1.54. GAMES: 459 (7). GOALS: 12.
HONOURS: European Cup 77/8, 80/1. UEFA Cup 75/6. League Championship 72/3, 75/6, 76/7, 78/9, 79/80, 81/2, 82/3. FA Cup 73/4. League Cup 80/1, 81/2. 42 England caps (76-82).

OTHER CLUBS: Sheffield United 84/5-85/6 (37, 0).

1971/72- 1982/83

CRAIG JOHNSTON

Craig Johnston was an Anfield enigma from first to last. He arrived in a whirlwind of raw energy and ebullience, threatening to turn the place upside down in the manner of Kevin Keegan; it didn't happen, but he stayed to win nine major honours in seven seasons – despite rarely being assured of a first-team place – and make his name as the most untypical Liverpool player of modern times. Finally, forever his own man, he effectively tore up his contract and walked out on the Reds to start a new life in Australia.

Bob Paisley paid Middlesbrough £575,000 for the South African-born attacking midfielder in the summer of 1981 and Craig started the new season as a substitute with high expectations. But it was not until mid March, with Liverpool just embarking on a surge that was to take them from an unaccustomed mid-table position to the title, that the effervescent newcomer ousted Terry McDermott. Raiding gleefully down the right, those long, curly, dark locks flying in his wake, Craig offered a fitful flair which was distinctly at odds with the Anfield tradition for consistency. His searing pace and exhilarating skill were a delight to behold, but often nothing would come of them; there was an all-too-frequent resemblance to a headless chicken as he disappeared into a blind alley or wasted a faultless dribble by capping it with a wayward cross.

Over the successful 1982/83 and 1983/84 campaigns, Craig – whose work-rate bore witness to his supreme fitness – was more often in the team than out of it, but both Paisley and his successor, Joe Fagan, were wary of his headstrong element. Bob, while a confirmed admirer of the overall Johnston package, aptly summed up the managerial dilemma: 'Putting Craig alongside ten men who were pacing themselves through a busy period was like throwing a firework into a box of safety matches.' As the Reds endured a disappointing season in 1984/85, Craig found himself on the fringe of the action, but Kenny Dalglish's appointment as manager the following term changed his luck and he became a regular in the side which won the League and FA Cup double. Kenny harnessed the midfielder's verve and persistence to the team effort and he became less unpredictable, more productive; one minute he would be winning the ball in his own half, the next scoring a vital goal such as the one which put Liverpool on top against Everton at Wembley.

Though Craig's name wasn't *always* on the teamsheet, a campaign of consolidation followed, and by 1987/88 he was at his peak. But Anfield security was not to be his; ironically soon after Craig's progress had been recognised by selection for an England squad, Dalglish bought Ray Houghton and the former Middlesbrough man returned to the periphery. In May 1988 he announced there was more to life than kicking a bag of wind and returned to Australia, where he had lived before moving to England, for domestic reasons. Craig became a full-time photographer and English football thus bade farewell to one of its more individual talents.

BORN: Johannesburg, 8.12.60. GAMES: 224 (36). GOALS: 39.
HONOURS: European Cup 83/4. League Championship 81/2, 82/3, 83/4, 85/6, 87/8. FA Cup 85/6. League Cup 82/3, 83/4.

OTHER CLUBS: Middlesbrough 77/8–80/1 (64, 16).

1981/82 – 1987/88

MARK LAWRENSON

There was a time in the mid eighties when Mark Lawrenson looked the equal of any central defender in the world. He had the lot: speed, power, ball control, anticipation, passing ability, strength in the air. There was no discernible defect, and together with the impeccable Alan Hansen he formed what was arguably the finest middle-of-the-back-four combination in British football history.

Bob Paisley broke the Reds' transfer record when he signed Mark from Brighton for £900,000 in August 1981, beating off stiff opposition from Manchester United and Arsenal. The Lancashire-born Eire international - an Irish father qualified him to play for the Republic - was undeniably a top-class addition to the Liverpool squad but with Hansen and Phil Thompson in consistently excellent form there were those who reckoned he was an ultra-expensive luxury. Bob reasoned, however, that such pedigree performers seldom became available and were not to be missed when they did. The manager's wisdom was borne out emphatically in the seasons that followed.

In his initial term at Anfield Mark demonstrated his versatility, flitting around the teamsheet like some latter-day Paul Madeley, the former Leeds United utility man. First came a stint replacing Alan Kennedy at left-back before relief duty took him to both midfield and centre-back. The opening months of 1982/83 told a similar story before a serious injury to Thompson allowed the ex-Seagull to cement the link with Hansen, which was not seriously disturbed for more than three years.

For most of that time the Reds revelled in a dominance of the First Division unequalled since the all-conquering exploits of Arsenal half a century earlier. With Mark's influence becoming ever more majestic, they completed a hat-trick of titles in his first three campaigns, monopolised the League/Milk Cup and in 1984 defeated Roma to lift the European Cup for the fourth time, a performance in which the tall defender's multiple talents were showcased to brilliant effect. In the second half of a tense struggle between two well-matched sides, Joe Fagan's men were often pinned back as the Italians strove to end the 1-1 deadlock, but Mark, a natural ball-winner through timing rather than ferocity, was immaculate in both the tackle and his reading of the game. If Graziani or Falcao seemed on the point of breaking through, a long Lawrenson leg would invariably snake out to frustrate them, and but for the inspired work of the Reds' number four the penalty shoot-out which landed the trophy might well not have been reached.

The first hint of a split in the partnership with Hansen appeared when Mark took a knock during a 6-0 thrashing of Oxford at Anfield in March 1986. Gary Gillespie stepped in and the Eire star might have missed the Wembley win over Everton which clinched the League and FA Cup double had his deputy not fallen ill. But the blow which was to lead to the premature end of a glittering career fell a year later in the home encounter with Wimbledon, when he sustained a serious Achilles tendon injury. Despite several short-lived comebacks, Mark had lost too much pace and power to continue playing and he turned to management, then broadcasting. No more would that gangling yet curiously graceful figure, sleeves pushed up and head rolling as he ran, patrol the Reds' back line. Club - and country - had been deprived of a true thoroughbred.

BORN: Preston, 2.6.57. GAMES: 332 (9). GOALS: 17. HONOURS: European Cup 83/4. League Championship 81/2, 82/3, 83/4, 85/6, 87/8. FA Cup 85/6. League Cup 81/2, 82/3, 83/4. 38 Republic of Ireland caps (77-87).

OTHER CLUBS: Preston North End 74/5-76/7 (73, 2); Brighton and Hove Albion 77/8-80/1 (152, 5). MANAGER: Oxford United 88; Peterborough United 89-90.

1981/82– 1987/88

DAVID HODGSON

1982/83 – 1983/84

Rangy front-runner David Hodgson, a £450,000 acquisition from Middlesbrough in the summer of 1982, started his Reds career with a flourish only to fizzle out in sad anti-climax within two seasons. Playing alongside Ian Rush and Kenny Dalglish, the robust England under-21 international notched four goals in his first six games. His most impressive display came at home to Nottingham Forest in September when his willingness to chase apparently lost causes brought him two goals in a 4-3 victory. David's greatest asset was his pace and he could be particularly dangerous cutting in from the flanks. But once in a threatening position he was often betrayed by a lack of finesse and the opening would be wasted. At times he was guilty of failing to do the basic things well, and faced with competition as a wide attacker from the more skilful Craig Johnston - with the intimidating presence of Ian and Kenny closing off other avenues of advance-ment - he was, perhaps, destined inevitably for a short Anfield tenure.

In David's opening campaign, manager Bob Paisley gave his fellow north-easterner plenty of chances to impress. In truth, he didn't disgrace himself during an unbroken midwinter spell of 15 matches and his title medal was well earned. But in 1983/84, with Joe Fagan now in charge and Michael Robinson on the scene, his opportunities were fewer and he accepted a £125,000 move to Sunderland. There followed spells with several other clubs but David still gave little sign of fulfilling the promise which had first prompted Paisley to take him from Ayrsome Park.

BORN: Gateshead, 1.11.60.
GAMES: 33 (14). GOALS: 10. HONOURS: League Championship 82/3.

OTHER CLUBS: Middlesbrough 78/9-81/2 (125, 16); Sunderland 84/5-85/6 (40, 5); Norwich City 86/7 (6, 1); Middlesbrough on loan 86/7 (2, 0); Jerez, Spain 87/8; Sheffield Wednesday 88/9 (11, 1); Metz, France; Swansea City 91/2 (3, 0).
MANAGER: Darlington 95 and 96-.

MICHAEL ROBINSON

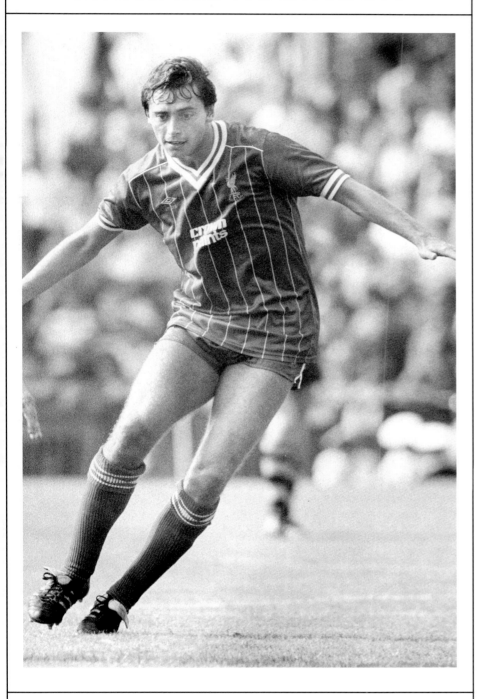

1983/84 – 1984/85

Four years after a rash gamble by Malcolm Allison had threatened to blight Michael Robinson's career, Liverpool offered the honest, uncomplicated, head-down-and-run striker a second chance at the top level. Big Mal had astounded the football world by paying £756,000 to take the then unknown youngster from Preston to Manchester City during one of the wildest spending sprees in the game's history. Understandable failure at Maine Road had been followed by a steady spell with Brighton when Joe Fagan spent £200,000 to make him a Red in August 1983.

Michael was pitched straight into first-team action, forming a joint spearhead with Ian Rush as Kenny Dalglish withdrew to a deeper position, and when he went eight games without a goal the tongues of the I-told-you-so brigade were wagging avidly. But then a European Cup brace at home to BK Odense of Denmark and a cracking League hat-trick at Upton Park three games later restored his credibility, and despite losing his place as the manager tried various permutations, the burly Eire international remained in the reckoning for most of the campaign.

Though capable of the occasional artistic touch, Michael was not blessed with a wide range of delicate skills and, with commendable common sense, played to his strengths. He liked to run on to the ball rather than have it played to his feet and was often at his best when foraging on the flanks. His whole-hearted efforts were deservedly rewarded with title and European Cup medals – he came on as substitute for Dalglish in the 1984 final against Roma – but it was no surprise when, half-way through his second season at Anfield, Michael was allowed to join Queen's Park Rangers for £100,000. Certainly he had proved a short-term investment, but, this time around in the big league, it would be an exceedingly exacting critic who called him a flop.

BORN: Leicester, 12.7.58. GAMES: 45 (6).
GOALS: 13. HONOURS: European Cup
83/4. League Championship 83/4.
23 Republic of Ireland caps (80-86).

OTHER CLUBS: Preston North End 75/6-
78/9 (48, 15); Manchester City 79/80 (30, 8);
Brighton and Hove Albion 80/1-82/3 (113,
37); Queen's Park Rangers 84/5-86/7 (48, 6);
Osasuna, Spain, 87/8.

BRUCE GROBBELAAR

Bouquets and brickbats rained on the head of Bruce Grobbelaar with equal intensity after that most eccentric of soccer entertainers succeeded Ray Clemence as Liverpool goalkeeper in 1981/82. Many shrewd observers claimed that, during his lengthy Anfield reign, he was the most accomplished custodian in the land and maintained that his habitual brilliance more than outweighed his well-publicised errors; others reckoned that his slapstick antics and catalogue of clangers prevented the Reds from lifting an even greater share of honours. Another strand to the debate went that, whatever his technical merits, football needed the Zimbabwe international for the sheer fun he brought to a game beset with problems.

Undoubtedly, that third standpoint received short shrift from Liverpool's pragmatic management; surely, the key lay in the fact that three bosses of England's most successful club were content with Bruce's unorthodox efforts in his prime. Had Bob Paisley, Joe Fagan and Kenny Dalglish in turn not been convinced that they had the best 'keeper available, he would have been ruthlessly replaced.

Bruce arrived at Anfield in March 1981 as a £250,000 signing from Vancouver Whitecaps, and had little time to settle before being pitchforked into regular first-team action. He might have benefited from a couple of seasons as understudy to his illustrious predecessor - as Ray had himself once learned from Tommy Lawrence - but with the England man moving to White Hart Lane that summer there was no such chance.

Liverpool supporters realised they were getting an unknown quantity but they were hardly prepared for the culture shock which Bruce represented. They loved the stunning saves, a product of a natural athlete's startlingly sharp reflexes, and were impressed by the way he sought to dominate his penalty area. They were not so sure, on the other hand, about the occasional flailing attempt to gather a cross which had passed way over his head or the disturbing tendency to leave his penalty area to snuff out an attack not far from the half-way line!

The acid test, however, was whether Liverpool won as many trophies with Grobbelaar as they did in the pre-Bruce days. And they certainly *did*. He was an ever-present in the five seasons between 1981/82 and 1985/86, during which the team lifted four League Championships and five major cups. Better still, the triumphs were spiced with humour, an irresistible combination to the Scouse legions. When Bruce was confronted with a penalty shoot-out at the end of the 1984 European Cup Final against Roma, he eased the tension with his famous leg-wobbling act - and, crucially, had the last laugh by finishing on the winning side. If he was pelted with coins on an away ground, as 'keepers are at times apt to be, he might pocket them to get the crowd on his side, and he was always ready with a spontaneous reaction to fans' banter.

After plentiful alarms and excursions in his early Anfield years, Bruce appeared more consistent in the mid-eighties, and after winning his place back from Mike Hooper after a bout of meningitis in 1988/89, he struck an inspired vein of form as the side went unbeaten for 22 games. Perversely, the odd howler crept back in during 1989/90 and the doubts resurfaced. Nevertheless, the old soldier battled on, increasingly error-prone and frequently irascible but in the side more often than out of it until spring 1994, when he was unseated finally by David James.

Given a free transfer that summer, Bruce joined Southampton and continued to hold his own in the top flight, even, for a time, after he was accused of accepting a bribe to fix Liverpool's game at Newcastle the previous term, a damning allegation which he denied strenuously and of which he was cleared. But whatever uncertainties might persist about Grobbelaar, no one should doubt that he took his trade seriously. As one former team-mate remarked: 'Inside that clown is a dedicated perfectionist.' On his day that perfection was sometimes achieved; on others ... well, at least it was never dull!

BORN: Durban, South Africa, 6.10.57. GAMES: 609. GOALS: 0. HONOURS: European Cup 83/4. League Championship 81/2, 82/3, 83/4, 85/6, 87/8, 89/90. FA Cup 85/6, 88/9, 91/2. League Cup 81/2, 82/3, 83/4. Zimbabwe caps.

OTHER CLUBS: Vancouver Whitecaps; Crewe Alexandra on loan 79/80 (24, 1); Stoke City on loan 92/3 (4, 0); Southampton 94/5-95/6 (32, 0); Plymouth Argyle 96/7 (36, 0); Oldham Athletic 97/8 (4, 0).

1981/82 – 1993/94

JAN MOLBY

Few top-flight managers could put their hands on their hearts and say they did not covet the ability of Jan Molby. Yet the Danish international midfielder, a rare and at times irresistible combination of dainty skills and bear-like strength, became a shadowy figure on the fringe of the Anfield action long before reaching the veteran stage and being freed to become player-boss of Swansea in February 1996.

Joe Fagan took him to Anfield as a £200,000 recruit from Ajax of Amsterdam in August 1984 and pitched him straight into the team. The initial impression was of a sluggish, rather corpulent individual who lacked the speed to make the most of his natural gifts. Jan played on for the first half of the campaign before being replaced by Kevin MacDonald, and a brief end-of-term reappearance as sweeper was not enough to prevent many critics from writing him off.

Never a man to be swayed by the media, Kenny Dalglish was of a different opinion. The new Liverpool manager installed a slightly slimmer Jan in his side for 1985/86, and his faith was quickly repaid. The Dane, having had time to adjust to the frenetic demands of the British game, exuded authority as the Reds' creative fulcrum, supplying Ian Rush in particular with a nourishing diet of exquisitely weighted through-balls. Like Souness before him, Jan laced his constructive merits with formidable power, and his dead-ball expertise – he scored nine of his 19 goals from the penalty spot – was indispensable. His finest hour came in the FA Cup Final at Wembley, in which Liverpool were distinctly second-best to Everton until the hefty schemer began to exert his influence. First he put Rush through to level the scores at one-apiece and then opened up the match with a succession of flowing crossfield passes, which led ultimately to two more goals.

Jan's Anfield future was apparently assured. Not only was he a success on the pitch, he also became a personal favourite with the fans, who delighted in his Danish-Scouse accent and general willingness to embrace the Merseyside way of life. The way ahead, however, was paved with problems. After playing well enough for a slightly below-par 'Pool in the following season, he broke his foot in training and missed most of the vintage 1987/88 campaign. Jan was back for 1988/89, deputising in defence for Alan Hansen, but soccer was forced to take a back seat as he was sentenced to three months in prison for a driving offence.

To his credit, Jan survived the trauma with dignity, returning to fight for his place. But, though arguably still the most artistic play-maker in the land – as he showed repeatedly during 1991/92, contributing hugely to Liverpool's FA Cup triumph – the affable Dane seemed to have lost the impetus of earlier days.

Part of the reason was his eternal battle with his weight – if he could have controlled that ample girth as ably as he mastered a football then, surely, Jan must have attained true greatness – but also he suffered appallingly with injuries throughout the first half of the nineties. In addition, there were times when the team's pattern of play, with so many attacking ideas stemming from more fleet-footed colleagues, simply did not suit his measured approach.

For all that, there is no escaping the truth that the sumptuous talents of Jan Molby remained frustratingly peripheral at a time when they should have been reaping their richest bounty. By any reckoning, that amounts to a dreadful waste.

BORN: Kolding, Denmark, 4.7.63. GAMES: 251 (30). GOALS: 58. HONOURS: League Championship 85/6, 89/90. FA Cup 85/6, 91/2. Denmark caps.

OTHER CLUBS: Ajax, Amsterdam; Barnsley *on loan* 95/6 (5, 0); Norwich City *on loan* 95/6 (3, 0); Swansea City 95/6-97/8 (42, 8). MANAGER: Swansea City 96-97.

1984/85 – 1994/95

STEVE NICOL

No player is indispensable at Liverpool. Neither the departure of Rush nor the retirement of Dalglish left a vacuum which was not filled swiftly and successfully; that is the Anfield way. But, throughout most of the eighties and the early nineties, if there was one performer who might have been missed more than any other, one for whom the manager might have longed most wistfully, especially in the depths of an injury crisis, that man was Steve Nicol.

The versatile Scottish international, Footballer of the Year in 1989, acquitted himself with distinction in every back-four and midfield position, and epitomised all that was best about the modern Reds. Enthusiastic and determined, Steve boasted a rich range of soccer assets: his touch on the ball - despite his need for size 14 boots - was sure and often subtle, his passing was accurate and imaginative, his tackle was firm. He was rarely found to lack power in the air or pace in a sprint, he possessed boundless stamina, and his classy finishing put many a striker to shame.

Steve was imported to Anfield as £300,000 worth of raw teenage talent from Ayr United in October 1981. Then principally a right-back, he immediately found himself in the shadow of the consistent Phil Neal and was consigned to the reserves to complete his soccer education. If there were ever any doubts about his potential they were quickly stilled in an early Central League encounter in which he picked up the ball in his own penalty box and beat five opponents as he ran the length of the field to score the winner.

His initial outings deputising for Neal, on the infrequent occasions that the England stalwart was injured, bode well for the future. Despite his inexperience, Steve revelled in the responsibility, revealing an eagerness for the ball and the initiative to use it constructively, and clearly it could not be long before he claimed a first-team place. The breakthrough came in October 1983 when Craig Johnston was injured and Steve slotted into midfield. His 19 League appearances were enough to earn a title medal and he went on to play his part in that term's European Cup Final, coming on as substitute against Roma and volunteering to take Liverpool's first penalty in the deadlock-breaking shoot-out. He missed, but still took home a winner's medal.

The following campaign saw him cement his place, mainly at the expense of Sammy Lee, before he reverted to right-back when Neal left the club early in the League/FA Cup double campaign of 1985/86. Back in his original role, Steve was magnificent, but any chance of settling there was destroyed by groin problems which kept him out of action for two thirds of the ensuing season. A return to full fitness saw him reach yet greater heights of form and over the next three years he gave full rein to his adaptability. A competent spell at centre-back in the absence of Alan Hansen revealed a new aspect of his talent, though the right side of midfield was perhaps his most effective niche. From that position he had the scope to be a potent attacking force and contributed some memorable goals, notably a crisp hat-trick - including a sublime chip over the advancing 'keeper - at Newcastle in September 1987, and the sweetest of lobs against Southampton in the FA Cup in February 1990.

The sight of Steve, spiky red hair dripping with sweat and huge feet dancing over the ball, became an inspiring and reassuring one for Reds fans during a period of fabulous success and on into leaner times. Injuries and the advancing years reduced his effectiveness slightly during his final days at Anfield, but often his experience proved priceless as the team underwent a time of transition. When he was freed to join Notts County in January 1995, Liverpool appeared not to be short of high-quality replacements. But, as events have proved, rare mettle indeed will be needed to equal the durability and achievements of Steve Nicol.

BORN: Irvine, Ayrshire, 11.12.61. GAMES: 437 (17). GOALS: 45.
HONOURS: European Cup 83/4. League Championship 83/4, 85/6, 87/8, 89/90.
FA Cup 85/6, 88/9, 91/2. 27 Scotland caps (84-91).

OTHER CLUBS: Ayr United 79/80-81/2 (70, 7); Notts County 94/5-95/6 (32, 2); Sheffield Wednesday 95/6-97/8 (49, 0); West Bromwich Albion *on loan* 97/8 (9, 0).

1982/83 – 1994/95

When England striker Paul Walsh left Luton for Liverpool in the close season of 1984, Reds fans drooled and rival supporters quaked. The prospect of a partnership between the waspish Walsh, then the most promising front-runner in the country, and the mighty Ian Rush seemed a breathtaking one for Kopites dreaming of ever more extravagant triumphs.

Paul, who shortly before his £700,000 move had been voted Young Player of the Year by his fellow professionals, was exquisitely equipped for the Anfield challenge. Quick, lithe and abundantly skilful, he was that increasingly rare phenomenon, a central attacker who ran at defenders and took the ball past them. In confined spaces he could turn to deadly effect, like some pencil-slim Sassenach version of Dalglish, and he possessed a rasping shot to cap his exciting approach work.

Expectations were sky-high, and Paul's early performances - while flawed by a slight inclination to over-elaborate and an occasional tendency to drift on the edge of the action - hinted at riches to come. After marking his home debut against West Ham with a goal after 15 seconds, the eel-like newcomer was working hard to establish an understanding with Rush when injury ruled him out for two months - and that was to set the sorry pattern for the rest of his Liverpool days. Whenever he managed to put together a run of matches, usually Paul would impress and the pundits would predict the long-awaited breakthrough; then he would be sidelined again and his impetus would be lost.

Despite such frustrations, 1984/85 saw Paul maintain his average career strike-rate of roughly one goal every three starts and in the following term, after again missing a clutch of matches, he ran into splendid early-winter form. Two goals at home to his former Luton team-mates began an almost unbroken, 16-game sequence in which he netted ten times, and in the November encounter with West Brom Paul was again at his irresistible best, setting up three and scoring one as the Kop roared its approval. There was another brilliant performance, crowned by two goals, against Watford at Vicarage Road in January 1986 before an Anfield injury a month later against Manchester United kept him out of the run-in to the League/FA Cup double.

There were similar tribulations in 1986/87, after which the advent of Peter Beardsley, John Aldridge and John Barnes relegated him to the role of perpetual substitute. Accordingly, in February 1988 Paul opted for a much-needed clean slate and accepted a £500,000 move to White Hart Lane. Roughly a third of his time at Anfield had been spent recovering from a cartilage injury, a hernia, torn ankle ligaments and a broken wrist, and he certainly deserved better fortune with Spurs. However, consistent first-team action continued to elude one of the top flight's most tantalising talents.

BORN: Plumstead, London, 1.10.62.
GAMES: 85 (18). GOALS: 35. HONOURS: League Championship 85/6. 3 England caps.

OTHER CLUBS: Charlton Athletic 79/80-81/2 (87, 24); Luton Town 82/3-83/4 (80, 24); Tottenham Hotspur 87/8-91/2 128 (19); Queen's Park Rangers on loan 91/2 (2, 0); Portsmouth 92/3-93/4 (73, 14); Manchester City 93/4-95/6 (53, 16); Portsmouth 95/6 (21, 5).

PAUL WALSH

1984/85 – 1987/88

JOHN WARK

1983/84 – 1987/88

There is no disguising the fact that John Wark was a disappointment at Anfield, partly through injury but also, perhaps, because his game lacked the all-round qualities needed to flourish with Liverpool.

He was signed from Ipswich Town in March 1984, three months before the much-dreaded departure of fellow Scottish midfielder Graeme Souness to Sampdoria of Italy. At Portman Road John had been a kingpin of Bobby Robson's refreshing side, scoring heavily with powerful shots and ferocious headers, and such was his reputation that Reds boss Joe Fagan was widely considered to have completed a sizeable coup in capturing the thrustful Glaswegian for £450,000.

Initial impressions were excellent as John slotted smoothly into the side, replacing Craig Johnston for the title run-in. He scored on his debut in a 2-0 win at Watford, and though there were not enough games left for him to win a medal in that campaign it seemed only a matter of time before his barrel chest would be covered in gongs. In the event, immediate life after Souness proved non-productive for Liverpool as they failed to lift an honour in 1984/85, but John acquitted himself with gusto, even excelling his Ipswich strike-rate with 18 League goals - highlighted by a hat-trick at West Brom and including only two penalties - in 40 games and contributing five more on the way to that ill-fated European Cup Final against Juventus at the Heysel Stadium.

Kenny Dalglish replaced Fagan for 1985/86 and, often deprived of John's services by niggling knocks, prospered without his countryman. The swarthy, moustachioed international's cup of woe finally ran over in March when he broke his leg, missing out not only on the League and FA Cup double but also Scotland's World Cup trip to Mexico. The following term presented the challenge of breaking back into the team but, though the Reds won no trophies, John was called up for only a handful of senior outings.

A magnificent striker of the ball who was at his most dangerous arriving late in the penalty area behind the front-runners, John had little outstanding to offer if his goals dried up. Admittedly he was strong in the air and firm in the tackle but his distribution lacked precision at times and he could match neither the vision of Molby nor the flair of Johnston.

In January 1988 he rejoined Ipswich for £100,000 and gave doughty and memorably lengthy service during two more stints at Portman Road, at first in his former role and later in defence, soldiering on gamely and effectively into his late thirties.

Looking back, John could count himself unlucky that his best Anfield term coincided with one of the Reds' rare barren seasons.

BORN: Glasgow, 4.8.57.
GAMES: 90 (12). GOALS: 42.
HONOURS: 29 Scotland caps (79-84).

OTHER CLUBS: Ipswich Town 74/5-83/4 (296, 94) and 87/8-89/90 (89, 23); Middlesbrough 90/1 (32, 2); Ipswich Town 91/2-96/7 (154, 18).

KEVIN MacDONALD

There were times during Kevin MacDonald's first 18 months at Anfield when his form emitted echoes - admittedly faint, but encouraging nevertheless - of that departed 'king' of playmakers, Graeme Souness. Joe Fagan paid £400,000 for the promising mid-fielder, who had caught the eye as an inspiring skipper of Leicester City, in November 1984 after the Reds' early-season progress had fallen short of expectations.

The newcomer was quickly introduced into a side suffering noticeably from the absence of Souness and, though short of pace, he soon impressed with his assured distribution and wiry strength. One display in the FA Cup quarter-final at Barnsley in March 1985, when his imaginative approach work played an influential part in a 4-0 victory, was particularly accomplished and Kevin seemed poised for success.

Somehow, however, the lanky Scot never quite became established and in 1985/86, with the likes of Jan Molby and Steve McMahon in direct competition, he slid out of the reckoning until injuries to team-mates precipitated a comeback during the run-in to the League/FA Cup double. He seized his opportunity and gave a series of enterprising performances, including an assertive contribution against Everton at Wembley.

That might have been the platform for greater things but all hopes of consolidation were smashed when he broke his leg at Southampton in September 1986, an accident which effectively ended his Anfield career. After two operations Kevin fought back to fitness with commendable determination, but the combination of a strong squad and further injury trouble denied him a Liverpool future. After spells on loan with former club Leicester and - ironically - Souness' Glasgow Rangers, he joined Coventry on a free transfer in the summer of 1989.

BORN: Inverness, 22.12.60. GAMES: 42 (14). GOALS: 3. HONOURS: League Championship 85/86. FA Cup 85/6.

OTHER CLUBS: Leicester City 80/1-84/5 (138, 8); Leicester City on loan 87/8 (3, 0); Glasgow Rangers on loan 88/9 (3, 0); Coventry City 89/90-90/1 (31, 0); Cardiff City on loan 90/1 (8, 0); Walsall 91/2-92/3 (53, 6).

1984/85 – 1988/89

JIM BEGLIN

1984/85 – 1987/88

All was right with Jim Beglin's world as he ran out for the Milk Cup quarter-final against Everton in January 1987. The 23-year-old Eire international, who had played a telling part in the League/FA Cup double of the previous campaign, was apparently on the threshold of a long career as the Reds' left-back. He was firmly established and there seemed little likelihood of a more accomplished rival emerging to fill what had often proved a problem position at Anfield. But by the end of that fateful Goodison encounter, Jim's leg had been shattered in a tackle with Gary Stevens – and with it his Liverpool ambitions.

Jim, who cost a small fee from Shamrock Rovers in May 1983, made his Reds debut 18 months later in midfield but was not tried in his favoured role until he deputised for Alan Kennedy at the end of 1984/85, a stint which culminated in the European Cup Final at the Heysel Stadium. Alan started 1985/86 back in favour but soon Jim ousted him for good and, apart from one four-match spell, the Irishman held sway for the rest of a triumphant term. His talents typified those demanded of a modern Liverpool defender: he had close control, used the ball with precision and intelligence – it was his interception and pass to Molby which initiated Rush's equaliser against Everton in the 1986 FA Cup Final – and read the game shrewdly. In addition Jim was fast, strong in the air and effective in attack. If he had a weakness it was when an opponent cut inside him, but he was working on that when injury struck.

While his leg was mending Jim suffered the frustration of watching a succession of youngsters – Ablett, Staunton, Burrows – impress in his job and when he regained fitness the old confidence was missing. In June 1989 he took a free transfer to Leeds, only for ligament problems and arthritis to force premature retirement. Happily, Jim found a new niche in broadcasting.

BORN: Waterford, 29.7.63. GAMES: 90. GOALS: 3. HONOURS: League Championship 85/6. FA Cup 85/6. 15 Republic of Ireland caps (84-86).

OTHER CLUBS: Shamrock Rovers; Leeds United 89/90 (19, 0); Plymouth Argyle on loan 89/90 (5, 0); Blackburn Rovers on loan 90/1 (6, 0).

STEVE McMAHON

Steve McMahon was a winner, plain and simple. The fact was etched in every flicker of expression, every gesture, every line of his combative frame as he patrolled the Reds' midfield like some hunter who knew that his prey was at his mercy and that it was only a matter of time before he claimed it. Like Graeme Souness before him, he exuded ruthlessness, and again like the formidable Scot, he had the footballing qualities to fulfil his ambitions.

Liverpool-born Steve took an unorthodox road to Anfield, joining Everton from school and serving as a Goodison Park ball-boy before becoming one of the most promising Blues of the early eighties. But he was not happy on Merseyside; after rejecting Howard Kendall's offer of a new contract, he also spurned the chance to join the Reds, electing instead to make a new start with Aston Villa in May 1983. Steve failed to settle in the Midlands, and when Kenny Dalglish offered £350,000 to take him home two years later, the deal was completed swiftly. It was the first signing by Liverpool's new boss, but few were to prove wiser.

Not that the blond play-maker immediately revealed the form which was to make him one of the club's most influential performers by the end of the decade. His abrasive ball-winning qualities, precise distribution and dynamic shooting – ironically his first goal for Liverpool was the winner at Goodison in September 1985 – were already in evidence, but the creative heights which transformed him into the hub of the side still lay ahead. In that first season as a Red he won a Championship medal, but vied for a place with Kevin MacDonald and missed the FA Cup Final victory against Everton. The following campaign, which brought no trophy, saw a maturing of his talents, and the through-pass which freed Ian Rush to score the opener in the Milk Cup Final clash with Arsenal was a foretaste of delights to come.

But it was not until 1987/88 – and the arrival of John Barnes and Peter Beardsley – that Steve began to realise his full potential. He was the perfect provider for the gifted newcomers and, as his confidence grew, so did his authority in the centre of midfield. Fierce tackling remained a basic part of his game, but now he revealed creativity and vision at which he had previously only hinted; his passing, both long and short, grew in control and penetration, and he carried the ball with both purpose and grace.

Though never a prolific scorer, Steve continued to contribute a significant quota of spectacular goals, possessing the enviable ability to hit his shots hard and low, a nightmarish combination for goalkeepers. Oxford United were on the receiving end of one particularly fearsome strike at the Manor Ground on Boxing Day 1987, and Manchester United's Chris Turner, rooted to his line as he was passed by a 25-yard piledriver at Anfield three months later, will also vouch for the velocity of McMahon's missiles. Power, however, did not provide his only means of finding the net, as he demonstrated with a cheeky chip in the 9-0 demolition of Crystal Palace in the autumn on 1989.

As the nineties dawned, Steve had broken into the England squad and had most of a five-year contract with the Reds to run. He was at his peak and still playing as though his life depended on it, but he never flourished under the leadership of new boss Graeme Souness, despite a spell as captain when Ronnie Whelan was injured.

As his form declined, he appeared to get tetchier on the field and, with the side struggling for direction, he was sold to Manchester City for £900,000 in December 1991. It was an anti-climactic exit for such an influential individual, who made little impact at Maine Road but went on to show promise as an abrasive (what else?) player-boss at Swindon.

Though never *quite* matching the omnipotence of Souness as a performer, Steve McMahon was close enough for the comparison to be made. And praise doesn't come much higher than that.

BORN: Liverpool, 20.8.61. GAMES: 264 (2). GOALS: 49. HONOURS: League Championship 85/6, 87/8, 89/90. FA Cup 88/9. 17 England caps (88-90).

OTHER CLUBS: Everton 80/1-82/3 (100, 11); Aston Villa 83/4-85/6 (75, 7); Manchester City 91/2-94/5 (87, 1); Swindon Town 94/5- (41, 0). MANAGER: Swindon Town 94-.

1985/86 – 1991/92

Gary Ablett did little wrong over six seasons in and out of the Liverpool team, picking up two Championship medals and one FA Cup winner's gong along the way. Yet, somehow, he never seemed destined to secure a regular long-term niche – and so it proved.

If the versatile defender ever harboured doubts about the paramount need for patience as he fought for that berth, the events of 1989/90 must have removed them unceremoniously. Gary, the first Liverpudlian since Sammy Lee to appear in more than a handful of matches for the Reds, had made steady progress since making his League debut at Charlton in December 1986. Deputising in both full-back slots and in the middle of the back four, he had distinguished himself with a succession of sound, composed performances.

Gaunt of build and spidery of movement, he was not the paciest of operators but he timed his tackles well, was solid in the air and boasted a neat line in unfussy distribution. His temperament was impeccable and, after missing only the first three League games of 1988/89, he might have been excused for feeling that he was established.

But nowhere is competition for places hotter than at Anfield. The arrival of Glenn Hysen, and the rapid progress of Steve Staunton and David Burrows, relegated Gary in the pecking order and his opportunities in the new campaign were limited. Yet a measure of his standing was that when Middlesbrough offered £700,000 for him, Kenny Dalglish said no, just as Joe Fagan had four years earlier when Gary had attracted a six-figure offer from Derby.

Liverpool's refusal to part must have given him confidence, and the England under-21 international continued to make the most of limited chances. Certainly he impressed when standing in at centre-back – arguably his best position – in the Littlewoods Cup defeat at Highbury in 1989, but when Hysen and Alan Hansen returned he was sidelined again.

Gary deserved better than to be a perpetual reserve and, after looking uncomfortable during the early months of the new Souness regime, he joined Everton for £750,000 in January 1992.

BORN: Liverpool, 19.11.65. GAMES: 135 (9). GOALS: 1. HONOURS: League Championship 87/8, 89/90. FA Cup 88/9. OTHER CLUBS: Derby County *on loan* 84/5 (6, 0); Hull City *on loan* 86/7 (5, 0); Everton 91/2-95/6 (128, 5); Sheffield United *on loan* 95/6 (12, 0); Birmingham City 96/7- (78, 1).

GARY ABLETT

1986/87 – 1991/92

NIGEL SPACKMAN

1986/87 – 1988/89

During the two eventful years they spent in each other's company, Nigel Spackman and Liverpool were undeniably good for each other. Kenny Dalglish parted with £400,000 to sign the tall, strong Chelsea stalwart in February 1987 when the Reds' midfield department was sorely depleted by injuries. Nigel's early performances demonstrated that while he might lack the creative skills to unlock a stubborn defence singlehandedly, there was no one more adept at doing the simple thing well. He had the underrated ability to play short passes quickly and with precision, and became a reliable foil for the more extravagant talents around him.

This was particularly evident in 1987/88 when the former Bournemouth man, who spent much of the season deputising for the injured Ronnie Whelan, was joined in the team by John Barnes and Peter Beardsley. Nigel played in more than half the matches as the Reds cruised exhilaratingly to the title, time and again proving the need for a workhorse among the artists. His stout attributes were never more sharply defined than in the much-lauded 5-0 demolition of Nottingham Forest at Anfield in April 1988 when, unselfish to a fault, he laid on two of the goals for colleagues when he might have found the net himself – especially admirable as Nigel was never to score in his 63 appearances for the club.

He went on to play in the FA Cup Final against Wimbledon, but in the subsequent season a fitter squad increased the manager's options and even the versatile Nigel, who helped out occasionally in defence, found it hard to win a place. In February 1989, his job done, he left for QPR (on his way to Ibrox, as it transpired) with a Championship medal and glorious memories; Liverpool had received two years' doughty service and now picked up a £100,000 profit - splendid business for all concerned.

BORN: Romsey, Hampshire, 2.12.60.
GAMES: 50 (13). GOALS: 0.
HONOURS: League Championship 87/8.

OTHER CLUBS: Bournemouth 80/1-82/3 (119, 10); Chelsea 83/4-86/7 (141, 12); Queen's Park Rangers 88/9-89/90 (29, 1); Rangers 89/90-92/3 (100, 1); Chelsea 92/3-95/6 (67, 0); Sheffield United 96/7 (23, 0). MANAGER: Sheffield United 97-98.

JOHN ALDRIDGE

It was like a worthy but run-of-the-mill county cricketer taking over from prince of batsmen Viv Richards, or a rookie rider climbing into the saddle of master jockey Lester Piggott; when John Aldridge replaced Ian Rush as Liverpool centre-forward public expectations were not especially high. But Scouser John had the perfect response. He scored so freely that Ian was not missed and when the prodigal hero *did* return after a frustrating year in the Italian sun he found that reclaiming the role of the Reds' goalscorer-in-chief was no formality. Indeed, a hefty slice of the Welshman's first campaign back at Anfield was spent on the bench as he languished in the shadow of his so-called stand-in.

John had achieved his lifetime ambition of joining Liverpool in January 1987 when, with Ian's departure in the offing, Kenny Dalglish signed him from Oxford United for £700,000. His Manor Ground strike-rate of around 1.5 goals every two games might have made him one of the most feared strikers in the land yet, strangely, there was widespread reticence in recognising his achievements. True, he had never played for a glamour club and his style was efficient rather than flashy, but that record – which included 18 months of First Division experience – would surely have made it surprising if he had failed at Anfield, instead of provoking the amazement in many quarters which followed his success.

In his first half-term as a Red, John started only two League matches but, significantly, scored in both, although it wasn't until 1987/88 that the headlines started coming his way. Even when he netted in the opening nine League matches – admittedly six of his strikes were from the penalty spot – he was accorded but a fraction of the acclaim deservedly bestowed on John Barnes. As the season wore on, however, it gradually dawned on the media that perhaps the unobtrusive front-runner who unfussily rounded off so many flowing moves should be given a share of the credit. After all, his finishing was clinical and he was better in the air than Rush; his selfless running created countless openings for Messrs Barnes and Beardsley and if John could match neither the ball skills of his team-mates nor the pace of his predecessor he made up for it with the positional sense of a born opportunist. Add to that his inbuilt passion for Liverpool – never more evident than in his utter devastation on missing his first penalty for the club in the 1988 FA Cup Final against Wimbledon – and his all-round value becomes apparent.

Despite the triumphs of his first full term at Anfield, in which he scored 26 times on the way to a title medal, it was widely predicted that he would quietly shuffle out of the limelight when Ian Rush returned for 1988/89. Once again John confounded the pundits. Ian spent most of the League opener against Charlton in the Selhurst Park dugout before replacing not Aldridge but Beardsley; John, meanwhile, was weighing in with a little matter of a hat-trick! That performance set the tone for a campaign in which 'Aldo' outscored an often unfit Ian and capped his Reds career by sweetly sweeping home the opening goal against Everton in the 1989 FA Cup Final.

Come 1989/90 it was clear that Dalglish must make a choice between the two men and, not surprisingly, he chose the one for whom he had paid more than £2 million. John, though, had one more moment of glory before joining Real Sociedad for £1 million. Just days before his September move, 'Pool were five up at home to Crystal Palace when they won a penalty and the Kop called for the Eire international. The boss betrayed evidence of a heart by sending him on, and he duly signed off with a goal; the man whom the critics had continually expected to fail had succeeded to the last.

Even then, Aldo's Merseyside exploits were not finished. After two years of prospering in Spain, he signed for Tranmere as a 32-year-old in 1991, going on to become player-boss and to register well in excess of a century of League strikes over the next seven campaigns. Wherever he has played, at whatever level, John Aldridge has scored freely; it is tempting to wonder just what he might have achieved had he been allowed to remain at Anfield in 1989.

BORN: Liverpool, 18.9.58. GAMES: 88 (15). GOALS: 61. HONOURS: League Championship 87/8. FA Cup 88/9. 69 Republic of Ireland caps (86-96). OTHER CLUBS: Newport County 79/80-83/4 (170, 69); Oxford United 83/4-86/7 (114, 72); Real Sociedad 89/90-90/1 (63, 33); Tranmere Rovers 91/2-97/8. (242, 138). MANAGER: Tranmere Rovers 96-.

1986/87 - 1989/90

JOHN BARNES

As the veteran John Barnes applied himself industriously to a comparatively unspectacular midfield anchor role during the Reds' attempted mid-nineties renaissance, it was inevitable that he was outshone by the generation of new stars shining incandescently around him. But it should never be forgotten that, not so long before, he had been hailed as one of the most brilliant entertainers to grace British football since the war. More than that, he achieved something which eluded every Anfield player before him: he became, for a while, *the* national symbol of the game at its most attractive. In the same way that George Best's name was once a byword for soccer excellence, even among people who didn't follow sport, so in the late eighties was that of the Jamaican-born England forward.

As an all-round performer he did not equal Dalglish at his peak, and for sheer pop-idol appeal, he did not match Keegan. But in terms of presence and charisma John left the Scotsman standing, and for all Kevin's admirable qualities, he lacked the magical skills with which the former Watford winger was so plenteously endowed. Thus, it was John Barnes, more than anyone else, who finally bestowed upon Liverpool the glitter and panache which had been the traditional preserve of Spurs and Manchester United.

Yet for all the plaudits heaped on his close-cropped head, John was seen as something of a gamble when he headed north for £900,000 in the summer of 1987. His extravagant talents were acknowledged, but at Vicarage Road these had been tempered with inconsistency and there were fears that he was not the Anfield type. Any misgivings, however, withered as John produced a string of scintillating early performances which dazzled even the sceptics. To say he gave the Reds a new dimension is a gross understatement. A big, powerful man blessed with a sublime first touch, he was lethal when he received the ball in a deep left-flank position and ran at defences. He had the guile to gull those who stood in his way, the strength to ride tackles and a deceptive pace which took him loping away from his stricken prey. One moment John would be hemmed in by several opponents, two feints later he would be yards away, jockeying for a shooting chance. And unlike many wingers, he could capitalise on his own approach work, scoring goals from almost any angle or distance. Indeed, so stunning was his marksmanship that some critics reckoned he was best employed as a central striker.

John's reward for his inspired efforts during that first Anfield campaign was a title medal and Footballer of the Year awards from fellow professionals and soccer writers alike. Understandably, much was expected of him in the 1988 European Championships but he disappointed, as he did often in the international arena, looking more like the wayward performer who had alternately thrilled and frustrated in his Watford days. Maybe he needed his regular top-class colleagues to bring the best out of him, for on his return to club duty he was as deadly as ever, apart from the occasional game when he seemed to drift.

Despite his catalogue of gifts, however, John experienced a relatively fallow career interlude, which coincided loosely with the Souness reign. Injuries laid him low and he put on weight, looking sluggish and ill at ease when he did play. Happily, he shed pounds and regained vitality in 1994, confounding the popular belief that he was finished, and became a subtly cohesive link-man, passing so beautifully that he was known to go through an entire game without losing possession.

Yes, there were times when he was overrun by heel-snapping speedsters, and some reckoned he was too cautious, not delivering enough 'killer' balls. There was no denying, either, that the 'miracle man' of yesteryear had gone forever. But in his place was a canny general, offering his precocious young lieutenants much-needed guidance, sometimes with a firmness surprising in one so placid, and it was clear that he had plenty to offer still. However, after he was dropped for the Cup Winners' Cup semi-final second leg against Paris St-Germain in April 1997, it became apparent that he was no longer wanted and come August, by then aged 33, he was freed to pursue an Indian summer at Newcastle. It is to be hoped that those fans who had noisily demanded his exit will now restore him, in their minds, to the place of honour his service merits. Truly, John Barnes was one of Liverpool's finest.

BORN: Jamaica, 7.11.63. GAMES: 399 (4). GOALS: 106. HONOURS: League Championship 87/8, 89/90. FA Cup 88/9. League Cup 94/5. 79 England caps (83-95).

OTHER CLUBS: Watford 81/2-86/7 (233, 65); Newcastle United 97/8- (26, 6).

1987/88 – 1996/97

PETER BEARDSLEY

Shoulders hunched and mouth habitually agape, Peter Beardsley hardly cuts an heroic figure on the field. Until, that is, the ball is at his feet. Then, suddenly, the multi-talented Geordie looks what he is - a daring, elusive firecracker of a player, lurking with intent on the very verge of world class.

For four seasons, presumed at the time to be his peak, he plied his trade to coruscating effect for Liverpool; then, having entered his 31st year and with his confidence evidently in decline, he was allowed to slip away. Wisdom comes easily after the event, but how ill-judged Graeme Souness's decision to sell him was to appear after Peter put in another half-decade and more of sheer magnificence for Everton and Newcastle, finding time to resurrect his England career along the way.

Peter's early days at Anfield were not easy. When he moved from Newcastle for £1.9 million in the summer of 1987, he carried the burdensome tag of Britain's most expensive footballer. As if that were not enough of a challenge, his arrival coincided with that of John Barnes, a circumstance which both helped and hindered his efforts to make an instant impact. The England winger's sensational form deflected much of the media attention from Peter, giving him much-needed extra time to bed in, but also it set a dauntingly high standard, especially as John's transfer fee had been less than half his own.

For several months, while by no means a flop, the stocky, deep-lying marksman failed to take the eye and by the turn of the year had contributed only four goals. The Reds, however, remained unbeaten in the League and Kenny Dalglish pronounced himself well satisfied with Peter's progress. As 1988 dawned, the manager's faith was shown to be cannily placed, his record signing turning in a sparkling New Year's Day performance against Coventry. The former Magpie - whose route to St James' Park had taken in a frustrating one-match sojourn at Old Trafford - scored twice and had the Kop purring with pleasure at his all-round skills as he began to fulfil his immense potential.

That day, and for the rest of the campaign, Peter was irresistible, whether employing his speed and ball control to skip past defenders as he ran from deep positions, or slicing deadly, perfectly angled passes through a crowded penalty area. With his self-belief at last sky-high, he revealed the full repertoire of tricks which had endeared him to Tyneside and, at Anfield later that month, Arsenal fell victim to a typical piece of Beardsley cheek. Nutmegging an astonished Michael Thomas, he moved forward to chip the ball over towering 'keeper John Lukic to put the match beyond the Gunners' reach.

Quick-witted and a great improviser, Peter confirmed his stature over subsequent seasons, though he would have risen to yet greater heights in a red shirt if his finishing had been more consistent. Often he would appear on the edge of the box, jink past a couple of defenders and then spoil his work with a weak attempt on goal. The Beardsley boot could dispatch a devastating shot, be it blistering drive or tantalising curler but, in those days at least, reliable it was not.

Unlike some gifted individuals, Peter could never be faulted for his work-rate, even if he did seem to run out of steam now and then. Also there were days when he was unable to get into the swing of the action, which resulted in periodic controversial omissions from an increasingly out-of-sorts side - by Anfield standards, that is - as the Dalglish era approached its stunning end. Those absences and occasional form-losses offered proof positive of Beardsley's enormous influence: when the England striker was sidelined or below-par, the Reds' overall performance suffered significantly, their attacking options drastically reduced without his normally incisive input.

For Liverpool fans who bemoan, to this day, what they lost after Peter's £1 million sale to Everton in August 1991, there is one telling consolation - at least they enjoyed four years of Beardsley brilliance. At Manchester his sole appearance ended in substitution; how United must rue the day they let him go after just one hour of first-team football.

BORN: Newcastle, 18.1.61. GAMES: 155 (15). GOALS: 58. HONOURS: League Championship 87/8, 89/90. FA Cup 88/9. 59 England caps (86-96). OTHER CLUBS: Carlisle United 79/80-81/2 (104, 22); Vancouver Whitecaps 82; Manchester United 82/3 (0, 0, one appearance in a cup-tie); Vancouver Whitecaps 83; Newcastle United 83/4-86/7 (147, 61); Everton 91/2-92/3 (81, 25); Newcastle United 93/4-96/7 (129, 47); Bolton Wanderers 97/8 (17, 2); Manchester City *on loan* 97/8 (6, 0); Fulham *on loan* 97/8 (8, 1).

1987/88 – 1990/91

RAY HOUGHTON

Kenny Dalglish's ceaseless quest for perfection took Ray Houghton to Anfield in the autumn of 1987. Even at that early stage of the season, the Reds were apparently cantering away with the Championship and playing some of the most exhilarating football the First Division had seen in years. Surely the manager could not ask for more? But, of course, he could!

Craig Johnston was doing a splendid job as a right-sided attacking midfielder, but Kenny believed that Ray would be an improvement. So, after a protracted cloak-and-dagger transfer saga, he paid £825,000 for the stocky Glaswegian.

Ray, who had been dumped by West Ham after one appearance and then rebuilt his career with Fulham and Oxford United, played his first match for Liverpool at home to Norwich and made an instant impact, the game finishing goalless through no fault of the newcomer. The Kop warmed to Ray as he created a series of chances with his busy runs and accurate crosses, and as the weeks went by it became clear that Dalglish had made yet another astute purchase.

The Eire international - he qualified for the Republic by virtue of an Irish father - was a tireless forager who liked to pick up the ball inside his own half and dribble it deep into opposition territory. On reaching his destination, he was less prone than Johnston to squander possession, and often startled goalkeepers with snap shots from outside the penalty area. He was in the habit, also, of popping up for vital close-range strikes, as he did twice with FA Cup goals in early 1988 - a header which beat Everton at Goodison and a mid-air sidefooted volley against Manchester City at Maine Road.

With Ray providing a thrustful threat on the right and John Barnes casting his magic spell on the left, the Reds were superbly balanced. They were ideally equipped to rip open the most clam-like of defences, and in that glorious 1987/88 campaign, they did so frequently.

Ray capped the impressive start to his Liverpool career with some enterprising performances for his adopted country, linking smoothly with clubmates John Aldridge and Ronnie Whelan in the 1988 European Championships. His dash and skill on the wider stage prompted the interest of assorted Italian clubs and huge sums were mentioned, but Dalglish understandably refused to part with his new-found gem. Ray confirmed his standing with exemplary form in the following term, being an ever-present in the team which narrowly failed to take the title and giving an outstanding display in the FA Cup Final win over Everton.

Injuries caused Ray to miss much of 1989/90, but he bounced back for the hectic climax to that title-winning season and was the Reds' most consistent performer during the two turbulent campaigns which followed. Accordingly, his £825,000 departure to Aston Villa in July 1992 provoked considerable consternation among Kopites, who were mystified by Graeme Souness' sale of a player who had so much still to offer at club and international level.

BORN: Glasgow, 9.1.62. GAMES: 191 (7). GOALS: 37.
HONOURS: League Championship 87/8, 89/90. FA Cup 88/9, 91/2.
73 Republic of Ireland caps (86-).

OTHER CLUBS: West Ham United 81/2 (1, 0); Fulham 82/3-85/6 (129, 16); Oxford United 85/6-87/8 (83, 10); Aston Villa 92/3-94/5 (95, 6); Crystal Palace 94/5-96/7 (72, 7); Reading 97/8- (25, 1).

1987/88 — 1992/93

RONNIE WHELAN

At best inspirational, at worst remarkably consistent, Ronnie Whelan was at the heart of almost every Liverpool triumph of the eighties. The Eire international's deceptively simple, almost matter-of-fact midfield method exerted a powerfully pervasive influence which increased with the passing years.

When the sandy-haired Dubliner breezed into Bob Paisley's side in 1981, he made an exciting impact with spectacular goals and an infectious, ambitious style of play which, though exhilarating when Ronnie was on song, sometimes resulted in the ball being lost unnecessarily. Maturity taught him to do the simple thing, and to do it well, with the result that he could be counted on to perform reliably in any company, on any occasion.

When Ronnie - whose father, Ron Snr, also wore the Republic's green shirt - left Home Farm in October 1979, his destination might have been Old Trafford rather than Anfield. He had spent three summer holidays with Manchester United as a schoolboy but was allowed to slip through their recruitment net. The Red Devils' loss was to be Liverpool's gain and, 18 months after crossing the Irish Sea, he marked his League debut - against Stoke in front of the Kop - with a goal. It was October 1981, however, before he outstripped his countryman Kevin Sheedy, who was later to build a successful career with Everton, in the race to replace Ray Kennedy on the left side of the Reds' midfield.

In his first campaign as a regular, Ronnie could do little wrong. As well as picking up a title medal, he scored twice in the Milk Cup victory over Spurs at Wembley and received a Young Player of the Year award. To cap it all, no less a judge than Joe Mercer compared him to that great Northern Irish inside-forward of several decades earlier, Peter Doherty. Ronnie maintained his progress the following season but suffered a setback in 1983/84 when a hand injury kept him out of the side until November. On his return he seemed to have lost impetus and there were fears that he was drifting out of long-term contention, but the exit of Graeme Souness changed all that.

In the absence of the former skipper, Ronnie tightened up his game and accepted new responsibility to become a better all-round player than ever before. His distribution became more efficient, his tackling attained a keenly abrasive edge, and there was a new purpose about everything he did. As a bonus, the new Whelan retained his habit of scoring sensational goals, none more breathtaking than the first-time 25-yard curler past Gary Bailey which took the 1985 FA Cup semi-final against Manchester United into extra time.

As his medal collection burgeoned, so did his versatility. At various times he occupied all the midfield positions and filled in effectively at left-back when Jim Beglin broke his leg in early 1987. Then, in the subsequent season when costly newcomers were grabbing all the headlines, Ronnie enjoyed his best term to date. Moving into a central role to create extra space for John Barnes on the left, he was a revelation, his quickfire passing and selfless running off the ball winning new and much-deserved acclaim. His enthusiasm and level-headed approach were rewarded with the captaincy when Alan Hansen was sidelined for most of 1988/89 and he led the Reds to FA Cup triumph over Everton at Wembley.

Come 1990, Ronnie was vastly experienced though not yet 30 and he was expected to play a pivotal role as Liverpool sought to extend their dominance of English football into a new decade. Sadly, his outings over ensuing seasons were to be curtailed cruelly by injuries, and, surprisingly, when he was fit he was not always selected by Souness. In September 1994, he was freed to join Southend United and 10 months later was promoted to player-boss. After an encouraging start, there followed difficult times at Roots Hall and come 1997 Ronnie Whelan was seeking a new arena in which to test his managerial mettle.

BORN: Dublin, 25.9.61. GAMES: 459 (17). GOALS: 73. HONOURS: European Cup 83/4. League Championship 81/2, 82/3, 83/4, 85/6, 87/8, 89/90. FA Cup 85/6, 88/9. League Cup 81/2, 82/3, 83/4. 53 Republic of Ireland caps (81-95).

OTHER CLUBS: Home Farm; Southend United 94/5-95/6 (34, 1).
MANAGER: Southend United (95-97).

1980/81– 1994/95

The shrewd acquisition of centre-back Gary Gillespie in July 1983 typified the meticulous planning which helped Liverpool retain their position of supremacy in English football for so long. When new manager Joe Fagan paid Coventry £325,000 to make Gary his first signing, it was hardly credible that the classy Scot was going to see first-team service in the foreseeable future. Joe was blessed already with the masterly combination of Alan Hansen and Mark Lawrenson, and despite five years' experience as a First Division defender, the tall, angular newcomer seemed destined to serve an Anfield 'apprenticeship' in the reserves.

Sure enough, a whole season passed in which the former midfielder and occasional full-back made but a solitary senior appearance, at home to Walsall in the Milk Cup semi-final first leg. But 1984/85 brought intermittent opportunities and Gary made the most of them. He revealed a commanding aerial presence in both penalty areas, cultured and precise distribution, and a penchant for loping forward like some runaway giraffe to play slick one-two passing combinations. His campaign culminated with a promising European Cup Final display against Juventus - despite conceding the penalty which cost Liverpool the match - after coming on for the injured Lawrenson just 90 seconds into the action. Of course, all footballing considerations had been rendered irrelevant by earlier events on that tragic Heysel night.

Gary was to get no further chance until January 1986, when he put together an impressive run - highlighted, uncharacteristically, by an Anfield hat-trick against Birmingham - and finally became established in the team. With Lawrenson sidelined once again, the former Sky Blue dovetailed seamlessly with Hansen and played enough matches to earn a title medal. Even when Mark was fit again, Gary retained his place and looked set to face Everton in the FA Cup Final, but he was laid low by a virus and missed what would have been his first Wembley date.

Over the next two terms he played some of the best football of his career, showing ever more skill and composure as his confidence grew. He was rewarded by international caps but this encouraging progress was interrupted by injuries which put him out of contention for most of 1988/89 and 1989/90. With Glenn Hysen added to the squad, Gary's prospects were suddenly not so bright, though he returned in the spring of 1990 to help clinch the Championship. However, he did not figure in Graeme Souness' plans and joined Celtic for £925,000 in August 1991.

BORN: Bonnybridge, Stirling, 5.7.60. GAMES: 197 (7). GOALS: 16. HONOURS: League Championship 85/6, 87/8, 89/90. 13 Scotland caps (87-90).

OTHER CLUBS: Falkirk 77/8 (22, 0); Coventry City 78/9-82/3 (172, 6); Celtic 91/2-93/4 (69, 3); Coventry City 94/5 (3, 0).

GARY GILLESPIE

1983/84 – 1990/91

BARRY VENISON

1986/87 – 1991/92

Barry Venison deserves top marks for initiative. In the summer of 1986 the England under-21 international full-back felt his career was going nowhere with Sunderland, who had narrowly escaped relegation to the Third Division. It had been a second successive disappointing campaign for Barry, who in 1985 had become the youngest captain in a Wembley final when the Wearsiders had tasted Milk Cup defeat *and* dropped out of the top flight. So he wrote to Liverpool to ask if he was wanted at Anfield; the result was a £250,000 transfer and a place in the first team at the start of the new term.

He settled in with a series of composed displays, usually at right-back but occasionally switching flanks, and missed only a handful of League games. Determined and positive in his approach, Barry tackled efficiently, linked well with his attack and often crossed the ball well, though his overall distribution was sometimes scrappy.

He started 1987/88 as the first choice right-back, but then injuries to an Achilles tendon and calf were followed by an appendix operation and his season was in tatters. As new defenders such as Gary Ablett, Steve Staunton and David Burrows came into the reckoning, it looked as though Barry might be pushed to regain his role. The next campaign, in which he started only 14 League matches but won an FA Cup medal, proved indeterminate, but in 1989/90 he enjoyed his most settled run for three years. His use of the ball, as exemplified by the pass which cut through the Chelsea rearguard to set up a goal for Peter Beardsley at Stamford Bridge in December 1989, was improving and he was beginning to look like a long-term proposition.

However, further injuries and stern competition for places precipitated a £250,000 transfer to Newcastle in July 1992 and it proved the making of him. Given extra responsibility with Kevin Keegan's Magpies, the forthright north-easterner excelled in both central defence and midfield, and earned a full England call-up in the latter role. Later Barry – whose flowing flaxen locks and flamboyant dress became familiar to viewers of Sky TV, for whom he showed promise as a summariser – played briefly under Graeme Souness in Turkey. Thereafter he took his considerable nous and experience to Southampton, only for a back problem to end his career prematurely.

BORN: Consett, County Durham, 16.8.64.
GAMES: 133 (18). GOALS: 2. HONOURS: League Championship 87/8, 89/90. FA Cup 88/9. 2 England caps (94).

OTHER CLUBS: Sunderland 81/2-85/6 (173, 2); Newcastle United 92/3-94/5 (109, 1); Galatasaray, Turkey, 95/6 (8, 0); Southampton 95/6-96/7 (24, 0).

The transfer of Steve Staunton to Aston Villa was arguably Liverpool's most ill-conceived sale since the war. As the nineties began, the callow Irishman had just broken into the Reds' senior side and it was clear that he possessed, in bountiful abundance, the talent, temperament and versatility to become an Anfield cornerstone until the turn of the century. Just a year later, in August 1991, new manager Graeme Souness struck a perplexing £1.1 million deal with Ron Atkinson and the 22-year-old duly developed into what many critics saw as the finest left-back in the Premiership. Meanwhile, for several seasons, Liverpool struggled depressingly for quality in what is often a problem position.

Of course, there were mitigating circumstances for letting Staunton go, although none that impressed the galled majority of Reds fans who watched the Eire international's predictably splendid progress at Villa Park. Liverpool, like other top clubs, were hamstrung by the restriction on non-English players that then pertained, and for this purpose Steve was classed as a 'foreigner'. Secondly, in Souness' judgement David Burrows was a more-than-adequate left-back and, in fairness, some people agreed. In addition, though Steve had already picked up League and FA Cup honours as a Red, his confidence had been buffeted by cruel barracking by a small but noisy section of 'supporters', who used him as a scapegoat for the team's indifferent form. On top of all that, the Anfield coffers were not exactly bulging in 1991 and, measly though the fee seems in retrospect, it was not negligible at the time.

Exactly what had Liverpool lost with Steve's departure? A defensively sound, tireless overlapper capable of truly destructive distribution - his speciality is the wickedly curling, low-trajectory cross into the box - who can also play in midfield, central defence or even up front; indeed, he helped himself to a Littlewoods Cup hat-trick when he came on as substitute for Ian Rush at Wigan in September 1989.

Ironically, he would have been ideally suited to Roy Evans' fluid 3-5-2 formation and in 1995 there were persistent rumours that the Anfield boss was negotiating for his return. But Steve signed a new contract with Villa and looked likely to remain, frustratingly for Liverpool, the one that got away.

BORN: Drogheda, Republic of Ireland, 19.1.69. GAMES: 75 (14). GOALS: 5. HONOURS: League Championship 89/90. FA Cup 88/9. 74 Republic of Ireland caps (88-).

OTHER CLUBS: Dundalk; Bradford City on loan 87/8 (8, 0); Aston Villa 91/2- (208, 16).

STEVE STAUNTON

1988/89 – 1990/91

DAVID BURROWS

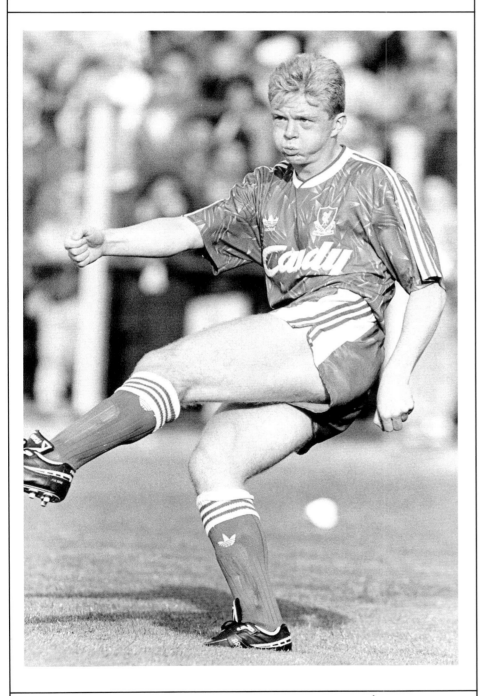

1988/89 – 1993/94

When Kenny Dalglish prised rookie defender David Burrows away from West Bromwich Albion for £500,000 in October 1988, dashing the hopes of a posse of rivals in the process, the word sped down the soccer grapevine that the Liverpool boss had pulled off a sizeable coup. The fiercely enthusiastic Midlander, already an England under-21 international despite having fewer than 50 League appearances under his belt, was viewed widely as one of the finest prospects outside the top flight.

Indeed, there was a certain something about 'Bugsy' which was reminiscent of another all-action youngster who, more than 20 years earlier, had also moved to Anfield for a hefty fee. In his unbridled sense of adventure, his almost frenzied commitment and his downright hatred of being beaten, David evoked memories of no less a competitor than Emlyn Hughes. Sadly, though the former Throstle gave the Reds five years of doughty service encompassing nearly 200 senior outings, he was never even to approach the standard set by his eminent predecessor.

Having arrived with Liverpool in the throes of an injury crisis, David found himself in immediate first-team action. Pressed into service at both left-back and the left side of midfield, he revealed bullish strength and enough skill to suggest that hard work could turn him into an accomplished player, despite a disturbing inclination to commit himself to horribly rash tackles. His long stride made him an effective overlapper and his galloping gait was becoming a familiar sight when returning regulars and the emergence of fellow hopeful Steve Staunton edged him out.

David fought back to play a full part in the title triumph of 1989/90 and was not often absent from the side for the next three seasons, impressing particularly as a midfield marker and proving a gutsy stand-in at centre-half. However, he remained headstrong, his tactical acumen seemed rudimentary and, overall, his game did not progress as expected. Accordingly, it was no surprise when he was dispatched to West Ham as a makeweight in the deal that took Julian Dicks to Anfield.

BORN: Dudley, Worcestershire, 25.10.68. GAMES: 178 (12). GOALS: 3. HONOURS: League Championship 89/90. FA Cup 91/2.

OTHER CLUBS: West Bromwich Albion 85/6-88/9 (46, 1); West Ham United 93/4-94/5 (29, 1); Everton 94/5 (19, 0); Coventry City 94/5- (73, 0).

IAN RUSH

Every now and then, no more than once or twice in a generation, there arises in top-flight football an individual with a certain predatory instinct; no matter how exciting or beautiful the talents of more artistic performers may be, this man's special gift - the knack of scoring goals in large numbers and at regular intervals - is *the* most valuable asset in the game. In modern times, certainly since the golden days of Greaves and Law, no British player has demonstrated a more ruthless aptitude for long-term net-finding than Ian Rush. The Welshman's record is all the more remarkable because so many of his goals have come in high-profile matches with trophies at stake, a testimony to temperament as well as supreme skill.

Yet there was a time, shortly after his £300,000 move from Chester in April 1980, that Ian looked destined to flop. In his early days at Anfield he could hardly manage to get on the Central League scoresheet, and there had even been talk of a swift exit. Then came a chance in the 1981 League Cup Final replay against West Ham and, suddenly, confidence seemed to surge through the rookie striker's lean frame. Streaking down the left flank, at last revealing a glimpse of the searing pace that was to make him feared throughout the football world, the raw Flintshire lad gave a broad hint that the Reds' investment had not been a rash one.

But it was not until the following campaign that the real Ian Rush stood up. Then the goals came with a vengeance; they started with a trickle, increased to a steady flow, and over the next five seasons swelled to a veritable torrent. Between 1981/82 and 1986/87 Ian hit the target nearly 200 times, averaging around two strikes every three games. Ironically, he was particularly pitiless towards Everton, whom he had supported as a boy, his most savage execution taking place at Goodison in 1982 when he scored four. Ian's most obvious asset was the speed which carried him beyond defenders, but it was by no means his only weapon. He was a clean, powerful striker of the ball and had the finely honed positional sense of all the best poachers; his first touch was usually sure and he was willing to forage for possession, though for a six-footer he was surprisingly weak in the air.

So integral was Ian to the Liverpool set-up that when it was revealed he was on his way to Juventus for £3.2 million - the deal was announced a year before he left in June 1987 - there was consternation on the Kop. In the event he was hardly missed, thanks to the Aldridge, Barnes and Beardsley triumvirate, and many observers thought the Reds were foolish to part with £2.8 million to get him back. After a year of frustration and illness, the old Rush fire needed patient rekindling and there were moments when it seemed the spark had gone. But now he was no longer merely a spearhead; instead he was leading the line, often receiving the ball with his back to goal, which demanded different skills. Naturally it took time to adapt, but two opportunist strikes which beat Everton in the 1989 FA Cup Final signalled that his rehabilitation was complete.

Thereafter, Ian proved a more accomplished all-rounder than ever before. His former pace never quite returned, his scoring-rate was not as formidable, but his own more-than-respectable tallies were augmented by the countless 'assists' he contributed to team-mates and by a capacity for work which seemed to grow as he got older.

But most telling of all was the way Ian Rush reacted to a challenge. When dropped by Graeme Souness he came back with all guns blazing to earn the captaincy, only to face an even more daunting double threat from Messrs Fowler and Collymore in 1995. With two such virile young bloods hunting his job, most thirtysomethings might have shuffled off to find a more comfortable berth. But not Rushie: he just battled harder, and first Robbie, then Stan, was omitted to accommodate the old fella. Eventually a cartilage injury cost him his place, but still Ian showed no signs of stepping meekly aside, continuing to give his all until accepting a free transfer to Leeds United in May 1996. True grit from a true great.

BORN: St Asaph, Flintshire, 20.10.61. GAMES: 616 (30). GOALS: 337. HONOURS: European Cup 83/4. League Championship 81/2, 82/3, 83/4, 85/6, 89/90. FA Cup 85/6, 88/9, 91/2. League Cup 80/1, 81/2, 82/3, 83/4, 94/5. 73 Wales caps (80-96).

OTHER CLUBS: Chester 78/9-79/80 (34, 14); Juventus 87/8 (29, 7); Leeds United 96/7 (36, 3); Newcastle United 97/8 (10, 0). Sheffield United *on loan* 97/8 (4, 0).

1980/81 – 1986/87 & 1988/89 – 1995/96

When Ronny Rosenthal was pitched into the title race in the spring of 1990 it was like a fistful of *Alka Seltzers* hitting a bucket of water. Not that Liverpool were ailing - they were firmly in pole position - but were in need of a tonic after the trauma of FA Cup semi-final defeat by Crystal Palace. Cue Ronny, an instant one-man pick-me-up.

Kenny Dalglish had signed the Israeli international striker on loan from Standard Liege just minutes ahead of the transfer deadline, eventually closing a £1 million deal the following summer after Ronny had proved his worth in stirring fashion. After impressing as a substitute against Southampton at Anfield, he was a sensation in his first full appearance, destroying Charlton at Selhurst Park with a scintillating hat-trick. It wasn't just the goals but the manner of them which captivated travelling Kopites; there was one with his left foot, one with his right and a diving header.

Through pace, verve and crisp finishing, he produced further crucial strikes that term and, though he might not have been the easiest man to play alongside - he was always full of running but not always in the right direction - Reds fans salivated at the thought of more defence-shredding cavalry charges to come.

However, it transpired that while he could lift crowds and colleagues alike, Ronny was at his most effective when rising from the bench, unpredictability being his chief virtue, and he remained on the fringe of the side for four years.

In January 1994, as one of his last acts as Liverpool boss, Graeme Souness sold the Israeli to Tottenham for £250,000. Ronny left Anfield declaring that he had never been given a fair chance, understandable from his standpoint but not a view shared by most observers.

At White Hart Lane, he found himself in a similar supporting role at first, until in 1995/96 he enjoyed his longest unbroken run of senior appearances since arriving in English football, playing a typically energetic part in Spurs' latest attempt at renaissance.

BORN: Haifa, Israel, 11.10.63. GAMES: 40 (55). GOALS: 22. HONOURS: Israel caps.

OTHER CLUBS: Macabbi, Haifa; FC Bruges, Belgium; Standard Liege, Belgium; Tottenham Hotspur 93/4-96/7 (87, 4); Watford 97/8- (25, 8).

RONNY ROSENTHAL

1989/90 – 1993/94

GLENN HYSEN

1989/90 – 1991/92

During the first of his three campaigns at Anfield, Glenn Hysen cut an imposing figure. Tall, muscular and handsome, he radiated authority and charisma – and that was before he ran on to the pitch. When Sweden's centre-half and captain actually began to play, the impression of power, almost majesty, tended to be reinforced. He was courageous, skilful and audaciously calm, accustomed to aerial dominance and resourceful enough to counter most ground-level thrusts. Accordingly, in stately tandem with Alan Hansen, he helped Liverpool lift the title in 1989/90.

But then, like a footballing enactment of The King's New Clothes, the hitherto regal Hysen was, quite simply, found out and his weaknesses exploited. That icy assurance appeared to evaporate, revealing a frequently disturbing clumsiness in its place; his lack of pace was laid bare; he appeared casual, at times to the point of complacency, and he was caught in possession with alarming frequency.

With his previous club, Fiorentina of Italy, Glenn had been the well-protected linchpin of a packed defence. Thus, surrounded by colleagues and threatened by comparatively fewer forwards, his physical presence and arrogant skill were enough to command most situations. But in the more frenetic, attack-minded English game, he found himself increasingly isolated and vulnerable as his flaws were rumbled.

Glenn had arrived on Merseyside in the summer of 1989 – thus jilting Manchester United, who had expected to sign him – and early indications were that Kenny Dalglish had acquired an accomplished and imperious leader for his £650,000. Hearteningly, too, the Nordic newcomer was willing to scrap, as he proved in two boneshaking confrontations with United's Mark Hughes. The combative Welshman put Glenn's resolve and ability to the most searching of tests and they were not found wanting.

Come 1991, though, that distinguished iron-grey head was looking ever more forlorn. Glenn did not relish the new Souness regime, and did not last long under it. He was stripped of the captaincy, dropped, then freed in January 1992 to complete a poignant fall from grace.

BORN: Gothenburg, Sweden, 30.10.59.
GAMES: 89 (2). GOALS: 3.
HONOURS: League Championship 89/90.
Sweden caps.

OTHER CLUBS: Warta, Sweden; IFK Gothenburg, Sweden (twice); PSV Eindhoven, Holland; Fiorentina, Italy; GAIS Gothenburg, Sweden.

DAVID SPEEDIE

David Speedie crackled into Anfield as a Championship shock-trooper, introducing himself in characteristically explosive fashion, only to fizzle out in dismal anti-climax and leave largely unmourned. Though there were few public hints of the Liverpool manager's desperation at the time, Kenny Dalglish was already under enormous personal pressure when he paid Coventry £700,000 for the aggressive, cocky little Scot in February 1991. The Reds were losing ground in the title race and the beleaguered boss thought, presumably, that the battle-scarred 30-year-old attacker might prove a short-term inspiration, perhaps do for Liverpool what Andy Gray had once done for Everton.

At first it seemed that Kenny had pulled a rabbit out of the hat, even if Speedie had more in common with a ferret. On his debut his volley secured a share of the spoils at Old Trafford, then he netted twice in three minutes - a deft header and an adroit sidefoot - to furnish victory in the Merseyside derby at Anfield. It was an astonishing start against the Reds' two fiercest rivals but, thereafter, it was all downhill. Dalglish departed and the Championship slipped away, while David floundered, particularly when deployed in midfield, where he worked hard but his technique was found to be wanting. He was an able harasser of opponents, and some might have been intimidated by his volcanic temperament, but he could not dovetail with the side's traditional passing game and it was no surprise when Graeme Souness sold him to Blackburn for £500,000 that August. Thus a prospective title talisman had become a gamble that failed, albeit a fascinating one.

BORN: Glenrothes, Fife, 20.2.60. GAMES: 9 (5). GOALS: 6. HONOURS: 10 Scotland caps (85-89).

OTHER CLUBS: Barnsley 78/9-79/80 (23, 0); Darlington 80/1-81/2 (88, 21); Chelsea 82/3-86/7 (162, 47); Coventry City 87/8-90/1 (122, 31); Blackburn Rovers 91/2 (36, 23); Southampton 92/3 (11, 0); Birmingham City *on loan* 92/3 (10, 2); West Bromwich Albion *on loan* 92/3 (7, 2); West Ham United *on loan* 92/3 (11, 4); Leicester City 93/4 (37, 12).

1990/91

JIMMY CARTER

Prodigiously pacy but plain and predictable, £800,000 winger Jimmy Carter was a relative unknown when he arrived at Anfield from Millwall in January 1991 and, sad to say, seemed hardly less anonymous when he departed some nine months and four senior starts later.

In retrospect it is easy to question Kenny Dalglish's judgement of the right-sided flankman, who had helped the Lions lift the Second Division crown in 1987/88, yet in the year before he became a Red, Jimmy had attracted substantial bids from Rangers, Arsenal and Coventry City.

Perhaps it was all a matter of confidence. Despite early encouragement from the Kop, the Londoner seemed tentative, as if terrified of failure. Somehow, too, despite those winged heels, there was a lack of urgency about his play and also the suspicion that he became disheartened rather too quickly when the ball didn't run his way. Harking back to happier days at The Den, Jimmy had displayed a delightful change of pace, neat footwork and reliable crossing ability. For Liverpool it appeared, at times, that his legs moved too fast for his footballing brain, while his control was barely adequate and his distribution erratic.

There had been suggestions that he was to be groomed as the long-term successor to John Barnes, who had been linked with a possible move abroad, but the very thought seemed increasingly preposterous. Soon it became apparent that Jimmy had no future at Anfield and Liverpool were relieved, perhaps, when Arsenal demonstrated their continued belief in the player by paying £500,000 for him in October 1991. However, he fared little better at Highbury before returning to the second flight.

BORN: Hammersmith, London, 9.11.65. GAMES: 4 (4). GOALS: 0.

OTHER CLUBS: Millwall 86/7-90/1 (110, 10); Arsenal 91/2-94/5 (25, 2); Oxford United *on loan* 93/4 (5, 0) and 94/5 (4, 0); Portsmouth 95/6-97/8 (72, 5).

1990/91 – 1991/92

MIKE HOOPER

As the man who kept both Bruce Grobbelaar and David James out of the Liverpool team on merit for substantial spells, Mike Hooper was clearly not short of goalkeeping quality. Unfortunately for the red-haired six-footer, natural talent alone is never enough at the top level, especially in such an exposed, high-pressure position. As indispensable as the knack of stopping shots or catching crosses is a generous supply of confidence, a commodity of which Mike appeared to be parlously short.

Unquestionably, he had plenty of opportunities to cement a regular place following his £50,000 arrival from Wrexham in October 1985. There were several competent stints deputising for Grobbelaar, followed by four months in 1988/89 when the personable Bristolian seemed on the verge of becoming the Reds' regular 'keeper. While Bruce fought to overcome meningitis, Mike enjoyed a sequence of 24 consecutive games in which he won praise for his safe handling and quick reactions, and turned in several outstanding displays. Even when Grobbelaar was fit, Kenny Dalglish persisted with Hooper, and an end to the long reign of the flamboyant Zimbabwe international was suddenly conceivable. But the presence of the still-eager veteran brought added tension, and after some uncertain showings, Mike was dropped.

Still the door remained ajar, though, with Graeme Souness preferring him to Grobbelaar and newcomer James for two months in mid 1992/93. However, Anfield was going through a harrowing interlude then, and as poor results produced inevitable criticism, Hooper was unseated again.

Undoubtedly his £550,000 move to Newcastle in September 1993 was in his best interests but, sadly, Mike was unable to make the most of it.

BORN: Bristol, 10.2.64. GAMES: 69 (1). GOALS: 0. OTHER CLUBS: Bristol City 84/5 (1, 0); Wrexham 84/5-85/6 (34, 0); Leicester City on loan 90/1 (14, 0); Newcastle United 93/4-94/5 (25, 0).

1986/87 – 1992/93

NICKY TANNER

Nicky Tanner was a moderately talented but exceptionally dedicated stopper who deserves credit for exceeding most expectations when Liverpool were hit by an appalling sequence of injuries during 1991/92. However, at a club accustomed to central defenders of the highest calibre, the tall, blond Bristolian didn't seem likely to retain his place when the crisis was past.

A £30,000 acquisition in the summer of 1988 from Bristol Rovers, for whom most of his outings had been at full-back or in midfield, Nicky made little initial impact at Anfield. Though competent in the air, competitive in the tackle and blessed with deceptive pace, his ball work and reading of the game left something to be desired. In short, he didn't look like a Liverpool player.

But when Mark Wright was sidelined in August 1991, obvious deputies were thin on the ground and Nicky had the chance of an extended run in the side. He responded nobly, playing the best football of his life by keeping it simple and eradicating risk. Two examples that come to mind are his efficient part in the away UEFA Cup win over Swarovski Tirol and his shackling of Gary Lineker at White Hart Lane, and his progress was duly rewarded by a new three-and-a-half-year contract in January 1992.

Though doubts persisted in many quarters, Nicky seemed to have arrived, but the reversal of fortune was short-lived. He lost his place through injury and, when fit again, looked ordinary in the extreme. Thereafter he slipped down the pecking order before being forced into premature retirement by a back problem.

BORN: Bristol, 24.5.65. GAMES: 50 (8). GOALS: 1.

OTHER CLUBS: Bristol Rovers 85/6-87/8 (107, 3); Norwich City on loan 89/90 (6, 0); Swindon Town on loan 90/1 (7, 0).

1989/90 – 1992/93

KEVIN KEWLEY

KEVIN SHEEDY

KEVIN KEWLEY 1977/78

Forward. BORN: Liverpool, 2.3.55. GAMES: 0 (1). GOALS: 0.

STEVE OGRIZOVIC 1977/78 - 1980/81

Goalkeeper. BORN: Mansfield, 12.9.57. GAMES: 4. GOALS: 0.
OTHER CLUBS: Chesterfield 77/8 (16, 0); Shrewsbury Town
82/3-83/4 (84, 0); Coventry City 84/5- (502, 1).

KEVIN SHEEDY 1980/81 - 1981/82

Midfielder. BORN: Builth Wells, 21.10.59. GAMES: 3 (2).
GOALS: 2. HONOURS: 45 Republic of Ireland caps (83-93).
OTHER CLUBS: Hereford United 75/6-77/8 (51, 4);
Everton 82/3-91/2 (274, 67); Newcastle United 91/2-92/3
(37, 4); Blackpool 93/4 (26, 1).

COLIN RUSSELL 1980/81

Forward. BORN: Liverpool 21.1.61. GAMES: 0 (1). GOALS: 0.
OTHER CLUBS: Huddersfield Town 82/3-83/4 (66, 23);
Stoke City *on loan* 83/4 (11, 2); Bournemouth 84/5-85/6
(68, 14); Doncaster Rovers 86/7-87/8 (43, 5);
Scarborough 87/8 (13, 2); Wigan Athletic 88/9 (8, 3).

MARK SEAGRAVES 1985/86

Defender. BORN: Bootle, 22.10.66. GAMES: 2. GOALS: 0.
OTHER CLUBS: Norwich City on loan 86/7 (3, 0); Manchester City
87/8-89/90 (42, 0); Bolton Wanderers 90/1-94/5 (157, 7); Swindon
Town 95/6-97/8 (60, 0).

ALAN IRVINE 1986/87 - 1987/88

Forward. BORN: Broxburn, West Lothian, 2.3.55.
GAMES: 0 (4). GOALS: 0.
OTHER CLUBS: Falkirk 82/3-85/6 (92, 13);
Shrewsbury Town 87/8-88/9 (37, 6).

STEVE OGRIZOVIC

COLIN RUSSELL

MARK SEAGRAVES

ALAN IRVINE

BRIAN MOONEY

ALEX WATSON

BARRY JONES

BRIAN MOONEY 1986/87

Midfielder. BORN: Dublin, 2.2.66. GAMES: 0 (1). GOALS: 0.
OTHER CLUBS: Wrexham *on loan* 85/6 (9, 2);
Preston North End 87/8-90/91 (128, 20); Sunderland 90/1-92/3
(27, 1); Burnley *on loan* 92/3 (6, 0).

JOHN DURNIN 1986/87 - 1988/89

Forward. BORN: Liverpool, 18.8.65
GAMES: 1 (1). GOALS: 0.
OTHER CLUBS: West Bromwich Albion *on loan* 88/9 (5, 2);
Oxford United 88/9-92/3 (161, 44); Portsmouth 93/4- (153, 24).

ALEX WATSON 1987/88 - 1988/89

Central Defender. BORN: Liverpool 6.4.68.
GAMES: 5 (3). GOALS: 0.
OTHER CLUBS: Derby County *on loan* 90/1 (5, 0); Bournemouth
90/1-94/5 (151, 5); Torquay United 95/6- (121, 4).

PHIL CHARNOCK 1992/93 -

Midfielder/defender. BORN: Southport, 14.2.75.
GAMES: 1 (1). GOALS: 0.
OTHER CLUBS: Blackpool *on loan* 95/6 (4, 0),
Crewe Alexandra 96/7- (65, 4).

BARRY JONES 1991/92

Defender. BORN: Prescot, 20.6.70. GAMES: 0 (1). GOALS: 0.
OTHER CLUBS: Wrexham 92/3-97/8 (195, 4);
York City 97/8- (23, 2).

LEE JONES 1994/95 -

Forward. BORN: Wrexham, 29.5.73. GAMES: 0 (4). GOALS: 0.
OTHER CLUBS Wrexham 90/1-91/2 (39, 10); Crewe Alexandra
on loan 93/4 (8, 1); Wrexham on loan 95/6 (20, 8), Wrexham *on loan*
96/7 (6,0); Tranmere Rovers 96/7- (42, 14).

JOHN DURNIN

PHIL CHARNOCK

LEE JONES

MIKE MARSH

1988/89 – 1993/94

Anyone who watched Mike Marsh in training during his two best seasons at Liverpool will be mystified by the comprehensively capable midfielder's failure to secure a long-term Anfield future. A superb passer and a game trier who never backed away from a challenge, the enthusiastic Scouser frequently dominated sessions at Melwood, his all-round skills standing out even among so many exalted colleagues.

Yet during 1991/92 and 1992/93, when he was rarely absent from Graeme Souness' line-ups, Mike transferred that outstanding form to matches only in fitful bursts. It wasn't that he let the side down, simply that he didn't live up to his vast potential, becoming frustratingly peripheral at times.

Of course, there were exceptions, notably one scintillating display against Crystal Palace at Anfield in November 1992. That night Mike was irresistible as he scored one goal - a fulminating 30-yard drive after an exquisite feint past an opponent - and set up two more with an immaculate through-ball to Ronny Rosenthal and a precise cross for Don Hutchison.

He was versatile, too, excelling in a spell as Rob Jones' deputy at right-back, defending stoutly and joining in attacks with commendable enterprise, such as when he headed a neat equaliser in the passionate home encounter with Auxerre during the 1991/92 UEFA Cup campaign.

However, Mike never quite made himself indispensable and when he was needed to help facilitate the purchase of Julian Dicks from West Ham in September 1993, he was dispatched to Upton Park, valued at £1 million. He didn't settle in London, nor in Coventry, nor with Souness in Turkey, but then, under the tutelage of former Liverpool hero Ronnie Whelan, he became an instant favourite at Southend.

Still it seemed, with all due respects to Roots Hall, that Mike Marsh's place was in the Premiership, but the matter became poignantly academic in 1997 when a knee injury ended his career when it should have been approaching its peak.

BORN: Kirkby, Liverpool, 21.7.69.
GAMES: 69 (31). GOALS: 6.

OTHER CLUBS: West Ham United 93/4–94/5 (49, 1); Coventry City 94/5 (15, 2); Galatasaray, Turkey, 95/6; Southend United 95/6–97/8 (83, 11).

DEAN SAUNDERS

1991/92 – 1992/93

Dean Saunders was a footballer of many admirable qualities, a vivacious entertainer and expert marksman with ample ability to have flourished at the top level. However, buying him for Liverpool, who did not play to his strengths, was a glaring mistake.

Graeme Souness beat Everton to the Saunders signature in July 1991, paying Derby County £2.9 million for a striker who had been excitingly successful in a struggling team. Just imagine, went the argument, what he could achieve alongside better players at Anfield.

Sadly, that theory neglected to take into account the two clubs' contrasting styles. During his Baseball Ground days, invariably Derby had been under pressure and many of his goals had come from latching on to clearances punted into vast areas of empty space. In such situations the dashing 'Deano' was undeniably deadly, his eager industry, searing pace and frequently clinical finish being exactly what was needed.

But Liverpool played a patient passing game, which demanded a surer first touch than the Welsh international possessed and a positional sense which he never seemed to acquire. All too often, beautifully measured moves would break down with the ball squirting tantalisingly out of his reach.

Oddly enough, though, once in possession he could run with the ball under control, sometimes taking on opponents to devastating effect. Indeed, it should be stressed that, despite his limitations, Dean was not an unmitigated flop. The crowd warmed to his engaging enthusiasm - his non-stop effort and tip-tap gait were positively Keeganesque - and, after all, his overall strike-rate *was* respectable, if massaged by a disproportionately prolific 1991/92 UEFA Cup campaign which featured several goals of the highest quality.

At his lowest ebb, during one especially arid scoring drought, Dean - whose father, Roy, was a Reds wing-half in the fifties - came under intense media pressure, and earned admiration for facing it so manfully. In October 1992, Souness tacitly owned up to his error by selling the troubled striker to Aston Villa for £2.3 million.

BORN: Swansea, 21.6.64. GAMES: 60. GOALS: 24. HONOURS: FA Cup 91/2. 61 Wales caps (86-). OTHER CLUBS: Swansea City 83/4-84/5 (49, 12); Cardiff City *on loan* 84/5 (4, 0); Brighton and Hove Albion 85/6-86/7 (72, 21); Oxford United 86/7-88/9 (59, 22); Derby County 88/9-90/1 (106, 42); Aston Villa 92/3-94/5 (112, 37); Galatasaray, Turkey, 95/6 (27, 25); Nottingham Forest 96/7-97/8 (42, 6); Sheffield United 97/8- (24, 9).

TORBEN PIECHNIK

ISTVAN KOZMA

Even by the wretched overall standard of Graeme Souness's transfer record as manager of the Reds, the unfortunate Torben Piechnik appears as a mammoth blot.

The 29-year-old central defender was signed from his hometown club, BK Copenhagen, in the wake of his finest hour, helping Denmark to amaze the soccer world by lifting the European Championship in the summer of 1992.

The £500,000 move was completed that September, and a few days later Torben was experiencing the first of too many embarrassing afternoons in a Liverpool shirt. It cannot have done much for the Anfield boss's peace of mind that the newcomer's tormentor-in-chief was the recently-sold Dean Saunders, but that day at Villa Park it was the Welshman's pace and nimbleness that exposed the Danish debutant most cruelly. While allowances could fairly be made for understandable first-match nerves, the omens were ominous.

As autumn turned to winter, the Piechnik purchase became ever more perplexing. At a time when, because of European competition rules, Liverpool were expected to seek young English talent, Souness had invested in an aging, dithering Dane who was adequate in the air but ponderous on the turn, an unreliable passer and not the best at positioning. In short, he looked hopelessly out of his depth.

Torben was dropped soon after suffering another chasing by Saunders in January and never regained a regular place. He was freed to return to Denmark during the 1994 close season.

BORN: Copenhagen, Denmark, 21.5.63. GAMES: 23 (1).
GOALS: 0. HONOURS: Denmark caps.
OTHER CLUBS: BK Copenhagen; Aarhus, both Denmark.

It would be easy to pillory Graeme Souness over his purchase of Istvan Kozma, the little-known play-maker who cost £300,000 from Dunfermline Athletic in January 1992, only to be freed just 20 months and three senior starts later. Of course, the manager was not blameless in the matter of the Hungarian's dismal failure, but he could be excused, perhaps, for being captivated by delicious ball skills that positively shamed the technique of most Britons.

Like some throwback to the 'Magnificent Magyars' of the 1950s, Istvan could mesmerise an opponent, charm a crowd, by his total command over a football. The trouble was, he appeared utterly unable to apply that rare mastery in the hectic arena of the English game. In many a reserve encounter, he would bemuse a defender with outrageous, two-footed trickery, but then, instead of delivering a telling pass, Istvan would pause, as though admiring his own work. In that instant, almost invariably, he would be robbed and left to shuffle ineffectually on the fringe of the action until his next moment of unproductive inspiration.

Sadly, as the months passed he showed few signs of adapting to his new circumstances and his passion for the job seemed questionable. Clearly, no English club, and certainly not Liverpool, could afford such a luxury and it is significant that by August 1993 Istvan had not played enough first-team games to qualify for a new work permit. Accordingly, Graeme - who had been impressed by the Kozma quality during meetings between Dunfermline and Glasgow Rangers, but whose judgement had been proved faulty - allowed the disenchanted schemer to return to his native land.

BORN: Paszto, Hungary, 3.12.64. GAMES: 3 (6). GOALS: 0.
HONOURS: Hungary caps.
OTHER CLUBS: Ujpest Dozsa, Hungary (twice); Bordeaux, France; Dunfermline Athletic 89/90-91/2 (90, 8).

1992/93 – 1993/94

1991/92 – 1992/93

NIGEL CLOUGH

DON HUTCHISON

He might have been made for Liverpool: a clean-cut, intelligent young man blessed with sumptuous natural ability, dedicated to the work ethic and with ambition to burn. His combination of vision and dexterity, flair and courage, marked him out as a thoroughbred footballer, the type who has flourished at Anfield since Bill Shankly readjusted the club's horizons. And that is why Nigel Clough qualifies as the saddest, most distressing example of Graeme Souness's transfer market travail. Signed from Nottingham Forest for £2.275 million in June 1993, Nigel began brilliantly, playing up front alongside Ian Rush and scoring twice on his debut at home to Sheffield Wednesday. Comparisons with Kenny Dalglish were invidious yet understandable, the newcomer's smoothness of touch and quickness of thought evoking echoes of the great man.

Disillusion was not far away, however. A lean spell of results presaged the rise of Robbie Fowler and Nigel was omitted, then employed in a midfield role. The team toiled, his confidence evaporated and suddenly his one major fault, his lack of pace, appeared to outweigh his catalogue of merits. Apart from a two-goal contribution to the rousing 3-3 draw with Manchester United in January 1994, Nigel was rarely to bestride centre stage with real certainty again. For two more years he strove manfully but vainly to gain a place, but seemed perpetually ill at ease, spawning theories that his subtle gifts were increasingly unsuited to the speed of the modern game. That theory gained poignant momentum when neither a £1 million move to Manchester City in early 1996, nor a subsequent loan spell with Forest, produced a reversal of fortune.

BORN: Sunderland, County Durham, 19.3.66. GAMES: 34 (10). GOALS: 9. HONOURS: 14 England caps (89-93). OTHER CLUBS: Nottingham Forest 84/5-92/3 (311, 101); Manchester City 95/6-96/7 (38, 4); Nottingham Forest *on loan* 96/7 (13, 1); Sheffield Wednesday *on loan* 97/8 (1, 0).

Liverpool fought a long, frequently tiresome battle to induce Don Hutchison to realise his extravagant potential. Disappointingly for the club, perhaps disastrously for the player, it was a conflict that ended in frustration and defeat as a sorry catalogue of unsavoury off-the-field incidents scuppered his Anfield career. The lean, leggy midfielder cost £300,000 from Hartlepool United in November 1990, an apparently shrewd investment. At the time he was touted as having talent to equal that of another, more famous north-easterner; unfortunately he shared certain other of Paul Gascoigne's characteristics, too.

After two years of honing his skills in the Central League, Don won a regular senior berth in 1992/93, and became one of the most eye-catching members of Graeme Souness's transitional side. A perceptive passer blessed with impeccable ball control, he was an expert finisher, too, and became noted for audacious runs ahead of his forwards which yielded 10 goals that term. Such form should have guaranteed Don a key long-term role in the new Liverpool, but the indiscretions continued until even the patient Roy Evans, who had replaced Souness as boss, could tolerate no more. Accordingly, the troubled midfield man was sold to West Ham for £1.5 million in August 1994 and, used frequently as a striker, made a major contribution to the Hammers' late escape from relegation. However, Don could not settle in the capital and moved down a division with Sheffield United before being given a further top-flight opportunity with Everton. It was one he could not afford to waste.

BORN: Gateshead, County Durham, 9.5.71. GAMES: 44 (15). GOALS: 10. OTHER CLUBS: Hartlepool United 89/90-90/1 (24, 2); West Ham United 94/5-95/6 (35, 11); Sheffield United 95/6-97/8 (78, 4); Everton 97/8- (11, 1).

1993/94 – 1995/96

1991/92 – 1993/94

It was easy to see why Liverpool bought Mark Walters. When Graeme Souness paid Rangers £1.25 million to be reunited with his former star in August 1991, he was acquiring an international winger in his prime, an enthralling entertainer and a match-winner, ostensibly the man to fill the void that seemed likely to be created by the oft-mooted departure of John Barnes. However, it didn't work out quite like that. Mark never played for England again, he thrilled only sporadically and made crucial contributions to only a handful of games. Oh yes, and John Barnes stayed. The relative failure of the gentle Brummie on Merseyside was perplexing, not least because there was no denying his abundance of natural talent. On song he could be an enchanting swashbuckler, all bewitching step-overs, outrageous backheels and venomous snap-shots, and it should be stressed that he *did* have his moments as a Red.

The most memorable of these climaxed what was probably the most joyous Anfield night during the Souness stewardship, when Liverpool came from behind to beat Auxerre in a 1990/91 UEFA Cup tie, Mark sliding home the winner with cool expertise while the Kop went wild. Other highlights included his two-goal home demolition of Blackburn in December 1992, and his mesmeric gulling of four Spurs defenders before laying on a goal for Robbie Fowler in an FA Cup quarter-final in March 1995. Sadly, such telling interventions were the exception rather than the rule. Too often, particularly when the team was struggling, Mark's influence was negligible and the fans let him know, in stringent terms, exactly what they thought about it. He was slammed for not going past defenders, for inaccurate crossing, for dallying ineffectually on the ball, for not scoring enough goals and, most damning of all, for not showing sufficient fire and determination.

Increasingly Mark became a scapegoat, at times almost an aunt-sally figure, and his confidence drained away until he was little more than a cipher. As Roy Evans' exciting new side took shape it became clear that the flankman's future lay away from Anfield and in January 1996 he joined Southampton on a free transfer. Mark Walters might have meant so much to Liverpool, but in the end he meant so little.

BORN: Birmingham, 2.6.64. GAMES: 81 (42). GOALS: 19. HONOURS: 1 England cap (91).

OTHER CLUBS: Aston Villa 81/2-87/8 (181, 39); Rangers 87/8-90/1 (106, 32); Stoke City *on loan* 93/4 (9, 2); Wolverhampton Wanderers *on loan* 94/5 (11, 3); Southampton 95/6 (5, 0); Swindon Town 96/7- (61, 13).

MARK WALTERS

1991/92 – 1994/95

STIG BJORNEBYE

1992/93 –

A cross from the left foot of Stig Inge Bjornebye can be a thing of rare, almost aesthetic beauty. It seems to float from the Norwegian's boot before curving inexorably away from the goalkeeper, arcing tantalisingly beyond the reach of desperately back-pedalling defenders to fall perfectly for an oncoming attacker to smack it netwards.

Never was this scenario realised more sweetly than on one tumultuous evening at Anfield in January 1994 when Stig's sublime delivery enabled Neil Ruddock to complete Liverpool's comeback from a three-goal deficit against Manchester United. Such precision was exactly what Graeme Souness paid Rosenborg £600,000 to acquire in December 1992, though it must be said that Stig was to suffer bouts of morale-sapping inconsistency between periods of admirable competence.

He had impressed with a fine display against England in the summer before the transfer and when David Burrows suffered a serious injury, the Reds boss felt the sturdy defender - who'd had five years of international experience at 23 - was ideal for the English game.

However, Stig took time to adjust to the pace of the Premier League and, during intermittent appearances over the next season and a half, was subjected to sometimes senseless criticism from fans. But 1994/95 brought a change of fortune, at least initially, as Stig secured a regular place at left wing-back. Strong, well balanced and composed, he tackled firmly and showed good ball control, although that was prone to slip under severe pressure. His passing, irreproachable at times, was prone to infuriating lapses of accuracy, as were the crosses which became his speciality.

Nevertheless, Stig was a respected member of the team that beat Bolton to lift the League Cup, his one Wembley disappointment coming when he shot against the post instead of breaking his scoring duck for Liverpool. That minor regret was placed in perspective a few days later when he broke his leg in a freak accident against Southampton, his studs sticking in the grass as he strained to reach the ball.

On recovery, he found himself in a daunting queue for a first-team place, but with Rob Jones and Steve Harkness unavailable for the start of 1996/97, he capitalised by earning a regular berth. That term Stig was a revelation, oozing quiet confidence at the back and attacking with consistent potency. However, his form dipped during 1997/98, when he was left out frequently for the feisty Harkness.

BORN: Trondheim, Norway, 11.12.69.
GAMES: 147 (6). GOALS: 4. HONOURS: League Cup 94/5. Norway caps. OTHER CLUBS: Strommen 88 (19, 0); Kongsvinger 89-91 (62, 3), Rosenborg, 92 (21, 3), all Norway.

JULIAN DICKS

Expensive signings tend to provoke avid and enjoyable anticipation among fans of the buying club, yet when Graeme Souness paid West Ham the equivalent of £2.5 million for Julian Dicks in September 1993, there was no shortage of Anfield regulars who cringed in disbelief. Not that anyone doubted the footballing credentials of the Hammers' left-back; his skill, power and commitment were all undeniable. Rather it was his appalling disciplinary record - eight sendings-off and 20 yellow cards in his career to that date - and his general image of crude machismo that filled them with dismay. The gyst of their feelings was 'Have Liverpool really come to this?', a feel-bad factor excacerbated by the departure of the popular Mike Marsh and David Burrows as part of the deal. Souness, though, was content with his capture, confident that he could moderate Julian's wilder excesses, and he predicted that the 25-year-old England 'B' international would go on to win full caps.

To be fair, though continuing to exude an aura of provocative bravado, the pugnacious Bristolian made a promising and peaceful start. Though his positional play gave cause for concern, his passing was assured, his tackling aggressive but usually fair, and he packed a savage left-foot shot. However, knee problems disrupted his training, which he had not appeared to relish anyway, and a subsequent fall-out over his fitness level with new boss Roy Evans led to the defender's £1 million return to Upton Park in October 1994. Had he joined a successful Liverpool side, rather than a transitional one, Julian *might* have met Souness's expectations. As it was, he is remembered at Anfield as a piece of very bad business.

BORN: Bristol, 8.8.68. GAMES: 28. GOALS: 3. OTHER CLUBS: Birmingham City 85/6-87/8 (89, 1); West Ham United 87/8-93/4 (159, 29) and 94/5- (94, 21).

1993/94

PAUL STEWART

Opinion was divided when Liverpool paid Spurs £2.3 million for England midfielder Paul Stewart in the summer of 1992. On the face of it, the burly but skilful Mancunian appeared to be a magnificent acquisition, just the player to replace the ball-winning bite so markedly missed since the departure of Steve McMahon. In addition, the former striker was expected to add to the Reds' goal power, probably operating just behind the front-men and making late runs into the box. However, amid the immediate euphoria of pipping rival clubs for the Stewart signature, there were those who warned that he was a costly flop waiting to happen. After all, he had endured dire periods at Tottenham before his conversion to the central role in which he had earned England caps and had yet to prove himself a long-term prospect at the top level.

In the event, the doubters were proved sadly but overwhelmingly correct. Throughout most of his troubled, injury-plagued Anfield sojourn, Paul looked sluggish and unimaginative, never mastering the Liverpool concept of pass-and-move, failing even to be an effective tackler. Following the sale of Dean Saunders, he was moved forward briefly to partner Ian Rush but that did not work and his lack of fulfilment became apparent in petulant on-the-field demeanour. He never returned to the senior side after 1993 and his value plummeted during two and a half years divided between treatment table, the Reds' reserves and loan stints elsewhere. A free transfer to Sunderland in 1996 must have come as a relief to all concerned.

BORN: Manchester, 7.10.64. GAMES: 37 (4). GOALS: 3. HONOURS: 3 England caps (91-92). OTHER CLUBS: Blackpool 81/2-86/7 (201, 56); Manchester City 86/7-87/8 (51, 26); Tottenham Hotspur 88/9-91/2 (131, 28); Crystal Palace *on loan* 93/4 (18, 3); Wolverhampton Wanderers *on loan* 94/5 (8, 2); Burnley *on loan* 94/5 (6, 0); Sunderland 95/6-96/7 (35, 5); Stoke City 97/8 (22, 3).

1992/93 – 1993/94

STEVE HARKNESS

1991/92 –

Steve Harkness had no rivals for the title of Liverpool's unluckiest player of 1995/96. After several frustrating seasons on the fringe of the side, the combative Cumbrian had confounded his critics by winning a regular berth, proving a revelation at wing-back on the left flank of Roy Evans' enterprising 3-5-2 formation. Having been given his chance through Stig Inge Bjornebye's broken leg, Steve performed so splendidly in defence, attack and all points between that he made it impossible for his manager to drop him, even when the Norwegian regained fitness. Clearly, only suspension or serious injury was going to unseat him - and he was destined to suffer both before the term was out.

After being ever-present until January, including an able emergency stint at centre-half, Steve was banned for collecting six bookings. The resultant reshuffle, which saw Rob Jones switch from right to left, proved so successful that 'Harkie' was out in the cold once more. Admittedly, it could be said that his sentence was self-inflicted but his misdemeanours owed far more to enthusiasm than malice and it was difficult not to feel sorry for him.

But even greater mortification was in store. An injury crisis won Steve a springtime recall which ended in agony, both physical and mental, when his leg was shattered by an uncharacteristically wild tackle from Coventry's John Salako. Ever resilient, he returned in early 1997, bypassing no less than Ruddock, Babb and Matteo to play in central defence. His progress continued as he unseated Bjornebye on the left of the rearguard during 1997/98, but while his passing and overlapping were periodically impressive, they were not as consistent as his doughty work at the back and further improvement may be needed if he is to cement a long-term berth.

Steve, a former England youth team skipper, was signed from his hometown club, Carlisle, for £75,000 in July 1989 and made his Reds debut some two years later. Playing as an orthodox left-back, he did well enough but wasn't quite ready for the top flight and was contemplating the possibility of a move when Stig's misfortune gave him a lifeline in April 1995. Thereafter Steve played like a man burning to prove a point and, though his raw aggression was channelled sensibly, brick walls with Harkness-shaped holes sprang irresistibly to mind. For the future, perhaps, something a little more sophisticated is in order.

BORN: Carlisle, Cumberland, 27.8.71.
GAMES: 113 (13). GOALS: 6.
OTHER CLUBS: Carlisle United 88/9 (13, 0);
Huddersfield Town *on loan* 93/4 (5, 0);
Southend United *on loan* 94/5 (6, 0).

MICHAEL THOMAS

After a beguilingly bright beginning, it took several seasons of debilitating, injury-induced frustration before Graeme Souness's judgement in paying Arsenal £1.5 million for Michael Thomas in December 1991 was borne out. But when vindication finally came, in the winter and spring of 1995/96, it was so handsome that the former England midfielder came close to winning an international recall.

Of course, the name of Thomas was already burned indelibly into the consciousness of Kopites, thanks to his barely credible, last-gasp Anfield strike which won the 1988/89 title for the Gunners, but all was forgiven as Michael emerged as one of Liverpool's FA Cup heroes of 1992. A precision-tooled quarter-final winner against Aston Villa was followed by a rasping 15-yard volley to open the Wembley scoring against Sunderland; the Londoner had completed the transition from bane to paragon and seemed set for a key role in Liverpool's future.

Then came sickening anti-climax. Fitness problems, mainly a snapped Achilles tendon, sidelined the newcomer for some two and a half campaigns and, with a wave of fabulous young players emerging, he missed out on the start of the renaissance inspired by new boss Roy Evans.

The torment ended with a worthy first-team run at the end of 1994/95 but it was not until the fitness gremlins transferred themselves to Jamie Redknapp in the following November that the real Michael Thomas had the opportunity to stand up. He seized it avidly, displaying all his former box-to-box athleticism, allied with smooth distribution, sure control and the type of stern tackling which enabled him to fill in as a full-back or central defender at need.

Though surrounded by extravagant talents, he contributed a succession of outstanding performances, often at his most impressive in a holding position which allowed John Barnes the freedom to attack. As a result, towards the end of the season he was offered a new contract which he duly signed, but only after protracted speculation that he wanted to play abroad, and reported feelings of insecurity regarding his Anfield future. Any such misgivings could only have heightened when he was dropped for the returning Redknapp after Liverpool's first defeat in 20 games, but they were not to linger into the subsequent campaign.

During 1996/97 a more contented Michael's well-grooved consistency proved a telling factor in the Reds' renewed drive for honours. He was ever-present until a suspension in January and the team never functioned more smoothly than when he was beavering unobtrusively at its hub. That often-underrated value was highlighted with vivid clarity in the FA Cup debacle against Chelsea, which saw a two-goal lead transformed into an astonishing 4-2 deficit. Had the reliable former Gunner been on duty, it is inconceivable that midfield possession would have been squandered with such wanton frequency on that sorry Sunday afternoon.

However, such is the uncertainty of football that he was unable to win back a regular place after his ban and, though he started 1997/98 in favour, the presence of Messrs Ince, Redknapp, Carragher, Murphy and Thompson facilitated a loan spell at Middlesbrough in the New Year. Clearly Michael's Anfield days were numbered.

BORN: Lambeth, London, 24.8.67. GAMES 128 (35): GOALS: 12. HONOURS: FA Cup 91/2. 2 England caps (88-89). OTHER CLUBS: Arsenal 86/7-91/2 (163, 24); Portsmouth *on loan* 86/7 (3, 0); Middlesbrough *on loan* 97/8 (10, 0).

1991/92 –

MARK WRIGHT

Consider the sorry plight of Mark Wright in the late summer of 1994. A former England centre-half in his 32nd year and niggled by injuries, he had spent three seasons at Liverpool during which he had not lived up to expectations. Now his aspirations and, no doubt, his pride had been dented massively by the expensive arrival of John Scales and Phil Babb, two of the League's most accomplished defenders. Already at Anfield were the fearsome Neil Ruddock and the talented youngster, Dominic Matteo. As if that wasn't enough, the one-time World Cup star had just clashed publicly with Reds boss Roy Evans, who had criticised his attitude and axed him from the senior squad. Job prospects? Forget them.

Yet, from that seemingly bottomless pit of professional and personal anguish, Mark emerged with a fresh outlook to play the finest football of his life. Indeed, in both 1995/96 and 1996/97 he was the pick of Liverpool's impressive posse of stoppers, a majestically assured performer whose class, strength and new-found maturity played an integral part in his club's spirited quest for honours and won him a richly-deserved international recall.

The sandy-haired six-footer was an international of seven years' standing when Graeme Souness signed him for £2.2 million from newly-relegated Derby County in July 1991. Anfield appeared the perfect platform for such a stylish individual approaching his prime, and when he skippered the side to FA Cup glory in his first campaign it was easy to assume that undiluted success would follow.

But something was not right. Even allowing for an Achilles problem that would not quite clear up, Mark did not exude true authority. Yes, there was a certain arrogance about him but - and this annoyed many fans - his form simply did not justify it. He was splendid in the air but his slowness on the turn made him horribly vulnerable when faced with nippy opponents, who would draw him out of position, then leave him for dead. And, though smoothly comfortable on the ball, he strolled so languidly at times that possession would be squandered dangerously.

This situation simmered frustratingly through 1992/93 and 1993/94 before coming to a head when the dissatisfied Evans dispensed his home truths to such devastating effect. Now Mark was faced with a stark choice: leave Liverpool on such a low note that it might prove difficult to resurrect his career, or stay and fight against overwhelming odds in a bid to make the most of his undeniable quality.

After what must have been some painful self-examination, Mark opted courageously for the latter course and he worked ferociously, only for injuries to make an already steep mountain all but unclimbable. There were few opportunities in 1994/95 but the ex-captain continued to buckle down and, gradually, the pendulum swung. With Scales sidelined at the start of the following term, Mark found himself in the team - and how he made the most of it.

Looking fit and alert, the old cockiness replaced by a more measured confidence, he was a goliath alongside Babb and Ruddock in the Reds' back-three formation and earned repeated man-of-the-match accolades. As aerially dominant as ever, now he was using his experience to read the game more astutely than ever before; tackles were timed to perfection, sloppiness was eradicated, passes were sensible or probing by turn, but never foolhardy. Indeed, it might have been an optical illusion, but such was Mark's aura of control that he even seemed to run faster than in the dark, ponderous days of previous campaigns.

As age and injuries were catching up with him during 1997/98, if he paused to consider what he might have achieved on Merseyside given a different approach from the beginning, he might have shuddered. But at least he could be proud of his response when granted a late shot at revealing his true worth. For that majestic resurrection in the twilight of his playing days, Mark Wright deserved eternal credit.

BORN: Dorchester, Oxfordshire, 1.8.63. GAMES: 205 (4). GOALS: 8.
HONOURS: FA Cup 91/2. 45 England caps (84-).
OTHER CLUBS: Oxford United 81/2 (10, 0); Southampton 81/2-87/8 (170, 7);
Derby County 87/8-90/1 (144, 10).

1991/92 —

ROB JONES

At a time when accolades have been showered like so much confetti on the vibrant new wave of multi-talented Reds, it is all too easy to treat Rob Jones a tad uncharitably, like some less-favoured sibling in a family of prodigies. But to do so is unfair, and quite monstrously so. The fact is that after bursting abruptly on to the Anfield stage as a 19-year-old virtually unknown outside the homely confines of Gresty Road, Crewe, then ascending to international heights within a few fantastic months, Rob has suffered a veritable catalogue of maladies, one of which was serious enough to threaten his football career. In such harrowing circumstances, it is hardly surprising that his form hit something of a plateau. It didn't mean that he was no longer one of the finest young full-backs to emerge since the war; merely that he was human after all, that his script was not penned by the same author as Roy of the Rovers and that he was being overshadowed, perhaps temporarily, by some brilliant team-mates.

Rob - the grandson of stalwart post-war Liverpool defender Bill Jones - was discovered by Graeme Souness he was weighing up the merits of another player. A deal was struck in October 1991, with Crewe receiving £300,000 down, £150,000 after the right-back had played 20 senior games, and a further £50,000 if he won five England caps. Though Rob was clearly an outstanding prospect, the Cheshire club could hardly have expected to pocket the full amount as soon as they did. Just two days after the deal was completed, the slim, pale rookie was thrown in at the deepest of ends, facing high-riding Manchester United at Old Trafford and astonishing seasoned observers with his poise and aplomb amid the non-stop frenzy which characterises clashes between the north-west rivals. Rob was skilful, tough and could run like the wind, and, not surprisingly with the team going through a lean period, he became a first-team regular on the spot.

By February he was a full international, in May he helped Liverpool beat Sunderland to win the FA Cup and Alexandra must surely have received the balance of the fee that summer but for Rob's affliction with shin splints, an agonising condition which left him barely able to walk after games. As it was he missed a substantial slice of 1992/93 and, while doing enough to demonstrate that his phenomenal potential was unimpaired, laboured a little to regain his early impetus, though still the Crewe coffers got their final instalment in 1994.

Thereafter, despite difficulties with knee and back and a worrying susceptibility to viruses, Rob began to acquire the top-flight experience he still lacked. Though he was no longer quite as prominent in a side in which the overall standard was steadily increasing, his maturity and pace, his acute positional sense in defensive situations and the impeccable timing of his tackles were as impressive as ever. Going forward he could take part delightfully in Liverpool's short-passing triangles, though his self-belief appeared to waver as he reached opponents' penalty areas. Indeed his crossing and shooting has continued to cry out for attention, especially when a 3-5-2 formation has involved more frequent overlapping, and he remained goalless after nearly 250 senior outings for the Reds.

Season 1995/96 brought competition in the shape of newcomer Jason McAteer, who emerged as a startlingly effective right-sided wing-back. As a result the thoroughly right-footed Rob was switched to the left flank, where he performed competently enough though with rather reduced impact, leaving an inescapable feeling that he had been marginalised. An even more distressing development was in store. The Jones back had been causing ever-worsening pain for a year and, only three days after facing Manchester United in the FA Cup Final, he was told to rest for six months or risk becoming a cripple. On his return to the squad, with McAteer and Bjornebye ensconced as wing-backs, Rob found himself out of the team, then suffered further niggling injuries. Once more he bounced back, unseating the Irishman at the outset of 1997/98, only to be sidelined again with a pulled hamstring. After recovering he was consigned to the reserves and there were rumours of a move to Fiorentina, but then McAteer broke a leg and the Welsh-born Englishman was restored to senior duty before succumbing to yet another fitness problem. Equipped with enormous talent, abundant grit and vast experience for a fellow in his mid-twenties, Rob Jones still has much to offer, but how he needs a change of luck. An injury-free 1998/99 would do for a start.

BORN: Wrexham, North Wales, 5.11.71. GAMES: 241 (2). GOALS: 0.
HONOURS: FA Cup 91/2; League Cup 94/5. 8 England caps (92-).
OTHER CLUBS: Crewe Alexandra 87/8-91/2 (75, 2).

1991/92 –

STEVE McMANAMAN

When Steve McManaman seemed set to join Barcelona in August 1997, and as transfer talk persisted ominously throughout the season that followed, the question was posed repeatedly: just what would Liverpool be losing if the £12 million move went through? As he enjoyed his most influential campaign to date, the popular answer, if not the unanimous one, was that despite occasional fitfulness, the mild-mannered Merseysider remains the most compelling home-grown entertainer British football has to offer. At his scintillating best, he makes matches dance to his tune, showing why terms like joy and beauty can be applied still to a game plagued by greed and fear and tawdriness. Even better, by doing so he achieves the well-nigh impossible: to all but the blind, the bigoted and the most chronically biased, Steve transcends allegiance. Okay, perhaps that last assertion is going a bit far, but let's put it this way – he *ought* to transcend allegiance.

What makes him special is his mesmerising knack of dribbling a football past opponent after opponent, not through awesome acceleration in the manner of, say, Andrei Kanchelskis, but through a heavenly alliance of touch and balance, wit and resilience and, most precious of all, sheer instinct. He lopes towards intended victims gently, like some inoffensive lone pedestrian almost begging to be mugged; he carries the ball so close to their feet that robbery with violence seems inevitable; then comes a seemingly effortless shuffle and they are tackling empty air while the floppy-haired England flankman skips lightly towards his next challenge. Like Stanley Matthews in another age, Steve employs a deceptively simple method of showing the ball to defenders, then snatching it away. But, thanks to his sublime timing, even though they know what's coming, more often than not they are helpless to prevent it.

When Liverpool are flying, McManaman is one of half a dozen potential match-winners, but it is when the Reds' rhythm is missing a beat that his value can be felt most keenly. Then he can turn a contest on its head, as he did by traversing half the length of Celtic Park before equalising against the Bhoys with an exquisite last-minute curler in September 1997. He has his faults, but one of them is not a proclivity for disappearing when the going gets tough. In all but a very few games – the 1996 FA Cup Final comes to mind – he *will* create chances sooner or later, thus providing appreciable insurance against a poor team display.

Those defects? Well, the argument goes that given the number of menacing positions his sorcery places him in, he does not score enough goals, though 11 strikes during 1997/98, many of them quite brilliant, went a long way towards answering that one. Another criticism voiced by ultra-demanding observers is that Steve surrenders possession too frequently with misplaced or underhit passes and crosses, a tendency that has been a touch too common for comfort in recent seasons. It is nothing that a little more care and concentration will not correct, but certainly it is worthy of attention.

Steve arrived on the top-flight scene as a clearly gifted but distinctly frail-looking 18-year-old in 1990/91 and despite his telling contribution to the FA Cup triumph against Sunderland in 1992, in ideal circumstances he might have been blooded rather more gradually than the club's prevailing injury situation permitted. As it was he did not progress as rapidly as expected over the next two campaigns. For all his fabulous skill, fears began to surface that he lacked direction, that he tended to be something of a blind-alley merchant, even that he appeared a tad too casual at times, though it would be unfair to equate languid body language with lack of commitment.

Come 1994/95, under Roy Evans, the situation changed. Whether the words boot and backside might reasonably have been applied in conjunction at this stage is not known, but now Steve was beginning to dominate games, especially when given a roving commission. In most matches that term and during the next three, he instigated the majority of Liverpool's attacks, despite being shadowed constantly by ruthless close-markers. What made his rise all the more meaningful to Kopites was that he was the first local lad since Sammy Lee to become fully established after working his way through the junior ranks. To the rest of the nation he was, purely and simply, a rare pleasure to watch. But as the Reds reached the end of another season of under-achievement, and with the prime of Steve McManaman beckoning, whether those delicious talents would remain accessible to English fans was less than clear.

BORN: Liverpool, 11.2.72. GAMES: 320 (13). GOALS: 60. HONOURS: FA Cup 91/2; League Cup 94/5. 20 England caps (94-).

1990/91 –

NEIL RUDDOCK

Neil Ruddock is a giant who has never attained his full footballing stature. He has it within him to be as dominating and talismanic a figure as say, Ron Yeats in the sixties, but despite spells of excellence - such as the 1994/95 season, when he was capped by England - the mountainous Londoner has continued to fall short of the consistently inspirational standard set by Bill Shankly's skipper.

At his best Neil is an awesome central defender, his implacable, rock-like presence, uplifting spirit and strident assertiveness combining with often underestimated natural ability to produce an abrasively dynamic focal point around which any team would unite.

But that is not always the Ruddock on view. Occasionally his concentration seems to desert him and his defects, mostly related to lack of pace, are thrown into sharp relief. Then he can be a lumbering, lunging figure, slow at closing down opponents worryingly vulnerable on the turn and prone to concede free-kicks in dangerous positions through rash challenges, though he should be congratulated for reining in the volatile temper which marred his early development.

Most Spurs fans would have been only too happy to bear with Neil's infrequent lapses when his £2.5 million move to Liverpool was agreed in July 1993. Having returned for a second stint with the North Londoners only a season earlier, he had played the finest football of his career and had assumed cult-hero status at White Hart Lane.

Kopites greeted him fervently. He was the warrior king they craved, perhaps a new heartbeat for their talented but slightly tentative team, but for some time he did not live up to such vivid billing. Though mighty in the air and comfortable enough against big men whom he could match physically, Neil was made to look clumsy by nippier strikers, and too often he would go for the same ball as his partner, Mark Wright. Maybe a mite complacent following his move to Merseyside, he put on weight, too, and it took a word in his ear from former mentor Terry Venables, among others, to help re-establish his priorities.

Indeed, had 'Razor' not sharpened up his act, he would surely have slipped prematurely out of the Liverpool reckoning in 1994/95. Top centre-backs John Scales and Phil Babb were recruited and the rumour machine had it that Neil would be shipped out, probably to Rangers. But the slimmed-down Ruddock would have none of it. He started the term in such majestic form that manager Roy Evans could not countenance dropping him, let alone selling him, and Neil settled seamlessly into a back-three system alongside the speedy newcomers, who offered ideal cover if he was caught flat-footed. Displaying immense composure on the ball - in fact, there were times when he was a little *too* laid-back - he also revealed impressive accuracy in his long-distance distribution. In particular, his trademark delivery, swept majestically from the left-back slot to the inside-right channel, offered telling and much-needed variety to Liverpool's short-passing game.

International recognition, deputy stints as Reds skipper and a League Cup winner's medal completed a memorable season. Thus the platform for consolidation as an Anfield cornerstone was in place but Neil's progress during 1995/96, a term complicated by personal problems, was not wholly smooth. He played fairly well, but could not make himself indispensable and had to endure spells in the reserves after returning from suspension. His first-team security was lessened by the phenomenal renaissance of Mark Wright and he was omitted from the 1996 FA Cup Final line-up.

The following campaign brought further chequered fortune, with Neil's chances being limited by the advance of Matteo and the arrival of Kvarme. Come 1997/98, however, he made the line-up for opening day, looking lean and hungry, only to suffer injury, after which he drifted tamely out of contention. He descended, in his own words, 'from hero to zero' and Liverpool fans who believed in Neil Ruddock as a potential touchstone for long-term glory felt disillusioned. After a loan spell with QPR, he seemed certain to leave Anfield and the sense of missed opportunity was overwhelming.

BORN: Wandsworth, London, 9.5.68. GAMES: 146 (6). GOALS: 12. HONOURS: League Cup 94/5. 1 England cap (94). OTHER CLUBS: Tottenham Hotspur 86/7-87/8 (9, 0); Millwall 88/9 (2, 1); Southampton 88/9-91/2 (107, 9); Tottenham Hotspur 92/3 (38, 3); Queen's Park Rangers *on loan* 97/8 (7, 0).

1993/94 –

JAMIE REDKNAPP

Where will Jamie Redknapp stand by the turn of the century? Will he have blossomed, as predicted widely for half a decade, into a midfield general capable of dictating the play for a Liverpool side of genuine Championship stature? Will he have departed for pastures new, perhaps hoping that a change of scene might coincide with better fortune on the fitness front? Or will he remain at Anfield, shining intermittently but never quite living up to that immense potential, an attractive footballer but one whose ultimate authority never quite matches his talent? Of course, the first scenario is idyllic; but if the second is regrettable, it is not as worrying as the third. That one would be irredeemably frustrating.

At times it has seemed that if Jamie were created for a work of fiction, he would be dismissed as too good to be true. The sumptuously sleek skills, the self-assurance untainted by arrogance, the personable character and matinee-idol looks: put them all together and they would beggar credibility. But Harry's boy is for real, and despite anxious interludes in the shadows following lengthy absences through injury, come 1998 both club and country continued to expect a mighty dividend from his prodigious ability.

Jamie has looked every inch a thoroughbred since making his League debut as a 16-year-old for Bournemouth, then managed by the senior Redknapp. Certainly Kenny Dalglish thought so, backing his judgement to the tune of £350,000 to take the novice to Anfield in January 1991, to the mortification of Spurs, for whom Jamie had played as a schoolboy. His natural gifts enhanced by above-average physique and maturity for his years, he made an instant impression on new Reds boss Graeme Souness, who gave him his senior debut in the taxing atmosphere of a UEFA Cup clash with Auxerre in Burgundy a mere nine months after his departure from Dean Court. Though he wasn't quite ready to express himself at that level, the experience did him no harm, and the following season he enjoyed a lengthy settled run in the senior side, his personal development mercifully unimpaired by the turmoil then gripping the club.

Thereafter, Jamie claimed a regular place, his game spiced deliciously with wit, guile and imagination, yet underpinned also with the more mundane, but equally important, attributes of stamina, strength and determination. Indeed, the Redknapp style has been buttressed so firmly by steel that certain pundits' earlier suspicions that he might lack a touch of 'devil' have been banished emphatically. Of course it is his control, breadth of vision and precision of distribution, both long and short, which offer particular delight, even if his repertoire of passes is not quite comprehensive. Maddeningly, he misses the occasional inviting opportunity to deliver a killing short through-ball around the edge of the box, the type at which Souness was the master, though it is reasonable to surmise that his creative armoury will not lack such a desirable sophistication indefinitely. Versatile enough for England boss Glenn Hoddle to experiment with him as a sweeper, Jamie is beautifully balanced, can feint past opponents on the run and is adept at supplying all manner of crosses. But for sheer crowd-pleasing spectacle, pride of place goes to his long-distance shooting, of which there has been no more sensational example than the fulminating 30-yarder away to Spartak Vladikavkaz in September 1995.

Are there no major flaws, then, in Jamie's ravishing cocktail of accomplishments? Well, he has been criticised for not getting forward enough, but was taking steps to rectify that as the nineties wore on, and in fairness it should be pointed out that at times he has been asked to play the role of deep-lying anchor. There have been occasional bouts of inconsistency, too, such as in February 1995 when he was relegated briefly to the bench, and some observers maintain that it is rare for him to turn a game that is not going Liverpool's way, that he is at his very best only when his side is already purring.

In recent seasons Jamie has been plagued by injuries, several of which have been received on England duty. On his return from the most serious of them, a broken leg suffered against South Africa in summer 1997, his eagerness to make up for lost time was almost tangible and he excelled periodically alongside new midfield partner Paul Ince. But no sooner was Jamie's career apparently back on track than knee trouble jolted his momentum in February 1998, then again in April. Now his first priority was to overcome that infuriating stop-go syndrome, paving the way for the main item on his agenda - showing once and for all how reliably fine and influential a player he can be. How desperately Liverpool need him to do that … but they can't wait forever.

BORN: Barton on Sea, Hampshire, 25.6.73. GAMES: 209 (28). GOALS: 27.
HONOURS: League Cup 94/5. 8 England caps (95-).
OTHER CLUBS: Bournemouth 89/90-90/1 (13, 0).

1991/92 –

In the space of one breathless year, Phil Babb went from being a promising but little-known youngster with Coventry to winning lavish acclaim in the World Cup finals and becoming, for a time, the most expensive defender in British football history. Perhaps understandably after such a demanding journey, the leggy, exceptionally pacy Londoner, who was once freed by Millwall, has yet to live up fully to the inevitable hype created by a combination of his international profile and the £3.75 million fee Liverpool paid for him in September 1994. Some would have it that Phil's luck has been out from the day he was asked to play on the left of the Reds' rearguard of three, rather than as a centre-back in a 4-4-2 formation. After all, the last-mentioned was the role in which he rose to prominence, and which left him less isolated and exposed, the play invariably coming on to him in a straightforward manner and posing less diverse problems than are faced on the flank.

In the immediate wake of his USA '94 exertions, Phil made a tentative start in a red shirt and before long his game was being placed under an uncharitable media microscope. Some criticised him for an inconsistent first touch and for rushing his creative passing, which led to mistakes; others drew attention to his questionable positional sense and felt he dwelt on the ball with apparent casualness when danger threatened. Against that, his phenomenal speed could get him out of most scrapes as well as offering superb cover to colleagues, his tackling technique was slickly effective, he was a smotheringly tight man-marker and he was able in the air.

Roy Evans was quick to deny speculation that Phil might make a rapid exit from Anfield and, despite formidable competition for his place and too many edgy displays for comfort, he missed few games over nearly two campaigns before he was injured in spring 1996. On his return to fitness he faced a stern challenge to become re-established. To his credit, he met it head on and was rewarded with an FA Cup Final slot at Neil Ruddock's expense.

Over the next two terms, during which he was plagued incessantly by injury, there was a gradual upturn in his form - especially after the reversion to 4-4-2 in 1997/98 - although still it came as no surprise when a string of solid performances was followed by a distinctly uneasy one. So, with new defensive recruits inevitable, Phil was facing a testing future.

BORN: Lambeth, London, 30.11.70. GAMES: 136 (4). GOALS: 1. HONOURS: League Cup 94/5. 24 Republic of Ireland caps (94-). OTHER CLUBS: Bradford City 90/1-91/2 (80, 14); Coventry City 92/3-94/5 (77, 3).

PHIL BABB

1994/95 –

JOHN SCALES

1994/95 – 1996/97

When he signed John Scales from Wimbledon in September 1994, Roy Evans reckoned his £3.5 million recruit had been the steadiest defender in the League for some time. Not many observers were arguing with the Liverpool manager then and, two seasons of immaculate service down the road, still fewer were taking issue. Yet early in 1996/97 a combination of three factors – nagging injuries, consequent loss of form and the forthcoming arrival of Bjorn Tore Kvarme – saw John join Spurs in an unexpected £2.5 million deal. Until then the athletic Yorkshireman had been an unflappable, speedy and almost metronomically reliable component of the Reds' back-three formation, whether operating at its heart or on its right side. His economical style – tackling cleanly, covering intelligently and eschewing risks by playing 'percentage' passes rather than succumbing to over-ambition – had meshed smoothly with a variety of partners. Indeed, the more swashbuckling Ruddock, the gifted but sedate Wright and the less experienced Babb and Harkness had all benefited immeasurably from the consummate Scales professionalism.

John, who won his first England cap in the summer of 1995, attained his eminence only after paying his dues in full. Rejected by Leeds as a teenager, he underwent footballing rehabilitation with Bristol Rovers, then continued his development with Wimbledon, for whom he appeared as a Wembley substitute to help foil Liverpool's League/FA Cup double aspirations in 1988.

For six more seasons Scales flourished as a steely but untypically restrained member of the Crazy Gang and his stature was underlined by a moving, near-tearful farewell from Sam Hammam. The Dons' owner mourned the loss of a gladiator and comrade-in-arms, honouring his exemplary attitude to the game, particularly his coolness under fire, and accurately predicting his international future.

Thereafter John settled quickly into the Reds' more sophisticated system, his solidity and common-sense offering reassuring security to an extravagantly entertaining side. Some believe he should have attacked more, but his safety-first approach worked admirably and he looked set for a lengthy Anfield sojourn. Then came that surprising exit.

BORN: Harrogate, Yorkshire, 4.7.66. GAMES: 93 (1). GOALS: 4. HONOURS: League Cup 94/5. 3 England caps (95-).

OTHER CLUBS: Bristol Rovers 85/6–86/7 (72, 2); Wimbledon 87/8–94/5 (240, 11); Tottenham Hotspur 96/7- (22, 1).

ROBBIE FOWLER

To the shell-shocked followers of Liverpool's rivals, it must seem so unfair. After more than a decade of being terrorised by Ian Rush, relief was in sight as the goal-scoring powers of the phenomenally prolific Welshman began finally to wane … and then along came Robbie Fowler. Whisper it softly but there must be a realistic chance that the nervelessly audacious young Scouser will place Rushie's numerous marksmanship records in grave danger come the early part of the 21st century. True, he has a long and pitfall-strewn road to travel if he is to come even close to emulating the ultimate achievements of his illustrious mentor, as his troubled 1997/98 campaign demonstrated all too vividly. But already he has beaten Ian to the 100-goal mark and, still only 23 as 1998/99 kicked off, he might have another decade of bountiful productivity ahead of him. Indeed, even though the Toxteth-born imp started slowly at full international level, it was being suggested that he could pass Bobby Charlton's 49-goal milestone to become the most successful England marksman of all time. Preposterous at this stage, of course, though it must be admitted that Robbie of the Reds has given a more than creditable impression of Roy of the Rovers to date.

After excelling for England under-18s in the summer of 1993, he was drafted into Graeme Souness's labouring team that autumn and, well, a star was born. A goal on debut against Fulham at Craven Cottage in the League Cup was followed by *five* in the return leg, before Robbie began his first settled sequence in the senior side. Though obviously uncut, he was so clearly a jewel that Kopites were dismayed when a hairline leg fracture interrupted his progress in January; in truth, it was a blessing, enabling him to draw much-needed breath. He was back in March and finished his first campaign with 18 goals in 34 outings, the majority of them plundered with his favoured left foot.

The second campaign is always testing for any youngster but for many months Robbie's self-possession was equal to the pressure, and so was his talent as he netted 31 times in 57 games. Of course, by now the hype which goes with such territory had intensified and, perhaps inevitably, as the season wore on the relentless exposure began to take its toll. Where there had been hunger, there was noticed a hint of complacency, and the goal-machine began to splutter.

Happily for the Liverpool cause, however, such wise men as Roy Evans and Ronnie Moran were alert to the danger signs and they acted decisively. After Robbie, by his own subsequent admission, had been taking his place for granted during the preparation for 1995/96, he was dropped to the bench for the first two matches of the new term, leaving new signing Stan Collymore to partner Ian Rush. He could have whinged, he could have asked for a move, but now Fowler showed his true mettle. When Stan was injured, Robbie resumed his place, displaying a vastly improved work-rate and attaining an enriched standard of all-round performance which he maintained for the rest of a term which brought him 36 senior goals. Many of them were breathtaking in both conception and execution, and there was still time for plenty of tap-ins along the way. The credits continued to pile up in 1996/97, another 31 of them, and Liverpool missed Robbie sorely, when suspension removed him from their abortive title run-in.

Naturally, a blip had to appear on the Fowler graph at some stage and that's what happened in 1997/98. Bearing in mind that he missed the start through injury and suffered knee damage in February which was expected to keep him out for some 10 months, his 13 strikes in 27 starts seem more than adequate at first glance. But the figures do not tell the full story. Perhaps his confidence was undermined by endless comparisions with Michael Owen, maybe he had private worries, only he knows. Certainly, though, on many occasions Robbie seemed at odds with himself and the world, unable to do justice to himself or his team. One view was that the enforced holiday from the game may help and Liverpool fans were praying that would be the case.

In the circumstances it is comforting to reflect on the cornucopia of qualities that has made Robbie special. He has speed, skill, vision, subtlety, strength, courage and just about every other footballing attribute to which a name has been put, yet somehow his command of the striker's art amounts to more than the sum of those assets. What distinguishes him can only be instinct, some untutored knack of perceiving the appropriate option and selecting it in the blink of an eye. If Robbie recovers completely from injury, and provided he can successfully complete the tricky business of growing up in public, then supporters of Manchester United, Everton and the rest should lie down in a darkened room before contemplating what he might achieve in the years ahead.

BORN: Liverpool, 9.4.75. GAMES: 211 (5). GOALS: 129.
HONOURS: League Cup 94/5. 7 England caps (96-).

1993/94 −

STAN COLLYMORE

After a brief but blissful honeymoon, the marriage between Stan Collymore and Liverpool was threatened by an ugly, embarrassingly public spat. Even at that early stage it seemed the differences might be irreconcilable, but a heart-to-heart talk and a little give and take on both sides soon had the partners kissing and making up. Alas, the cosy concord was not to last. Thereafter the relationship was intermittently fulfilling but strained by periodic turbulence, and friends of the handsome couple were not surprised when it culminated in sudden divorce.

Yet the initial consummation had been joyful, indeed. It took place on a sunny afternoon at Anfield in August 1995, just 60 playing minutes into the Reds career of the multi-talented striker for whom Roy Evans had obliterated the British transfer record by paying Nottingham Forest £8.5 million a few weeks earlier.

Stan was heavily marked as he received the ball with his back to goal some 25 yards out; he turned sinuously, held off one challenger and feinted past another before calmly dispatching the most delicious of top-corner curlers with his unfavoured left foot. He was the match-winner, he ran to the crowd, he was received with rapture. Happy ever after? Not a bit of it.

The next outing brought injury, then Stan suffered illness and there followed a run of anonymous performances, leavened by only one more goal, another 'miracle' strike at home to Blackburn. Now, for the most part, the tall Midlander was looking like some moody stranger with a grudge against the world. An undercurrent of impatience began to emanate from the stands and he was dropped.

Stan's predicament was that he was used to being the focal point of Forest's counter-attacking game, with the whole team playing to his main strength, which was dashing thrillingly at and past defenders. Liverpool espoused a more intricate, patient build-up, involving long passing sequences which, at this stage, were alien to him.

A sensitive fellow who had encountered a number of personality clashes during his progress through six clubs in the previous six years, he became so disillusioned with the Anfield experience that he talked of quitting, which was bad enough. What made it many times worse, however, was that he chose to bare his soul in a magazine, his morose reflections being seized upon and magnified by the rest of the media. As the debate raged about who was to blame, player or club, Glenn Moore of *The Independent* likened Roy Evans to a man who had discovered his bold new Ikea sofa did not match his pretty-pattern Laura Ashley fittings, an eloquently telling summation. Suddenly, unthinkably, a split was not out of the question.

But Stan, clearly chastened by a 'headmaster's study' session with his manager, apologised for his indiscretion and then regained his first-team place following injury to Ian Rush. Now, slowly but inexorably, he began to settle. He adapted his approach to suit Liverpool and, to a certain extent, the Reds bent to accommodate their costly acquisition.

At last there was a spring in the Collymore step and he began to integrate into the team pattern; an understanding with Robbie Fowler started to flower, the side flourished and Stan was scoring goals again. Hitherto disgruntled fans began to sing his praises as they revelled in his pace, power and control, his exciting excursions to either flank and the high-quality crosses he supplied to his predatory partner. Stan's off-the-ball work improved, too, especially his defending from the front, yet all this was achieved without sacrificing his glorious capacity for the unexpected which could turn a game on its head.

During 1996/97 there were spells when the ex-Forest star remained peripheral, listless, even disenchanted, and he was ousted occasionally by Patrik Berger. But he scored prolifically as the Reds strove for the title, upped his all-round involvement and won an England recall in the spring. It seemed the general trend was positive and that, having survived some debilitatingly stormy interludes, Stan Collymore just might be staying at Anfield. But then, two days after season's end, nuptial vows were exchanged with Aston Villa, a £7 million settlement was arranged and another honeymoon began …

BORN: Stone, Staffordshire, 22.1.71. GAMES: 71 (10). GOALS: 35. HONOURS: 3 England caps (95-). OTHER CLUBS: Crystal Palace 90/1-92/3 (20, 1); Southend United 92/3 (30, 15); Nottingham Forest 93/4-94/5 (65, 41); Aston Villa 97/8- (25, 6).

1995/96 – 1996/97

JASON McATEER

In this cynical modern world, where so much of the romance and wonder has been squeezed out of football and everything else, Jason McAteer was the type of signing about which any manager might fantasise. Yes, he's a lovely player, enormously talented and endlessly industrious, but that was only the half of it. More than anything else, the bright-eyed, self-confident Scouser *wanted to play* for Liverpool, the club he'd worshipped for as long as he could remember.

To get his wish, he turned down chances to join reigning champions Blackburn Rovers, run by his boyhood idol Kenny Dalglish, and Arsenal, where he would have been reunited with Bruce Rioch, the man under whom he had played a major role in the recent renaissance of Bolton Wanderers. Both offers must have been hugely tempting but when Roy Evans came along, there could be only one outcome. As Jason reflected after the £4.5 million deal ended months of intense speculation in September 1995: 'I've been waiting for this all my life, it's a dream come true.'

That being so, it would be surprising if McAteer's travails of 1997/98, during which he was dropped at the outset in favour of Rob Jones, then suffered a broken leg at home to Blackburn in February, culminated in a change, either of outlook or club. Yet there were moments during the campaign when the media debated a move and his uncharacteristically passive demeanour during autumn stand-in duty fuelled the rumours. However, to his credit he worked hard, gained possession of the right-back berth on merit and was in buoyant form at the time of the accident. Three months after *that* he was fit again and completed the season in the first-team.

Looking back, it was that sort of commitment, together with the Republic of Ireland international's dynamic all-round ability, which gave rise to mammoth expectation following his Anfield arrival, and after the Reds boss had made up his mind where to use him, the eager newcomer did not disappoint. Though Jason had thrived in central midfield at Bolton, terrorising opponents with his driving runs and employing his box-to-box energy to compelling effect, he slotted into the Liverpool jigsaw as a right-sided wing-back, initially because of injury to Jones. However, it wasn't long before his zest and verve in that key position won him preference. His defensive work was generally competent, if occasionally naive, but it was his attractively direct attacking contribution that captured the imagination and offered a pleasingly invigorating counter-balance to what seemed, at times, a surfeit of pretty passing in the centre of the pitch.

Not that Jason does not fit admirably into Liverpool's traditional smooth rhythm, his impeccable control and sharp intelligence making him an able participant in the team's customary sweet moves. He carries a fierce, if too-frequently wayward shot, too, and is capable of nipping past top-quality defenders with the ball at his feet. But the McAteer speciality, which has marked him out above all else as an exceptional acquisition, is his mastery of what is in danger of becoming a dying art in today's game, that of dispatching an accurate cross. Any professional can manage the occasional pearler, but what makes Jason special is his consistency and variety, whether on the run or stationary, under pressure or in acres of space. He can float them, drive them or whip them in with a wicked bend, such as the glorious delivery which laid on an equaliser for Stan Collymore as the classic Anfield encounter with Newcastle in March 1996 boiled towards its frenzied finish.

Ironically, a few years earlier the Reds could have enlisted Jason's services for nothing. After his mother had refused to let him follow his boxing uncles, Pat and Les McAteer, into the ring, he concentrated on soccer but, at that stage, lacked the self-belief to capitalise on his natural gifts. Accordingly, he had problems establishing himself even with the Merseyside-based non-League club, Marine, and it was in their reserves that he began to attract attention, notably after one display against Manchester United's 'A' side, during which he had given a severe chasing to a certain Lee Sharpe.

Eventually he came to the notice of former Anfield favourite Phil Neal, then boss of Bolton, and he moved to Burnden Park. After starring in the Trotters' progress to the 1995 League Cup Final - they lost to Liverpool - and subsequent promotion to the top flight, the refreshingly eager 24-year-old arrived at his spiritual home. He accepted a five-year contract, but as far as Jason McAteer was concerned, it might as well have been for life.

BORN: Birkenhead, Cheshire, 18.6.71. GAMES: 107 (10). GOALS: 6.
HONOURS: 24 Republic of Ireland caps (94-).
OTHER CLUBS: Bolton Wanderers 92/3-94/5 (110, 8).

1995/96 —

DAVID JAMES

A catalogue of calamitous blunders in the spring of 1997, and the consequent aura of fallibility which gathered like an ominous raincloud above his head, reduced David James from his widely perceived status as England's finest young 'keeper to a forlorn, almost abject figure, utterly bereft of confidence and an accident waiting to happen on the Liverpool goal-line. Throughout this period of public purgatory, David remained a magnificent shot-stopper but his ineptitude at dealing with crosses became a millstone to a title-chasing side, begging the question: why had the Reds no experienced reserve to spare the 6ft 5in international such prolonged embarrassment? To his credit, he soldiered on with dignity, interspersing some spellbinding saves with the demoralising misjudgements, and when manager Roy Evans recruited Brad Friedel in December 1997, in a belated attempt to provide meaningful competition, David responded in commendable manner. Indeed, he produced his finest form for more than a year and kept the American on the sidelines for several months before being forced aside.

However, it must be admitted that the crisis of 1997 was not the first James had faced since his £1.3 million transfer from Watford in July 1992. At that time he was pressed straight into senior action in Graeme Souness's struggling team and was found to be out of his depth. He proved particularly vulnerable in the air, losing his place first to Bruce Grobbelaar, then to Mike Hooper, before earning a late-season recall. Though immensely promising, the newcomer languished in the Zimbabwean's intimidating shadow during 1993/94 and he came close to joining Southampton, remaining at Anfield only after a swap deal involving Tim Flowers fell through.

The turning point for David, who took over once more when Grobbelaar was injured in the February, came the following summer when Bruce left the club. With the spectre of yet another return by his ultra-competitive predecessor no longer haunting him, the younger man began to flourish, exuding presence and charisma that had previously lurked behind a somewhat brooding public demeanour. He was an ever-present during 1994/95, making several fine saves during the League Cup Final victory over Bolton, and his game continued to progress apace in the subsequent term. David seemed to fill the goal, barring the way like some huge and muscular spider, whether arching his back to make stupendously agile stops or plucking shots from the air with deceptively casual ease. He improved in one-on-one situations and the speed of his reflexes when adjusting his direction to deal with deflections could be phenomenal.

Still, though, there persisted doubts about his aerial prowess. Though more reliable than in earlier campaigns, he continued to lose his way a little too often for comfort during 1995/96. Unfortunately for Liverpool, there was one vivid example in the FA Cup Final against Manchester United, when his disastrous dash and weak punch led to Eric Cantona's winning goal, thus marring an otherwise faultless display. It should be said that there was solid evidence of David's progress, too, with his fellow professionals naming him as the season's best goalkeeper in the Premiership, though with the likes of Peter Schmeichel and David Seaman on the scene, the players' verdict seemed a tad perplexing.

And so to 1996/97 which, to be fair, James began in splendid style, maintaining generally excellent form until the turn of the year. There were signs of the jitters in the League Cup upset at Middlesbrough in January but it was not until March that alarm bells began to ring. Errors in the seven-goal thriller against Newcastle set the tone, before mistakes at Nottingham Forest, at home to Coventry, away to Paris St-Germain, then most excruciatingly of all in the crucial Anfield clash with Manchester United, piled up in painful procession. His ability to catch high crosses under challenge appeared to have vanished, taking his self-belief along with it, a mystifying and debilitating situation as the campaign approached its climax.

Ironically, he was called up for his full England debut during this traumatic interlude and though Glenn Hoddle left him out of his next squad, Roy Evans retained faith in the troubled custodian, hoping to reap the benefit in 1997/98. Unfortunately, his inconsistency continued unabated, yet David remains a huge natural talent and a self-critical perfectionist who will strive diligently to get back on track. It has to be acknowledged, though, that instead of charging headlong towards his pomp as expected at this stage of his development, he finds himself, at least temporarily, in the doldrums.

BORN: Welwyn Garden City, Hertfordshire, 1.8.70. GAMES: 244 (1). GOALS: 0.
HONOURS: League Cup 94/5. 1 England cap (97).
OTHER CLUBS: Watford 90/1-91/2 (89, 0).

1992/93 –

DOMINIC MATTEO

Had Roy Evans opted to sell Dominic Matteo in the summer of 1996 - and Liverpool received no less than 30 inquiries about the leggily coltish 22-year-old - there would have been no public outcry. Oh, there might have been some well-intentioned remarks about another promising youngster who hadn't quite made the Anfield grade, and then Kopites would have turned their attention to the next multi-million-pound transfer target.

But the Reds' shrewd boss saw what most fans didn't and refused to part with one of his most versatile assets, a stylish performer who had impressed in brief stints as central-defender, left-back and midfielder since making his debut nearly three years earlier.

Now as it happened, Dominic had passed the 1996 close-season soul-searching over why he had not emulated his chum, Robbie Fowler, in claiming a regular senior berth. Accordingly, he emerged from the break burning with renewed enthusiasm to prove himself, and virtue had its own reward when injuries to Ruddock and Scales offered an immediate back-three opportunity.

Dominic had never looked out of his depth during his sporadic first-team outings to date; but now, having added some muscle to a previously spindly physique and with a distinctly more ruthless approach, he was a revelation. Whether operating in the centre or on the left, he exuded calm authority, tackling and heading in approved stopper fashion and displaying enviable pace and athleticism for such a tall fellow. He read the game intelligently, was immensely comfortable on the ball and could use it with crisp perception.

Crucially, too, he could surge forward in possession, not indiscriminately but at telling junctures, as Chelsea discovered at Anfield in the September. After intercepting confidently, Dominic ran practically from box to box before choosing the optimum moment to release Patrik Berger for a lovely goal.

That sequence of action spoke volumes for the Matteo potential, which was duly recognised by selection for the England squad, for which he was eligible despite being Scottish born of Italian extraction.

After missing the start of 1997/98 through injury, he embarked on the longest unbroken senior run of his career, continuing to impress individually though occasionally implicated in overall defensive slackness. Perhaps what he lacks is the aura of invincibility that all great centre-halves carry with them, but that should come if he finds himself in a truly assured rearguard. Dominic remains a superb prospect.

BORN: Dumfries, Scotland, 28.4.74. GAMES: 86 (12). GOALS: 0. OTHER CLUBS: Sunderland *on loan* 94/5 (1, 0).

1993/94 –

PATRIK BERGER

1996/97 –

Patrik Berger is a captivating, if inconsistent, footballer, a swashbuckling Pied Piper who seduces the eye as he sways and darts behind enemy lines, all athletic grace topped off by the threat of imminent explosion. But, sadly for the Liverpool fans who came to love him, he lost impetus after a high-octane start and, by the spring of 1998, appeared ready to leave.

He had joined at a cost of £3.25 million from Borussia Dortmund in the wake of Euro '96, during which he had helped the Czech Republic reach the final without quite fulfilling his boundless potential as an entertainer.

However, it wasn't long before his new followers were enraptured by the Berger repertoire. Patrik arrived as a major force at Filbert Street in September, appearing after the interval as a substitute for the troubled Stan Collymore. Almost instantly he transformed a hitherto drab stalemate with a joyous infusion of attacking bravado, running at and past Leicester defenders seemingly at will and contributing two brilliant goals to a 3-0 victory. Lest anyone feared that Patrik's performance was a fluke, he repeated the dose in the next game against Chelsea, then made it five goals in two-and-a-half outings with a strike against MyPa-47 of Finland.

Kopites rejoiced and wondered: had they found their talisman, an Anfield answer to Cantona who would change the balance of power on the English soccer scene? After all, the Czech was endowed with sumptuous skills, endearing enthusiasm – clearly he wasn't the type to sulk when things went wrong – and thrilling verve. Messiah material, surely.

In fact, it was not quite that simple. Despite his early impact as a marksman, Patrik is actually a left-sided play-maker rather than a specialist front-runner. He is in his element operating just behind the main striker, often a crowded area given Liverpool's plethora of attackers, and vacancies proved hard to find. Thus, after a short run of senior starts in which his influence was fitful as he adjusted to the English game, Patrik was used more sparingly, frequently entering the fray from the bench.

His vision, passing and crossing remained exquisite at times and there was always the hint of the unexpected. But he tired of life on the periphery and, understandably enough, when Benfica came a-calling, he expressed eagerness to go. With the season's climax approaching, the Reds refused to release Patrik, but it seemed likely that a diverting, if enigmatic, Anfield sojourn was about to end.

BORN: Prague, 10.11.73. GAMES: 32 (30). GOALS: 13. HONOURS: Czech Republic caps. OTHER CLUBS: Slavia Prague, Czech Republic, 91/2-94/5 (69, 21); Borussia Dortmund 95/6 (27, 4).

PAUL INCE

Paul Ince did not have a bad first campaign as an Anfield Red, injecting extra bite and dynamism into a midfield unit not always renowned for those qualities in the past. But did he consistently exert the same towering, passionate influence as in his Old Trafford pomp? Were there many games which he seized and shaped to his will, simply refusing to countenance defeat? While not precluding a future return to his irresistible peak, at which he hinted as the season wore on, the answer has got to be in the negative.

When the England star came on the market in the summer of 1997, the newspapers linked his name with the majority of England's leading clubs, though there was a peculiar hiatus when it seemed nobody was that interested. Certainly Manchester United didn't want him back and as other feasible employers began to rule themselves out, there was a suggestion that he might remain in Italy after all. However, lurking in the background were Liverpool, for whom he seemed ideally suited.

For a long time the Merseysiders had craved a warrior at the team's heart, a man who would lead by rousing personal example, who could sort out the physical side but also play some football. A second Graeme Souness would have been perfect, but in the absence of such an improbable being, Paul Ince was eminently acceptable. A fee of £4.2 million - an absolute bargain at today's prices - was agreed with Inter Milan, then followed excruciatingly protracted negotiations over personal terms until, finally, a wisp of white smoke appeared over Anfield and Roy Evans announced that the Reds had a new captain.

Despite his wide experience in the English top flight with West Ham and Manchester United, it was reasonable to suppose that Paul would need some sort of re-acclimatisation period following his two-year Italian sojourn. After all, although he believed he was both a more complete player and a more mature character in the wake of his San Siro service, the pace in *Serie A* was not as frenetic as the Premiership's.

It was not surprising, therefore, that as he strove to make an early impression, he received a string of bookings which resulted in suspension by November. His footballing input, meanwhile, was worthy enough but a tad pallid in comparison with the expectations of Kopites who recalled, all too vividly, the United swashbuckler of seasons past. He was hard, undeniably improving the side's competitiveness, yet he seemed uncharacteristically tentative about pressing forward, perhaps reasonably given the wealth of attacking talent on parade.

However, come the turn of the year, with Liverpool clearly off the pace in the Championship race, Paul appeared to shrug off any inhibitions and threw himself into the fray as of yore. No doubt encouraged by a growing understanding with Jamie Redknapp - the Reds were unbeaten in the 15 League games the two England men started in harness - he became a more dominant figure, especially in the attacking half.

One welcome upshot was a spell of three imporant springtime goals, a close-range equaliser in a pulsating Anfield clash with Everton, a thundering header in the 2-1 home victory over Bolton and a balletic overhead kick from six yards in the stirring 3-3 encounter with Tottenham at White Hart Lane.

As he appeared steadily to gather momentum ahead of England's summer assault on World Cup glory in France, the snarl seemed to be back on the face of the tiger, which was wonderful news, indeed, for the Anfield camp. Still only 30 as 1998/99 got under way, Paul Ince should have plenty left to give. If he can recover the form and display the naked desire which earned him the cordial loathing of Kopites in the early and mid-nineties, then he might just be the man who brandishes the bauble those same supporters yearn for so desperately. For all concerned, nothing but the title will suffice.

BORN: Ilford, Essex, 21.10.67. GAMES: 40. GOALS:8.
HONOURS: 38 England caps (92-).
OTHER CLUBS: West Ham United 86/7-89/90 (72, 7);
Manchester United 89/90-94/5 (206, 25);
Inter Milan 95/6-96/7.

1997/98 —

OYVIND LEONHARDSEN

Oyvind Leonhardsen appeared to be exactly what Liverpool needed. A buzzing fetcher and carrier in the Ray Houghton mould, he combines pace and directness with immense technical skill and formidable physical presence. At Wimbledon he proved himself in the Premiership fire as a driving midfielder whose range of operations stretched from ahead of his side's front-men to his own goal-line and the Norwegian's half-century of international caps served to underline his genuine quality.

Yet there is no disguising the fact that Oyvind endured a disappointing first season at Anfield following his arrival from Selhurst Park in the summer of 1997. He got off to an unfortunate start, missing the first two months of the campaign with a hamstring injury, but when he enjoyed a typically sparky debut in a 2-0 League Cup victory at West Bromwich in October, it seemed only a matter of a little bedding-in time before the Reds started reaping a royal benefit from their £4.5 million investment.

Quite simply, it never happened. Though Oyvind was as eager and energetic as expected, his contribution to match after match was largely anonymous. That is not to say much of his work wasn't valuable, but it was mainly of an unobtrusive nature, covering for defensive colleagues when they ventured forward, and he received precious little credit from the fans.

So why was such an experienced performer, who had excelled so comprehensively with the Dons, under-achieving on the grander stage with Liverpool? The simple answer appears to be that he spent most of his time playing out of position. As a right-footer on the left flank his options were limited and he became numbingly predictable, always being forced to cut inside where, invariably, he would be crowded out.

Of course, his preferred right-sided position was occupied by the wandering Steve McManaman, while Jamie Redknapp and Paul Ince tied up the middle, so it could be argued that manager Roy Evans had little choice. For Oyvind, this must have been supremely frustrating.

However, all is not lost. The man who helped Rosenborg lift three successive domestic titles and who excelled for his country in the 1994 World Cup finals is a player of true pedigree and can be expected to come to terms successfully with the situation in 1998/99. There is always the possibility, too, of personnel changes at Anfield which might lead to a different role for the ultra-professional Norwegian. Either way, it's a fair bet that the best of Oyvind Leonhardsen is yet to come.

BORN: Rosenborg, Norway, 17.8.70.
GAMES: 33 (3). GOALS: 6.
HONOURS: Norway caps. OTHER CLUBS: Molde, Norway, 89-91 (64, 9); Rosenborg, Norway, 92-94 (63, 20); Wimbledon 94/5-96/7 (76, 13).

1997/98 —

KARLHEINZ RIEDLE

1997/98 –

It is more of a compliment to Michael Owen than a condemnation of Karlheinz Riedle that the star German marksman, who has been everywhere and done everything, languished in the shadow of the English *wunderkind* for much of 1997/98.

When Liverpool announced their £1.8 million purchase of Karlheinz from Borussia Dortmund in July 1997, a tremor of apprehension intruded on the annual summer celebration of Manchester United supporters, and on the followers of others clubs with genuine title aspirations. Clearly the Reds were not messing about: they had signed a man whose goals had just secured the European Cup, who had helped to win the World Cup in 1990, who had played and prospered in Italy's ultra-demanding *Serie A*. True, he was nearly 32 and past his absolute pomp but it was easy to imagine this tall, dark stranger having the same sort of impact as did Jurgen Klinsmann during his first coming at White Hart Lane.

As it turned out, the phenomenal Owen advance combined with the presence of Robbie Fowler confined Karlheinz to the sidelines far more frequently than expected, but that is not to denigrate the newcomer's exceptional class or his impeccable influence as a professional athlete of the highest order.

To run through the Riedle roster of attributes is to describe the well-nigh ideal centre-forward. Superb in the air and possessed of beautiful all-round technique, he plays with a sophisticated amalgam of delicacy and power, intelligence and style. His awareness of the overall attacking picture, abhorrence of wasting possession and commendable unselfishness make him an impeccable team man, while his flashes of individual brilliance offer a thrilling bonus. Of these, none was more compelling than his first Premiership goal at Elland Road in August, which he secured with a ravishing 20-yard chip after gulling a Leeds defender. For a moment, it was as though Kenny Dalglish, no less, had reappeared in a red shirt.

However, the presence of the two young Englishmen and a succession of niggling injuries limited his senior starts to less than a dozen after October and as the season ended there was an unavoidable feeling that Liverpool had not garnered a full harvest of the Riedle bounty. Still, with a year yet to run on his contract, there was time for this outstanding footballer to leave a more significant mark on the Anfield scene.

BORN: Simmerberg-weiler, Germany, 16.9.65. GAMES: 22 (12). GOALS: 7. HONOURS: 42 Germany caps. OTHER CLUBS: Augsburg, Blau-Weiss Berlin, Werder Bremen, all Germany; Lazio, Italy; Borussia Dortmund, Germany.

BJORN TORE KVARME

The rickety form of Bjorn Tore Kvarme during his first full Premiership campaign was rendered all the more mortifying by memories of his unflappable excellence in the months immediately following his arrival at Anfield in January 1997. Indeed, after looking faintly bemused by the pace of proceedings during the first 10 minutes of his debut at home to Aston Villa, the blond Norwegian international defender went on to be voted the man of that particular match. Thereafter, he performed so efficiently on the right of Liverpool's back three that, by May, it appeared that Roy Evans had pulled off a major coup, especially as new European transfer regulations meant that no fee had changed hands. Furthermore, Bjorn was fiercely committed to the cause, having been so keen to join the Reds that he had left Rosenborg as the Trondheimers were preparing for a European Cup quarter-final against Juventus.

There was nothing complicated about the Kvarme method: when his team had the ball he defended sensibly; when Liverpool were in possession he slotted easily into their smooth passing game. Quick, strong and exceptionally calm, he tackled forcefully, displayed power and timing in the air, and took up intelligent covering positions. Add to that an assured touch, tidy distribution and the versatility to double as a full-back, and the picture seemed satisfyingly complete. Yes, there had been a few isolated moments of aberration, but they had been deemed permissible for a foreigner settling in.

However, the new season brought sharp disillusionment. It wasn't that Bjorn became a duffer overnight, but mistakes became unacceptably frequent. At Everton in October, he dithered over a clearance, allowing Danny Cadamarteri to run on and score; at home to Manchester United in December, Andy Cole dispensed similar treatment. As winter wore on Bjorn's displays became increasingly ragged until his reputation was finally shredded by Darren Huckerby during the January FA Cup knockout at home to Coventry.

After that, he was dropped for the first time since joining the Reds, but not the last. Recalled when colleagues were injured in February, Bjorn looked devoid of confidence and soon he was axed again. It represented a demoralising turnaround for an experienced performer, who had looked more comfortable in his back-three slot than in the middle of a back four, to which Roy Evans had switched in the autumn. Can he recover lost ground? Bjorn was only 26 as 1998/99 began so youth was on his side, but with new recruits expected, opportunities may be at a premium.

BORN: Trondheim, Norway, 17.7.72.
GAMES: 45 (1). GOALS: 0. HONOURS: Norway caps. OTHER CLUBS: Rosenborg, Norway, 91-96 (88, 2).

1996/97 –

JAMIE CARRAGHER

1996/97 –

Every time Jamie Carragher opens his mouth, he leaves no conceivable room for doubt as to his city of origin; just as every time the young Scouser walks on to the pitch, his football proclaims his affiliation to Liverpool FC. A tall, strong midfielder who can also operate comfortably in central defence, he is both skilful and tough, a neat and sensible passer who looks first for the forward option and has the technique to capitalise on his initiative.

Jamie has excelled at every level of his development. A key member of the Reds' 1996 FA Youth Cup-winning combination, he went on to experience a steady introduction to the big time as a second-half substitute for Rob Jones in the League Cup quarter-final defeat at Middlesbrough in January 1997. Not for one moment of a tense evening did he look out of place as he performed the simple tasks well in time-honoured Liverpool tradition.

His full debut, filling in for John Barnes 10 days later at home to Aston Villa, was considerably more eventful. In the first minute he was booked for a foul but he appeared utterly unfazed, turning in a confident, competent all-round performance which he capped with the first goal of the match shortly after the interval. Jamie's strike, a firm header from six yards, was of crucial psychological importance, freeing Liverpool from mounting anxiety at not scoring earlier and paving the way for an ultimately comfortable 3-0 victory.

In 1997/98 his progress continued apace as he became an England 'B' international and enjoyed some 20 senior outings for the Reds, spread between defence and midfield. However, while the Carragher versatility is a boon to his manager, it might be preferable for Jamie in the long term if he specialised. Which to choose? Well, his strength and composure fits him admirably for a rearguard role, for which the competition, while decidedly brisk, might be a little less demanding. However, many canny judges believe him best suited as an anchorman in front of the back line, which utilises effectively the aforementioned qualities but allows more creative scope.

Given that he is not afraid to air his views during a match, even to far more seasoned team-mates, he might make a future skipper, too. Thus, in the fullness of time, it is not inconceivable that Jamie Carragher will inherit the two mantles currently resting on the shoulders of Paul Ince. At this early point in the young man's career that is not a prediction, but it does seem worthy of thought.

BORN: Bootle, Merseyside, 28.1.78.
GAMES: 21 (5). GOALS: 1.

MARK KENNEDY

'It seems I'm good enough to play for Ireland, but not good enough for Liverpool.' Thus spoke a frustrated Mark Kennedy during 1997/98, his final season at Anfield, and his assessment, which might or might not have been intended ironically, was spot on.

Yet after arriving on Merseyside as British football's most expensive teenager in March 1995, the confident Dubliner had set about justifying his £2 million fee in refreshingly sparky manner. Just 19 days after his move from Millwall, the left-sided raider, still overwhelmed at joining the club he had worshipped as a boy, was called on as a substitute at home to Leeds. He tormented the visitors' defence with the pace, strength and unpredictability of his dashing runs and only the crossbar prevented a sensation a 30-yard debut goal. Mark, a former centre-forward, consolidated with several more cameo gems on the left flank before season's end and the feeling was that, before long, the Reds' hefty investment would be considered a steal. True, he was naive in his work off the ball, which was only to be expected in one so young, but he was willing, fearless and gifted, an irrresistible combination.

But Mark's meteoric rise was destined for a summary halt. Injury disrupted his preparation for the 1995/96 campaign in which so much was expected of him and, thereafter, his form proved so indifferent that he was unable to advance beyond the fringe of Roy Evans' side, where he was to remain until his £1.75 million transfer to Wimbledon in March 1998.

BORN: Dublin, 15.5.76. GAMES: 5 (16). GOALS: 0. HONOURS: 17 Republic of Ireland caps (95-). OTHER CLUBS: Millwall 92/3-94/5 (43, 9); Queen's Park Rangers on loan 97/8 (8, 2); Wimbledon 97/8- (4, 0).

1994/95 – 1997/98

DANNY MURPHY

Five minutes after Danny Murphy was called from the bench to make his Premiership debut, Liverpool were awarded a penalty. With regular spot-kicker Robbie Fowler absent, the sassy newcomer piped up to volunteer his services, and although the job went to Michael Owen, the incident offered a vivid illustration of the former Crewe midfielder's astonishing confidence. Indeed, after the game, against Wimbledon at Selhurst Park in August 1997, Roy Evans declared that from the moment of Murphy's £1.5 million arrival that summer, it seemed like he had been at the club for years.

An articulate, intelligent fellow, Danny is a lovely footballer, too, creative and combative, endowed with delicious skills and positively consumed with a driving desire to succeed. At Gresty Road, where he was a hugely dynamic influence as the Alex won promotion to the First Division in 1997, he thrived as a central play-maker, which is his preferred position. But when pressed into duty as a stand-in front-man at Old Trafford in April, the England under-21 international shone, even when operating in virtual isolation following the dismissal of Owen. Danny Murphy relishes centre stage, and it will be major surprise if he does not enjoy it regularly in a Liverpool shirt in the seasons ahead.

BORN: Chester, Cheshire, 18.3.77. GAMES: 6 (11). GOALS: 0. OTHER CLUBS: Crewe Alexandra 93/4-96/7 (134, 27).

1997/98 –

BRAD FRIEDEL

Life in limbo decame distressingly familiar to Brad Friedel during the autumn and winter of 1997/98. After a tortuous three-month saga during which Liverpool laboured ceaselessly to secure a work permit for the USA international goalkeeper, his December arrival provoked a dramatic improvement in the hitherto erratic form of incumbent custodian David James.

Thus Brad, signed for £1 million from Columbus Crew, was consigned to the Anfield sidelines and for a time it seemed that his drawn-out acquisition might prove to be little more than an expensive charade. But then David faltered again and the 26-year-old newcomer was called up on the last day of February, at home to Aston Villa, and retained his place until season's end.

The verdict? He made a solid start and he deserves a portion of the perseverance enjoyed by James. Though the Reds leaked plenty of springtime goals, Brad was blameless for most of them and his brilliant block on Ryan Giggs at Old Trafford in April typified his expertise in one-on-one situations.

Provided he suffers no further grief from red tape - and his employment status was unclear at the time of writing - Brad Friedel may prove well worth Liverpool's wait.

BORN: Lakewood, Ohio, USA, 18.5.71. GAMES: 11. GOALS: 0.
HONOURS: United States caps. OTHER CLUBS: Brondby, Denmark; Galatasaray, Turkey; Columbus Crew, United States.

1997/98 –

DAVID THOMPSON

It might have been a goal fashioned by any of Liverpool's great midfield combinations of the past few decades. David Thompson seized possession of the ball in centre-pitch, sprayed it wide to Steve McManaman on the right, then sprinted into the opponents' penalty box to slide home the return pass from six yards. Beautifully simple, devastatingly effective.

The younger of the two Merseysiders' contribution to that late winner at home to Crystal Palace in April 1998 was a particular joy. David appears to be in the traditional mould of vintage Reds such as Sammy Lee and Ray Houghton, a skilful and intelligent workaholic who embodies the timeless 'pass-and-move' philosophy, and his burgeoning development was one of the major pluses from another disappointing Anfield campaign.

A bouncily robust character, David produced such outstanding form during a lengthy loan stint at Swindon that Robins boss Steve McMahon was keen to buy him. But Roy Evans called him back and he impressed in each of a handful of senior outings in the spring. Liverpool's latest Thompson can be expected to figure significantly as the Reds renew their assault on the top honours and if he does half as well as his eminent namesakes, Peter and Phil, then seasoned Kopites will be well satisfied.

BORN: Birkenhead, Merseyside, 12.9.77.
GAMES: 1 (6). GOALS: 1.

1996/97 –

MICHAEL OWEN

He began the 1997/98 campaign as an unproven rookie, albeit one of prodigious potential; he ended it as one of the most exciting players in the world and England's youngest full international of the century. By any standard, Michael Owen is a remarkable footballer.

Not for half a lifetime has a teenage goal-scoring phenomenon erupted on to the British scene with such compelling force, and while Jimmy Greaves was a marksman of a vastly different type, in terms of sheer impact the comparison is valid. Of course, the impish Londoner was an incomparable opportunist in confined areas rather than a taker and maker of chances like Michael, who is at his most lethal when running into space. But both caught the imagination of a public who were ready to believe that, for them, nothing was impossible; both were quicksilver in thought and deed, able to transform any match with a split-second of inspiration; both were brimming with exuberant vitality, incapable of being overawed.

Similarities abounded, too, in the influence they wielded at their respective clubs. Jimmy carried a ho-hum Chelsea side in the late fifties and, while the Liverpool of 40 years later were hugely superior, all too often during 1997/98 they relied on their own boy wonder with a completeness which was little short of embarrassing. After all, it was a season in which he had been slated for a bit part, being phased in gradually as support for Robbie Fowler and Karlheinz Riedle. In the event, with both experienced men suffering injuries, and Fowler frequently out of sorts anyway, Michael became an increasingly dominant figure. Indeed, where the Reds might have finished without his 21 goals and numerous 'assists' does not bear contemplation.

At Anfield, where the talents of Hunt, Rush and Fowler have been nurtured, they know a thing or two about strikers and the backroom staff are not known for dispensing fulsome praise. Yet even before he had kicked a ball at senior level, they were as thrilled about Michael as they had ever been about any of his illustrious predecessors. Having netted 11 times in five outings during Liverpool's triumphant FA Youth Cup campaign of 1996, the Welsh-born front-runner made his Premiership debut during the closing stages of the crucial confrontation with Wimbledon at Selhurst Park in May 1997. Within minutes of taking the field he had stroked a lovely goal with the icy aplomb of a veteran and came close to forcing the draw which would have extended the title race.

Unveiled to a national audience that evening were his deft technique, startling change of pace and astonishing strength for one so slightly built, while aficionados were gasping, too, over his uncanny knack of taking up dangerous positions. Michael's father, Terry, was a winger who enjoyed a worthy professional career, including a brief spell at Everton. But with every respect to Owen Snr, it was abundantly evident during that fleeting cameo performance that his gifted son would be plying his trade on an altogether more exalted plane.

Roy Evans stressed that such a talent would need cautious handling and sparing early use, but the Reds' injury situation dictated that Michael would start the new season in the first team. Pretty soon, it was unthinkable that he should be anywhere else as he settled quickly to reveal his extensive range of attacking abilities. As fast and tricky as any winger but with the instinct of a striker, he inspires fear in defenders who know that once he steals ahead of them they can never catch him. His movement off the ball is unfailingly intelligent, offering a constant passing option for team-mates, and his vision means that he creates almost as many goals as he scores. In addition, he is physically resilient, more than willing to mix it with opponents far bigger than he, and as for the Owen finish, it makes the purists drool. He has scored with chips, flicks, drives, lobs, volleys, curlers, even an iso-lated header, though it's fair to say that his aerial work needs developing.

The fairytale nature of the story intensified in February when, at 18 years and 59 days, he became the youngest recipient of a full England cap since Tot Rostron in 1881 and, astonishingly enough, there was no outward sign of weariness as a hectic term drew to a close. His seemingly unstoppable rise was likely to continue with the World Cup finals, though that lay ahead at the time of writing. Just how far can Michael Owen go? Barring mishaps, all the way.

BORN: Hawarden, Clwyd, 14.12.79. GAMES: 42 (4). GOALS: 24.
HONOURS: 3 England caps (98-).

1996/97 –

BILL SHANKLY

Liverpool and Bill Shankly were made for each other. When they joined forces in December 1959, the club was a slumbering mass of unfulfilled potential, the man a soccer boss of only moderate success. But Bill had a vision, and when he set eyes on Anfield he knew he had found the setting for his life's great work. The stadium was a mess and the training ground a wasteland, the team mediocre and the board complacent – but those fans, their spirit and that all-consuming thirst for a football team worthy of the name . . . ah, now they were really something.

The story of Bill's transformation of the Reds has passed into folklore, but what was his secret? How did he do it? Well, to begin with, he was a motivator and psychologist supreme. His players respected him, and some of them might even have feared him a little bit. Eventually, most of them loved him. Above all, no one wanted to let him down. Often outrageous, eternally indomitable, the Ayrshire miner's son built up his men until they felt like giants. Before the 1965 FA Cup Final he told them: 'You are the best. Leeds are honoured to be on the same pitch.' And after watching his side be annihilated 5–1 by Ajax in a 1966 European Cup tie he rasped: 'We've got their measure now. We can still beat them.' Men who played under Bill swear that most of his lurid statements were not made for mere effect; he actually believed them!

Then there was his knowledge of the game. His brain was an encyclopaedia of footballers, their strengths and weaknesses, likes and dislikes – any scrap of information which might one day further the Liverpool cause. His long career as an abrasive wing-half for Carlisle, Preston and Scotland, and his management experience at Carlisle, Grimsby, Workington and Huddersfield inspired his creed for playing the game, which was deceptively simple: 'Get the ball, pass it to the nearest red shirt, and then move into space. It all comes down to give and take.' Bill possessed strong socialist ideals and carried them into his football; the work was shared by everyone in the team and there was no room for prima donnas, though he always resented the description of his side as mechanical, seeing this as an unjust slur.

The Shankly wit, of course, is synonymous with the man, as the Liverpool directors quickly discovered when they asked him if he wanted to take over the best club in the country. 'Why, is Matt Busby packing up?' was his quickfire reply. Having accepted the job, though, Bill knew that he would need more than jokes to resurrect the Reds. He began by retaining the backroom staff; then he set to work on the players. A chosen few stayed, but over the next couple of seasons most of the men who had struggled unavailingly to lift the club out of the Second Division departed. In came the likes of St John and Yeats, and the playing foundations of the most successful soccer dynasty in the history of the British game were laid.

Promotion came in 1961/62 and was swiftly followed by unprecedented glories as the sixties unfolded. The Reds' first FA Cup triumph was sandwiched by two League Championships and there was a series of enthralling European adventures to fire the imagination of the most passionate supporters in the land. Shanks was placed on a pedestal from which not even a barren patch towards the end of the decade could remove him. He went on to build a second fine side and register further triumphs before stunning the soccer world with his retirement – immediately after lifting his second FA Cup – in 1974.

His subsequent relations with the club he had turned into an international institution were tainted with misunderstandings, and perhaps a little more tact might have been exercised on both sides. Bill died of a heart attack in 1981, and the Shankly Gates – inscribed with the legend 'You'll Never Walk Alone' – stand as an appropriate tribute at his beloved Anfield. But his ultimate memorial is something grander, more all-embracing than that – no less than Liverpool FC itself, the club Bill Shankly built.

MANAGER 1959 – 1974

BOB PAISLEY

When Bob Paisley moved into the manager's chair unexpectedly vacated by Bill Shankly in the summer of 1974, most pundits saw the modest north-easterner as a two-way loser. If the Reds continued in their winning ways, it would be a case of yet more triumphs for the team that Shanks had created; if, on the other hand, the flow of trophies dried up, then poor old Bob would take the blame. But it didn't happen quite like that.

After one barren campaign, the man who had served Liverpool as player, coach and assistant manager since 1939 began putting his own stamp on the side. Six Championships, three European Cups, one UEFA Cup and three League Cups later, he retired as the most successful boss in English football history. And no one could seriously suggest that his incredible record was the result of anyone's efforts but his own. Of course, Bob was the first to acknowledge that Bill had laid the foundations, although as number two in the Anfield hierarchy he had undeniably put in much of the spadework himself. With characteristic diffidence, he was reluctant to take the job when it was thrust upon him, even urging his predecessor to change his mind about stepping down. In the end, he said he'd do his best …

Bob started with the respect of his players, though there may have been traces of resentment in some quarters as a result of tough decisions he had been called on to implement as first lieutenant during the Shankly regime. Probably he suffered some early embarrassment, too, when Bill, on appearing at the training ground, was addressed as 'Boss' by some of his former charges. Undaunted, he soldiered on, sensibly deciding not to compete with the wisecracking Scot for the fans' affections. He was no extrovert and had no intention of pretending to be one; 'I'll let the players on the pitch do my talking for me,' he said at the time, and over the seasons that followed their statements were eloquent indeed. To begin with, however, they were not quite so communicative, with no silverware being added to the Anfield collection in 1974/75. The prophets of doom had a field day, predicting that the new manager would prove little more than a caretaker and that some top name was being lined up.

The Paisley way was not to panic. He responded by quietly enhancing his legacy of players, adding the likes of Neal and McDermott to his squad and – a master stroke, this – converting Ray Kennedy from a struggling striker into a vastly influential left-sided midfielder. In 1975/76 he began to enjoy the fruits, with a title and UEFA Cup double to match Bill's identical achievement of three years earlier. Thereafter he began to break new ground, the subsequent campaign yielding the ultimate prize which had perpetually eluded Shanks - the European Cup. As his confidence grew, Bob even began to unbend a little in public, and when asked for his views before that greatest ever British football triumph on Italian soil, he revealed his own brand of wry humour: 'The last time I was in Rome was 33 years ago. I helped to capture it.'

As the honours mounted, the extent of Bob's soccer expertise became ever more apparent. He preached a gospel of control and movement, and made sure that he had the right men to put it into practice, bringing such outstanding talents as Dalglish, Souness and Hansen to the club. A meticulous planner, shrewd tactician and canny judge of a player's strengths and weaknesses, also he was an authority on football injuries, often able to diagnose problems before they became serious. Refreshingly, he was willing also to own up to his rare mistakes, taking the blame for changing his formation from 4-4-2 to 4-3-3 for the 1979 FA Cup semi-final replay against Manchester United, a switch which he believed cost the Reds the match.

Bob retired in 1983 after nine years in charge, coming back two years later to advise Kenny Dalglish, and eventually taking a seat on the board. In summing up the Paisley career, some years before Bob's death in 1996, Brian Clough said it all: 'He is a great man, and has once and for all broken the myth that nice guys don't win anything.'

MANAGER 1974 – 1983

JOE FAGAN

Joe Fagan was faced with the seemingly impossible task of following not one, but two legends as boss of the Reds. How did he react? Why, by instantly outdoing them, how else? In his first campaign, Joe achieved what neither Bill Shankly nor Bob Paisley had managed – he led Liverpool to three major honours, the European Cup, the League Championship and the Milk Cup. It was the perfect riposte to critics who had said that not even the all-conquering Anfield outfit could promote from within for a second time and maintain success.

To people who knew the club, though, his triumphs came as no surprise. Joe, whose son Chris made one senior appearance for the Reds in 1971, had been a Liverpool coach since 1958 and had moved up to become Bob's assistant after Bill's retirement. As such, he was imbued with all things Liverpool and was already a vital part of the set-up, albeit a publicly silent one. He had the golden knack of getting the best out of the players in his charge and, in many cases, he was a mixture of friend and adviser to them.

It was from this position of strength that his reign began, inauspiciously as it turned out, with a Charity Shield defeat by Manchester United. But when the real business got under way the status quo of Liverpool dominance was soon restored, and a glorious 1983/84 came to a climax with that nerve-tingling penalty shoot-out to decide the European Cup Final against AS Roma in Rome. And when Alan Kennedy slotted home the winner, Joe's familiar cheeky grin dominated the celebrations as the enormity of his triple triumph began to sink in.

But there were clouds on the horizon. With his imperious skipper Graeme Souness leaving for Italy, Joe was always going to face a more demanding term in 1984/85, and so it proved. His early years in the game - when he had been an enthusiastic, if moderate performer for Manchester City and Bradford - had taught Joe the virtues of pragmatism, and he declared: 'Souness has gone; forget about him, we've got a job to do without him.' That, however, was easier said than done.

John Wark and Paul Walsh were added to the squad but, partly through injuries, neither player had the hoped-for impact. An appalling League start saw the Reds drop into the bottom three by October, and although they recovered to finish as runners-up, the title slipped across Stanley Park to Everton. There was an early Milk Cup exit at the hands of Tottenham, and when progress towards the FA Cup Final was halted by Manchester United in a semi-final replay, all that was left was the European Cup. That Liverpool eventually lost the final to Juventus counted for nothing; that lives were lost when a wall collapsed during crowd trouble at the Heysel Stadium cast a blight over the football world.

Joe, who had decided already to retire, shed tears of despair on that grievous night as he confirmed his decision to step down. So honest, knowledgeable and respected throughout the game, he did not deserve such a dire departure. But despite the trauma of Heysel, Joe Fagan can look back with pride on his two years in charge at Anfield. One former Liverpool star once described him as the top coach in Europe, perhaps the world; another called him a gentleman and a gentle man. Few managers have left their desks with warmer tributes.

MANAGER 1983 – 1985

KENNY DALGLISH

It had to happen, sooner or later. Someone in the mad, mad world that professional soccer has become was bound to crack. Unreal expectations fuelled by the spiralling financial stakes, the constant tension endured in the media's unforgiving glare, the consequent pressure on family and friends … they combined to make it inevitable. Thus, when it finally came to pass in February 1991, the only surprise was the identity of the victim: Kenny Dalglish.

At the time Liverpool were reigning champions, they were top of the League yet again and among the favourites for the FA Cup. Their manager was perceived universally as impregnably self-sufficient, his strength of character and *sang-froid* not in doubt after more than two decades of top-class competition. If his communication skills left something to be desired and his barbs of arid humour, aimed mainly at pressmen, were becoming ever more venomous, then what of it? Kenny was the master, Kenny had done it all, Kenny could cope …

In retrospect, however, it is possible to discern a significant difference in the Dalglish demeanour during the fateful months leading to his dramatic departure. Though the Reds continued to ride high, they were nowhere near as convincing as they had been a couple of years previously and their boss had been the butt of steady criticism. At various times Kenny was slammed for negative tactics, peculiar selections, bizarre purchases and, most persistently, for his periodic dropping of Peter Beardsley.

It must be remembered that throughout a dazzling career with Celtic and Liverpool, just about everything had gone right for the multi-gifted Glaswegian. The game's most glittering prizes were piled high around him, he was deluged with bouquets, it was all one way. Now, with a degree of flak beginning to fly in his direction at last, he faced an unfamiliar set of circumstances and, it would appear, was not equipped to deal with them.

Weighed down by the cares that goes with the territory of being a figurehead for any large organisation - and there were stories of some almighty behind-the-scenes rows at the club - he became increasingly tetchy and defensive in public, until the day he could take no more.

Despite Kenny's subdued but emotional protestations that there was no ulterior motive behind his decision to quit the Reds as the season approached its climax - indeed, an FA Cup tie with Everton was still unresolved, his bombshell being dropped the morning after a 4-4 draw at Goodison - speculation was rife, not only on a stunned Merseyside but throughout the football world. However, no credible alternative theory has ever been advanced and, for what it's worth, this observer is happy to take the situation at face value. Here was a fellow at the end of his tether, like so many in the unforgiving modern world; just another man whose job had become too much for him but who was in an enviable position of security which emabled him to walk away.

After all, apart from the everyday stress of managing a top club, Kenny had lived through the traumas of Heysel and, even more drainingly, of Hillsborough. For his compassion, dignity and selflessless in the aftermath of the Sheffield tragedy, he had earned widespread respect and affection and was praised for his immense strength, though who can say what kind of long-term toll was exacted?

But whatever the ins and outs of his exit, what remains indisputable is the eminence of his record during his five and a half years at the Anfield helm. The vultures had gathered when Liverpool gave him the the task of succeeding Joe Fagan in the summer of 1985, especially as he was to continue as a player. A popular reaction was that after successfully replacing first Bill Shankly and then Bob Paisley by promoting long-time loyal servants, the board should have chosen another graduate from the legendary bootroom, probably Ronnie Moran. How could a man with no management experience possibly cope with one of the most demanding positions in football? The directors, however, knew a thing or two about Kenny Dalglish. They had perceived the leadership potential and other personal attributes which made them comprehensively worthy of following his illustrious predecessors.,

Kenny's subsequent progress speaks for itself. In 1985/86 his side claimed the coveted League and FA Cup double, something even Liverpool had never done before; season 1986/87 brought only League Cup Final defeat, though it moved the manager to create, by means of Barnes and company, one of the most exciting combinations in Anfield history. That team won the League and lost the FA Cup Final in 1987/88, then missed the title by the narrowest margin but won the FA Cup in 1988/89. The following term they were champions *again*, albeit a little less stylishly, and then came that final harrowing campaign.

Kenny had never been afraid to back his judgement and for a long time his transfer acquisitions - the likes of McMahon, Barnes, Beardsley, Aldridge - bore the hallmark of inspiration. Only later, when such names as Speedie and Carter appeared on the Anfield roster, were questions raised and by then, maybe, the boss wasn't quite himself.

What cannot be contradicted is that, by his managerial deeds alone, he attained soccer greatness. Indeed, if the enormity of his sudden farewell had been allowed to sink in gradually, had there been no return to hugely lucrative employment with Blackburn Rovers some nine months later, then his god-like status on Merseyside would have remained undiminished. As it is there persists a bitter resentment among some fans, who maintain that he let them down at a time when his club was approaching a period of transition, and was desperate for stable and expert leadership.

Astonishingly, his tenure at Ewood Park produced a similar tale of fabulous achievement followed by controversial withdrawal, albeit in different circumstances. And so to Newcastle and the next fascinating chapter in the story of Kenny Dalglish, one of the truly great football men of this or any other age.

MANAGER 1985 – 1991

GRAEME SOUNESS

There were certain extenuating circumstances, it's true, but nothing can alter the unadorned truth that, as Liverpool managers go, Graeme Souness was a rank failure. He spent a fortune on new players, yet not since pre-Shankly days - and perhaps not even then - had such empty, frustrating, downright upsetting seasons been endured at Anfield. Worse still, the man who had skippered the Reds to untold glory, whose midfield mastery and uplifting leadership had been hailed throughout the soccer world, became widely despised, partly on non-footballing grounds, by the very people who had once revered him the most. Poignantly persuasive evidence of his fall was offered by the vehement reaction of a lifelong Liverpool fanatic and Anfield season-ticket holder during the strife-torn 1992/93 campaign. Wincing at the enormity of sentiments he would once have regarded as sacrilege, he declared: 'I'd like to see the lads lose 10 games on the trot - if it meant we could get rid of Graeme Souness.'

Alienated supporters and discontented players, embarrassingly public wrangles and perceived weakness in the boardroom, 'Souness must stay' T-shirts selling merrily outside Old Trafford ... a nightmare scenario had developed from the jubilant press conference in April 1991 at which Graeme was announced as the successor to his friend and countryman, Kenny Dalglish. Fresh from an avalanche of domestic trophies with Rangers, he brought charisma, pride and exceptional strength of character with him, but how relevant were the Scottish achievements to the task at hand? Well, none could deny that at Ibrox he had comprehensively revived a once-great club, backing his judgement with massive outlay in the transfer market, but there were lingering doubts. Was the competition up there much to shout about? Why had a significant number of his acquisitions been dumped so soon? Why had Rangers nosedived in Europe?

Graeme, the first Liverpool boss since Shanks with previous managerial experience elsewhere, reckoned that he was also the first new Anfield incumbent since the great man with a major job to do, and he declared that fresh faces were needed.

Accordingly the merry-go-round cranked up: in came Mark Wright, Dean Saunders, Mark Walters and the splendid Rob Jones, out went Peter Beardsley, Steve Staunton and Gary Gillespie in short order. However, those changes and others could not lift the Reds above what was, for them, a mediocre sixth place in the League and although the FA Cup was won - a trifle fortuitously, it must be admitted - the side and its football left much to be desired. Less than a month before the final, however, all that was overshadowed by the startling news that Graeme was entering hospital for a triple-bypass heart operation at the age of 38. Incredibly, he turned up at Wembley, flanked by two anxious medicos, and every twist and turn of the game was mirrored on his strained features. Foolhardy, maybe, but characteristically courageous, and he vowed to be back at his desk, and on the training ground, in time for the 1992/93 season.

He was, too, but what a tumultuous term was in store. Before it began he dispensed with Ray Houghton, Barry Venison and the aforementioned Saunders, drafting in Paul Stewart, David James and more, but the blend was wrong, individuals failed to live up to their potential and Premier League non-achievement was compounded by FA Cup defeat at Bolton. In fairness, it must be stated that the club was assailed by a chronic injury crisis, though there were those ready to apportion much of the blame for that on Souness-inspired changes to the training regime, alterations which he has subsequently denied making. What could not be gainsayed, though, was the disharmony within the camp. The manager adopted a confrontational style and became involved in well-publicised differences with several senior players. Indiscipline occurred both on and off the field to a degree hitherto unthinkable at Anfield and, most telling of all, the fans' resentment was smouldering dangerously. In fact, the roots of increasingly rampant public discontent lay not in disappointment with the Reds' lacklustre football, but in Graeme's close relationship with the *Sun* newspaper, a publication reviled on Merseyside for its controversial treatment of the Hillsborough disaster. Following one ill-judged series of paid-for articles, he apologised and made a donation to a children's hospital from the proceeds, but by then offence had been given. Arguably, from that moment, Graeme was living on borrowed time as manager of Liverpool. Not surprisingly, in the spring of 1993, the board decided that the situation was out of hand and that Souness should be sacked. But then, amidst a confusing welter of negotiations over compensation and doubt about the succession, there was a humiliating U-turn. Graeme would stay, but with Roy Evans promoted to be his assistant.

Granted another new start, Graeme signed Nigel Clough, Neil Ruddock and, a little later, Julian Dicks and his revamped team topped the table after three matches of 1993/94. But it was a false dawn. A run of four League defeats shattered pipedreams of a dramatic recovery and an anti-climactic autumn dragged into an ominous winter. Then, in January, FA Cup defeat by Bristol City presaged the end of the sad second liaison between Graeme Souness and Liverpool FC. At last he was forced to admit defeat, resigning ahead of the inevitable axe, and many thousands of Reds supporters emitted a huge sigh of collective relief. Of course, the svelte Scot had not been all bad. He had been brave beyond measure and both his desire for success and his dedication in working towards that goal had been immense. Also, he had espoused an attractive passing game and blooded some of the brilliant youngsters who have since become household names. Undoubtedly, he felt let down by certain of his charges, whom he believed to be mercenary and less professional than himself. But, in the final reckoning, he was paid to get the best from his footballers and he did not make a good job of it.

During his 33 months of power, he paid £21.25 million for 15 players, recouping some £12 million by way of sales. By the time compensation had been paid by the club at each end of his contract, he had proved astronomically expensive, and with precious little glory to show for it. Did Graeme buy badly? Or did he buy wisely and manage badly? After all, there was nothing intrinsically wrong with the people he brought in. To a lesser or greater degree, they had all succeeded elsewhere and several of them blossomed anew at Anfield after a change of boss. Did he sell badly, dispensing with high-quality performers such as Beardsley, Houghton and Staunton unnecessarily? Was the root of the problem that he *had* to do everything his way? Was he simply the victim of his own ego? Whatever the answers, he arrived as a hero and departed as a villain. Some years earlier he had written that being successful was more important than being popular. Unfortunately, by the time he left Anfield, Graeme Souness was neither.

MANAGER 1991 — 1994

ROY EVANS

Fourth, third, fourth, third – not some obscure marching chant but a chronological list of Liverpool's Premiership finishing positions during the four full seasons of Roy Evans' managerial reign. To the followers of most clubs it would make eminently satisfactory reading and equate with comfortable security of tenure for the man in charge; for Reds fans weaned on a veritable surfeit of trophies, a season-after-season glut that turned their major rivals green with envy, it represented nothing less than an indictment.

At the time of writing it was not known whether Roy would keep his job. His contract still had time to run so, arguably, it should not have been an issue, but throughout 1997/98, a season in which Liverpool did not even come close to lifting silverware, the chorus calling for his dismissal had grown increasingly strident. Even with months of the campaign to run there was open discussion about possible successors. The likes of Gullit, Heynckes, Toshack, Jansen, Dalglish, Keegan and Frenchman Gerard Houillier were all mentioned, though it was some sort of tribute to an agreeable, unassuming, wholly decent man that most of the attacks on his record contained more regret than venom.

With so much ravishing attacking talent at Roy's disposal and with the steely addition of Paul Ince in the summer, it was predicted widely that the Reds had reached their turning point, that 1997/98 would see them overhaul their bitterest rivals, Manchester United. The Anfield boss, so endearingly honest, cranked up the pressure on himself at the outset by declaring that this was the term in which he had to deliver. Well, the Old Trafford club did not win the title for once, but it was Arsenal who supplanted them as champions, while Liverpool were barely in the hunt.

But why? Is Evans simply too nice to handle a bunch of hugely-paid young men, some of whom are perceived by the public - rightly or wrongly - to be so preoccupied with matters other than football that they were dubbed The Spice Boys? Is Roy, who has never worked for anyone but Liverpool FC and been at Anfield since the Shankly days, a relic of a bygone age? With the whiff of a new European league ever more pungent, do the Reds need new and innovative leadership from a Continental coach? More specifically, what about a defence packed with individually accomplished players but which collectively is prone to chronic under-achievement? As the last ball was kicked, such questions took on a new urgency, and the answers supplied by the Liverpool board will shape the immediate future of the club.

Whatever else can be levelled at Bootle-born Roy, none can question his commitment to the cause. He enjoyed a modest career as a full-back with the Reds before being convinced by Bob Paisley that his future lay in coaching; then, after much heart-searching, the 25-year-old ditched his playing ambitions in 1974 and embarked on the road that was to lead to management. At the time, with most attention focused on the retirement of Shankly and the accession of Paisley, little heed was paid to Roy's appointment as reserve team trainer. Yet no less canny a judge of character than Sir John Smith, then the club chairman, predicted that one day the young man would boss Liverpool.

First, though, there were extensive dues to pay and Roy did so comprehensively, presiding over a phenomenal succession of Central League title triumphs before being promoted to help Ronnie Moran with the first team in 1983. His name was mentioned in dispatches when the Reds needed a new manager in 1985, and again in 1991, and when he was passed over both times he must have wondered if the Smith prophecy would ever be fulfilled.

However, with the Souness momentum faltering, Roy became assistant manager in the spring of 1993, some nine months before inheriting the top job. Inevitably, he was placed under minute media scrutiny and a picture emerged of an engaging, bloke-next-door type, an amiable fellow

MANAGER 1994 –

but one blessed with inner strength aplenty. It was an appealing image which contrasted vividly with the popular perception of his more showy predecessor and which gave him a head start with Liverpool fans who yearned for the old values.

Crucially, Roy didn't have to earn the respect of his charges - he already had it. Practically overnight he restored morale among the players, removed the fear of failure which had engulfed some of them, and made training more stimulating by placing less emphasis on sometimes confusing theory and more on working out problems through five-a-sides. Suddenly, Anfield and Melwood were happier places.

After taking over in February 1994, he used the rest of that campaign to give everyone a fair chance, but having decided that certain areas of the side needed drastic surgery, he didn't shrink from wielding the scalpel. Roy bought boldly, acquiring expensive central defenders Scales and Babb in time for the new term, and had the courage to opt for the 3-5-2 formation which he believed would be most effective in the modern game. There were hiccups, but in general the system was positive and frequently exhilarating, providing a fluid framework for the uplifting talents of McManaman, Redknapp, Fowler *et al*, although one frequent criticism was that the team 'passed itself to death'. Whatever, in autumn 1997 Roy reverted to 4-4-2, but with no noticeable improvement in results.

On a personal level, Roy has demonstrated that he can handle a disparate collection of strong personalities. Indeed, when Mark Wright and Julian Dicks displeased him by their attitude and fitness respectively during the preparation for 1994/95, he simply dropped them, making it abundantly clear that no one was indispensable. Later, when certain others allowed their egos too much rein, he was equally firm, asserting his authority quietly and privately, but absolutely.

However, Roy remained acutely aware that his Reds needed to improve dramatically. The way the team fell away in the latter months of 1994/95 following the Wembley victory over Bolton and the mortifying fade-outs when their League challenges withered in each of the next three campaigns suggested a lack of backbone and concentration that was totally unacceptable. He has been able to spend lavishly (£8.5 million for Stan Collymore, seemingly a desirable acquisition at the time, was a British record) and yet, in general, his acquisitions have proved only adequately or partially successful rather than inspired. Indeed, he has found the club's flourishing youth system to be far more productive.

None would deny that Roy has made his mistakes, such as taking so long to procure experienced goalkeeping cover during the tribulations of David James. Yet despite the disappointments, nothing should ever detract from his sterling achievement in launching the Reds' renaissance in the aftermath of the traumatic Souness regime. Equally, though, nothing can disguise the truth that in 1998 the Reds were lagging behind not only United but also the imaginatively reconstructed Arsenal. Another chance for Roy Evans? The heart says yes, but in these impatient times, when the big decisions are made the heart is not always consulted …

RONNIE MORAN

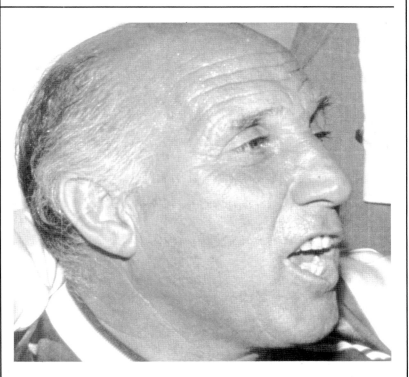

After the disruptive, disorientating departure of Kenny Dalglish, and the rather more predictable but hardly less traumatic exit of Graeme Souness, Liverpool could not have wished for a steadier hand on the Anfield tiller than that of Ronnie Moran.
Having spent his entire working life as a Red, Ronnie had become the high priest of Shanklyism, an ineffably wise sergeant-major cum soccer sage whom many pundits believe should have been offered the boss's chair when Joe Fagan retired in 1985.
Intense and hard to satisfy but essentially golden-hearted, Ronnie is a shrewd coach and an ego-deflater supreme whose creed both for football and life is based on collective effort.
Throughout Liverpool's great years, as he moved from player to youth coach (1966), then took over the reserves (1971), began working with the first-team (1976) and finally became chief coach (1983), he preached that the most important game was the next one. Everyone gets the same down-to-earth treatment from Ronnie, who dispensed his level-headed philosophy to the exuberant class of 1995 as they partied in the dressing room after beating Crystal Palace in the League Cup semi-final. He called them to order, pointing out simply: 'You've won nothing yet.'
When he stepped into the breach created by Dalglish, he began by presiding over three successive defeats but, typically refusing to panic, restored equilibrium to revive realistic title hopes, although Arsenal were to prove uncatchable. In 1994 his spell in control was too short to do any more than keep things ticking over until Roy Evans was appointed.
Would Ronnie have been a success as top man? Probably. But maybe his forte was in a supporting role, creating a bridge between players and management, busying himself with the minutae of everyday football life.
The Reds' final link with the fifties, he has served the club under eight managers - Don Welsh, Phil Taylor, Bill Shankly, Bob Paisley, Joe Fagan, Kenny Dalglish, Graeme Souness and now Roy Evans - and he has been utterly loyal to each one, whether he agreed with him or not.
Ronnie Moran remains at Anfield as chief coach. The day he leaves, Liverpool will lose more than any words can express.

CARETAKER MANAGER 1991 & 1994

PLAYERS' STATISTICS

Player	Seas	LEAGUE			FA CUP			L CUP			EUROPE			TOTAL		
		Ap	Sb	Gl	Ap	Sb	Gl	Ap	Sb	Gl	Ap	Sb	Gl	Ap	Sb	Gl
Ablett G	86-91	103	(6)	1	16	(2)	0	10	(1)	0	6	(0)	0	135	(9)	1
A'Court A	52-64	355	(0)	61	24	(0)	2	2	(0)	0	1	(0)	0	382	(0)	63
Aldridge J	86-89	69	(14)	50	12	(0)	8	7	(1)	3	0	(0)	0	88	(15)	61
Arnell A	53-60	69	(0)	33	6	(0)	2	0	(0)	0	0	(0)	0	75	(0)	35
Arnold S	1970	1	(0)	0	0	(0)	0	0	(0)	0	0	(0)	0	1	(0)	0
Arrowsmith A	61-67	43	(4)	20	6	(0)	4	0	(0)	0	1	(0)	0	50	(4)	24
Babb P	94-	100	(3)	1	11	(0)	0	16	(0)	0	9	(1)	0	136	(4)	1
Banks A	58-60	8	(0)	6	0	(0)	0	0	(0)	0	0	(0)	0	8	(0)	6
Barnes J	87-96	310	(4)	84	51	(0)	16	22	(6)	3	2	(0)	3	399	(4)	6
Beardsley P	87-90	120	(11)	46	22	(3)	11	13	(1)	1	0	(0)	0	155	(15)	58
Beglin J	84-87	64	(0)	2	10	(0)	0	13	(0)	0	3	(0)	1	90	(0)	3
Berger P	96-	19	(26)	9	1	(2)	0	5	(1)	2	7	(1)	2	32	(30)	13
Bjornebye S	92-	112	(4)	2	9	(2)	0	14	(0)	0	12	(0)	2	147	(6)	4
Boersma P	9-75	73	(9)	17	7	(3)	1	5	(3)	3	13	(6)	8	98	(21)	29
Brownbill D	1973	1	(0)	0	0	(0)	0	0	(0)	0	0	(0)	0	1	(0)	0
Burrows D	88-93	135	(11)	3	16	(1)	0	16	(0)	0	11	(0)	0	178	(12)	3
Byrne G	57-68	273	(1)	2	29	(0)	0	5	(0)	0	22	(0)	1	329	(1)	3
Callaghan I	59-77	637	(3)	50	77	(1)	2	42	(0)	7	87	(1)	10	843	(5)	69
Campbell R	59-60	14	(0)	1	0	(0)	0	0	(0)	0	0	(0)	0	14	(0)	1
Carragher J	96-	18	(4)	1	0	(0)	0	2	(1)	0	1	(0)	0	21	(5)	1
Carter J	90-91	2	(3)	0	2	(0)	0	0	(0)	0	0	(1)	0	4	(4)	0
Case J	74-80	170	(16)	23	20	(2)	7	21	(1)	3	25	(6)	12	236	(25)	45
Charnock P	1992	0	(0)	0	0	(0)	0	1	(0)	0	0	(1)	0	1	(1)	0
Chisnall P	64-65	6	(0)	1	0	(0)	0	0	(0)	0	2	(0)	1	8	(0)	2
Clemence R	68-80	470	(0)	0	54	(0)	0	55	(0)	0	77	(0)	0	656	(0)	0
Clough N	93-95	29	(10)	7	2	(0)	0	3	(0)	2	0	(0)	0	34	(10)	9
Cohen A	79-80	16	(2)	1	1	(0)	0	1	(0)	0	2	(1)	0	20	(3)	1
Collymore S	95-96	55	(6)	26	9	(0)	7	2	(2)	0	5	(2)	2	71	(10)	35
Cormack P	72-75	119	(6)	21	14	(0)	2	20	(0)	1	15	(3)	2	168	(9)	26
Dalglish K	77-89	342	(13)	118	36	(0)	13	57	(2)	27	46	(1)	10	481	(16)	168
Dicks J	1993	24	(0)	3	1	(0)	0	3	(0)	0	0	(0)	0	28	(0)	3
Durnin J	86-88	0	(0)	0	0	(0)	0	1	(1)	0	0	(0)	0	1	(1)	0
Evans A	68-71	77	(2)	21	9	(2)	3	7	(0)	2	11	(2)	7	104	(6)	33
Evans R	69-73	9	(0)	0	0	(0)	0	1	(0)	0	1	(0)	0	11	(0)	0
Fagan C	1970	1	(0)	0	0	(0)	0	0	(0)	0	0	(0)	0	1	(0)	0
Fairclough D	75-82	64	(36)	34	10	(4)	4	7	(13)	10	7	(9)	4	88	(62)	52
Ferns P	62-64	27	(0)	1	1	(0)	0	0	(0)	0	0	(0)	0	28	(0)	1
Fowler R	93-	156	(4)	92	17	(0)	9	25	(0)	20	13	(1)	8	211	(5)	129
Friedel B	97-	11	(0)	0	0	(0)	0	0	(0)	0	0	(0)	0	11	(0)	0
Furnell J	61-63	28	(0)	0	0	(0)	0	0	(0)	0	0	(0)	0	28	(0)	0
Gayle H	1980	3	(1)	1	0	(0)	0	0	(0)	0	0	(1)	0	3	(2)	1
Gillespie G	83-90	152	(4)	4	21	(2)	0	22	(0)	2	2	(1)	0	197	(7)	16
Graham R	64-71	96	(5)	31	7	(2)	4	7	(1)	2	13	(0)	5	123	(8)	42
Grobbelaar B	81-93	440	(0)	0	2	(0)	0	70	(0)	0	37	(0)	0	609	(0)	0
Hall B	68-75	140	(13)	15	17	(2)	3	12	(1)	1	27	(8)	2	196	(24)	21
Hansen A	77-89	435	(2)	7	59	(1)	2	68	(0)	1	42	(1)	3	604	(4)	13
Harkness S	91-	86	(10)	3	4	(0)	0	11	(1)	3	12	(2)	0	113	(13)	6
Harrower J	57-60	96	(0)	21	6	(0)	1	3	(0)	0	0	(0)	0	105	(0)	22
Hateley T	67-68	42	(0)	17	7	(0)	8	2	(0)	0	5	(0)	3	56	(0)	28
Heighway S	70-80	312	(17)	50	33	(3)	8	38	(0)	7	61	(3)	11	444	(23)	76
Hickson D	59-60	60	(0)	37	4	(0)	0	3	(0)	1	0	(0)	0	67	(0)	38
Hignett A	1964	1	(0)	0	0	(0)	0	0	(0)	0	0	(0)	0	1	(0)	0
Hodgson D	82-83	21	(7)	4	3	(0)	1	6	(3)	3	3	(4)	2	33	(14)	10
Hooper M	86-92	50	(1)	0	5	(0)	0	10	(0)	0	4	(0)	0	69	(1)	0
Houghton R	87-91	147	(6)	28	26	(1)	1	4	(0)	3	4	(0)	2	191	(7)	37
Hughes E	66-78	474	(0)	35	62	(0)	1	46	(0)	3	75	(0)	9	657	(0)	48
Hutchison D	91-93	33	(12)	7	1	(2)	0	7	(1)	2	3	(0)	1	44	(15)	10
Hunt R	59-69	401	(3)	245	44	(0)	18	10	(0)	5	29	(2)	17	484	(5)	285
Hysen G	89-91	70	(2)	2	13	(0)	0	6	(0)	1	0	(0)	0	89	(2)	3
Ince P	97-	31	(0)	8	1	(0)	0	4	(0)	0	4	(0)	0	40	(0)	8
Irvine A	86-87	0	(2)	0	0	(1)	0	0	(1)	0	0	(0)	0	0	(4)	0
Irwin C	79-80	26	(3)	3	4	(0)	0	6	(0)	0	4	(1)	0	40	(4)	3
James D	92-	187	(1)	0	18	(0)	0	22	(0)	0	17	(0)	0	244	(1)	0
Johnson D	76-81	128	(20)	55	17	(2)	6	15	(3)	9	14	(5)	8	174	(30)	78
Johnston C	81-87	165	(25)	30	14	(4)	4	32	(3)	3	13	(4)	2	224	(36)	39
Jones A	59-62	5	(0)	0	0	(0)	0	0	(0)	0	0	(0)	0	5	(0)	0
Jones B	1991	0	(0)	0	0	(0)	0	0	(0)	0	0	(1)	0	0	(1)	0
Jones J	75-77	72	(0)	3	9	(0)	0	4	(0)	0	12	(0)	0	97	(0)	3
Jones L	94-96	0	(3)	0	0	(0)	0	0	(1)	0	0	(0)	0	0	(4)	0
Jones R	91-	182	(1)	0	27	(0)	0	21	(1)	0	11	(0)	0	241	(2)	0
Keegan K	71-76	230	(0)	68	28	(0)	14	23	(0)	6	40	(0)	12	321	(0)	100
Kennedy A	78-85	247	(2)	15	21	(0)	0	45	(0)	2	34	(0)	4	347	(2)	21
Kennedy M	94-96	5	(11)	0	0	(1)	0	0	(2)	0	0	(2)	0	5	(16)	0

PLAYERS' STATISTICS

Player	Seas	LEAGUE			FA CUP			L CUP			EUROPE			TOTAL		
		Ap	Sb	Gl	Ap	Sb	Gl	Ap	Sb	Gl	Ap	Sb	Gl	Ap	Sb	Gl
Kennedy R	74-81	272	(3)	51	28	(0)	3	35	(0)	6	46	(0)	12	381	(3)	72
Kettle B	75-76	3	(0)	0	0	(0)	0	0	(0)	0	1	(0)	0	4	(0)	0
Kewley K	1977	0	(1)	0	0	(0)	0	0	(0)	0	0	(0)	0	0	(1)	0
Kozma I	91-92	3	(3)	0	0	(2)	0	0	(1)	0	0	(0)	0	3	(6)	0
Kvarme B	96-	37	(1)	0	2	(0)	0	2	(0)	0	4	(0)	0	45	(1)	0
Lane F	1972	1	(0)	0	0	(0)	0	1	(0)	0	0	(0)	0	2	(0)	0
Lawler C	62-75	406	(0)	41	47	(0)	4	27	(0)	5	66	(0)	11	546	(0)	61
Lawrence T	62-70	306	(0)	0	42	(0)	0	6	(0)	0	33	(0)	0	387	(0)	0
Lawrenson M	81-87	233	(8)	11	24	(0)	2	49	(0)	2	26	(1)	2	332	(9)	17
Lee S	77-85	190	(7)	13	17	(0)	0	39	(0)	2	3	(0)	4	279	(7)	19
Leishman T	59-62	107	(0)	6	9	(0)	0	3	(0)	1	0	(0)	0	119	(0)	7
Leonhardsen O	97-	27	(1)	6	1	(0)	0	3	(2)	0	2	(0)	0	33	(3)	6
Lewis K	60-62	71	(0)	39	8	(0)	3	2	(0)	2	0	(0)	0	81	(0)	44
Liddell W	45-60	495	(0)	216	42	(0)	13	0	(0)	0	0	(0)	0	537	(0)	229
Lindsay A	69-76	168	(2)	12	22	(0)	1	23	(0)	1	31	(0)	4	244	(2)	18
Livermore D	67-70	13	(3)	0	0	(0)	0	1	(0)	0	0	(0)	0	14	(3)	0
Lloyd L	69-73	150	(0)	4	16	(0)	0	20	(0)	0	31	(0)	1	217	(0)	5
Lowry T	1964	1	(0)	0	0	(0)	0	0	(0)	0	0	(0)	0	1	(0)	0
McAteer J	95-	78	(9)	3	10	(0)	3	10	(1)	0	9	(0)	0	107	(10)	6
McDermott T	74-82	221	(11)	54	23	(0)	4	36	(0)	5	30	(1)	12	310	(12)	75
MacDonald K	84-88	29	(11)	1	9	(0)	1	1	(3)	1	3	(0)	0	42	(14)	3
McLaughlin J	69-74	38	(2)	2	4	(0)	1	3	(0)	0	8	(0)	0	53	(2)	3
McMahon S	85-91	202	(2)	29	30	(0)	7	27	(0)	13	5	(0)	0	264	(2)	49
McManaman S	90-	233	(11)	41	28	(1)	5	32	(1)	10	27	(0)	4	320	(13)	60
Marsh M	88-93	42	(27)	2	6	(2)	0	10	(1)	3	11	(1)	1	69	(31)	6
Matteo D	93-	64	(11)	0	4	(1)	0	9	(0)	0	9	(0)	0	86	(12)	0
Melia J	55-63	269	(0)	76	18	(0)	2	0	(0)	0	0	(0)	0	287	(0)	78
Milne G	60-66	234	(2)	18	27	(0)	1	0	(0)	0	16	(0)	0	277	(2)	19
Molby J	84-94	195	(23)	44	24	(4)	4	25	(3)	9	7	(0)	1	251	(30)	58
Molyneux J	55-61	229	(0)	2	17	(0)	1	3	(0)	0	0	(0)	0	249	(0)	3
Molyneux W	1964	1	(0)	0	0	(0)	0	0	(0)	0	0	(0)	0	1	(0)	0
Money R	1980	12	(2)	0	1	(0)	0	1	(0)	0	1	(0)	0	15	(2)	0
Mooney B	1986	0	(0)	0	0	(0)	0	0	(1)	0	0	(0)	0	0	(1)	0
Moran R	52-64	343	(0)	14	32	(0)	2	0	(0)	0	4	(0)	0	379	(0)	16
Morris F	58-59	47	(0)	14	1	(0)	0	0	(0)	0	0	(0)	0	48	(0)	14
Morrissey J	57-60	36	(0)	6	1	(0)	0	0	(0)	0	0	(0)	0	37	(0)	6
Murphy D	97-	6	(10)	0	0	(1)	0	0	(0)	0	0	(0)	0	6	(11)	0
Neal P	74-85	453	(2)	41	45	(0)	3	66	(0)	4	69	(0)	12	633	(2)	60
Nicol S	82-94	328	(15)	36	50	(0)	3	42	(0)	4	17	(2)	2	437	(17)	45
Ogrizovic S	77-80	4	(0)	0	0	(0)	0	0	(0)	0	0	(0)	0	4	(0)	0
Ogston J	1966	1	(0)	0	0	(0)	0	0	(0)	0	0	(0)	0	1	(0)	0
Owen M	96-	35	(3)	19	0	(0)	0	4	(0)	4	3	(1)	1	42	(4)	24
Peplow S	1969	2	(0)	0	0	(0)	0	0	(0)	0	1	(0)	0	3	(0)	0
Piechnik T	92-93	16	(1)	0	2	(0)	0	5	(0)	0	0	(0)	0	23	(1)	0
Redknapp J	91-	154	(23)	19	15	(1)	2	25	(0)	5	15	(4)	1	209	(28)	27
Riedle K	97-	18	(7)	6	1	(0)	0	2	(3)	0	1	(2)	1	22	(12)	7
Robinson M	83-84	26	(4)	6	2	(0)	1	11	(1)	4	6	(1)	2	45	(6)	13
Rosenthal R	89-93	32	(42)	21	5	(3)	0	2	(7)	1	1	(3)	0	40	(55)	22
Ross I	66-71	42	(6)	2	9	(1)	1	3	(0)	0	5	(2)	1	59	(9)	4
Ruddock N	93-	111	(4)	11	11	(0)	0	19	(1)	1	5	(1)	0	146	(6)	12
Rush I	80-86 and 88-95	448	(22)	229	55	(6)	9	78	(0)	48	35	(2)	21	616	(30)	337
Russell C	1980	0	(1)	0	0	(0)	0	0	(0)	0	0	(0)	0	0	(1)	0
Rylands D	1973	0	(0)	0	1	(0)	0	0	(0)	0	0	(0)	0	1	(0)	0
St John I	61-70	334	(2)	95	48	(1)	12	6	(0)	1	30	(2)	10	418	(5)	118
Saunders D	91-92	42	(0)	11	8	(0)	2	5	(0)	2	5	(0)	9	60	(0)	24
Scales J	94-96	65	(0)	2	14	(0)	0	10	(0)	2	4	(1)	0	93	(1)	4
Seagraves M	1985	0	(0)	0	1	(0)	0	1	(0)	0	0	(0)	0	2	(0)	0
Sealey J	1964	1	(0)	1	0	(0)	0	0	(0)	0	0	(0)	0	1	(0)	1
Sheedy K	80-81	1	(2)	0	0	(0)	0	2	(0)	2	0	(0)	0	3	(2)	2
Slater B	59-61	99	(0)	0	9	(0)	0	3	(0)	0	0	(0)	0	11	(0)	0
Smith T	62-77	467	(0)	36	52	(0)	2	30	(0)	2	83	(1)	8	632	(1)	48
Souness G	77-83	246	(1)	38	24	(0)	2	45	(0)	9	35	(1)	7	350	(2)	56
Spackman N	86-88	39	(12)	0	5	(0)	0	6	(1)	0	0	(0)	0	50	(13)	0
Speedie D	1990	8	(4)	6	1	(1)	0	0	(0)	0	0	(0)	0	9	(5)	6
Staunton S	88-90	55	(10)	0	14	(2)	1	6	(2)	4	0	(0)	0	75	(14)	5
Stevenson W	62-67	188	(0)	15	24	(0)	1	0	(0)	0	25	(1)	1	237	(1)	17
Stewart P	92-93	28	(4)	1	1	(0)	0	6	(0)	0	2	(0)	2	37	(4)	3
Storton T	72-73	5	(0)	0	1	(0)	0	4	(0)	0	1	(1)	0	11	(1)	0
Strong G	64-69	150	(5)	29	23	(0)	1	4	(0)	0	16	(0)	2	193	(5)	32
Tanner N	89-92	36	(4)	1	2	(0)	0	6	(2)	0	6	(2)	0	50	(8)	1
Thomas M	91-	96	(28)	9	15	(2)	2	7	(3)	1	10	(2)	0	128	(35)	12
Thompson D	96-	1	(6)	1	0	(0)	0	0	(0)	0	0	(0)	0	1	(6)	1
Thompson M	73-75	1	(0)	0	0	(0)	0	0	(0)	0	0	(1)	0	1	(1)	0

PLAYERS' STATISTICS

Player	Seas	LEAGUE			FA CUP			L CUP			EUROPE			TOTAL		
		Ap	Sb	Gl	Ap	Sb	Gl	Ap	Sb	Gl	Ap	Sb	Gl	Ap	Sb	Gl
Thompson Peter	63-71	318	(4)	41	37	(1)	5	9	(0)	2	40	(3)	6	404	(8)	54
Thompson Phil	71-82	337	(3)	7	3	(0)	0	42	(1)	1	44	(3)	4	459	(7)	12
Thomson R	62-63	6	(0)	0	1	(0)	0	0	(0)	0	0	(0)	0	7	(0)	0
Toshack J	70-77	169	(3)	74	24	(0)	8	13	(0)	3	30	(6)	10	26	(9)	95
Venison B	86-91	103	(7)	1	16	(5)	0	14	(3)	0	0	(3)	1	133	(18)	2
Waddle A	73-76	11	(5)	1	2	(0)	0	3	(0)	0	0	(1)	0	16	(6)	1
Wall P	67-69	31	(0)	0	6	(0)	0	2	(0)	0	3	(0)	0	42	(0)	0
Wallace G	62-66	19	(1)	3	0	(0)	0	0	(0)	0	1	(0)	2	2	(1)	5
Walsh P	84-87	63	(14)	25	6	(2)	3	10	(2)	4	6	(0)	3	85	(18)	35
Walters M	91-94	58	(36)	14	6	(3)	0	10	(2)	4	7	(1)	1	81	(42)	19
Wark J	83-86	64	(6)	28	11	(2)	6	6	(4)	3	9	(0)	5	90	(12)	42
Watson A	87-88	3	(1)	0	1	(1)	0	1	(1)	0	0	(0)	0	5	(3)	0
Wheeler J	56-61	164	(0)	21	10	(0)	2	3	(0)	0	0	(0)	0	177	(0)	23
Whelan R	80-93	351	(11)	46	40	(1)	7	46	(4)	14	22	(1)	6	459	(17)	73
White D	55-61	203	(0)	0	10	(0)	1	3	(0)	0	0	(0)	0	216	(0)	1
Whitham J	70-71	15	(0)	7	0	(0)	0	1	(0)	0	0	(0)	0	16	(0)	7
Wilson D	1966	0	(1)	0	0	(0)	0	0	(0)	0	0	(0)	0	0	(1)	0
Wright M	91-	156	(2)	5	18	(0)	0	14	(2)	1	17	(0)	2	205	(4)	8
Yeats R	61-70	357	(1)	13	50	(0)	0	7	(0)	0	36	(0)	2	450	(1)	15

Dates shown indicate first years of each season. Thus 70-77 means 1970/71 to 1977/78. A single entry indicates one season only, eg 1964 refers to 1964/65.

slow-cooker
COMFORT FOOD

THE AUSTRALIAN WOMEN'S WEEKLY
TRIPLE TESTED
TEST KITCHEN

PUBLISHED IN 2017 BY BOUNTY BOOKS BASED ON MATERIALS LICENSED TO IT BY BAUER MEDIA BOOKS, AUSTRALIA.

BAUER MEDIA BOOKS ARE PUBLISHED BY
BAUER MEDIA PTY LIMITED
54 PARK ST, SYDNEY; GPO BOX 4088,
SYDNEY, NSW 2001 AUSTRALIA
PHONE +61 2 9282 8618; FAX +61 2 9126 3702
WWW.AWWCOOKBOOKS.COM.AU

PUBLISHER
JO RUNCIMAN

EDITORIAL & FOOD DIRECTOR
PAMELA CLARK

DIRECTOR OF SALES, MARKETING & RIGHTS
BRIAN CEARNES

CREATIVE DIRECTOR
HANNAH BLACKMORE

DESIGNER
MENG KOACH

SENIOR EDITOR
STEPHANIE KISTNER

JUNIOR EDITOR
AMANDA LEES

FOOD EDITORS
REBECCA MELI, ALEXANDRA ELLIOTT

OPERATIONS MANAGER
DAVID SCOTTO

PRINTED IN CHINA
BY LEO PAPER PRODUCTS LTD

PUBLISHED AND DISTRIBUTED IN THE
UNITED KINGDOM BY BOUNTY BOOKS,
A DIVISION OF OCTOPUS PUBLISHING GROUP LTD
CARMELITE HOUSE
50 VICTORIA EMBANKMENT
LONDON, EC4Y 0DZ
UNITED KINGDOM
INFO@OCTOPUS-PUBLISHING.CO.UK;
WWW.OCTOPUSBOOKS.CO.UK

INTERNATIONAL FOREIGN LANGUAGE RIGHTS
BRIAN CEARNES, BAUER MEDIA BOOKS
BCEARNES@BAUER-MEDIA.COM.AU

A CATALOGUE RECORD FOR THIS BOOK IS
AVAILABLE FROM THE BRITISH LIBRARY.

ISBN: 978-0-7537-3243-4

© BAUER MEDIA PTY LTD 2017
ABN 18 053 273 546

THE AUSTRALIAN
Women's Weekly

slow-cooker

COMFORT FOOD

Bounty
BOOKS

CONTENTS

Comfort made easy 06

COMFORT *Made* EASY

Slow cookers are available in a range of shapes and sizes and come with a variety of features. We tested the recipes in this cookbook using either a **4.5-litre (18-cup) slow cooker or a 5-litre (20-cup) slow cooker**. If you have a smaller or larger cooker you will have to **decrease or increase** the quantity of food, and almost certainly the **liquid content,** in the recipes. The first step when using your slow cooker is to **read the manufacturer's instructions** as each cooker will differ depending on its features. They will also outline appropriate safety measures, such as not leaving the appliance unattended at any time.

Some cookers heat from the base and side, while others heat just from the base; some have timers that cut off after the cooking time has expired, while others have timers that will keep the food warm by reducing the temperature until you're ready to eat.

SLOW COOKER SETTINGS

Generally, the longer meat takes to cook the more tender and more intense the flavours will be; so if you have the time, set your cooker to a low setting. However, if you're pressed for time, setting the slow cooker on high will halve the cooking time. No matter which setting you use, the food will reach simmering point. Some slow cookers have a warm setting; this is not used for cooking but rather to maintain the temperature of the food until it's time to eat. Over time you will find what works best for you and your slow cooking needs.

BEST CUTS FOR
Slow cooking

Long, slow cooking will tenderise even the toughest cut of meat. Stewing or braising cuts are the best choices. Tough cuts are usually inexpensive, but cutting the meat off the bone yourself can usually save you more money, as you're not paying for the convenience of pre-cut meat. Cutting up the meat yourself also gives you the opportunity to trim off visible fat and make the pieces a uniform size.

THE BEST CUTS OF MEAT TO USE ARE

Beef topside, oyster, blade, skirt, round, chuck, gravy beef.

Veal osso buco, shanks, shoulder.

Lamb neck chops, boneless shoulder, shanks, boneless forequarter.

Pork forequarter chops, neck, belly, shoulder.

Chicken any pieces on the bone, such as drumsticks, thighs, marylands.

Seafood is generally not suitable for slow cooking as it toughens quickly. However, there are many recipes for sauces that can be cooked in the slow cooker; add the seafood just before serving. Large octopus will cook and become tender in a slow cooker.

BROWN THE MEAT FIRST

As straightforward as most slow cooking recipes are, it is best not to just throw all your ingredients in. Browning the meat first enhances the flavour and gives the meat a beautiful rich colour. Do this in a heated, oiled, large frying pan, adding the meat in batches, and turning it so that it browns evenly. Make sure there is a sufficient amount of oil in the pan so that the meat caramelises rather than scorches. Be sure to have the pan heated before adding the meat – it's also important to maintain the heat during the browning process; if the pan is not hot enough the meat will stew rather than brown. Some slow cookers have a sauté mode, which can be used to brown meat – do this in batches as you would in a frying pan.

THICKENING THE SAUCE

Coating the meat in flour before browning will result in a sauce that is thick enough to make a light coating gravy. If the recipe does not suggest coating the meat, then it is a good idea to thicken the sauce using plain flour or cornflour.

Blending the flour or cornflour with butter or a cold liquid such as water or some of the cooled juices from the cooker will help it combine with the cooking juices when stirred into the pan at the end of the cooking time. Put the lid back on and leave the sauce to thicken while the slow cooker is on the highest setting – this will take around 10-20 minutes.

Another trick to thicken the sauce is to blend some of the cooked vegetables until smooth, and then stir them into the cooking juices.

TIPS FOR FREEZING

Throughout this book we've suggested whether or not recipes are suitable to freeze. We've chosen to say 'not suitable' when coconut milk or large quantities of mushrooms and potatoes are used, and often when large pieces of meat are an ingredient. However, if you don't mind the food looking a bit sad after it's thawed, almost anything will tolerate freezing.

Slow-cooked meals will freeze for up to three months. There is usually a large quantity of liquid, so transfer the meat and vegetables to appropriate-sized freezer-friendly containers, then pour in enough of the liquid to cover the meat etc. Leave a 2.5cm (1-inch) space between the food and the lid to allow for expansion then seal the container. Label and date the container before placing in the freezer.

A NOTE ON DRIED BEANS

Some dried beans need to be cooked before adding to a slow cooker because of a certain chemical they contain. Kidney-shaped beans of all colours and sizes are related to each other and MUST be washed, drained and boiled in fresh water until tender. Add the cooked beans to the slow-cooked dish, just like canned beans.

Dried, unsoaked chickpeas and soya beans are fine to use in the slow cooker, just rinse them well first; there is no need for you to soak them overnight before cooking.

BEEF

BEEF KORMA

PREP + COOK TIME 8 HOURS 20 MINUTES   SERVES 4

¼ cup (35g) plain (all-purpose) flour

2 tablespoons vegetable oil

800g (1½ pounds) diced beef

3 teaspoons ground coriander

3 teaspoons ground cumin

½ teaspoon ground turmeric

1 teaspoon paprika

¼ teaspoon ground cinnamon

4 cardamom pods, bruised

1 fresh long green chilli, chopped finely

2 medium brown onions (300g), chopped finely

3 cloves garlic, crushed

1 teaspoon poppy seeds

1 fresh long green chilli, extra, sliced thinly

1 Place flour in a large bowl; season.

2 Heat oil in a 4.5-litre (18-cup) slow cooker on sear (HIGH) setting. Coat beef in flour; shake off excess. Cook beef, stirring, for 10 minutes, or until browned.

3 Add spices, chilli, onion and garlic to cooker; cook, stirring, for 5 minutes or until softened and fragrant.

4 Cook, covered, on low, for 8 hours.

5 Serve korma sprinkled with poppy seeds and extra chilli.

SERVING SUGGESTIONS

Accompany with steamed rice sprinkled with extra poppy seeds, pappadums, flatbread or dhal, and yoghurt topped with mango chutney.

• Suitable to freeze at the end of step 4.

TEX-MEX BEEF & SWEET POTATO STEW

PREP + COOK TIME 8 HOURS 30 MINUTES **SERVES** 4

800g (1½ pounds) beef chuck steak, cut into 5cm (2-inch) pieces

1 medium orange sweet potato (400g), unpeeled, cut into 5cm (2-inch) pieces

1 medium brown onion (150g), cut into wedges

400g (12½ ounces) canned diced tomatoes

2 teaspoons ground cumin

1 teaspoon dried oregano

2 teaspoons Mexican chilli powder

1 fresh long green chilli, chopped finely

3 cloves garlic, crushed

⅔ cup (130g) drained chargrilled capsicum (bell peppers), chopped coarsely

½ cup (125ml) beef stock

⅔ cup coarsely chopped fresh coriander (cilantro)

1 Place beef, sweet potato, onion, tomatoes, cumin, oregano, chilli powder, chilli, garlic, capsicum and stock in a 4.5-litre (18-cup) slow cooker. Cook, covered, on low, for 8 hours. Season to taste.

2 Stir in half the coriander. Serve topped with remaining coriander and a dollop of sour cream, if you like.

SERVING SUGGESTION

Accompany with grilled corn on the cob, sliced pickled jalapeños, sour cream and lime wedges.

• Suitable to freeze at the end of step 1.

BEEF RENDANG

PREP + COOK TIME 8 HOURS 30 MINUTES SERVES 4

½ cup (40g) desiccated coconut

10cm (4-inch) stick fresh lemon grass (20g), chopped finely

1 tablespoon finely grated fresh ginger

4 cloves garlic, quartered

3 fresh long red chillies, chopped coarsely

1 medium brown onion (150g), chopped coarsely

1½ tablespoons olive oil

800g (1½ pounds) beef chuck steak, cut into 5cm (2-inch) pieces

2 teaspoons ground coriander

1 tablespoon grated palm sugar

1 tablespoon tamarind puree

1 cinnamon stick

1 cup (250ml) coconut milk

2 tablespoons fresh micro herbs, to serve

1 green onion (scallion), sliced thinly, to serve

1 Process coconut, lemon grass, ginger, garlic, chilli, brown onion and oil until smooth.

2 Heat a 4.5-litre (18-cup) slow cooker on sear (HIGH) setting; cook paste, stirring, for 5 minutes or until well toasted and fragrant. Add beef; cook, stirring, for 8 minutes or until browned.

3 Add remaining ingredients to cooker; stir to combine. Cook, covered, on low, for 8 hours. Season.

4 Serve rendang topped with micro herbs and green onion.

SERVING SUGGESTION

Accompany with flatbread or steamed rice mixed with red lentils.

• Suitable to freeze at the end of step 3.

BRAISED BEEF

PREP + COOK TIME 8 HOURS 45 MINUTES SERVES 4

2 tablespoons plain (all-purpose) flour

2 tablespoons olive oil

2 x 250g (8-ounce) beef cheeks, halved

3 cloves garlic, crushed

1 medium brown onion (150g), chopped finely

1 stalk celery (150g), trimmed, chopped finely

1 medium carrot (120g), chopped finely

3 sprigs fresh thyme

2 fresh bay leaves

1 teaspoon cracked black pepper

1 cup (250ml) dry red wine

¼ cup (70g) tomato paste

2 tablespoons fresh micro herbs

1 Place flour in a large bowl; season.

2 Heat oil in a 4.5-litre (18-cup) slow cooker on sear (HIGH) setting. Coat beef in flour; shake off excess. Cook beef, for 5 minutes each side, or until well browned. Remove from cooker.

3 Add garlic, onion, celery, carrot, thyme, bay leaves and pepper to cooker; cook, stirring, for 5 minutes or until vegetables soften. Add wine and paste; stir to combine. Return beef to cooker.

4 Cook, covered, on low, for 8 hours. Discard thyme and bay leaves; season to taste.

5 Serve braised beef sprinkled with micro herbs.

SERVING SUGGESTION

Accompany with orange sweet potato and pan-fried mushrooms.

• Suitable to freeze at the end of step 4.

OSSO BUCO WITH LEMON & FENNEL SALAD

PREP + COOK TIME 9 HOURS   SERVES 6

¼ cup (35g) plain (all-purpose) flour

2 teaspoons fennel seeds

2 tablespoons olive oil

12 small pieces beef osso buco (1.8kg)

1 medium brown onion (150g), chopped coarsely

1 baby fennel bulb (130g), trimmed, chopped coarsely

2 rindless bacon slices (130g), chopped coarsely

3 cloves garlic, crushed

2 dried bay leaves

pinch saffron threads

½ cup (125ml) dry white wine

1½ cups (375ml) beef stock

1 sprig fresh rosemary

LEMON & FENNEL SALAD

1 baby fennel bulb (130g)

⅓ cup loosely packed fresh flat-leaf parsley leaves

1 tablespoon finely sliced lemon rind (see tips)

2 teaspoons lemon juice

2 teaspoons olive oil

1 Combine flour and fennel seeds in a large bowl; season.

2 Heat oil in a 4.5-litre (18-cup) slow cooker on sear (HIGH) setting. Coat beef in flour mixture; shake off excess (reserve excess flour). Cook beef, in batches, for 5 minutes each side or until well browned. Remove from cooker.

3 Add onion, fennel, bacon, garlic, bay leaves and saffron to cooker; cook, stirring, for 5 minutes or until vegetables soften. Sprinkle with reserved excess flour; cook, stirring, for 3 minutes. Gradually stir in wine and stock; bring to the boil. Add rosemary.

4 Return beef to cooker, packing tightly in cooker. Cook, covered, on low, for 8 hours. Discard bay leaves and rosemary; season to taste.

5 Just before serving, make lemon and fennel salad.

6 Serve osso buco topped with salad.

LEMON & FENNEL SALAD Trim fennel, reserve fronds. Using a mandoline or V-slicer, shave fennel finely. Combine fennel with reserved fronds, rind, parsley juice and oil in a medium bowl; season to taste.

TIPS

Ask the butcher for small pieces (about 3cm/1¼ inches) of either beef or veal shin (osso buco). Use a zesting tool to make long thin strips of lemon rind. If you don't have one you can thinly peel the rind from the lemon, avoiding any white pith, then finely slice the rind into long thin strips.

SERVING SUGGESTIONS

Accompany with creamy polenta, mashed potato or crusty bread to mop up the juices.

• Suitable to freeze at the end of step 4.

CARNE GUISADA WITH POLENTA

PREP + COOK TIME 8 HOURS 15 MINUTES **SERVES** 4

¼ cup (35g) plain (all-purpose) flour

2 teaspoons ground cumin

2 teaspoons smoked paprika

2 teaspoons dried oregano

2 tablespoons olive oil

1.2kg (2½ pounds) beef chuck steak, trimmed,
cut into 3cm (1¼-inch) pieces

2 cured chorizo sausages (340g), sliced thinly

1 large red onion (300g), sliced thinly

1 small red capsicum (bell pepper) (150g),
chopped coarsely

1 small yellow capsicum (bell pepper) (150g),
chopped coarsely

1 small green capsicum (bell pepper) (150g),
chopped coarsely

3 cloves garlic, crushed

¾ cup (180ml) dry red wine

¾ cup (180ml) beef stock

400g (12½ ounces) canned diced tomatoes

1 tablespoon sriracha chilli sauce

⅓ cup loosely packed fresh coriander (cilantro) leaves

POLENTA DUMPLINGS

¾ cup (110g) self-raising flour

½ cup (85g) polenta (cornmeal)

50g (1½ ounces) cold butter, chopped

½ cup (50g) pizza cheese

2 tablespoons finely chopped fresh coriander (cilantro)

1 egg, beaten lightly

2 tablespoons milk, approximately

1 Combine flour, cumin, paprika and oregano in a large bowl; season.

2 Heat oil in a 4.5-litre (18-cup) slow cooker on sear (HIGH) setting. Coat beef in flour mixture; shake off excess (reserve excess flour). Cook beef, in batches, turning, for 5 minutes, or until well browned. Remove from cooker.

3 Cook chorizo in cooker, stirring, for 5 minutes or until browned. Remove from cooker.

4 Reduce cooker to sauté (MEDIUM) setting. Cook onion, capsicums and garlic, stirring, for 5 minutes or until vegetables soften. Sprinkle with reserved excess flour; cook, stirring, for 3 minutes. Gradually stir in wine, then stock, tomatoes and chilli sauce; bring to the boil.

5 Return beef and chorizo to cooker. Cook, covered, on low, for 7 hours. Season to taste.

6 Make polenta dumpling mixture just before serving.

7 Drop level tablespoons of dumpling mixture, about 2cm (¾-inch) apart, on top of beef mixture. Cook, covered, on high, for 30 minutes or until dumplings are firm to touch and cooked through.

8 Serve beef stew topped with dumplings and sprinkled with coriander.

POLENTA DUMPLINGS Place flour and polenta in a medium bowl; using your fingertips, rub in butter. Add cheese and coriander; stir to combine. Stir in egg and enough of the milk to make a soft, sticky dough.

SERVING SUGGESTION

Accompany with cooked black beans and sliced avocado.

• Not Suitable to freeze.

FLEMISH BEEF STEW (CARBONNADE)

PREP + COOK TIME 8 HOURS 30 MINUTES **SERVES** 4

¼ cup (35g) plain (all-purpose) flour

¼ cup (60ml) olive oil

1.2kg (2½ pounds) gravy beef, trimmed, cut into 3cm (1¼-inch) pieces

4 rindless bacon slices (260g), chopped coarsely

1 large brown onion (200g), sliced thinly

3 cloves garlic, crushed

1 teaspoon caraway seeds

1½ cups (375ml) Belgian-style beer

1 cup (250ml) beef stock

¼ cup (70g) tomato paste

2 tablespoons brown sugar

2 tablespoons apple cider vinegar

2 sprigs fresh thyme

2 sprigs fresh tarragon

1 tablespoon fresh thyme leaves, extra

1 tablespoon small tarragon leaves, extra

1 Place flour in a large bowl; season.

2 Heat 2 tablespoons of the oil in a 4.5-litre (18-cup) slow cooker on sear (HIGH) setting. Coat beef in flour; shake off excess (reserve excess flour). Cook beef, in batches, turning, for 5 minutes, or until well browned. Remove from cooker.

3 Reduce cooker to sauté (MEDIUM) setting. Heat remaining oil in cooker; cook bacon, stirring, for 5 minutes until browned. Add onion, garlic and caraway seeds; cook, stirring, for 5 minutes or until onion softens. Sprinkle with reserved excess flour; cook, stirring, for 3 minutes. Gradually stir in beer, then stock, paste, sugar and vinegar; bring to the boil. Add thyme and tarragon.

4 Return beef to cooker. Cook, covered, on low, for 8 hours. Discard thyme and tarragon; season to taste.

5 Serve beef stew topped with extra thyme and tarragon.

TIP

This classic Belgian dish is known for its rich, sweet sour flavour, relying heavily on the deep, dark Belgian-style beer.

SERVING SUGGESTIONS

Accompany with creamy mashed potato or grilled crusty bread to mop up the juices.

• Suitable to freeze at the end of step 4.

BEEF WITH BOURBON & COKE

PREP + COOK TIME 9 HOURS SERVES 4

⅓ cup (50g) plain (all-purpose) flour

2 tablespoons olive oil

4 beef cheeks (2kg)

1 medium brown onion (150g), sliced thinly

4 cloves garlic, crushed

½ cup (125ml) bourbon

½ cup (125ml) beef stock

1 cup (250ml) coca cola

⅓ cup (95g) tomato paste

1 tablespoon honey or pure maple syrup

4 sprigs fresh thyme

1 tablespoon fresh thyme leaves, extra

CELERIAC MASH

1 celeriac (celery root) (750g), trimmed, chopped coarsely

2 medium potatoes (300g), chopped coarsely

50g (1½ ounces) butter

½ cup (125ml) pouring cream, warmed

1 Place flour in a large bowl; season.

2 Heat half the oil in a 4.5-litre (18-cup) slow cooker on sear (HIGH) setting. Coat beef in flour; shake off excess (reserve excess flour). Cook beef, in batches, for 5 minutes each side, or until well browned. Remove from cooker.

3 Reduce cooker to sauté (MEDIUM) setting. Heat remaining oil in cooker; cook onion, and garlic, stirring, for 5 minutes or until onion softens. Sprinkle with reserved excess flour; cook, stirring, for 3 minutes. Gradually stir in bourbon, then stock, cola, paste, honey and thyme; bring to the boil.

4 Return beef to cooker. Cook, covered, on low, for 8 hours. Discard thyme; season to taste.

5 Just before serving, make celeriac mash.

6 Serve celeriac mash topped with beef cheeks and sauce; sprinkle with extra thyme.

CELERIAC MASH Boil, steam or microwave celeriac and potato until tender; drain. Mash celeriac and potato with butter and cream in a medium bowl until smooth; season to taste.

SERVING SUGGESTIONS

Accompany with steamed trimmed baby carrots and green beans or halved sugar snap peas.

• Suitable to freeze at the end of step 4.

JAMAICAN OXTAIL WITH BLACK-EYED BEANS

PREP + COOK TIME 8 HOURS 45 MINUTES **SERVES** 6

1 tablespoon olive oil

1.6kg (3¼ pounds) beef oxtail

1 large brown onion (200g), chopped coarsely

4 cloves garlic, crushed

3 stalks celery (450g), trimmed, chopped coarsely

2 medium carrots (240g), chopped coarsely

1 tablespoon finely grated fresh ginger

2 teaspoons dried chilli flakes

2 teaspoons ground allspice

400g (12½ ounces) canned black-eyed beans

400g (12½ ounces) canned diced tomatoes

6 sprigs fresh thyme

2 tablespoons worcestershire sauce

¾ cup (180ml) coconut water

2 tablespoons finely shredded fresh mint leaves

⅓ cup (15g) toasted flaked coconut

1 Heat oil in a 4.5-litre (18-cup) slow cooker on sear (HIGH) setting; cook oxtail, in batches, turning, for 15 minutes, or until well browned. Remove from cooker.

2 Carefully drain excess fat from cooker, leaving about 2 teaspoons of fat in cooker. Heat cooker on sauté (MEDIUM) setting; cook onion, garlic, celery, carrot and ginger, stirring, for 5 minutes or until vegetables soften. Add chilli and allspice; cook, stirring, for 2 minutes or until fragrant. Return oxtail to cooker with beans, tomatoes, thyme, sauce and coconut water; bring to the boil.

3 Cook, covered, on low, for 8 hours or until oxtail is very tender.

4 Skim fat from surface of oxtail stew. Discard thyme; season to taste.

5 Serve oxtail stew topped with mint and coconut.

TIP

Be careful of the bones when eating this dish; the meat will be so tender that it will be falling off them.

SERVING SUGGESTIONS

Accompany with steamed or roasted sweet potato, rice or couscous, and with lime wedges.

• Suitable to freeze at the end of step 4.

MASSAMAN BEEF CURRY

PREP + COOK TIME 8 HOURS 45 MINUTES   SERVES 6

2 tablespoons peanut oil

2 large brown onions (400g), cut into thin wedges

1kg (2 pounds) gravy beef, chopped coarsely

⅔ cup (200g) massaman curry paste

1 cup (250ml) coconut milk

1½ cups (375ml) chicken stock

2 cinnamon sticks

2 dried bay leaves

3 medium potatoes (600g), peeled, chopped coarsely

½ cup (70g) roasted unsalted peanuts

2 tablespoons brown sugar

1 tablespoon fish sauce

⅓ cup loosely packed fresh coriander (cilantro) leaves

2 tablespoons fried shallots

2 tablespoons roasted unsalted peanuts, extra

1 Heat half the oil in a 4.5-litre (18-cup) slow cooker on sauté (MEDIUM) setting; cook onion, stirring, for 10 minutes or until browned lightly. Remove onion from cooker.

2 Heat remaining oil in cooker on sear (HIGH) setting; cook beef, in batches, turning, for 5 minutes, or until browned. Add paste; cook, stirring, for 1 minute or until fragrant.

3 Return onion to cooker with coconut milk, stock, cinnamon, bay leaves, potato and peanuts. Cook, covered, on low, for 8 hours.

4 Discard cinnamon sticks. Stir in sugar and sauce.

5 Serve curry topped with coriander, fried shallots and extra peanuts.

TIP
Chuck steak is also suitable for this recipe, if you prefer.

SERVING SUGGESTION
Accompany with steamed jasmine rice, roti bread and lime wedges.

• Not suitable to freeze.

LAMB&GOAT

LAMB SHANKS WITH TOMATO, CHILLI & FETTA

PREP + COOK TIME 8 HOURS 45 MINUTES   SERVES 4

¼ cup (35g) plain (all-purpose) flour

2 tablespoons olive oil

4 french-trimmed lamb shanks (800g)

1 medium brown onion (150g), sliced thinly

2 small fennel bulbs (400g), sliced thinly, fronds reserved

1 medium carrot (120g), chopped finely

2 cloves garlic, crushed

1 fresh long red chilli, sliced thinly

½ cup (125ml) dry white wine

410g (13 ounces) canned tomato puree

75g (2½ ounces) fetta, crumbled

¼ cup finely chopped fresh-flat leaf parsley

1   Place flour in a large bowl; season.

2   Heat half the oil in a 4.5-litre (18-cup) slow cooker on sear (HIGH) setting. Coat lamb in flour; shake off excess. Cook lamb, turning, in batches, for 15 minutes, or until well browned. Remove from cooker.

3   Heat remaining oil in cooker on sauté (MEDIUM) setting; cook onion, fennel, carrot, garlic and half the chilli, stirring, for 5 minutes or until vegetables soften.

4   Add wine and tomato puree; stir to combine. Return lamb to slow cooker. Cook, covered, on low, for 8 hours. Season to taste.

5   Serve lamb shanks sprinkled with fetta, parsley, remaining chilli and reserved fronds.

SERVING SUGGESTIONS

Accompany with mashed potato, cooked pasta or sautéed cavolo nero.

• **Suitable to freeze at the end of step 4.**

MOROCCAN GOAT STEW

PREP + COOK TIME 9 HOURS SERVES 4

800g (1½ pounds) boneless
  goat shoulder, cut into
  5cm (2-inch) pieces

1 medium brown onion (150g),
  chopped coarsely

3 cloves garlic, crushed

1 tablespoon finely grated
  fresh ginger

¼ teaspoon saffron threads

¼ teaspoon cayenne pepper

2 teaspoons ground coriander

1 cinnamon stick

½ cup (125ml) chicken stock

400g (12½ ounces) canned
  chickpeas (garbanzo beans),
  drained, rinsed

⅔ cup (100g) dried apricots

1 cup (150g) green olives

1 green onion (scallion),
  sliced thinly (see tip)

2 tablespoons pine nuts, toasted

1 Place goat, brown onion, garlic, ginger, spices, stock and chickpeas in a 4.5-litre (18-cup) slow cooker. Cook, covered, on low, for 8 hours.

2 Stir in apricots and olives. Cook, covered, on high, for 15 minutes or until apricots soften. Discard cinnamon; season to taste.

3 Serve stew topped with green onion and pine nuts.

TIP

To make green onions curl, place the sliced onions in a small bowl of iced water for 30 minutes; drain.

SERVING SUGGESTIONS

Accompany with pearl couscous, naan or steamed baby potatoes.

• **Suitable to freeze at the end of step 1.**

LAMB & FENNEL RAGÙ

PREP + COOK TIME 8 HOURS 45 MINUTES **SERVES** 6

¼ cup (35g) plain (all-purpose) flour

2 tablespoons olive oil

1kg (2 pounds) boneless lamb shoulder, cut into 2.5cm (1-inch) pieces

1 medium brown onion (150g), chopped finely

3 cloves garlic, crushed

6 anchovy fillets, chopped finely

½ teaspoon dried chilli flakes

1 teaspoon fennel seeds, crushed lightly

400g (12½ ounces) canned diced tomatoes

⅔ cup (160ml) dry red wine

½ cup (40g) grated parmesan

½ cup loosely packed fresh basil leaves

1 Place flour in a large bowl; season.

2 Heat oil in a 4.5-litre (18-cup) slow cooker on sear (HIGH) setting. Coat lamb in flour; shake off excess. Cook lamb, stirring, for 15 minutes, or until well browned.

3 Add onion, garlic, anchovy, chilli, fennel seeds, tomatoes and wine; bring to the boil. Cook, covered, on low, for 8 hours. Season to taste.

4 Serve ragù sprinkled with parmesan and basil leaves.

SERVING SUGGESTION

Accompany with cooked pappardelle, mashed potato or crusty bread.

• Suitable to freeze at the end of step 4.

LAMB MADRAS

PREP + COOK TIME 8 HOURS 30 MINUTES **SERVES** 4

1 tablespoon olive oil

800g (1½ pounds) diced lamb

2 medium brown onions (300g),
sliced thinly

3 cloves garlic, sliced thinly

1 tablespoon finely grated
fresh ginger

¼ teaspoon ground cinnamon

⅓ cup (100g) madras curry paste

½ cup (125ml) beef stock

2 tablespoons flaked almonds,
toasted

⅓ cup loosely packed fresh
coriander (cilantro) leaves

1 Heat oil in a 4.5-litre (18-cup) slow
cooker on sear (HIGH) setting; cook
lamb, stirring, for 15 minutes, or until
well browned. Add onion, garlic,
ginger and cinnamon. Cook, stirring
for 1 minute or until fragrant.

2 Add curry paste and stock; stir to
combine. Cook, covered, on low, for
8 hours. Season to taste.

3 Serve sprinkled with almonds and
coriander leaves.

SERVING SUGGESTION

Accompany with steamed rice and
pappadums.

• Suitable to freeze at the end of step 2.

SPICY BARBECUE GOAT SLIDERS WITH SLAW

PREP + COOK TIME 10 HOURS 30 MINUTES **MAKES** 10

1 large brown onion (200g), sliced thinly

1.4kg (2¾ pound) goat shoulder

1 teaspoon cayenne pepper

2 sprigs fresh rosemary

½ cup (140g) smokey barbecue sauce

1 tablespoon honey

2 cloves garlic, crushed

1 tablespoon wholegrain mustard

10 brioche buns (500g), split

RED APPLE SLAW

1 small apple (130g)

1 medium carrot (120g)

2 green onions (scallions)

¼ small red cabbage (300g), shredded finely

2 tablespoons olive oil

2 tablespoons lemon juice

1 teaspoon wholegrain mustard

1 Spread onion over the base of a 4.5-litre (18-cup) slow cooker. Place goat on top of onion; sprinkle cayenne pepper all over goat, season with salt. Top with rosemary.

2 Combine sauce, honey, garlic and mustard in a small jug; pour over goat. Cook, covered, on low, for 10 hours or until meat is falling off the bone.

3 Meanwhile, make red apple slaw.

4 Transfer goat shoulder to a large bowl; shred meat using two forks. Discard bones.

5 Return shredded goat meat to sauce mixture in cooker; cook, covered, on high until heated through.

6 Divide goat and slaw between buns to serve.

RED APPLE SLAW Using a julienne peeler or a mandoline or V-slicer with a julienne attachment, cut unpeeled apple and carrot into matchsticks. Slice onion thinly. Combine apple, carrot and onion with remaining ingredients in a medium bowl; season to taste. Refrigerate slaw until ready to assemble buns.

SERVING SUGGESTION

Accompany with potato crisps and dill pickles.

• Goat mixture is suitable to freeze at the end of step 5.

LAMB KLEFTIKO WITH POTATOES

PREP + COOK TIME 10 HOURS SERVES 6

2 tablespoons olive oil

1.4kg (2¾-pound) lamb shoulder

1kg (2 pounds) red and white-skinned baby potatoes

1 large brown onion (200g), sliced thinly

2 dried bay leaves

1 cinnamon stick

⅓ cup (80ml) dry white wine

⅓ cup (80ml) chicken stock

1 tablespoon finely grated lemon rind

2 tablespoons lemon juice

3 cloves garlic, crushed

1 tablespoon rigani (see tips) or dried oregano

⅓ cup loosely packed fresh oregano leaves

1 Heat half the oil in a large frying pan over medium-high heat; cook lamb, turning, for 20 minutes or until well browned.

2 Meanwhile, heat remaining oil in a 4.5-litre (18-cup) slow cooker on sauté (MEDIUM) setting; cook potatoes, onion, bay leaves and cinnamon, stirring, for 10 minutes or until browned.

3 Place lamb on top of potatoes in cooker. Combine wine, stock, rind, juice, garlic and rigani in a small jug; pour over lamb. Cook, covered, on low, for 9 hours or until meat is falling off the bone.

4 Serve lamb with potatoes and a little of the cooking liquid. Sprinkle with fresh oregano.

TIPS

Depending on the size and shape of your cooker, you may be able to brown the lamb in the cooker in step 1, if you prefer. Rigani is Greek-style dried oregano; it is available from specialty food stores and delicatessens. You can use dried oregano instead.

SERVING SUGGESTIONS

Accompany with a greek salad or steamed continental beans and lemon halves.

• **Not suitable to freeze.**

GOAT MAVROU

PREP + COOK TIME 8 HOURS 30 MINUTES   SERVES 4

2 tablespoons olive oil

1.2kg (2½ pounds) boneless diced goat

1 large brown onion (200g), chopped coarsely

3 cloves garlic, crushed

2 medium carrots (240g), chopped coarsely

2 teaspoons smoked paparika

2 teaspoons ground cinnamon

2 teaspoons ground cumin

2 teaspoons ground ginger

1 teaspoon ground cardamom

1 teaspoon ground turmeric

1 teaspoon dried chilli flakes

400g (12½ ounces) canned diced tomatoes

1 cup (250ml) beef stock

⅓ cup loosely packed fresh coriander (cilantro) sprigs

1 Heat half the oil in a 4.5-litre (18-cup) slow cooker on sear (HIGH) setting; cook goat, in batches, turning, for 10 minutes, or until well browned. Remove from cooker.

2 Heat remaining oil in cooker on sauté (MEDIUM) setting; cook onion, garlic and carrot, stirring, for 5 minutes or until vegetables soften. Add spices and chilli; cook, stirring, for 2 minutes or until fragrant. Return goat to cooker with tomatoes and stock; bring to the boil.

3 Cook, covered, on low, for 8 hours. Season to taste.

4 Serve goat topped with coriander.

TIP

You can use diced lamb shoulder or leg instead of the goat; reduce cooking time to about 8 hours.

SERVING SUGGESTIONS

Accompany with steamed saffron rice or couscous, yoghurt and lemon wedges.

• Suitable to freeze at the end of step 3.

LAMB WITH KALE & POMEGRANATE

PREP + COOK TIME 8 HOURS 30 MINUTES   **SERVES** 4

1.2kg (2½ pounds) boneless lamb shoulder, cut into 10cm (4-inch) chunks

2 teaspoons ground cumin

2 teaspoons ground allspice

2 teaspoons fennel seeds

1 teaspoon smoked paprika

1 teaspoon dried chilli flakes

2 tablespoons olive oil

1 medium pomegranate (320g)

1 large brown onion (200g), sliced thickly

3 cloves garlic, crushed

2 teaspoons finely grated fresh ginger

1 cup (250ml) beef stock

2 tablespoons pure maple syrup

1 tablespoon pomegranate molasses

4 medium kale leaves (140g), trimmed, shredded coarsely

¼ cup (20g) flaked almonds, toasted

1 Combine lamb with spices and chilli in a large bowl; season. Heat half the oil in a 4.5-litre (18-cup) slow cooker on sear (HIGH) setting; cook lamb, in batches, turning, for 10 minutes, or until well browned. Remove from cooker.

2 Meanwhile, cut pomegranate in half. Hold pomegranate, cut-side down over a sieve into a medium bowl and hit the back of the pomegranate with a wooden spoon to release the juice and seeds. Reserve ¼ cup (60ml) juice and ⅓ cup seeds separately. Refrigerate seeds until required.

3 Heat remaining oil in cooker on sauté (MEDIUM) setting; cook onion, garlic and ginger, stirring, for 5 minutes or until onion softens. Stir in stock, maple syrup, molasses and reserved pomegranate juice. Return lamb to cooker; bring to the boil.

4 Cook, covered, on low, for 8 hours.

5 Add kale to cooker; cook, covered, on high for 5 minutes or until kale is wilted. Season to taste.

6 Serve lamb topped with reserved pomegranate seeds and almonds.

TIPS

Wear gloves in step 2 when preparing the pomegranate or it will stain your hands. You can use a teaspoon to scrape the seeds out of the cut pomegranate halves if you prefer.

SERVING SUGGESTIONS

Accompany with steamed pearl couscous, quinoa or rice, and lemon wedges.

• Suitable to freeze at the end of step 4.

RUSTIC ITALIAN LAMB SHANKS WITH BARLEY

PREP + COOK TIME 8 HOURS 30 MINUTES **SERVES** 4

½ cup (100g) pearl barley

2 tablespoons olive oil

4 french-trimmed lamb shanks (800g)

1 large brown onion (200g), sliced thinly

2 stalks celery (300g), chopped coarsely

2 medium carrots (240g), sliced thickly

1 large red capsicum (bell pepper) (350g), chopped coarsely

4 cloves garlic, crushed

2 teaspoons fennel seeds

1 teaspoon smoked paprika

2 dried bay leaves

⅓ cup (95g) tomato paste

400g (12½ ounces) canned diced tomatoes

3 cups (750ml) beef stock

2 tablespoons coarsely chopped fresh flat-leaf parsley leaves

⅓ cup (25g) grated parmesan

1 Rinse barley in a sieve under cold running water; drain well.

2 Heat half the oil in a 4.5-litre (18-cup) slow cooker on sear (HIGH) setting; cook lamb, in batches, turning, for 15 minutes, or until well browned. Remove from cooker.

3 Heat remaining oil in cooker on sauté (MEDIUM) setting; cook onion, celery, carrot and capsicum, stirring, for 5 minutes or until vegetables soften. Add garlic, fennel seeds, paprika and bay leaves; cook, stirring, for 2 minutes or until fragrant. Add paste; cook, stirring, for 2 minutes. Stir in tomatoes, stock and barley. Return lamb to cooker; bring to the boil.

4 Cook, covered, on low, for 8 hours. Discard bay leaves; season to taste.

5 Serve lamb mixture topped with parsley and parmesan.

SERVING SUGGESTION

Accompany with a bitter leaf salad.

• Not suitable to freeze.

LAMB & GOAT   53

POULTRY

WHITE CHILLI CHICKEN STEW

PREP + COOK TIME 9 HOURS SERVES 4

1 tablespoon olive oil

1 medium brown onion (150g), chopped finely

1 stalk celery (150g), trimmed, chopped finely

1 large red capsicum (bell pepper) (350g), chopped finely

2 teaspoons Mexican chilli powder

1 teaspoon ground coriander

1 teaspoon ground cumin

1 fresh long green chilli, chopped finely

400g (12½ ounces) canned black beans, drained, rinsed

1.2kg (2½-pound) whole chicken

2 cups (500ml) water

1½ tablespoons lime juice

⅓ cup coarsely chopped fresh coriander (cilantro)

⅓ cup loosely packed fresh coriander sprigs

1 Heat oil in a 4.5-litre (18-cup) slow cooker on sear (HIGH) setting; cook onion, celery and capsicum, stirring, for 3 minutes or until vegetables soften. Add chilli powder, coriander, cumin and fresh chilli; cook, stirring, for 1 minute or until fragrant. Add black beans, chicken and the water. Cook, covered, on low, for 8 hours.

2 Carefully remove chicken from cooker; shred meat coarsely using two forks. Discard skin and bones.

3 Return chicken to cooker with juice; stir to combine. Cook, covered, on high, for 15 minutes or until heated through. Stir in chopped coriander; season to taste.

4 Serve chilli chicken topped with coriander sprigs.

SERVING SUGGESTION

Accompany with steamed rice, grilled tortillas and lime wedges.

• **Not suitable to freeze.**

PHO GA

PREP + COOK TIME 9 HOURS 15 MINUTES SERVES 4

1.2kg (2½-pound) whole chicken

1 large brown onion (200g), chopped coarsely

5cm (2-inch) piece fresh ginger, sliced thinly

2 litres (8 cups) water

3 star anise

3 green onions (scallions), cut into 5cm (2-inch) lengths

2 cinnamon sticks

10cm (4-inch) stick fresh lemon grass, bruised

1 tablespoon coriander seeds

¼ cup (60ml) fish sauce

¼ (60ml) lime juice

2 tablespoons brown sugar

200g (6½ ounces) rice stick noodles

2 cups (160g) bean sprouts

½ cup loosely packed small fresh mint leaves

½ cup loosely packed small fresh coriander (cilantro) leaves

½ cup loosely packed fresh thai basil leaves

1 fresh long red chilli, seeded, sliced thinly lengthways

1 green onion (scallion), extra, sliced thinly

1 Place chicken, brown onion, ginger, the water, star anise, green onion, cinnamon, lemon grass and coriander seeds in a 4.5-litre (18-cup) slow cooker. Cook, covered, on low, for 8 hours.

2 Carefully remove chicken from cooker; shred meat coarsely using two forks. Discard skin and bones.

3 Add sauce, juice and sugar to stock mixture in cooker; stir to combine. Strain cooking liquid through a muslin-lined sieve into a large heatproof bowl; discard solids.

4 Place noodles in a medium heatproof bowl, cover with boiling water; stand for 15 minutes or until tender, drain.

5 Divide noodles and shredded chicken into serving bowls. Ladle hot soup over noodles; serve topped with sprouts, herbs, chilli and extra green onion.

• **Not suitable to freeze.**

TURKEY WITH ALMOND PICADA

PREP + COOK TIME 8 HOURS 30 MINUTES SERVES 4

1 cup firmly packed fresh
flat-leaf parsley leaves

2 cloves garlic, quartered

½ cup (80g) smoked almonds

2 teaspoons finely grated
lemon rind

1 tablespoon lemon juice

1kg (2-pound) turkey breast
roast, skin on

1 tablespoon olive oil

1 large brown onion (200g),
sliced thickly

¾ cup (180ml) dry white wine

¾ cup (180ml) chicken stock

400g (12½ ounces) brussels
sprouts, trimmed

400g (12½ ounces) baby carrots,
trimmed

30g (1 ounce) butter, chopped

1 Process parsley, garlic, almonds and rind until finely chopped. Transfer ¼ cup of mixture to a small bowl; refrigerate until required. Add juice to remaining mixture in processor; process until combined. Season to taste.

2 Place turkey, skin-side down, on a chopping board. Starting from one long edge, slice through the centre, horizontally, not quite through to other side, to open up flat. Spread with almond picada mixture. Tightly roll turkey up to secure filling. Using kitchen string, tie into a neat roll at 2.5cm (1-inch) intervals.

3 Heat oil in a 4.5-litre (18-cup) slow cooker on sear (HIGH) setting; cook turkey, turning occasionally, for 20 minutes, or until well browned all over. Remove from cooker.

4 Place onion in base of cooker; top with turkey. Pour combined wine and stock over turkey. Cook, covered, on low, for 7 hours.

5 Remove turkey from cooker; cover to keep warm. Add sprouts and carrots to cooker; cook, covered, on high, for 30 minutes or until vegetables are tender. Season to taste. Remove vegetables from cooker. Add butter to cooker; stir until melted.

6 Slice turkey thickly. Serve turkey slices with vegetables and some of the cooking liquid. Sprinkle with reserved almond picada.

SERVING SUGGESTIONS

Accompany with mashed potato or creamy polenta.

• **Not suitable to freeze.**

HEARTY CHICKEN & CORN CHOWDER

PREP + COOK TIME 9 HOURS   SERVES 4

1 tablespoon olive oil

1 medium brown onion (150g),
   chopped finely

2 rindless bacon slices (130g),
   cut into 2cm (¾-inch) pieces

1 stalk celery (150g), trimmed,
   chopped finely

3 sprigs fresh thyme

2 fresh bay leaves

1.2kg (2½-pound) whole chicken

2 trimmed corn cobs (500g)

500g (1 pound) potatoes,
   cut into 2cm (¾-inch) pieces

1.25 litres (5 cups) chicken stock

1 cup (250ml) milk

2 tablespoons cornflour
   (cornstarch)

⅓ cup finely chopped fresh chives

1 Heat oil in a 4.5-litre (18-cup) slow cooker on sear (HIGH) setting; cook onion, bacon, celery, thyme and bay leaves, stirring, for 5 minutes or until vegetables soften. Add chicken, corn cobs, potato and stock. Cook, covered, on low, for 8 hours.

2 Carefully remove chicken and corn from cooker. Shred chicken coarsely using two forks; discard skin and bones. Using a small sharp knife, cut kernels from corn cobs. Discard cobs.

3 Stir milk and cornflour in a small bowl until combined. Return chicken and corn to cooker with cornflour mixture. Increase heat to reduce setting on low; simmer, uncovered, for 10 minutes or until chowder thickens. Season to taste.

4 Serve chowder sprinkled with fresh chives.

SERVING SUGGESTIONS
Accompany with crackers or grilled crusty bread.

• Not suitable to freeze.

CHICKEN CONGEE

PREP + COOK TIME 8 HOURS 45 MINUTES   SERVES 4

1.2kg (2½-pound) whole chicken

1 medium brown onion (150g), chopped finely

50g (1½ ounces) fresh ginger, sliced thinly

1.5 litres (6 cups) water

2 cloves garlic, bruised

1 cup (200g) white long-grain rice

2 teaspoons peanut oil

150g (4½ ounces) fresh shiitake mushrooms, halved if large

1 dried chinese sausage (lap chong) (30g), sliced thinly

2 teaspoons chilli oil

2 tablespoons fried shallots

2 green onions (scallions), sliced thinly

1 Place chicken, brown onion, ginger, the water and garlic in a 4.5-litre (18-cup) slow cooker. Cook, covered, on low, for 6 hours.

2 Carefully remove chicken from cooker; shred meat coarsely using two forks. Discard skin and bones. Strain cooking liquid through a muslin-lined sieve into a large heatproof bowl; discard solids.

3 Return stock mixture to cooker with shredded chicken and rice. Cook, covered, on low, for 2 hours.

4 Just before serving, heat peanut oil in a medium frying pan over medium-high heat; cook mushrooms and sausage, stirring, for 5 minutes or until mushrooms are lightly browned and tender.

5 Divide congee between serving bowls. Drizzle with chilli oil. Serve topped with mushroom mixture, shallots and green onion.

• **Not suitable to freeze.**

CHICKEN, GREEN OLIVE & PRESERVED LEMON TAGINE

PREP + COOK TIME 9 HOURS SERVES 6

2 tablespoons olive oil

2 teaspoons ground cinnamon

2 teaspoons ground cumin

2 teaspoons ground coriander

1.8kg (3½-pound) whole chicken

1 large brown onion (200g),
sliced thickly

3 cloves garlic, crushed

2 teaspoons finely grated
fresh ginger

1 teaspoon dried chilli flakes

½ teaspoon ground turmeric

800g (1½ pounds) baby potatoes,
halved

½ cup (125ml) chicken stock

1 tablespoon honey

1 cup (120g) seeded green olives

1 tablespoon lemon juice

2 tablespoons coarsely chopped
fresh flat-leaf parsley

2 tablespoons coarsely chopped
fresh coriander (cilantro)

1 tablespoon finely sliced
preserved lemon rind (see tip)

1 Heat half the oil in a 4.5-litre (18-cup) slow cooker on sear (HIGH) setting. Rub combined cinnamon, cumin and coriander all over chicken. Cook chicken, turning, for 20 minutes, or until well browned all over. Remove from cooker.

2 Heat remaining oil in cooker on sauté (MEDIUM) setting; cook onion, garlic, ginger, chilli and turmeric, stirring, for 5 minutes or until onion softens. Add potatoes; cook, stirring, for 5 minutes or until browned. Add stock. Place chicken on top of potatoes; drizzle with honey. Cook, covered, on low, for 8 hours.

3 Carefully remove chicken from cooker; cover to keep warm. Add olives and juice to potato mixture in cooker. Season to taste.

4 Cut chicken into pieces. Serve chicken with potatoes and sauce mixture; sprinkled with combined herbs and rind.

TIP

Preserved lemons are available from delicatessens, specialty food shops and large supermarkets. Use the rind only; discard the flesh and rinse the rind well under cold water before using.

SERVING SUGGESTION

Accompany with chickpeas and steamed couscous.

• **Not suitable to freeze.**

THAI BASIL & CHILLI CHICKEN WITH CASHEWS

PREP + COOK TIME 9 HOURS SERVES 6

1.8kg (3½-pound) whole chicken

1 medium red onion (170g), sliced thickly

1 medium red capsicum (bell pepper) (200g), sliced thickly

1 medium yellow capsicum (bell pepper) (200g), sliced thickly

2 medium carrots (240g), halved, sliced thickly diagonally

4 cloves garlic, quartered

10cm (4-inch) stick fresh lemon grass (20g), sliced thinly

4cm (1½-inch) piece fresh galangal, sliced thinly

3 fresh small red thai chillies, chopped coarsely

2 tablespoons fish sauce

2 tablespoons grated palm sugar

1 tablespoon vegetable or peanut oil

¾ cup (180ml) chicken stock

2 fresh kaffir lime leaves

2 tablespoons cornflour (cornstarch)

¼ cup (60ml) water

115g (3½ ounces) baby corn, halved

400g (12½ ounces) gai lan, trimmed, cut into 5cm (2-inch) lengths

½ cup (75g) roasted salted cashews

½ cup loosely packed thai basil leaves

1 Remove as much skin as possible from chicken; refrigerate skin until required. Place chicken in a 4.5-litre (18-cup) slow cooker. Top with onion, capsicums and carrot.

2 Process garlic, lemon grass, galangal, chilli, sauce, sugar and oil until smooth. Stir in stock, then pour mixture over chicken in cooker. Add lime leaves to cooker; cook, covered, on low, for 8 hours. Skim excess oil away from surface.

3 Carefully remove chicken from cooker; break chicken into large chunks. Discard bones. Discard lime leaves.

4 Stir cornflour and the water in a small bowl until combined; add cornflour mixture to cooker with corn and gai lan. Increase heat to reduce setting on low; simmer, uncovered, for 15 minutes, stirring occasionally, or until sauce thickens. Return chicken to cooker; simmer until heated through. Season to taste.

5 Meanwhile, preheat grill (broiler).

6 Place reserved chicken skin on an oven tray; season. Grill about 15 minutes or until golden and crisp. Drain on paper towel; break crispy skin into pieces.

7 Serve chicken mixture topped with crispy chicken skin, cashews and thai basil.

SERVING SUGGESTIONS
Accompany with steamed jasmine rice or roti bread.

• **Not suitable to freeze.**

PORK

SOY-BRAISED PORK

PREP + COOK TIME 8 HOURS 30 MINUTES SERVES 4

1kg (2-pound) piece pork
  scotch fillet (neck)

2 cinnamon sticks

2 star anise

½ cup (125ml) salt-reduced
  soy sauce

½ cup (125ml) chinese cooking
  wine (shao hsing)

⅓ cup (75g) firmly packed
  brown sugar

30g (1-ounce) piece fresh ginger,
  sliced thinly

3 cloves garlic, bruised

1 medium red onion (170g),
  cut into wedges

2 teaspoons sesame seeds, toasted

¼ cup loosely packed fresh micro
  coriander (cilantro) leaves

1 Place all ingredients, except
sesame seeds and coriander, in
a 4.5-litre (18-cup) slow cooker.
Cook, covered, on low, for 8 hours.

2 Remove pork from cooker; cover to
keep warm. Increase heat to reduce
setting on high; simmer, uncovered,
about 10 minutes or until cooking
liquid thickens slightly.

3 Serve sliced pork with a little of
the cooking liquid; sprinkled with
sesame seeds and coriander.

SERVING SUGGESTION

Accompany with steamed rice,
Asian greens, snow peas and
sugar snap peas.

• Not suitable to freeze.

HAM & CHICKPEA STEW

PREP + COOK TIME 8 HOURS 40 MINUTES SERVES 4

1.5 litres (6 cups) water

2 ham hocks (1.5kg),
  rind removed

400g (12½ ounces) canned
  chickpeas (garbanzo beans),
  drained, rinsed

4 sprigs fresh thyme

2 fresh bay leaves

1 medium brown onion (150g),
  chopped finely

500g (1 pound) potatoes,
  chopped coarsely

½ cup (60g) frozen peas, thawed

¼ cup small fresh thyme sprigs

1 Place the water, ham hocks,
chickpeas, thyme, bay leaves, onion
and potato in a 4.5-litre (18-cup)
slow cooker. Cook, covered, on low,
for 8 hours.

2 Carefully remove ham hocks from
cooker; shred meat coarsely using
two forks. Discard bones, thyme and
bay leaves. Return ham to cooker with
peas; stand covered for 5 minutes or
until peas are heated through.

3 Serve stew topped with thyme;
season with pepper.

SERVING SUGGESTIONS

Accompany with cheese toasts or
crusty bread to mop up the juices.

• Suitable to freeze at the end of step 2.

RED WINE-BRAISED PORK WITH CRISPY PANCETTA

PREP + COOK TIME 8 HOURS 30 MINUTES **SERVES** 4

¼ cup (35g) plain (all-purpose) flour

2 tablespoons olive oil

1kg (2 pounds) boneless pork shoulder, cut into 5cm (2-inch) pieces

1 medium brown onion (150g), chopped finely

1 stalk celery (150g), trimmed, chopped finely

1 medium carrot (120g), chopped finely

2 cloves garlic, crushed

1 tablespoon finely chopped fresh rosemary

410g (13 ounces) canned crushed tomatoes

½ cup (250ml) dry red wine

2 tablespoons tomato paste

3 slices pancetta (45g)

12 fresh sage leaves

1 Place flour in a large bowl; season.

2 Heat half the oil in a 4.5-litre (18-cup) slow cooker on sear (HIGH) setting. Coat pork in flour; shake off excess. Cook pork, in batches, stirring, for 15 minutes, or until well browned. Remove from cooker.

3 Add onion, celery, carrot, garlic and rosemary to cooker; cook, stirring, for 5 minutes or until vegetables soften. Return pork to cooker with tomatoes, wine and paste; stir to combine. Cook, covered, on low, for 8 hours. Season to taste.

4 Meanwhile, heat remaining oil in a medium frying pan over medium-high heat; cook pancetta, turning, for 2 minutes or until golden and crisp. Drain on paper towel. Add sage to pan; cook for 30 seconds or until crisp. Drain on paper towel. Tear pancetta into pieces.

5 Serve stew sprinkled with pancetta and sage.

SERVING SUGGESTION
Accompany with roasted parsnips.

• Suitable to freeze at the end of step 3.

MULLED WINE PORK WITH RED CABBAGE

PREP + COOK TIME 8 HOURS 30 MINUTES **SERVES** 6

3 star anise

2 cinnamon sticks

2 teaspoons caraway seeds

6 whole cloves

2 sprigs fresh rosemary, chopped coarsely

2 sprigs fresh tarragon, chopped coarsely

2 cloves garlic, quartered

2 medium red onions (340g), cut into thick wedges

1.4kg (2¾-pound) piece boneless pork shoulder, rind removed

1 cup (250ml) dry red wine

1 cup (250ml) chicken stock

2 tablespoons worcestershire sauce

2 tablespoons brown sugar

2 tablespoons balsamic vinegar

½ small red cabbage (600g), cut into 6 thick slices

2 tablespoons fresh tarragon leaves, extra

SWEET POTATO MASH

2 medium orange sweet potatoes (800g), chopped coarsely

1 large potato (300g), chopped coarsely

60g (2 ounces) butter

1 Tie spices, herbs and garlic in a muslin bag; secure with kitchen string. Place onion in base of a 4.5-litre (18-cup) slow cooker. Top with muslin bag and pork. Pour combined wine, stock, sauce, sugar and vinegar over pork. Cook, covered, on low, for 7 hours 30 minutes. Add cabbage; cook, covered, on low for a further 30 minutes. Discard muslin bag; season to taste.

2 Just before serving, make sweet potato mash.

3 Carefully remove pork from cooker; break into large chunks.

4 Serve pork with sweet potato mash and cabbage and onion mixture; drizzled with some of the cooking liquid. Top with extra tarragon.

SWEET POTATO MASH Boil, steam or microwave sweet potato and potato until tender; drain. Mash vegetables with butter in a medium bowl until smooth; season to taste.

SERVING SUGGESTION

Accompany with baby spinach and crusty bread to mop up the juices.

• **Not suitable to freeze.**

PORK IN GINGER BEER

PREP + COOK TIME 8 HOURS **SERVES** 6

2 tablespoons olive oil

1.5kg (3-pound) piece pork
scotch fillet (neck)

12 shallots (300g), halved

100g (3 ounces) sliced prosciutto,
chopped coarsely

2 cloves garlic, crushed

2 teaspoons fennel seeds

1 teaspoon ground ginger

1 teaspoon ground cinnamon

1½ cups (375ml) ginger beer

⅓ cup (80ml) chicken stock

¼ cup (55g) firmly packed dark
brown sugar

2 sprigs fresh rosemary

2 tablespoons fresh micro herbs

1 Heat half the oil in a 4.5-litre (18-cup) slow cooker on sear (HIGH) setting. Season pork; cook pork, turning occasionally, for 20 minutes, or until well browned. Remove pork from cooker.

2 Heat remaining oil in cooker; cook shallots and prosciutto, stirring, for 5 minutes or until browned lightly. Add garlic and spices; cook, stirring, for 1 minute or until fragrant. Stir in ginger beer, stock, sugar and rosemary. Return pork to cooker. Cook, covered, on low, for 7 hours 15 minutes.

3 Carefully remove pork from cooker; cover to keep warm. Increase heat to reduce setting on high; simmer, uncovered, for 20 minutes or until sauce thickens slightly. Discard rosemary; season to taste.

4 Slice pork thickly. Serve pork topped with some of the cooking liquid; sprinkled with micro herbs.

SERVING SUGGESTION

Accompany with steamed green beans and buttered rye toast.

• Not suitable to freeze.

SPICY ITALIAN SAUSAGE, FENNEL & TOMATO RAGÚ

PREP + COOK TIME 8 HOURS 30 MINUTES   SERVES 4

1 tablespoon olive oil

12 Italian-style pork and veal sausages (850g)

1 medium fennel bulb (300g), trimmed, sliced thickly

4 cloves garlic, crushed

2 teaspoons dried chilli flakes

½ cup (125ml) dry white wine

800g (1½ pounds) canned diced tomatoes

2 sprigs fresh basil

¼ cup (20g) grated parmesan

¼ cup loosely packed fresh small basil leaves

1 Heat half the oil in a 4.5-litre (18-cup) slow cooker on sear (HIGH) setting; cook sausages, turning occasionally, for 8 minutes, or until well browned. Remove from cooker.

2 Heat remaining oil in cooker; add fennel, garlic and chilli, stirring, for 5 minutes or until fennel is softened and golden. Return sausages to cooker with wine, tomatoes and basil sprigs. Cook, covered, on low, for 8 hours.

3 Increase heat to reduce setting on high; simmer, uncovered, for 20 minutes or until sauce thickens slightly. Discard basil; season to taste.

4 Serve ragù sprinkled with parmesan and basil leaves.

SERVING SUGGESTIONS

Accompany with cooked gnocchi, creamy polenta or chop the sausages into chunks and serve the sauce over cooked pasta.

• **Suitable to freeze at the end of step 3.**

MEXICAN PULL-APART PORK

PREP + COOK TIME 8 HOURS 30 MINUTES **SERVES** 6

2 medium red capsicums (bell peppers) (400g), sliced thinly

2 medium brown onions (300g), sliced thinly

375g (12 ounces) bottled chunky mild tomato salsa

1 cup (280g) barbecue sauce

4 cloves garlic, crushed

3 teaspoons ground cumin

2 teaspoons cayenne pepper

1 teaspoon dried oregano

1kg (2-pound) boneless pork shoulder

12 large flour tortillas (600g)

1 cup (240g) sour cream

1 cup loosely packed fresh coriander (cilantro)

1 lime (65g), cut into wedges

1 Combine capsicum, onion, salsa, sauce, garlic, cumin, cayenne pepper and oregano in a 4.5-litre (18-cup) slow cooker; add pork, turn to coat in mixture. Cook, covered, on low, for 8 hours.

2 Carefully remove pork from cooker; shred meat using two forks. Return pork to cooker; stir gently. Season to taste.

3 Divide pork mixture between tortillas; top with sour cream and coriander. Serve with lime wedges.

TIP
Peel the capsicum with a vegetable peeler if you don't like the skin peeling off when it's cooked.

• **Suitable to freeze at the end of step 2.**

BEST-EVER BOLOGNESE SAUCE

PREP + COOK TIME 10 HOURS 40 MINUTES   SERVES 6

1 tablespoon olive oil

125g (4-ounce) piece prosciutto, chopped finely

2 medium brown onions (300g), chopped finely

1 large carrot (180g), chopped finely

2 stalks celery (300g), trimmed, chopped finely

2 cloves garlic, crushed

500g (1 pound) minced (ground) pork

500g (1 pound) minced (ground) veal

1 cup (250ml) dry red wine

1½ cups (375ml) beef stock

½ cup (140g) tomato paste

1kg (2 pounds) ripe tomatoes, peeled, seeded, chopped coarsely

⅓ cup finely chopped fresh basil leaves

2 tablespoons finely chopped fresh oregano

½ cup (40g) shaved parmesan

½ cup loosely packed fresh basil leaves, extra

1 Heat half the oil in a 4.5-litre (18-cup) slow cooker on sauté (MEDIUM) setting; cook prosciutto, stirring, until crisp. Add onion, carrot, celery and garlic; cook, stirring, until vegetables soften. Remove from cooker.

2 Heat remaining oil in cooker; cook pork and veal, stirring, for 5 minutes or until browned. Add wine; bring to the boil. Return vegetable mixture to cooker; stir in stock, paste and tomato. Cook, covered, on low, for 10 hours.

3 Stir in chopped basil and oregano; cook, covered, on high, for about 10 minutes. Season to taste.

4 Serve bolognese topped with parmesan and extra basil leaves.

TIPS

Prosciutto can be replaced with bacon. Fresh tomatoes can be replaced with 800g (1½ pounds) canned diced tomatoes.

SERVING SUGGESTION

Accompany with spaghetti or your favourite pasta.

• **Suitable to freeze at the end of step 2.**

VEGETARIAN

MINESTRONE

PREP + COOK TIME 9 HOURS SERVES 4

3 cloves garlic, crushed

1 medium brown onion (150g), chopped finely

1 stalk celery (150g), trimmed, chopped finely

1 medium carrot (120g), chopped finely

2 cups (500ml) vegetable stock

2 tablespoons tomato paste

410g (13 ounce) canned crushed tomatoes

400g (12½ ounces) canned cannellini beans

2 cups (500ml) water, approximately

¾ cup (100g) dried small pasta tubes

150g (4½ ounces) green beans, trimmed, cut into 3cm (1¼-inch) lengths

½ cup (60g) frozen green peas

¼ small cabbage (300g), shredded finely

⅓ cup (25g) finely grated parmesan cheese

½ cup loosely packed small fresh flat-leaf parsley leaves

1 Place garlic, onion, celery, carrot, stock, paste and tomatoes in a 4.5-litre (18-cup) slow cooker. Cook, covered, on low, for 6 hours.

2 Add cannellini beans and enough of the water to make a thick soup consistency. Cook, covered, on low, for 2 hours. Season to taste.

3 Meanwhile, cook pasta in a large saucepan of boiling salted water until just tender, adding green beans and peas for the last 2 minutes of cooking time; drain.

4 Divide pasta, green beans, peas and cabbage among serving bowls; ladle soup mixture into bowls. Serve minestrone topped with parmesan and parsley.

SERVING SUGGESTION

Accompany with toasted crusty bread.

• Suitable to freeze at the end of step 2.

POTATO & CHEDDAR SOUP

PREP + COOK TIME 8 HOURS 45 MINUTES SERVES 4

1 stalk celery (150g), trimmed, chopped coarsely

1kg (2 pounds) potatoes, chopped coarsely

2 medium brown onions (300g), chopped coarsely

½ small cauliflower (500g), chopped coarsely

3 cloves garlic, sliced thinly

2 cups (500ml) vegetable stock

2 cups (500ml) water

1½ cups (180g) coarsely grated cheddar

⅓ cup (80ml) thickened (heavy) cream

¼ cup loosely packed fresh micro herbs

1 Place celery, potato, onion, cauliflower, garlic, stock and the water in a 4.5-litre (18-cup) slow cooker. Cook, covered, on low, for 8 hours.

2 Add cheddar; stir until cheddar melts. Cool soup for 10 minutes. Using a stick blender, blend soup until smooth. Season to taste.

3 Serve topped with cream and micro herbs.

SERVING SUGGESTION
Accompany with herb bread.

• Suitable to freeze at the end of step 2.

CHICKPEA CURRY

PREP + COOK TIME 8 HOURS 30 MINUTES SERVES 6

1½ tablespoons finely grated
fresh ginger

2 cloves garlic, crushed

1 medium brown onion (150g),
chopped finely

1 large red capsicum (bell pepper)
(350g), chopped finely

2 tablespoons mild Indian
curry paste

800g (1½ pounds) canned
chickpeas (garbanzo beans),
drained, rinsed

1 medium orange sweet potato
(400g), chopped coarsely

410g (13 ounces) canned
tomato puree

½ cup (125ml) water

150g (4½ ounces) green beans,
trimmed, cut into 5cm
(2-inch) lengths

¼ cup loosely packed fresh
micro herbs

1 Place ginger, garlic, onion,
capsicum, paste, chickpeas, sweet
potato, puree and the water in a
4.5-litre (18-cup) slow cooker. Cook,
covered, on low, for 8 hours.

2 Season to taste. Stir in green beans.

3 Serve chickepea curry topped with
micro herbs.

SERVING SUGGESTIONS

Accompany with steamed couscous,
basmati rice or warmed naan bread.

• Suitable to freeze at the end of step 2.

TOMATO SOUP WITH BASIL DUMPLINGS

PREP + COOK TIME 9 HOURS SERVES 4

1kg (2 pounds) over-ripe roma (egg) tomatoes, cored

400g (12½ ounces) canned whole tomatoes

3 cloves garlic, peeled

2 medium brown onions (300g), quartered

1 fresh long red chilli, chopped coarsely

1 stalk celery (150g), trimmed, chopped coarsely

1 cup (200g) drained roasted red capsicum (bell pepper), chopped coarsely

¼ cup loosely packed fresh small basil leaves or micro basil

BASIL DUMPLINGS

1 cup (150g) self-raising flour

60g (2 ounces) cold butter, chopped

1 egg, beaten lightly

2 tablespoons basil pesto

2 tablespoons milk, approximately

1 Place tomatoes, garlic, onion, chilli, celery and capsicum in a 4.5-litre (18-cup) slow cooker. Cook, covered, on low, for 7 hours.

2 Cool soup for 10 minutes. Using a stick blender, blend soup until smooth. Season to taste.

3 Make basil dumpling mixture.

4 Carefully drop level tablespoons of the basil dumpling mixture, about 2cm (¾-inch) apart, on top of soup. Cook, covered, on low, for 1 hour or until dumplings are firm to touch and cooked through.

5 Serve soup with dumplings and sprinkled with basil.

BASIL DUMPLINGS Place flour in a medium bowl; using your fingertips, rub in butter. Stir in egg, pesto and enough of the milk to make a soft, sticky dough.

SERVING SUGGESTION

Top with halved mixed baby tomatoes.

• **Suitable to freeze at the end of step 2.**

BASIL, CHICKPEA & VEGETABLE STEW

PREP + COOK TIME 8 HOURS 30 MINUTES SERVES 4

1 large brown onion (200g), chopped coarsely

3 cloves garlic, crushed

600g (1¼ pounds) small potatoes, halved

1 large orange sweet potato (500g), chopped coarsely

1 medium red capsicum (bell pepper) (200g), chopped coarsely

800g (1½ pounds) canned chickpeas (garbanzo beans), drained, rinsed

1½ cups (375ml) vegetable stock

½ cup (125ml) verjuice

150g (4½ ounces) basil pesto

60g (2 ounces) baby spinach leaves

½ cup (120g) crème fraîche

1 Place onion, garlic, potato, sweet potato, capsicum, chickpeas, stock, verjuice and ⅓ cup of the pesto in a 4.5-litre (18-cup) slow cooker; stir to combine. Cook, covered, on low, for 8 hours.

2 Stir in spinach; cook, covered, on high, for 5 minutes or until spinach wilts. Season to taste.

3 Serve stew topped with crème fraîche and remaining pesto.

SERVING SUGGESTION
Accompany with crusty bread to mop up the juices.

• **Not suitable to freeze.**

LOADED VEG 'BOLOGNESE' BAKED POTATOES

PREP + COOK TIME 8 HOURS 30 MINUTES SERVES 4

1 medium brown onion (150g), chopped finely

3 cloves garlic, crushed

1 small eggplant (230g), chopped finely

1 small red capsicum (bell pepper) (150g), chopped finely

1 stalk celery (150g), chopped finely

1 medium carrot (120g), grated coarsely

1 medium zucchini (120g), grated coarsely

400g (12½ ounces) canned diced tomatoes

¼ cup (70g) tomato paste

2 sprigs fresh rosemary

1 cup (250ml) vegetable stock

4 large potatoes (1.2kg), unpeeled

¼ cup coarsely chopped fresh flat-leaf parsley

1 Place onion, garlic, eggplant, capsicum, celery, carrot, zucchini, tomatoes, paste, rosemary and stock in a 4.5-litre (18-cup) slow cooker; stir to combine.

2 Wrap each potato, separately, in foil; place on top of vegetable mixture in cooker. Cook, covered, on low, for 8 hours.

3 Carefully remove potatoes; when cool enough to handle, discard foil. Season vegetable 'bolognese' to taste.

4 Cut lengthways down centre of each potato; press down lightly on a board to open potato slightly. Place potatoes on serving plates; top with vegetable 'bolognese' and parsley.

TIP
You can make the baked potatoes this way and use any filling you like. This would be a great way to make baked potatoes for a large crowd, filling your cooker with potatoes until three-quarters full. Serve them straight from the cooker.

SERVING SUGGESTION
Accompany wtith parmesan crisps and sour cream.

• Vegetable 'bolognese' mixture is suitable to freeze at the end of step 3.

BEETROOT & ONION SOUP WITH MINTY WHIPPED FETTA

PREP + COOK TIME 10 HOURS SERVES 6

1 tablespoon olive oil

2 large brown onions (400g), sliced thinly

¼ cup (60ml) balsamic vinegar

2 tablespoons brown sugar

4 medium parsnips (1kg), unpeeled, scrubbed, chopped coarsely

1kg (2 pounds) baby beetroots (beets), trimmed, unpeeled, scrubbed, chopped coarsely, small leaves reserved

2 cloves garlic, crushed

4 sprigs fresh thyme

1 litre (4 cups) water

MINTY WHIPPED FETTA

180g (5½ ounces) persian fetta, drained (see tips)

⅓ cup (95g) no-fat Greek-style yoghurt

2 tablespoons finely chopped fresh mint

1 Heat oil in a 4.5-litre (18-cup) slow cooker on sauté (MEDIUM) setting; cook onion, stirring, for 15 minutes or until softened and lightly caramelised. Add vinegar and sugar; cook, stirring, for 2 minutes. Add parsnip, beetroot, garlic, thyme and the water; stir to combine. Cook, covered, on low, for 8 hours.

2 Cool soup for 10 minutes. Using a stick blender, blend soup until smooth (see tips). Season to taste.

3 Meanwhile, make minty whipped fetta.

4 Serve soup topped with minty whipped fetta and reserved beetroot leaves.

MINTY WHIPPED FETTA Blend or process fetta and yoghurt until smooth; stir in mint. Season to taste.

TIPS
Reserve some of the marinating oil from the fetta and drizzle over bowls of soup to serve. You may need to add a little extra boiling water if you would like a thinner soup.

SERVING SUGGESTION
Accompany with crusty bread.

• **Suitable to freeze at the end of step 2.**

SPICY CORN CHOWDER WITH AVOCADO CRÈME

PREP + COOK TIME 8 HOURS SERVES 6

---

1 tablespoon olive oil

6 trimmed corn cobs (1.5kg), kernels removed

2 medium brown onions (300g), chopped coarsely

2 cloves garlic, crushed

1 teaspoon ground cumin

1 teaspoon dried oregano

½ teaspoon smoked paprika

1 teaspoon dried chilli flakes

1.25 litres (5 cups) vegetable stock or water

300ml pouring cream

½ cup (60g) corn nuts (salted roasted corn kernels)

⅓ cup loosely packed fresh coriander (cilantro) sprigs

AVOCADO CRÈME

1 small avocado (200g), chopped

⅓ cup (80g) sour cream

2 tablespoons lime juice

1 Heat oil in a 4.5-litre (18-cup) slow cooker on sauté (MEDIUM) setting; cook corn, onion, garlic, cumin, oregano, paprika and chilli, stirring, for 15 minutes or until softened and lightly caramelised. Add stock and cream. Cook, covered, on low, for 7 hours 30 minutes.

2 Cool soup for 10 minutes. Using a stick blender, blend soup until smooth. Season to taste.

3 Meanwhile, make avocado crème.

4 Serve soup topped with avocado crème, corn nuts and coriander. Season with cracked pepper.

AVOCADO CRÈME Blend or process ingredients until smooth. Season to taste.

TIP
You can leave the chilli out for the littlies or those who don't like it spicy.

• **Suitable to freeze at the end of step 2.**

BEEF&VEAL

COTTAGE PIE

PREP + COOK TIME 3 HOURS 45 MINUTES **SERVES** 6

1 tablespoon olive oil

1 medium brown onion (150g), chopped finely

3 cloves garlic, crushed

1kg (2 pounds) minced (ground) beef

2 teaspoons paprika

2 teaspoons cracked black pepper

2 tablespoons plain (all-purpose) flour

1 stalk celery (150g), trimmed, chopped finely

1 medium carrot (120g), chopped finely

2 tablespoons worcestershire sauce

¼ cup (70g) tomato paste

1 cup (250ml) beef stock

1kg (2 pounds) potatoes, chopped coarsely

60g (2 ounces) butter, chopped

⅓ cup (80ml) milk, warmed

1 cup (120g) coarsely grated cheddar

¼ cup finely chopped fresh flat-leaf parsley

1 Heat oil in a 4.5-litre (18-cup) slow cooker on sear (HIGH) setting; cook onion and garlic, stirring, for 5 minutes or until softened. Add beef; cook, stirring, for 5 minutes or until browned. Drain excess oil, if needed.

2 Add paprika and pepper; cook, stirring, for 1 minute or until fragrant. Add flour; cook, stirring, for 1 minute. Add celery, carrot, sauce, paste and stock. Cook, covered, on low, for 3 hours. Season to taste.

3 Meanwhile, place potato in a large saucepan with enough cold water to barely cover potato; bring to the boil. Boil, uncovered, over medium heat, for 15 minutes or until potato is tender; drain. Mash potato in a large bowl until smooth; stir in butter and milk. Season to taste.

4 Preheat grill (broiler).

5 Transfer beef mixture to a 2.5-litre (10-cup) capacity ovenproof dish. Top with potato mash; sprinkle with cheddar. Cook under grill for 5 minutes or until cheddar melts and potato is warmed through. Serve pie sprinkled with parsley.

TIP

A handful of peas can be added to the beef mixture at the end of step 2.

SERVING SUGGESTION

Accompany with a watercress salad.

• Beef mixture is suitable to freeze at the end of step 2.

SLOPPY JOES

PREP + COOK TIME 6 HOURS 20 MINUTES **SERVES** 4

1 tablespoon olive oil

2 medium brown onions (300g), chopped finely

2 cloves garlic, crushed

375g (12 ounces) minced (ground) pork

375g (12 ounces) minced (ground) veal

3 teaspoons paprika

¼ teaspoon ground cinnamon

¼ cup (90g) golden syrup

½ cup (125ml) apple cider vinegar

½ cup (140g) tomato paste

1 Heat oil in a 4.5-litre (18-cup) slow cooker on sear (HIGH) setting; cook onions, garlic, pork and veal, stirring, for 5 minutes or until browned. Add spices; cook, stirring, for 1 minute or until fragrant.

2 Add syrup, vinegar and paste. Cook, covered, on low, for 6 hours.

3 Increase heat to reduce setting on high; simmer, uncovered, for 10 minutes or sauce is thick. Season to taste.

TIP

For a Mexican version, add a drained can of kidney beans and serve with pickled jalapeños.

SERVING SUGGESTION

Serve in soft brioche rolls or long hot dog rolls, or on mashed potato or with french fries. If serving in rolls, sandwich with sliced red radish, shredded iceberg lettuce and small fresh flat-leaf parsley leaves.

• Suitable to freeze at the end of step 3.

BEER-BRAISED CHILLI MEATBALLS

PREP + COOK TIME 3 HOURS 45 MINUTES SERVES 4

1kg (2 pounds) minced (ground) beef

2 eggs, beaten lightly

1 cup (70g) fresh sourdough breadcrumbs (see tips)

⅔ cup (50g) finely grated parmesan

½ cup finely chopped fresh flat-leaf parsley

¼ cup (60ml) olive oil

2 medium brown onions (300g), chopped finely

4 cloves garlic, crushed

2 fresh long red chillies, chopped finely

2 tablespoons plain (all-purpose) flour

1½ cups (375ml) beer

1 cup (250ml) beef consommé

¼ cup (70g) barbecue sauce

1 tablespoon worcestershire sauce

¼ cup parsley leaves

2 tablespoons finely sliced lemon rind (see tips)

1 Combine beef, egg, breadcrumbs, parmesan and parsley in a medium bowl; season. Roll rounded tablespoons of mixture into balls. Place on a tray.

2 Heat half the oil in a 4.5-litre (18-cup) slow cooker on sear (HIGH) setting; cook meatballs, in batches, turning, for 10 minutes, or until browned. Remove from cooker.

3 Reduce cooker to sauté (MEDIUM) setting. Heat remaining oil in cooker; cook onion, garlic and chilli, stirring, for 5 minutes or until onion softens. Add flour; cook, stirring, for 2 minutes. Gradually stir in beer, then consommé and sauces; bring to the boil.

4 Return meatballs to cooker. Cook, covered, on low, for 3 hours. Season to taste.

5 Serve meatballs with sauce; top with parsley and rind.

TIPS

Fresh breadcrumbs are best made from 2-3 day-old bread. If you only have fresh bread, leave the slices out on the bench for a few hours to stale. Process the bread, with or without crusts, into coarse or fine crumbs. If you don't have sourdough, white sandwich bread or another crusty bread, such as ciabatta, are fine to use. Use a zesting tool to make long thin strips of lemon rind. If you don't have one you can thinly peel the rind from the lemon, avoiding any white pith, then finely slice the rind into long thin strips. If you like a thicker sauce, remove meatballs and cook sauce for a further 10 minutes.

SERVING SUGGESTIONS

Accompany with mashed potato or crusty bread to mop up the juices.

• Suitable to freeze at the end of step 4.

VEAL & TOMATO MEATLOAF

PREP + COOK TIME 4 HOURS 45 MINUTES **SERVES** 4

500g (1 pound) pork and fennel sausages, casings removed

500g (1 pound) minced (ground) veal

2 tablespoons tomato paste

½ cup (35g) fresh breadcrumbs (see tip)

2 teaspoons fresh thyme leaves

2 tablespoons finely chopped fresh basil

1 egg, beaten lightly

400g (12½ ounces) mixed baby tomatoes

¼ cup loosely packed fresh micro herbs

1 Combine sausage meat, veal, paste, breadcrumbs, thyme, basil and egg in a large bowl; season. Shape mince mixture into a 9cm x 20cm (3 ¾-inch x 8-inch) log. Carefully place meatloaf in base of a 4.5-litre (18-cup) slow cooker. Place half of the tomatoes around meatloaf. Cook, covered, on low, for 3 hours 30 minutes. Add the remaining tomatoes. Cook, covered, on low, for a further 30 minutes. Season to taste.

2 Using two spatulas remove meatloaf from cooker. Serve slices of meatloaf with tomatoes and micro herbs.

TIP

Fresh breadcrumbs are best made from 2-3 day-old bread. If you only have fresh bread, leave the slices out on the bench for a few hours to stale. Process the bread, with or without crusts, into coarse or fine crumbs. White sandwich bread or crusty bread, such as ciabatta or sourdough, are all fine to use.

SERVING SUGGESTION

Accompany with mashed potato and steamed greens.

• Not suitable to freeze.

TEXAS-STYLE BRISKET WITH CORN & SLAW

PREP + COOK TIME 7 HOURS 45 MINUTES   **SERVES** 6

2 teaspoons chilli powder

2 teaspoons garlic salt

2 teaspoons onion powder

2 teaspoons smoked paprika

1 teaspoon mustard powder

1 teaspoon ground cumin

2 teaspoons dark brown sugar

1.2kg (2½ pounds) thick piece beef brisket

⅔ cup (190g) smokey barbecue sauce

1 tablespoon olive oil

½ cup (125ml) beef stock

4 corn cobs (1.6kg), quartered

40g (1½ ounces) butter, softened

1 clove garlic, crushed

2 tablespoons finely chopped fresh coriander (cilantro)

pinch chilli powder, extra

SILVER BEET SLAW

2 tablespoons olive oil

2 tablespoons apple cider vinegar

2 teaspoons honey

5 medium silver beet (swiss chard) leaves (325g), stalks removed, shredded finely (see tip)

2 medium carrots (240g), cut into matchsticks

4 green onions (scallions), sliced thinly

1 Combine chilli, spices and sugar in a small bowl. Brush beef all over with 1 tablespoon of the sauce; sprinkle spice mixture all over beef to coat.

2 Heat oil in a 4.5-litre (18-cup) slow cooker on sear (HIGH) setting. Cook beef for 3 minutes each side or until well browned. Add stock; cook, covered, on low, for 7 hours.

3 Remove beef from cooker; rest, covered, for 10 minutes.

4 Add remaining sauce to juices in cooker. Increase heat to reduce setting on medium; bring to the boil.

5 Just before serving, make silver beet slaw. Boil, steam or microwave corn until tender; drain. Combine butter, garlic, coriander and extra chilli in a small bowl. Spread corn with butter mixture.

6 Slice beef thinly; serve beef drizzled with sauce, accompanied with corn and slaw.

SILVER BEET SLAW Whisk oil, vinegar and honey in a large jug to combine. Place remaining ingredients in a large bowl; drizzle with dressing, toss to combine. Season to taste.

TIP

You need about half a bunch of silver beet (swiss chard) (approximately 3 cups of shredded) for this recipe.

SERVING SUGGESTIONS

Accompany with steamed baby carrots and green beans or halved sugar snap peas.

• Suitable to freeze at the end of step 2.

CANNELLONI `STRAIGHT-UP`

PREP + COOK TIME 5 HOURS SERVES 8

2 tablespoons olive oil

1.25kg (2½ pounds) minced (ground) beef

2 medium brown onions (300g), chopped finely

3 cloves garlic, crushed

2 medium carrots (240g), grated coarsely

2 medium zucchini (240g), grated coarsely

½ cup (140g) pizza sauce or tomato paste

700g (1½ pounds) bottled passata

400g (12½ ounces) canned diced tomatoes

¾ cup (180ml) beef stock

2 x 250g (8-ounce) packets cannelloni tubes

500g (1 pound) fresh ricotta

300ml pouring cream

2 egg yolks

1 cup (100g) pizza cheese

1 Heat oil in a 4.5-litre (18-cup) slow cooker on sear (HIGH) setting; cook beef, stirring, for 10 minutes, or until browned. Remove from cooker. Add onion, garlic, carrot and zucchini, stirring, for 5 minutes or until onion softens. Add sauce; cook, stirring, for 2 minutes. Return beef to cooker with passata, tomatoes and stock; bring to the boil. Season to taste.

2 Remove three-quarters of the beef mixture from cooker; reserve. Stand cannelloni tubes upright in cooker, pressing gently into mixture, allowing a little room between them to expand. Spoon reserved beef mixture into tubes, gently shaking the cooker insert to settle mixture.

3 Combine ricotta, cream and egg yolks in a large bowl until smooth. Pour mixture over cannelloni; sprinkle with pizza cheese. Cook, covered, on low, for 4 hours. Stand 10 minutes.

4 Preheat grill (broiler).

5 Carefully remove cooker insert and cook cannelloni under grill for 5 minutes or until browned lightly. Stand for 5 minutes before serving.

TIPS

You could use a large piping bag to fill the tubes with the beef mixture. Check the manufacturer's instructions before placing your cooker insert under the grill.

SERVING SUGGESTION

Accompany with a rocket salad.

• Suitable to freeze at the end of step 5. Meat sauce is suitable to freeze separately at the end of step 1.

VEAL ROLLS WITH PROSCIUTTO & SAGE

PREP + COOK TIME 6 HOURS 40 MINUTES   **SERVES** 4

8 slices prosciutto (120g)

8 veal schnitzels (800g)

⅔ cup (130g) drained chargrilled capsicum (bell pepper) strips

8 large fresh sage leaves

1 tablespoon olive oil

1 medium brown onion (150g), chopped finely

2 cloves garlic, crushed

¼ cup (60ml) dry red wine

400g (12½ ounces) bottled tomato pasta sauce

1 Place prosciutto slices on a chopping board; top each slice with a schnitzel. Place capsicum across centre of schnitzels. Top each with a sage leaf. Roll to enclose filling; secure veal rolls with toothpicks or kitchen string.

2 Heat oil in a 4.5-litre (18-cup) slow cooker on sear (HIGH) setting; cook veal rolls, turning, for 10 minutes or until well browned. Add onion, garlic, wine and sauce. Cook, covered, on low, for 6 hours. Season to taste.

3 Serve veal rolls with sauce.

SERVING SUGGESTIONS

Accompany with soft polenta, cooked pasta, mashed potato or crusty bread, and topped with gremolata and fried sage leaves

• **Not suitable to freeze.**

HAWAIIAN-STYLE BARBECUE BEEF RIBS WITH PINEAPPLE

PREP + COOK TIME 6 HOURS 30 MINUTES **SERVES** 4

1 small pineapple (900g)

2 medium red onions (340g), chopped coarsely

8 beef short ribs (1.6kg)

3 cloves garlic, crushed

2 teaspoons finely grated fresh ginger

¾ cup (180ml) japanese soy sauce

½ cup (110g) firmly packed brown sugar

½ cup (125ml) rice wine vinegar

2 teaspoons sriracha chilli sauce

⅓ cup (95g) barbecue sauce

COCONUT SLAW

1 medium carrot (120g), cut into matchsticks

⅓ cup loosely packed fresh coriander (cilantro) leaves

½ cup (45g) shaved fresh coconut (see tips)

2 green onions (scallions), cut into long thin strips (see tips)

1 tablespoon lime juice

1 Peel, quarter and core pineapple; chop pineapple into 2.5cm (1-inch) pieces.

2 Place onion in base of a 4.5-litre (18-cup) slow cooker. Top with beef, sprinkle with pineapple. Combine remaining ingredients in a large jug; pour over beef in cooker.

3 Cook, covered, on low, for 6 hours or until beef is tender.

4 Preheat grill (broiler).

5 Carefully remove beef from cooker to an oven tray; cook under grill, for 5 minutes, turning halfway, until browned, basting with sauce occasionally.

6 Meanwhile, skim fat from surface of remaining sauce mixture in cooker; simmer sauce, on reduce setting, uncovered, for 15 minutes or until sauce thickens slightly.

7 Just before serving, make coconut slaw.

8 Serve beef drizzled with some of the sauce mixture; top with slaw.

COCONUT SLAW Combine ingredients in a large bowl; season to taste.

TIPS

To open a coconut, push or hammer a metal skewer or screwdriver into the "eyes" in the coconut. Drain the water into a jug. Place the coconut on a board; use the blunt back of a large knife or hammer to tap firmly around the centre of the coconut until it splits. Or, place coconut in a strong plastic bag and throw it firmly on a hard surface. Use a butter knife to prise the flesh from the shell. Peel the skin with a peeler or knife and shave the flesh with a vegetable peeler. We placed our green onion strips in a bowl of iced water for about 30 minutes to make them curl.

SERVING SUGGESTIONS

Accompany with steamed rice, mashed or roasted taro, roasted potatoes or crusty bread to mop up the juices.

• Suitable to freeze at the end of step 3.

LAMB

SPANISH-STYLE LAMB MEATBALLS

PREP + COOK TIME 7 HOURS SERVES 4

500g (1 pound) bottled passata

½ teaspoon dried chilli flakes

1 sprig fresh rosemary

1 medium red capsicum
(bell pepper) (200g),
chopped coarsely

600g (1¼ pounds) minced
(ground) lamb

2 teaspoons paprika

½ cup finely chopped fresh
flat-leaf parsley

⅓ cup finely chopped fresh mint

2 cloves garlic, crushed

1 medium brown onion (150g),
chopped finely

¼ cup (35g) slivered almonds,
chopped coarsely

¼ cup (35g) slivered almonds,
toasted, extra

¼ cup loosely packed fresh
micro herbs

1 Place passata, chilli, rosemary
and capsicum in a 4.5-litre (18-cup)
slow cooker.

2 Combine remaining ingredients,
except extra almonds and micro
herbs, in a medium bowl; season.
Roll level tablespoons of mixture into
balls; place in cooker. Cook, covered,
on low, for 6 hours. Discard rosemary;
season to taste.

3 Serve meatballs topped with extra
almonds and micro herbs.

SERVING SUGGESTIONS

Accompany with toasted crusty bread
or couscous and mixed salad leaves.

• Suitable to freeze at the end of step 2.

LAMB WITH CURRANTS & TUSCAN CABBAGE

PREP + COOK TIME 6 HOURS 45 MINUTES **SERVES** 4

¼ cup (35g) plain (all-purpose) flour

½ teaspoon ground cinnamon

pinch chilli powder

2 tablespoons olive oil

1.2kg (2½ pounds) diced lamb leg

1 large red onion (300g), sliced thickly

1 medium carrot (120g), chopped coarsely

1 stalk celery (150g), trimmed, sliced thickly

3 cloves garlic, crushed

½ cup (125ml) dry red wine

1 cup (250ml) beef stock

¼ cup (60ml) balsamic vinegar

¼ cup (55g) firmly packed brown sugar

¼ cup (70g) tomato paste

2 tablespoons dried currants

1 dried bay leaf

250g (8 ounces) cavolo nero (tuscan cabbage), trimmed, (see tips)

CREAMY POLENTA

2 cups (500ml) chicken or vegetable stock

2 cups (500ml) milk

1 cup (170g) polenta (cornmeal)

30g (1 ounce) butter, chopped

½ cup (40g) grated parmesan

1 Combine flour, cinnamon and chilli in a large bowl; season.

2 Heat oil in a 4.5-litre (18-cup) slow cooker on sear (HIGH) setting. Coat lamb in flour; shake off excess (reserve excess flour). Cook lamb, in batches, for 5 minutes, turning, or until well browned. Remove lamb from cooker.

3 Reduce cooker to sauté (MEDIUM) setting. Cook onion, carrot, celery and garlic, stirring, for 5 minutes or until vegetables soften. Sprinkle with reserved excess flour; cook, stirring, for 3 minutes. Gradually stir in wine, then stock, vinegar, sugar, paste, currants and bay leaf; bring to the boil.

4 Return lamb to cooker. Cook, covered, on low, for 6 hours. Discard bay leaf; season to taste.

5 Just before serving, make creamy polenta.

6 Coarsely shred 2 cavolo nero leaves. Reserve for garnish. Coarsely chop remaining cavolo nero leaves. Add chopped leaves to cooker; cook, covered, on high, for 5 minutes or until cavolo nero wilts. Serve creamy polenta topped with lamb mixture and shredded cavolo nero.

CREAMY POLENTA Bring stock and milk to the boil in a large saucepan; gradually add polenta, whisking until mixture comes to the boil. Reduce heat to low; cook, stirring, for 5 minutes or until soft and thick. Stir in butter and parmesan; season to taste. Adjust consistency with a little extra milk, if necessary.

TIP

You will need 1 bunch of cavolo nero for this recipe; you can use kale or silver beet instead.

• Suitable to freeze at the end of step 4.

LAMB KEEMA

PREP + COOK TIME 5 HOURS   SERVES 4

1 tablespoon olive oil

1 medium brown onion (150g), chopped finely

2 cloves garlic, crushed

600g (1¼ pounds) minced (ground) lamb

1 tablespoon finely grated fresh ginger

2 fresh long green chillies, sliced thinly

2 teaspoons garam masala

2 teaspoons ground coriander

1 teaspoon ground turmeric

1 teaspoon cumin seeds

2 tablespoons plain (all-purpose) flour

800g (1½ pounds) canned diced tomatoes

½ cup (60g) frozen peas, thawed

1 tablespoon lemon juice

½ cup finely chopped fresh coriander (cilantro)

½ cup (140g) Greek-style yoghurt

¼ cup (20g) flaked almonds, toasted

2 tablespoons thinly sliced preserved lemon rind

1 Heat oil in a 4.5-litre (18-cup) slow cooker on sear (HIGH) setting; cook onion and garlic, stirring, for 5 minutes or until onion softens. Add lamb; cook, stirring, for 5 minutes or until browned.

2 Add ginger, chilli and spices; cook, stirring, for 1 minute or until fragrant. Add flour; cook, stirring for 1 minute. Add tomatoes. Cook, covered, on low, for 4 hours. Season to taste.

3 Increase heat to reduce setting on high; simmer, uncovered, for 10 minutes or until sauce is thick.

4 Stir in peas, juice and half the fresh coriander. Serve topped with yoghurt, remaining coriander, almonds and preserved lemon.

SERVING SUGGESTIONS
Accompany with grilled roti, couscous or steamed greens.

• Suitable to freeze at the end of step 3.

CRANBERRY & RED WINE GLAZED LAMB CHOPS

PREP + COOK TIME 6 HOURS 30 MINUTES **SERVES** 4

2 tablespoons plain (all-purpose) flour

2 tablespoons olive oil

8 lamb forequarter chops (2kg)

¼ cup (80g) whole cranberry sauce

1 tablespoon wholegrain mustard

½ cup (125ml) dry red wine

¾ cup (180ml) chicken stock

1 large red onion (300g), sliced thinly

2 stalks celery (300g), trimmed, sliced thickly

2 sprigs fresh rosemary

1 Place flour in a large bowl; season.

2 Heat oil in a 4.5-litre (18-cup) slow cooker on sear (HIGH) setting. Trim excess fat from lamb. Coat lamb in flour mixture; shake off excess. Cook lamb, in batches, for 5 minutes each side or until well browned. Remove from cooker.

3 Meanwhile, whisk sauce, mustard, wine and stock in a large jug until combined.

4 Place 4 lamb chops in base of cooker. Sprinkle half the onion, half the celery and half the rosemary over chops. Repeat layering with remaining lamb, onion, celery and rosemary. Pour stock mixture into cooker. Cook, covered, on low, for 6 hours.

5 Remove lamb from cooker; cover to keep warm. Skim fat from surface of sauce; season to taste. Serve lamb with sauce.

TIP

Lamb neck chops, shoulder chops and chump chops are also suitable for this recipe.

SERVING SUGGESTION

Accompany with mashed peas and steamed dutch carrots.

• Suitable to freeze at the end of step 4.

TURKISH LAMB WITH EGGS

PREP + COOK TIME 4 HOURS 45 MINUTES **SERVES** 4

1 tablespoon olive oil

1 large brown onion (200g), chopped finely

4 cloves garlic, crushed

500g (1 pound) minced (ground) lamb

2 teaspoons ground cinnamon

2 teaspoons ground coriander

2 teaspoons smoked paprika

½ teaspoon cayenne pepper

400g (12½ ounces) canned diced tomatoes

1 cup (240g) drained chargrilled capsicum (bell pepper), chopped finely

½ cup (125ml) beef stock

4 eggs

450g (14½ ounces) loaf turkish bread, split, toasted

⅓ cup loosely packed fresh micro herbs

1 Heat oil in a 4.5-litre (18-cup) slow cooker on sear (HIGH) setting; cook onion and garlic, stirring, for 3 minutes or until onion softens. Add lamb and spices; cook, stirring, for 5 minutes or until well browned. Add tomatoes, capsicum and stock; bring to the boil.

2 Cook, covered, on low, for 4 hours. Season to taste.

3 Make four indents in lamb mixture with the back of a spoon. Carefully crack eggs into indents; season eggs. Cook, covered, on high, for 10 minutes or until egg whites have set but yolks are still runny.

4 Serve bread topped with lamb and eggs; sprinkled with micro herbs.

LAMB CHOPS WITH RATATOUILLE

PREP + COOK TIME 6 HOURS 45 MINUTES SERVES 4

2 tablespoons plain (all-purpose) flour

1 tablespoon olive oil

4 lamb forequarter chops (1kg)

1 large eggplant (500g), cut into 2.5cm (1-inch) pieces

1 medium zucchini (120g), chopped coarsely

1 medium red onion (170g), cut into wedges

1 medium yellow capsicum (bell pepper) (200g), chopped coarsely

4 anchovy fillets, chopped finely

2 cloves garlic, crushed

700g (1½ pounds) bottled passata

250g (8 ounces) cherry tomatoes

⅓ cup (40g) pitted kalamata olives

1 Place flour in a large bowl; season.

2 Heat oil in a 4.5-litre (18-cup) slow cooker on sear (HIGH) setting. Coat lamb in flour; shake off excess. Cook lamb, in batches, for 5 minutes each side, or until well browned. Return lamb to cooker.

3 Add eggplant, zucchini, onion, capsicum, anchovies, garlic and passata to cooker; top with tomatoes. Cook, covered, on low, for 6 hours.

4 Stir in olives; season to taste.

SERVING SUGGESTION
Accompany with roasted potatoes and a chunky basil pesto.

• **Not suitable to freeze.**

HONEYED LAMB WITH PUMPKIN & CHICKPEAS

PREP + COOK TIME 6 HOURS 30 MINUTES SERVES 6

1.2kg (2½ pounds) diced lamb

1 medium red onion (170g),
  cut into thin wedges

3 cloves garlic, crushed

2 teaspoons garam masala

1 teaspoon ground cumin

1 teaspoon ground ginger

1 teaspoon chilli powder

400g (12½ ounces) canned
  diced tomatoes

400g (12½ ounces) canned
  chickpeas (garbanzo beans),
  drained, rinsed

800g (1½ pounds) pumpkin,
  peeled, cut into 5cm
  (2-inch) pieces

2 tablespoons honey

½ cup (125ml) pouring cream

500g (1 pound) spinach, trimmed

¼ cup micro mint

¼ cup (20g) slivered almonds,
  toasted

1 lime, cut into cheeks

1 Place lamb, onion, garlic, spices, tomatoes, chickpeas, pumpkin, honey and cream in a 4.5-litre (18-cup) slow cooker. Cook, covered, on low, for 6 hours.

2 Add spinach to cooker; cook, covered, on high, for 5 minutes or until spinach wilts. Season to taste.

3 Serve sprinkled with mint and almonds, accompany with lime cheeks.

TIP
You will need 1 bunch of spinach for this recipe; you can use 150g (4½ ounces) baby spinach leaves instead, if you like.

SERVING SUGGESTIONS
Accompany with couscous or basmati rice and warmed naan bread.

• Not suitable to freeze.

POULTRY

PAPRIKA CHICKEN

PREP + COOK TIME 5 HOURS SERVES 4

¼ cup (35g) plain (all-purpose) flour

1 tablespoon olive oil

8 chicken thigh cutlets (1.6kg), skin removed

1 medium brown onion (150g), chopped finely

1 large green capsicum (bell pepper) (350g), chopped finely

¼ teaspoon dried chilli flakes

1 tablespoon paprika

2 tablespoons tomato paste

1 cup (250ml) water

⅓ cup (80g) crème fraîche

¼ cup loosely packed fresh micro herbs

1 Place flour in a large bowl; season.

2 Heat oil in a 4.5-litre (18-cup) slow cooker on sear (HIGH) setting. Coat chicken in flour; shake off excess. Cook chicken, in batches, for 5 minutes each side or until well browned. Remove from cooker.

3 Add onion, capsicum, chilli and paprika to cooker; cook, stirring, for 5 minutes or until vegetables soften. Add paste and the water; stir to combine. Return chicken to cooker. Cook, covered, on low, for 4 hours. Transfer chicken to a plate; cover with foil to keep warm.

4 Stir crème fraîche into cooker. Increase heat to reduce setting on high; simmer, uncovered, for 10 minutes or until sauce thickens. Season to taste. Return chicken to cooker; coat in sauce.

5 Serve chicken with sauce, sprinkled with micro herbs.

SERVING SUGGESTIONS
Accompany with cooked egg noodles, pasta or mashed potato.

• **Suitable to freeze at the end of step 4.**

ITALIAN-STYLE CHICKEN WITH TOMATOES & PEPPERONI

PREP + COOK TIME 3 HOURS 35 MINUTES   SERVES 4

1 tablespoon olive oil

8 chicken thigh fillets (1.3kg), halved

125g (4 ounces) sliced pepperoni

1 medium brown onion (150g), sliced thinly

1 teaspoon fennel seeds, crushed lightly

3 teaspoons finely chopped fresh rosemary

2 medium red capsicums (bell peppers) (400g), sliced thinly

400g (12½ ounces) canned diced tomatoes

½ cup (125ml) chicken stock

¼ cup finely chopped fresh chives

1 Heat oil in a 4.5-litre (18-cup) slow cooker on sear (HIGH) setting; cook chicken, in batches, turning, for 10 minutes, until well browned. Remove from cooker.

2 Add pepperoni, onion, fennel seeds and rosemary; cook, stirring, for 5 minutes or until onion softens. Add capsicum, tomatoes and stock; stir to combine. Cook, covered, on low, for 3 hours.

3 Increase heat to reduce setting on high; simmer, uncovered, about 15 minutes or until sauce thickens. Season to taste. Serve sprinkled with chives.

SERVING SUGGESTIONS

Accompany with mashed potato, steamed baby potatoes, steamed green beans or crusty bread.

• **Suitable to freeze at the end of step 3.**

GARAM MASALA CHICKEN & POTATOES

PREP + COOK TIME 6 HOURS SERVES 4

8 chicken thigh fillets (1.3kg), halved

1 tablespoon garam masala

1 tablespoon olive oil

500g (1 pound) potatoes, unpeeled, chopped coarsely

1 medium red onion (170g), cut into wedges

1 tablespoon finely grated fresh ginger

3 cloves garlic, crushed

410g (13 ounces) canned tomato puree

⅔ cup (80g) frozen peas

1 Coat chicken in garam masala.

2 Heat oil in a 4.5-litre (18-cup) slow cooker on sear (HIGH) setting; cook chicken, in batches, turning, for 10 minutes, until browned. Remove from cooker.

3 Add potato, onion, ginger, garlic and puree to cooker; stir to combine. Return chicken to cooker. Cook, covered, on low, for 5 hours.

4 Add peas. Increase heat to reduce setting on high; simmer, uncovered, for 5 minutes or until sauce thickens slightly. Season to taste.

SERVING SUGGESTION

Accompany with steamed couscous and yoghurt, and top with a tomato, cucumber, red onion and baby basil leaf salad.

• **Suitable to freeze at the end of step 3**

TURKEY WITH PLUM & STAR ANISE

PREP + COOK TIME 7 HOURS SERVES 4

2 turkey drumsticks (1.6kg)

1 tablespoon peanut oil

825g (1¾ pounds) canned whole plums in natural juice

1 medium red onion (170g), sliced thinly

1 small red capsicum (bell pepper) (150g), sliced thinly

1 small yellow capsicum (bell pepper) (150g), sliced thinly

1 small green capsicum (bell pepper) (150g), sliced thinly

4 star anise

4 cloves garlic, crushed

1 tablespoon finely grated fresh ginger

1 fresh long red chilli, chopped finely

⅓ cup (80ml) soy sauce

¼ cup (60ml) rice wine vinegar

2 tablespoons grated palm sugar or brown sugar

1 Remove and discard skin from turkey drumsticks.

2 Heat oil in a 4.5-litre (18-cup) slow cooker on sear (HIGH) setting; cook turkey, in batches, turning, for 15 minutes, until well browned.

3 Meanwhile, drain plums over a medium bowl; reserve plums and 1 cup juice.

4 Return turkey to cooker; top with onion, capsicum, star anise and plums. Combine garlic, ginger, chilli, sauce, vinegar, sugar and reserved juice in a jug; pour into cooker. Cook, covered, on low, for 6 hours.

5 Carefully remove turkey from cooker; shred meat into large chunks. Discard bones and star anise. Return turkey to cooker. Season to taste.

TIP

Depending on the size and shape of your cooker, you may be need to brown the turkey in a large frying pan in step 2, then transfer to the slow cooker.

SERVING SUGGESTION

Accompany with steamed rice, steamed baby pak choy, fresh coriander (cilantro) sprigs and lime wedges.

• Not suitable to freeze.

SOY-GLAZED CHICKEN WINGS WITH NOODLES

PREP + COOK TIME 4 HOURS 30 MINUTES   SERVES 4

1 tablespoon vegetable oil

1kg (2 pounds) chicken wings

1 medium brown onion (150g), sliced thinly

1 small red capsicum (bell pepper) (150g), sliced thinly

2 cloves garlic, crushed

2 teaspoons finely grated fresh ginger

1 teaspoon sriracha chilli sauce

1 teaspoon sesame oil

¼ cup (60ml) soy sauce

¼ cup (60ml) rice wine vinegar

2 tablespoons honey

250g (8 ounces) baby choy sum, halved (see tips)

375g (12 ounces) fresh Singapore-style noodles

2 green onions (scallions), sliced thinly (see tips)

2 teaspoons toasted sesame seeds

1 Heat vegetable oil in a 4.5-litre (18-cup) slow cooker on sear (HIGH) setting; cook chicken, in batches, turning, for 10 minutes, until well browned. Remove from cooker.

2 Place brown onion and capsicum in base of cooker; top with chicken. Combine garlic, ginger, chilli sauce, sesame oil, soy sauce, vinegar and honey in a jug; pour into cooker. Cook, covered, on low, for 3 hours 30 minutes.

3 Preheat grill (broiler).

4 Carefully remove chicken from cooker to an oven tray; cook under grill, for 5 minutes, turning halfway, until browned and skin is crisp.

5 Meanwhile, skim fat from surface of remaining sauce mixture in cooker. Add choy sum and noodles to cooker; simmer, on reduce setting, uncovered, for 5 minutes or until heated through.

6 Serve noodles and choy sum topped with chicken, green onions and seeds.

TIPS

You will need 1 bunch baby choy sum for this recipe. To make green onions curl, place the sliced onions in a small bowl of iced water for 30 minutes to curl; drain.

• **Not suitable to freeze.**

CHICKEN WITH LENTILS, PORT & PANCETTA

PREP + COOK TIME 3 HOURS 45 MINUTES SERVES 4

1 cup (200g) French-style
green lentils

2 tablespoons olive oil

8 chicken drumsticks (1.2kg)

2 medium leeks (700g), white
part only, sliced thinly

2 medium carrots (240g), halved,
sliced thinly

2 stalks celery (300g), trimmed,
sliced thickly

100g (3 ounces) sliced pancetta,
chopped coarsely

⅓ cup (95g) tomato paste

2½ cups (625ml) port

1½ cups (375ml) chicken stock

4 sprigs fresh thyme

1 cup (120g) frozen peas, thawed

1 tablespoon fresh thyme leaves,
extra

1 Rinse lentils well; drain.

2 Heat oil in a 4.5-litre (18-cup)
slow cooker on sear (HIGH) setting;
cook chicken, in batches, turning,
for 10 minutes, or until well browned.
Remove from cooker.

3 Reduce cooker to sauté (MEDIUM)
setting. Cook leek, carrot, celery and
pancetta, stirring, for 5 minutes or
until vegetables soften. Add paste;
cook, stirring, for 3 minutes. Stir in
port, stock, thyme and lentils.

4 Return chicken to cooker. Cook,
covered, on low, for 3 hours.

5 Discard thyme. Add peas to cooker;
stand, covered, for 5 minutes. Season.
Serve sprinkled with extra thyme.

SERVING SUGGESTIONS

Accompany with creamy polenta,
mashed potato or crusty bread to
mop up the juices.

• **Not suitable to freeze.**

CHICKEN WITH SPECK, LEEK & TARRAGON SCONES

PREP + COOK TIME 5 HOURS SERVES 4

¼ cup (60ml) olive oil

1kg (2 pounds) chicken thigh fillets, halved

150g (4½-ounce) piece speck, chopped finely

2 medium leeks (700g), white part only, sliced thinly

2 cloves garlic, crushed

¼ cup (35g) plain (all-purpose) flour

½ cup (125ml) dry white wine

1½ cups (375ml) chicken stock

⅓ cup (80ml) pouring cream

1 tablespoon wholegrain mustard

½ cup (60g) frozen peas

TARRAGON SCONES

1 cup (150g) self-raising flour

50g (1½ ounces) cold butter, chopped

⅓ cup (25g) finely grated parmesan

2 teaspoons finely chopped fresh tarragon

1 egg, beaten lightly

2 tablespoons buttermilk, approximately

1 Heat 1 tablespoon of the oil in a 4.5-litre (18-cup) slow cooker on sear (HIGH) setting; cook chicken, in batches, for 5 minutes, turning, or until well browned. Remove from cooker.

2 Heat remaining oil in cooker on sauté (MEDIUM) setting; cook speck, leek and garlic, stirring, for 5 minutes or until leek softens. Add flour; cook, stirring, for 3 minutes. Gradually stir in wine, then stock, cream and mustard; bring to the boil.

3 Return chicken to cooker. Cook, covered, on low, for 4 hours. Season.

4 Make tarragon scone mixture just before serving.

5 Add peas to chicken mixture; stir to combine. Drop level tablespoons of scone mixture, about 2cm (¾ inch) apart, on top of chicken mixture. Cook, covered, on high, for 30 minutes or until scones are firm to touch and cooked through.

6 Serve chicken mixture topped with scones.

TARRAGON SCONES Place flour in a medium bowl; using your fingertips, rub in butter. Stir in parmesan and tarragon. Stir in egg and enough of the buttermilk to make a soft, sticky dough.

SERVING SUGGESTION

Accompany with a leafy green salad and top with crispy fried shredded leek.

• **Not suitable to freeze.**

BUTTER CHICKEN

PREP + COOK TIME 4 HOURS 45 MINUTES (+ REFRIGERATION) SERVES 6

12 chicken thigh cutlets (2.4kg), skin removed

2 tablespoons lemon juice

1 teaspoon chilli powder

¾ cup (200g) Greek-style yoghurt

1 tablespoon finely grated fresh ginger

2 teaspoons garam masala

45g (1½ ounces) butter

1 tablespoon vegetable oil

1 medium brown onion (150g), chopped finely

4 cloves garlic, crushed

1 teaspoon ground coriander

1 teaspoon ground cumin

1 teaspoon paprika

2 tablespoons tomato paste

410g (13 ounces) canned tomato puree

⅔ cup (160ml) chicken stock

2 tablespoons honey

1 cinnamon stick

⅓ cup (80ml) pouring cream

½ cup loosely packed fresh coriander (cilantro) leaves

⅓ cup (50g) toasted cashews

1 Combine chicken, juice and chilli powder in a large bowl. Cover, refrigerate for 30 minutes.

2 Stir yoghurt, ginger and half the garam masala into chicken mixture.

3 Heat butter and oil in a 4.5-litre (18-cup) slow cooker on sear (HIGH) setting; cook chicken, turning, in batches, for 15 minutes, until well browned. Remove from cooker.

4 Add onion and garlic to cooker; cook, stirring, for 5 minutes or until onion softens. Add remaining garam masala, coriander, cumin and paprika; cook, stirring, for 1 minute or until fragrant. Stir in paste, puree, stock, honey and cinnamon. Return chicken to cooker. Cook, covered, on low, for 4 hours.

5 Stir in cream; season to taste.

6 Serve topped with coriander leaves and cashews.

SERVING SUGGESTION

Accompany with basmati rice, warm naan bread and lime wedges.

• Suitable to freeze at the end of step 4.

APRICOT CHICKEN

45g (1½-ounce) packet cream of chicken simmer soup mix

405ml (13½ ounces) canned apricot nectar

6 chicken marylands (2.1kg)

1 medium leek (350g), white part only, sliced thickly

2 cloves garlic, crushed

¾ cup (75g) dried apricot halves

¼ cup (20g) slivered almonds, toasted

2 tablespoons fresh micro herbs

1 Place soup mix in a 4.5-litre (18-cup) slow cooker. Gradually whisk in nectar until smooth.

2 Remove and discard fat and skin from chicken. Place chicken, leek, garlic and apricots in cooker. Cook, covered, on low, for 4 hours. Season to taste.

3 Sprinkle chicken with almonds and micro herbs to serve.

TIP
Chicken maryland is a traditional crumbed-chicken dish in America, but in Australia it refers to a cut of chicken consisting of the leg (drumstick) and thigh in one piece with the skin and bone intact. It is available from chicken shops and supermarkets.

SERVING SUGGESTION
Accompany with almond couscous and steamed green beans.

• Suitable to freeze at the end of step 2.

PORK

SWEET & SOUR PORK

PREP + COOK TIME 6 HOURS 45 MINUTES **SERVES** 4

8 boneless pork spare ribs (1kg)

1 medium red onion (170g), cut into wedges

1 medium red capsicum (bell pepper) (200g), chopped coarsely

2 cloves garlic, crushed

½ teaspoon dried chilli flakes

⅔ cup (160ml) salt-reduced soy sauce

⅔ cup (160ml) salt-reduced tomato sauce

¼ cup (60ml) white wine vinegar

¼ cup (55g) firmly packed light brown sugar

½ cup (125ml) apple and pineapple juice (see tips)

2 tablespoons water

1½ tablespoons cornflour (cornstarch)

½ small pineapple (450g), peeled, cored, chopped coarsely

2 teaspoons sesame seeds, toasted

2 green onions (scallions), sliced thinly (see tips)

1 Place pork, red onion, capsicum, garlic, chilli, sauces, vinegar, sugar and juice in a 4.5-litre (18-cup) slow cooker. Cook, covered, on low, for 6 hours.

2 Combine the water and cornflour in a small bowl until smooth. Stir cornflour mixture and pineapple into cooker. Increase heat to reduce setting on low; simmer, uncovered, about 10 minutes or until sauce thickens and pineapple is heated through.

3 Serve pork topped with sesame seeds and green onion.

TIPS

If apple and pineapple juice is unavailable, use apple or pineapple juice. We placed our green onion strips in a bowl of iced water for about 30 minutes to make them curl.

SERVING SUGGESTION

Accompany with steamed jasmine rice and Asian greens.

• Suitable to freeze at the end of step 1.

SMOKED SAUSAGES WITH LENTILS

PREP + COOK TIME 3 HOURS 45 MINUTES SERVES 4

1 tablespoon olive oil

8 schinkengriller sausages (600g)

1 cup (200g) green lentils

1½ cups (375ml) chicken stock

1 stalk celery (150g), trimmed, chopped finely

1 medium carrot (120g), chopped finely

1 medium brown onion (150g), chopped finely

2 sprigs fresh thyme

2 cloves garlic, crushed

400g (12½ ounces) canned diced tomatoes

1 tablespoon wholegrain mustard

1 Heat oil in a 4.5-litre (18-cup) slow cooker on sear (HIGH) setting; cook sausages, in batches, turning, for 5 minutes or until well browned. Remove from cooker.

2 Add lentils and stock to cooker; stir to combine. Add celery, carrot, onion, thyme, garlic, tomatoes and sausages. Cook, covered, on low, for 3 hours.

3 Remove sausages from cooker; cover to keep warm. Discard thyme. Stir mustard into lentil mixture; season to taste.

4 Serve lentil mixture with sausages.

SERVING SUGGESTIONS

Accompany with a fennel, apple and curly endive salad, mashed potato, steamed baby potatoes or crusty bread.

• Not suitable to freeze.

CARAMEL GINGER & CHILLI PORK

PREP + COOK TIME 4 HOURS 45 MINUTES **SERVES** 6

1.2kg (2½ pounds) boneless pork shoulder, cut into 3cm (1¼-inch) pieces

1 medium brown onion (150g), chopped finely

3 cloves garlic, crushed

1 fresh long red chilli, chopped finely

1 tablespoon finely grated fresh ginger

2 teaspoons fish sauce

⅓ cup (80ml) soy sauce

1 tablespoon peanut oil

⅔ cup (160ml) salt-reduced chicken stock

¼ cup (55g) firmly packed dark brown sugar

10cm (4-inch) stick fresh lemon grass (20g), halved, bruised

2 star anise

1 cinnamon stick

2 x 5cm (2-inch) strips lime rind

2 tablespoons lime juice

2 green onions (scallions), sliced thinly

¼ cup (35g) roasted unsalted peanuts

1 fresh long red chilli, sliced thinly

1 Combine pork, brown onion, garlic, chopped chilli, ginger, fish sauce and half the soy sauce in a large bowl; toss to coat pork.

2 Heat oil in a 4.5-litre (18-cup) slow cooker on sear (HIGH) setting; cook pork, in batches, stirring, for 10 minutes or until well browned. Return pork to cooker.

3 Add remaining soy sauce, stock, sugar, lemon grass, star anise, cinnamon and rind. Cook, covered, on low, for 4 hours. Discard lemon grass, star anise, cinnamon and rind; stir in juice.

4 Serve pork topped with green onion, peanuts and sliced chilli.

SERVING SUGGESTIONS

Accompany with steamed jasmine rice or noodles.

• Suitable to freeze at the end of step 3.

SATAY PORK STEW

PREP + COOK TIME 4 HOURS 45 MINUTES **SERVES** 4

700g (1½ pounds) pork scotch fillet (neck), cut into 5cm (2-inch) pieces

1 medium red onion (170g), cut into wedges

1 large red capsicum (bell pepper) (350g), sliced thickly

250g (8 ounces) canned satay sauce

2 tablespoons salt-reduced soy sauce

½ fresh long red chilli, chopped finely

2 tablespoons lime juice

1 green onion (scallions), sliced thinly

¼ cup (35g) coarsely chopped roasted unsalted peanuts

½ fresh long red chilli, sliced thinly

2 tablespoons micro herbs

1 Place pork, red onion, capsicum, satay sauce, soy sauce and chopped chilli in a 4.5-litre (18-cup) slow cooker. Cook, covered, on low, for 4 hours. Season to taste.

2 Increase heat to reduce setting on high; simmer, uncovered, about 10 minutes or until sauce thickens slightly.

3 Stir in juice and green onion. Serve stew topped with peanuts, sliced chilli and micro herbs.

SERVING SUGGESTIONS
Accompany with jasmine rice or fried noodles and cucumber sticks.

• Suitable to freeze at the end of step 2.

HAM & CHEESE TORTELLINI BROTH

PREP + COOK TIME 5 HOURS 45 MINUTES   SERVES 4

3 cloves garlic, crushed

1 medium brown onion (150g), sliced thinly

400g (12½-ounce) piece smoked ham

2 tablespoons tomato paste

1 litre (4 cups) chicken stock

3 cups (750ml) water

400g (12½ ounces) canned diced tomatoes

200g (6½ ounces) green peas

300g (9½ ounces) ham and cheese tortellini

¼ small cabbage (300g), shredded finely

⅓ cup (25g) shaved parmesan

1 Place garlic, onion, ham, paste, stock, the water and tomatoes in a 4.5-litre (18-cup) slow cooker. Cook, covered, on low, for 5 hours. Season.

2 Remove ham from cooker; shred meat coarsely using two forks. Return to cooker with peas. Cook, covered, on high, for 10 minutes or until peas are tender.

3 Meanwhile, cook pasta in a large saucepan of boiling salted water until just tender; drain. Divide among serving bowls.

4 Ladle broth over tortellini. Serve topped with cabbage and parmesan.

SERVING SUGGESTION
Accompany with crusty olive bread.

• Not suitable to freeze.

SPANISH SMOKY RIBS WITH CHORIZO

PREP + COOK TIME 4 HOURS 45 MINUTES SERVES 4

2 tablespoons olive oil

2 cured chorizo sausages (260g), sliced thinly

1.5kg (3 pounds) American-style pork ribs, cut into 3-rib portions

1 large red onion (300g), sliced thinly

1 large red capsicum (bell pepper) (300g), sliced thinly

3 cloves garlic, crushed

2 teaspoons smoked paprika

1 teaspoon Mexican chilli powder

400g (12½ ounces) canned diced tomatoes

1 cup (250ml) beef stock

1 tablespoon brown sugar

1 tablespoon sherry vinegar (see tip)

2 green onions (scallions), sliced thinly

1 Heat half the oil in a 4.5-litre (18-cup) slow cooker on sear (HIGH) setting; cook chorizo, stirring, for 10 minutes or until well browned. Drain on paper towel.

2 Heat remaining oil in cooker; cook pork, in batches, turning, for 10 minutes or until well browned. Remove from cooker.

3 Add red onion, capsicum, garlic, paprika and chilli to cooker; cook, stirring, for 5 minutes or until vegetables soften. Stir in tomatoes, stock, sugar and vinegar. Return pork to cooker. Cook, covered, on low, for 4 hours. Season to taste.

4 Serve topped with green onion.

TIP
You can use balsamic or red wine vinegar if you can't get sherry vinegar.

SERVING SUGGESTIONS
Accompany with steamed white rice or flour tortillas and lime wedges.

• Not suitable to freeze

CHILLI MARMALADE & FIVE-SPICE PORK CHOPS

PREP + COOK TIME 5 HOURS SERVES 4

4 pork forequarter chops (1kg)

2 cloves garlic, crushed

2 teaspoons finely grated
fresh ginger

2 teaspoons sriracha chilli sauce

2 teaspoons five-spice powder

1 tablespoon vegetable oil

½ cup (170g) orange marmalade

½ cup (125ml) salt-reduced
chicken stock

¼ cup (60ml) kecap manis

500g (1 pound) baby choy sum,
trimmed (see tip)

¼ cup loosely packed fresh small
mint sprigs

¼ cup loosely packed fresh small
coriander sprigs

¼ cup (35g) coarsely chopped
roasted unsalted peanuts

1 fresh long red chilli,
sliced thinly

1 Combine pork, garlic, ginger, chilli
sauce and five-spice in a large bowl;
toss to coat pork.

2 Heat oil in a 4.5-litre (18-cup) slow
cooker on sear (HIGH) setting; cook
pork, in batches, for 4 minutes each
side or until well browned. Remove
from cooker.

3 Combine marmalade, stock, and
kecap manis in cooker; return pork
to cooker. Cook, covered, on low,
for 4 hours.

4 Just before serving, boil, steam
or microwave choy sum until tender;
drain.

5 Carefully remove pork from cooker;
cover to keep warm. Skim fat from
surface of sauce. Serve pork with
sauce and choy sum, topped with
mint, coriander, peanuts and chilli.

TIP

You will need two bunches of choy
sum for this recipe.

SERVING SUGGESTIONS

Accompany with steamed jasmine
rice or noodles.

• Not suitable to freeze.

SMOKY STICKY PORK RIBS WITH COLESLAW

PREP + COOK TIME 4 HOURS 15 MINUTES **SERVES** 4

2kg (4 pounds) American-style pork ribs

3 cloves garlic, crushed

1 cup (280g) barbecue sauce

¼ cup (60ml) lemon juice

¼ cup (55g) brown sugar

2 teaspoons sweet smoked paprika

1 teaspoon Tabasco sauce

CHEESY COLESLAW

¼ small green cabbage (300g), shredded finely

¼ small red cabbage (300g), shredded finely

1 large carrot (180g), grated coarsely

½ small red onion (50g), sliced thinly

1 cup (120g) coarsely grated vintage cheddar

2 tablespoons coarsely chopped fresh chives

¾ cup (225g) mayonnaise

¼ cup (60ml) cider vinegar

1 Cut pork into pieces that will fit into a 4.5-litre (18-cup) slow cooker.

2 Combine remaining ingredients in a large shallow dish; add pork, turn to coat in marinade. Transfer pork and marinade to cooker. Cook, covered, on high, for 3 hours 30 minutes. Turn ribs twice during cooking time for even cooking.

3 Make cheesy coleslaw.

4 Carefully remove ribs from cooker; cover to keep warm. Increase heat to reduce setting on high; boil sauce, uncovered, skimming fat from surface, for 10 minutes or until sauce has reduced to 1 cup.

5 Drizzle pork with sauce. Serve with coleslaw.

CHEESY COLESLAW Place ingredients in a large bowl; toss to combine. Season to taste.

TIP
Ask the butcher to cut the ribs into pieces that will fit into your slow cooker.

SERVING SUGGESTION
Accompany with jacket potatoes topped with sour cream and chives.

• **Not suitable to freeze.**

VEGETARIAN

BARLEY & FENNEL RISOTTO

PREP + COOK TIME 2 HOURS 45 MINUTES   SERVES 4

1 tablespoon olive oil

20g (¾ ounce) butter

1 medium brown onion (150g),
chopped finely

2 small fennel bulbs (400g),
sliced thinly

2 cloves garlic, crushed

2 teaspoons fresh thyme leaves

1 teaspoon fennel seeds,
crushed lightly

1 cup (200g) pearl barley

2½ cups (625ml) vegetable stock

½ cup (60g) frozen peas, thawed

½ cup (40g) finely grated
parmesan

60g (2 ounces) snow pea tendrils

2 teaspoons long strips lemon rind

1 Heat oil and butter in a 4.5-litre
(18-cup) slow cooker on sear (HIGH)
setting; cook onion, sliced fennel,
garlic, thyme and fennel seeds,
stirring, for 5 minutes or until
vegetables soften. Add barley; cook,
stirring, for 2 minutes or until barley
is toasted lightly. Add stock. Cook,
covered, on low, for 2 hours.

2 Add peas and half the parmesan;
season to taste. Stand, covered, for
5 minutes or until peas are heated
through.

3 Serve risotto sprinkled with
remaining parmesan, pea tendrils
and rind.

SERVING SUGGESTION
Accompany with grilled bread.

• **Not suitable to freeze.**

MUSHROOM STROGANOFF

PREP + COOK TIME 3 HOURS 15 MINUTES SERVES 4

¼ cup (60ml) olive oil

12 shallots (300g), halved

200g (6½ ounces) button mushrooms

200g (6½ ounces) swiss brown mushrooms

375g (12 ounces) portobello mushrooms, quartered

500g (1 pound) cup mushrooms, halved

3 cloves garlic, sliced thinly

2 tablespoons finely chopped fresh thyme

1 tablespoon finely chopped fresh rosemary

2 teaspoons paprika

2 fresh bay leaves

1 cup (250ml) dry white wine

1 tablespoon dijon mustard

1 tablespoon worcestershire sauce

½ cup (120g) crème fraîche

1 tablespoon plain (all-purpose) flour

¼ cup finely chopped fresh chives

1 Heat 1 tablespoon of the oil in a 4.5-litre (18-cup) slow cooker on sear (HIGH) setting; cook shallots and one-third of the mushrooms, stirring, for 5 minutes or until browned. Remove from cooker. Repeat twice with remaining oil and mushrooms.

2 Return mushroom mixture to cooker with garlic, half of the thyme, rosemary, paprika, bay leaves and wine; bring to the boil. Boil, uncovered, for 5 minutes or until wine reduces by half.

3 Add mustard and sauce; stir to combine. Cook, covered, on high, for 2 hours. Discard bay leaves.

4 Combine crème fraîche and flour in a small bowl. Stir crème fraîche mixture into mushroom mixture. Increase heat to reduce setting on high; simmer, uncovered, for about 10 minutes or until sauce boils and thickens. Season to taste.

5 Serve stroganoff sprinkled with chives and remaining thyme.

TIP
Use any combination of mushrooms that you prefer.

SERVING SUGGESTION
Accompany with buttered pasta.

• **Not suitable to freeze.**

INDIAN-STYLE LENTIL STEW

PREP + COOK TIME 2 HOURS 30 MINUTES SERVES 4

1 tablespoon olive oil

1 medium brown onion (150g),
    chopped finely

3 cloves garlic, crushed

½ teaspoon dried chilli flakes

1 teaspoon ground turmeric

1 tablespoon black mustard seeds

1 cinnamon stick

2 teaspoons ground cumin

1 tablespoon ground coriander

1½ cups (300g) green lentils

2½ cups (625ml) vegetable stock

1 cup (250ml) canned
    coconut cream

150g (4½ ounces) baby
    spinach leaves

½ cup (120g) natural yoghurt

2 tablespoons micro herbs

1 Heat oil in a 4.5-litre (18-cup) slow cooker on sear (HIGH) setting; cook onion and garlic, stirring, for 5 minutes or until softened.

2 Add chilli, turmeric, mustard seeds, cinnamon, cumin and coriander to cooker; cook, stirring, for 1 minute or until fragrant.

3 Add lentils, stock and coconut cream; stir to combine. Cook, covered, on low, for 2 hours.

4 Discard cinnamon. Stir in spinach; season to taste. Serve topped with yoghurt and micro herbs.

SERVING SUGGESTION
Accompany with cauliflower rice and grilled roti bread.

• **Not suitable to freeze.**

COCONUT PUMPKIN SOUP

PREP + COOK TIME 4 HOURS 45 MINUTES SERVES 4

3 cloves garlic, crushed

½ teaspoon dried chilli flakes

1.5kg (3 pounds) pumpkin, chopped coarsely

1 large brown onion (200g), chopped coarsely

1 cup (250ml) coconut milk

2 cups (500ml) vegetable stock

2 tablespoons roasted unsalted peanuts

1 fresh long red chilli, sliced thinly

¼ cup loosely packed small fresh coriander (cilantro) leaves

1 Place garlic, dried chilli, pumpkin, onion, coconut milk and stock in a 4.5-litre (18-cup) slow cooker. Cook, covered, on high, for 4 hours.

2 Cool soup for 10 minutes. Using a stick blender blend soup until smooth. Season to taste.

3 Serve soup topped with peanuts, fresh chilli and coriander.

SERVING SUGGESTION
Accompany with thin slices of toasted baguette and lime wedges.

• Suitable to freeze at the end of step 2.

QUINOA, BLACK BEAN & CHIPÓTLE CHILLI

PREP + COOK TIME 3 HOURS 15 MINUTES   SERVES 4

½ cup (100g) tri-colour quinoa

1 tablespoon olive oil

1 medium brown onion (150g),
chopped finely

1 medium red capsicum (bell
pepper) (200g), chopped finely

1 medium green capsicum (bell
pepper) (200g), chopped finely

3 cloves garlic, crushed

2 teaspoons ground cumin

2 teaspoons dried oregano

½ teaspoon Mexican chilli powder

375g (12 ounces) bottled chipotle
thick and chunky salsa

2½ cups (625ml) vegetable stock

910g (1¾ pounds) canned black
beans, drained, rinsed

2 trimmed corn cobs (500g),
kernels removed

½ cup loosely packed fresh
coriander (cilantro) sprigs

1   Rinse quinoa well; drain.

2   Heat oil in a 4.5-litre (18-cup) slow
cooker on sear (HIGH) setting; cook
onion, capsicum and garlic, stirring,
for 5 minutes or until vegetables
soften. Add cumin, oregano and
chilli; cook, stirring, for 1 minute
or until fragrant.

3   Add quinoa, salsa, stock and beans;
stir to combine. Cook, covered, on
low, for 2 hour 30 minutes.

4   Add corn to cooker; cook, covered,
on high, for 30 minutes or until corn
is tender. Season to taste.

5   Serve chilli topped with coriander.

SERVING SUGGESTION

Accompany with guacamole, corn
chips, sour cream and lime cheeks.

• Not suitable to freeze.

LENTIL & CAULIFLOWER STEW WITH CARROT-TOP PISTOU

PREP + COOK TIME 5 HOURS 45 MINUTES SERVES 4

¾ cup (150g) French-style
green lentils

400g (12½ ounces) baby (dutch)
carrots with tops

1 tablespoon olive oil

2 medium leeks (700g),
white part only, sliced thinly

3 cloves garlic, crushed

2 stalks celery (300g), trimmed,
sliced thickly

4 sprigs fresh thyme

2 dried bay leaves

1 cup (250ml) dry white wine

2 cups (500ml) vegetable stock

½ medium cauliflower (750g),
cut into medium florets

2 medium kale leaves (70g), stalks
removed, shredded coarsely

CARROT-TOP PISTOU

1½ cups coarsely chopped
reserved carrot tops

1 cup loosely packed fresh
mint leaves

2 teaspoons finely grated
lemon rind

1 tablespoon lemon juice

1 clove garlic, quartered

½ cup (125ml) olive oil

1 Rinse lentils well; drain.

2 Trim carrots, reserving tops to
make pistou.

3 Heat oil in a 4.5-litre (18-cup) slow
cooker on sauté (MEDIUM) setting;
cook leek and garlic, stirring, for
10 minutes or until lightly golden.
Add carrot, celery, thyme and bay
leaves; cook, stirring, for 5 minutes
or until vegetables soften. Add wine;
bring to the boil. Boil, uncovered,
for 1 minute.

4 Add stock, cauliflower and lentils;
stir to combine. Cook, covered, on
low, for 5 hours, stirring occasionally.

5 Discard thyme and bay leaves.
Add kale to cooker; cook, covered,
on high, for 10 minutes or until kale
wilts. Season to taste.

6 Meanwhile, make carrot-top
pistou.

7 Serve stew topped with pistou.

CARROT-TOP PISTOU Blend or process
reserves carrot tops, mint, rind, juice
and garlic until finely chopped. With
motor operating, add oil, in a thin,
steady stream; process until smooth.
Season to taste.

SERVING SUGGESTIONS
Accompany with brown rice or crusty
bread to mop up the juices.

• **Not suitable to freeze.**

BEAN BOURGUIGNON

PREP + COOK TIME 4 HOURS 15 MINUTES SERVES 4

600g (1¼ pounds) swiss brown mushrooms, halved if large

3 x 400g (12½ ounces) canned butter beans, drained, rinsed

8 shallots (200g), halved

4 cloves garlic, crushed

2 dried bay leaves

6 sprigs fresh thyme, plus extra small sprigs to serve

1½ cups (375ml) dry red wine

410g (13 ounces) canned tomato puree

1 Place mushrooms, beans, shallots, garlic, bay leaves, thyme, wine and puree in a 4.5-litre (18-cup) slow cooker. Cook, covered, on high, for 4 hours.

2 Discard bay leaves and thyme; season to taste. Serve bourguignon topped with extra thyme.

SERVING SUGGESTIONS
Accompany with mashed potato, wilted spinach or toasted crusty bread to mop up the juices.

• **Not suitable to freeze.**

EGGPLANT PARMIGIANA

PREP + COOK TIME 6 HOURS 45 MINUTES SERVES 4

⅔ cup (160ml) olive oil

1 medium brown onion (150g), chopped finely

2 cloves garlic, crushed

400g (12½ ounces) canned diced tomatoes

1 cup (260g) bottled passata

¼ teaspoon dried chilli flakes

2 medium eggplants (600g), sliced thickly

¼ cup (35g) plain (all-purpose) flour

⅔ cup loosely packed fresh basil leaves, plus extra, to serve

400g (12½ ounces) bocconcini, torn

⅔ cup (50g) finely grated parmesan

½ teaspoon sweet paprika

1 Heat 1 tablespoon of the oil in a large frying pan over medium heat; cook onion, stirring, for 5 minutes or until onion softens. Add garlic; cook, stirring, for 1 minute or until fragrant. Stir in tomatoes, passata and chilli. Transfer to a medium jug.

2 Toss eggplant in flour to coat, dust off excess. Heat remaining oil in same pan; cook eggplant, in batches, for 3 minutes each side or until browned. Drain on paper towel.

3 Layer half the eggplant in a 4.5-litre (18-cup) slow cooker; season. Top with half the tomato mixture, basil and bocconcini. Repeat layering, finishing with parmesan. Sprinkle with paprika. Cook, covered, on low, about 6 hours.

4 Serve sprinkled with extra basil.

SERVING SUGGESTION
Top with toasted coarse breadcrumbs and serve with salad leaves.

• Not suitable to freeze.

MIXED BEAN, SPINACH & PANEER RÓGAN JOSH

PREP + COOK TIME 4 HOURS 30 MINUTES SERVES 4

½ cup (150g) rogan josh
curry paste

2 large brown onions (400g),
sliced thinly

2 teaspoons finely grated
fresh ginger

3 cloves garlic, crushed

400g (12½ ounces) canned
diced tomatoes

840g (1¾ pounds) canned
four-bean mix, drained, rinsed

2 dried bay leaves

2 cups (500ml) vegetable stock

150g (4½ ounces) baby
spinach leaves

200g (6½ ounces) paneer,
crumbled

¼ cup loosely packed fresh
micro herbs

1 Heat a 4.5-litre (18-cup) slow cooker on sauté (MEDIUM) setting; cook curry paste, stirring for 5 minutes or until fragrant. Add onion, ginger, garlic, tomatoes, beans, bay leaves and stock; stir to combine. Cook, covered, on low for 4 hours.

2 Stir in spinach; cook, covered, on high, for 5 minutes or until spinach wilts. Season to taste.

3 Serve curry topped with paneer and micro herbs.

SERVING SUGGESTIONS

Accompany with warmed naan bread, steamed basmati rice, lime wedges or natural yoghurt

• **Suitable to freeze at the end of step 1.**

BREADS & CONDIMENTS

APPLE BUTTER

PREP + COOK TIME 7 HOURS   MAKES 3 CUPS

1kg (2 pounds) apples, peeled, cored, sliced thinly

¼ cup (55g) caster (superfine) sugar

1 teaspoon ground ginger

½ teaspoon ground cinnamon

¼ teaspoon cooking (kosher) salt

1 cup (250ml) apple juice

4 whole cloves

1 vanilla bean, split lengthways

1 Combine apples, sugar, ginger, cinnamon, salt, juice and cloves in a 4.5-litre (18-cup) slow cooker. Cook, covered, on high, for 6 hours.

2 Uncover, add vanilla bean. Increase heat to reduce setting on medium; boil, uncovered, for 20 minutes, stirring, until thick and browned. Discard cloves.

3 Pour hot apple butter into hot sterilised jars (see glossary, page 235); seal immediately. Label and date jars when cold.

SERVING SUGGESTION

Serve on porridge sprinkled with sunflower seeds, pepitas (pumpkin seed kernels), cinnamon and honey.

MIXED BERRY JAM

PREP + COOK TIME 4 HOURS 45 MINUTES **MAKES** 4 CUPS

1.25kg (2½ pounds) mixed
  fresh berries

1kg (2 pounds) white
  (granulated) sugar

¼ cup (60ml) lemon juice

1 Place berries, sugar and juice in
a 4.5-litre (18-cup) slow cooker; stir
to coat. Cook, covered, on high, for
4 hours.

2 Uncover, increase heat to reduce
setting on high; boil, uncovered,
stirring occasionally, for 30 minutes
or until jam jells when tested.

3 Pour hot jam into hot sterilised
jars (see glossary, page 235); seal
immediately. Label and date jars
when cold.

TIP

This jam has a softer set than
commercial jams.

BACON JAM

PREP + COOK TIME 7 HOURS **MAKES** 5 CUPS

1kg (2 pounds) rindless bacon slices, sliced thinly, excess fat trimmed

3 brown onions (450g), sliced thinly

4 cloves garlic, sliced thinly

⅔ cup (160ml) cider vinegar

⅔ cup (150g) firmly packed brown sugar

⅔ cup (160ml) pure maple syrup

1 tablespoon wholegrain mustard

4 sprigs fresh thyme

1 teaspoon instant coffee granules

⅓ cup (80ml) warm water

1 Heat a large frying pan over medium-high heat. Cook bacon, in batches, until browned lightly. Drain on paper towel.

2 Transfer bacon to a 4.5-litre (18-cup) slow cooker. Add onion, garlic, vinegar, sugar, syrup, mustard, thyme, coffee and the water. Cook, covered, on high, for 6 hours. Discard thyme; skim excess fat. Season with pepper.

3 Process bacon mixture until finely chopped, but not pureed. Spoon hot jam into hot sterilised jars (see glossary, page 235); seal immediately. Label and date jars when cold.

SERVING SUGGESTION

Serve on toasted bread with roasted tomatoes, fried egg and baby spinach leaves.

ORANGE MARMALADE

1kg (2 pounds) oranges

1 litre (4 cups) water

4½ cups (1kg) white (granulated) sugar, approximately

1 Peel oranges, removing rind and white pith separately; slice rind thinly, reserve half the pith. Quarter oranges; slice flesh thinly, reserve any seeds. Tie reserved pith and seeds in muslin.

2 Combine rind, flesh, muslin bag and the water in a 4.5-litre (18-cup) slow cooker. Cook, covered, on high, for 2 hours. Discard muslin bag.

3 Measure fruit mixture, allow 1 cup sugar for each cup of fruit mixture. Return orange mixture and sugar to slow cooker. Increase heat to reduce setting on high; boil, uncovered, for 40 minutes or until marmalade jells when tested.

4 Pour hot marmalade into hot sterilised jars (see glossary, page 235); seal immediately. Label and date jars when cold.

TIP
This method of making marmalade will work with most citrus fruits or a combination of various citrus fruits.

CHERRY CHUTNEY

PREP + COOK TIME 5 HOURS **MAKES** 5 1/2 CUPS

1kg (2 pounds) frozen pitted cherries, thawed

5 medium red apples (750g), peeled, chopped coarsely

2 medium red onions (340g), chopped coarsely

3 cloves garlic, crushed

1 tablespoon finely grated fresh ginger

1 cinnamon stick

2 cardamom pods, bruised

½ cup (110g) caster (superfine) sugar

1 cup (250ml) apple cider vinegar

1 Combine ingredients in a 4.5-litre (18-cup) slow cooker. Cook, covered, on high, for 4 hours.

2 Discard cinnamon and cardamom. Increase heat to reduce setting on high; boil mixture, uncovered, about 30 minutes or until chutney is thick, stirring occasionally.

3 Spoon hot chutney into hot sterilised jars (see glossary, page 235); seal immediately. Label and date jars when cold.

Spread chutney on crusty bread slices; top with ham and cheese and grill until cheese has melted.

PICKLED ONIONS

PREP + COOK TIME 3 HOURS (+ STANDING) MAKES 6 CUPS

You will need to start this recipe a day ahead.

1kg (3 pounds) baby brown
  onions (small pickling onions)

½ cup (140g) cooking
  (kosher) salt

2 cups (500ml) boiling water

1 cup (250ml) cold water

2 cloves garlic, bruised

1 teaspoon whole black
  peppercorns

3 cups (750ml) white wine
  vinegar

1 cup (250ml) white vinegar

1 cup (220g) caster (superfine)
  sugar

6 sprigs fresh rosemary

6 sprigs fresh thyme

2 dried bay leaves

1 Place onions in a large heatproof non-metallic bowl, cover with boiling water; stand for 30 minutes, drain. Peel onions, leaving root ends intact; return to bowl.

2 Combine salt and the boiling water in a large heatproof jug; stir until salt dissolves. Add the cold water; pour over onions. Cover with a large plate or a sealed plastic bag half-filled with water to keep onions submerged; stand overnight.

3 Place garlic, peppercorns, vinegars, sugar and 2 sprigs of both rosemary and thyme in a 4.5-litre (18-cup) slow cooker. Cook, covered, on high, for 2 hours.

4 Meanwhile, rinse and drain onions; pat onions dry with paper towel. Pack onions, bay leaves and remaining rosemary and thyme into hot sterilised jars (see glossary, page 235).

5 Discard rosemary, thyme and garlic from vinegar mixture. Pour enough vinegar mixture into jars to cover onions; seal immediately. Label and date jars when cold.

TIP

Discard any excess pickling liquid.

TOMATO SAUCE (KETCHUP)

PREP + COOK TIME 4 HOURS 30 MINUTES MAKES 6 CUPS

1 medium brown onion (150g), chopped finely

1 stalk celery (150g), trimmed, chopped finely

3 x 400g (12½ ounces) canned diced tomatoes

1 teaspoon celery salt

1 teaspoon mustard powder

½ teaspoon ground allspice

2 fresh or dried bay leaves

½ cup (125ml) white wine vinegar

410g (13 ounce) canned tomato puree

½ cup (110g) firmly packed brown sugar

1 Place ingredients in a 4.5-litre (18-cup) slow cooker. Cook, covered, on high, for 4 hours.

2 Discard bay leaves; season to taste. Using a stick blender, blend sauce until smooth.

3 Increase heat to reduce setting on high; boil, uncovered, for 10 minutes or until thickened slightly.

4 Pour sauce into hot sterilised bottles (see glossary, page 235); seal immediately. Label and date bottles when cold.

PICKLED BEETROOT

PREP + COOK TIME 4 HOURS 20 MINUTES **MAKES** 5 CUPS

750g (1½ pounds) trimmed,
beetroot (beets), peeled,
cut into wedges

2 cloves garlic, crushed

2 sprigs fresh thyme, plus extra
thyme leaves, to serve

2 sprigs fresh rosemary

1 teaspoon mustard seeds

1 teaspoon fennel seeds

1 cup (220g) caster (superfine)
sugar

1¼ cups (310ml) white
wine vinegar

1¼ cups (310ml) water

1 Place beetroot, garlic, thyme, rosemary, mustard seeds and fennel seeds in a 4.5-litre (18-cup) slow cooker. Cook, covered, on high, for 4 hours.

2 Just before beetroot is ready, place sugar, vinegar and the water in a small saucepan over medium heat; cook, stirring, for 2 minutes or until sugar dissolves.

3 Discard thyme and rosemary. Spoon beetroots into hot sterilised jars (see glossary, page 235). Pour enough hot vinegar mixture into jars to cover beetroots; seal immediately. Label and date jars when cold. Serve sprinkled with extra thyme.

TIP

Discard any excess pickling liquid.

PASSATA

PREP + COOK TIME 8 HOURS 30 MINUTES   **MAKES** 6 CUPS

1 tablespoon olive oil

2.5kg (5 pounds) ripe roma (egg) tomatoes, cored

1½ teaspoons salt

1 Place oil in base of a 4.5-litre (18-cup) slow cooker. Add tomatoes to cooker; sprinkle with salt. Cook, covered, on low, for 8 hours, do not stir.

2 Carefully transfer tomatoes to a sieve with a slotted spoon; discard liquid in cooker. Blend or process tomatoes, in batches, in a high-powered blender until smooth.

3 Return passata to cooker, increase heat to reduce setting on high; bring to the boil.

4 Pour hot passata into hot sterilised bottles (see glossary, page 235); seal immediately. Label and date bottles when cold.

TIPS

If you don't have a high-powered blender you may need to strain the passata mixture to remove any skins. You can add any flavours you like to the passata such as onion, garlic or basil; or use the passata in other recipes.

• Suitable to freeze at the end of step 2.

CHUNKY QUINCE, ROSÉ & VANILLA PRESERVE

PREP + COOK TIME 8 HOURS MAKES 7 CUPS

2kg (4 pounds) quince

2 cups (500ml) rosé wine

1 vanilla bean, split lengthways, seeds scraped

1 cinnamon stick

6 cups (1.3kg) white (granulated) sugar, approximately

½ cup (125ml) lemon juice

1 Peel, quarter and core quinces; reserve cores. Tie reserved cores in muslin. Chop quince coarsely.

2 Combine quince, muslin bag, wine, vanilla bean and seeds, and cinnamon in a 4.5-litre (18-cup) slow cooker; stir to combine. Cook, covered, on high, for 6 hours, stirring occasionally for even cooking, or until quince is tender and ruby-coloured. Discard muslin bag, vanilla bean and cinnamon.

3 Measure fruit mixture, allow 1 cup sugar for each cup of fruit mixture. Return quince mixture and sugar to cooker; add juice. Increase heat to reduce setting on high; boil, stirring frequently, for 1 hour or until mixture jells when tested.

4 Pour hot quince mixture into hot sterilised jars (see glossary, page 235); seal immediately. Label and date jars when cold.

SERVING SUGGESTION

Accompany with a sharp cheese and crackers.

TEAR & SHARE PIZZA SUPREME

PREP + COOK TIME 2 HOURS **SERVES** 6

½ cup (135g) drained canned pineapple pieces, chopped coarsely

2 cups (300g) self-raising flour

½ teaspoon bicarbonate of soda (baking soda)

50g (1½ ounces) cold butter, chopped

¾ cup (180ml) buttermilk, approximately

2 tablespoons pizza sauce with herbs and garlic

2 tablespoons barbecue sauce

½ small red onion (50g), sliced thinly

½ small green capsicum (bell pepper) (75g), sliced thinly

50g (1½ ounces) sliced pepperoni, chopped coarsely

50g (1½ ounces) shaved ham, chopped coarsely

50g (1½ ounces) sliced mushrooms

1½ cups (100g) pizza cheese

1 Drain pineapple on paper towel.

2 Preheat a 4.5-litre (18-cup) slow cooker on high for 30 minutes. Line cooker with a piece of baking paper.

3 Meanwhile, sift flour and soda into a large bowl; using your fingertips, rub in butter. Stir in enough of the buttermilk to make a soft, sticky dough.

4 Turn dough onto a floured surface; knead lightly until smooth. Flatten into a 25cm x 30cm (10-inch x 12-inch) rectangle. Spread dough with combined sauces; top with red onion, capsicum, pepperoni, ham, mushrooms, pineapple and half the cheese.

5 Roll up dough, using long side, to enclose fillings. Cut dough into six scrolls. Place scrolls, just touching, cut-side up, in cooker. Sprinkle with remaining cheese. Cook, covered, on high, for 1 hour 30 minutes or until cooked through.

6 Preheat grill (broiler).

7 Carefully lift scrolls, on baking paper, from cooker; place on an oven tray. Cook under grill for 5 minutes or until browned lightly.

TIP

You can use any fillings you like but be careful not to overload the scrolls or they will not cook through.

SERVING SUGGESTION

Accompany with a leafy green salad.

• **Not suitable to freeze.**

CHEESY SEED DAMPER

PREP + COOK TIME 3 HOURS 30 MINUTES **SERVES** 12

3 cups (450g) self-raising flour

2 teaspoons sea salt

40g (1½ ounces) cold butter, chopped

¼ cup (65g) pepitas (pumpkin seed kernels)

¼ cup (35g) sunflower seeds

2 tablespoons linseeds

¼ cup (50g) roasted buckwheat

1½ cups (100g) pizza cheese

¾ cup (180ml) buttermilk

½ cup (125ml) water, approximately

1 Preheat a 4.5-litre (18-cup) slow cooker on high for 30 minutes.

2 Meanwhile, sift flour and salt into a large bowl, using your fingertips; rub in butter. Stir in seeds, buckwheat and cheese. Stir in buttermilk and enough of the water to make a soft, sticky dough.

3 Turn dough onto a floured surface; knead lightly until smooth. Shape dough into a 16cm (6½-inch) round on a piece of baking paper. Brush with a little extra buttermilk, sprinkle with a little extra flour; cut a 1cm (½ inch) deep, 10cm (4-inch) wide cross in top of dough.

4 Lift dough, on baking paper, into cooker. Cook, covered, on high, for 3 hours or until damper sounds hollow when tapped with fingers.

5 Preheat grill (broiler).

6 Carefully lift damper, on baking paper, from cooker; place on an oven tray. Cook under grill for 5 minutes or until browned lightly.

TIP

Damper is best made on day of serving or reheat, wrapped in foil, in the oven for 15 minutes or until warmed through.

SERVING SUGGESTION

Accompany with butter and loads of golden syrup; or serve with soups and stews.

• Suitable to freeze at the end of step 6.

CORN BREAD

PREP + COOK TIME 2 HOURS 30 MINUTES **SERVES** 10

1½ cups (225g) self-raising flour

1 cup (170g) polenta (cornmeal)

2 teaspoons sea salt

¼ cup finely chopped fresh
  flat-leaf parsley

½ cup (60g) coarsely grated
  cheddar

250g (8 ounces) canned corn
  kernels, drained, rinsed

250g (8 ounces) canned
  creamed corn

2 eggs, beaten lightly

50g (1½ ounces) butter, melted

½ cup (125ml) buttermilk

1 Oil the insert bowl of a 4.5-litre (18-cup) slow cooker; preheat cooker on high for 30 minutes.

2 Meanwhile, combine flour, polenta, salt, parsley, cheddar and corn kernels in a large bowl. Combine creamed corn, egg, butter and buttermilk in a large jug. Add buttermilk mixture to flour mixture; stir until just combined.

3 Spread mixture into cooker bowl; smooth top. Cook, covered, on high, for 2 hours or until bread sounds hollow when tapped with fingers.

4 Preheat grill (broiler).

5 Carefully turn corn bread, top-side up, onto an oven tray. Cook under grill for 5 minutes or until bread is browned lightly.

TIP
Bread is best made on day of serving or reheat, wrapped in foil, in the oven for 15 minutes or until warmed through.

SERVING SUGGESTION
Serve with soups and stews.

• Suitable to freeze at the end of step 5.

IRISH SODA RYE BREAD

PREP + COOK TIME 3 HOURS 30 MINUTES **SERVES** 12

2½ cups (375g) white plain (all-purpose) flour

2⅔ cups (420g) rye flour

2 teaspoons sea salt

1 teaspoon bicarbonate of soda (baking soda)

2¾ cups (680ml) buttermilk, approximately

1 Oil the insert bowl of a 4.5-litre (18-cup) slow cooker; preheat cooker on high for 30 minutes.

2 Meanwhile, sift flours, salt and soda into a large bowl; stir in enough of the buttermilk to make a firm dough.

3 Turn dough onto a floured surface; knead lightly until smooth. Shape dough into a 20cm (8-inch) round. Brush with a little extra buttermilk, sprinkle with a little extra flour; cut 1cm (½ inch) deep scores, in a criss-cross pattern, in top of dough.

4 Carefully lift dough round into cooker. Cook, covered, on high, for 3 hours or until bread sounds hollow when tapped with fingers.

5 Preheat grill (broiler).

6 Carefully turn bread, top-side up, onto an oven tray. Cook under grill for 5 minutes or until browned lightly.

TIP
Bread is best made on day of serving or reheat, wrapped in foil, in the oven for 15 minutes or until warmed through.

SERVING SUGGESTION
Accompany with butter and any spread you like; or serve with soups and stews.

• Suitable to freeze at the end of step 6.

STOCKS

CHICKEN

PREP + COOK TIME 2 HOURS 15 MINUTES
MAKES 3.5 LITRES (14 CUPS)

2kg (4 pounds) chicken bones

2 medium onions (300g),
chopped coarsely

2 celery stalks (300g), trimmed,
chopped coarsely

2 medium carrots (240g),
chopped coarsely

3 bay leaves

2 teaspoons black peppercorns

5 litres (20 cups) water

1 Combine ingredients in a large
saucepan or stockpot; bring to the boil.
Reduce heat; simmer, uncovered, about
2 hours, skimming surface occasionally.

2 Strain stock through a fine sieve into
a large heatproof bowl; discard solids.
If not using immediately, cool slightly,
then refrigerate stock to cool completely.
Skim and discard surface fat before using.
Store, refrigerated, for up to 1 week or
freeze for up to 1 month. Bring to the
boil before using.

BEEF

PREP + COOK TIME 5 HOURS 15 MINUTES
MAKES 3.5 LITRES (14 CUPS)

2kg (4 pounds) meaty beef bones

2 medium brown onions (300g),
chopped coarsely

5.5 litres water (22 cups)

2 celery stalks (300g), trimmed,
chopped coarsely

2 medium carrots (240g),
chopped coarsely

3 bay leaves

2 teaspoons black peppercorns

3 litres water (12 cups), extra

1 Preheat oven to 200°C/400°F.

2 Roast bones for 1 hour or until
browned.

3 Transfer bones to a large saucepan or
stockpot. Add onion, the water, vegetables,
bay leaves and peppercorns; bring to the
boil. Reduce heat; simmer, uncovered, about
3 hours, skimming surface occasionally.
Add extra water; simmer, uncovered,
about 1 hour.

4 Strain stock through a fine sieve into
a large heatproof bowl; discard solids.
If not using immediately, cool slightly,
then refrigerate stock to cool completely.
Skim and discard surface fat before using.
Store, refrigerated, for up to 1 week or
freeze for up to 1 month. Bring to the boil
before using.

VEGETABLE

PREP + COOK TIME 1 HOUR 45 MINUTES
MAKES 3.5 LITRES (14 CUPS)

2 large carrots (360g),
chopped coarsely

2 large parsnips (700g),
chopped coarsely

4 medium onions (600g),
chopped coarsely

10 celery stalks (1.5kg), trimmed,
chopped coarsely

4 bay leaves

2 teaspoons black peppercorns

6 litres (24 cups) water

1 Combine ingredients in a large
saucepan or stockpot; bring to the boil.
Reduce heat; simmer, uncovered, about
1½ hours, skimming surface occasionally.

2 Strain stock through a fine sieve into
a large heatproof bowl; discard solids.
If not using immediately, cool slightly,
then refrigerate to cool completely. Store,
refrigerated, for up to 1 week or freeze
for up to 1 month.

GLOSSARY

ALLSPICE also called pimento or jamaican pepper; tastes like a combination of nutmeg, cumin, clove and cinnamon. Available whole or ground.

ALMONDS flat, pointy-tipped nuts having a pitted brown shell enclosing a creamy white kernel which is covered by a brown skin.

flaked paper-thin slices.

slivered small pieces cut lengthways.

ANCHOVIES small oily fish. Anchovy fillets are preserved and packed in oil or salt in small cans or jars, and are strong in flavour. Fresh anchovies are much milder in flavour.

BARLEY a nutritious grain used in soups and stews. Hulled barley, the least processed, is high in fibre. Pearl barley has had the husk removed then been steamed and polished so that only the 'pearl' of the original grain remains, much the same as white rice.

BASIL

sweet the most common type of basil; used extensively in Italian dishes and one of the main ingredients in pesto.

thai also known as horapa; different from holy basil and sweet basil in both look and taste, with smaller leaves and purplish stems. It has a slight aniseed taste and is one of the identifying flavours of Thai food.

BAY LEAVES aromatic leaves from the bay tree available fresh or dried; adds a strong, slightly peppery flavour.

BEANS

black also called turtle beans or black kidney beans; an earthy-flavoured dried bean completely different from the better-known Chinese black beans (fermented soybeans). Used mostly in Mexican and South American cooking.

black-eyed also called black-eyed peas or cow peas. Mild-flavoured and thin-skinned, so they cook faster than most other beans.

butter cans labelled butter beans are, in fact, cannellini beans. Confusingly butter is also another name for lima beans, sold both dried and canned; a large beige bean having a mealy texture and mild taste.

cannellini a small white bean similar in appearance and flavour to other white beans (great northern, navy or haricot), all of which can be substituted for the other. Available dried or canned.

green also known as french or string beans, this long thin fresh bean is consumed in its entirety once cooked.

sprouts tender new growths of assorted beans and seeds germinated for consumption as sprouts.

BEETROOT (BEETS) firm, round root vegetable.

BICARBONATE OF SODA (BAKING SODA) a raising agent.

BUCKWHEAT a herb in the same plant family as rhubarb; not a cereal so it is gluten-free. Available as flour; ground (cracked) into coarse, medium or fine granules (kasha) and used similarly to polenta; or groats, the whole kernel sold roasted as a cereal product.

BUK CHOY also known as bok choy, pak choi, Chinese white cabbage or Chinese chard; has a fresh, mild mustard taste. Use stems and leaves, stir-fried or braised. Baby buk choy, also known as pak kat farang or shanghai bok choy, is much smaller and more tender. Its mildly acrid, distinctively appealing taste has made it one of the most commonly used Asian greens.

BUTTER use salted or unsalted (sweet) butter; 125g (4 ounces) is equal to one stick of butter.

BUTTERMILK originally the term given to the slightly sour liquid left after butter was churned from cream, today it is made from no-fat or low-fat milk to which specific bacterial cultures have been added. Despite its name, it is actually low in fat.

CAPSICUM (BELL PEPPER) also called pepper. Comes in many colours: red, green, yellow, orange and purplish-black. Be sure to discard seeds and membranes before use.

CARAWAY SEEDS the small, half-moon-shaped dried seed from a member of the parsley family; adds a sharp anise flavour when used in both sweet and savoury dishes.

CARDAMOM a spice native to India and used extensively in its cuisine; can be purchased in pod, seed or ground form. Has a distinctive aromatic, sweetly rich flavour.

CELERIAC (CELERY ROOT) tuberous root with knobbly brown skin, white flesh and a celery-like flavour. Keep peeled celeriac in acidulated water to stop it discolouring.

CHEESE

bocconcini walnut-sized, baby mozzarella; a delicate, semi-soft, white cheese traditionally made from buffalo milk. Sold fresh, it spoils rapidly so will only keep, refrigerated in brine, for 1 or 2 days at the most.

cheddar the most common cows' milk 'tasty' cheese; should be aged, hard and have a pronounced bite.

fetta Greek in origin; a crumbly textured goat- or sheep-milk cheese having a sharp, salty taste. Ripened and stored in salted whey; particularly good cubed and tossed into salads.

fetta, persian a soft, creamy fetta marinated in a blend of olive oil, garlic, herbs and spices; available from most major supermarkets.

parmesan also called parmigiano; is a hard, grainy cow-milk cheese originating in the Parma region of Italy.

pizza cheese a commercial blend of varying proportions of processed grated mozzarella, cheddar and parmesan.

CHICKPEAS (GARBANZO BEANS) also called hummus or channa; an irregularly round, sandy-coloured legume used extensively in Mediterranean, Indian and Hispanic cooking. Firm texture even after cooking, a floury mouth-feel and robust nutty flavour; available canned or dried (reconstitute for several hours in cold water before use).

CHILLI
cayenne pepper a thin-fleshed, long, extremely hot dried red chilli, usually purchased ground.
chipotle pronounced cheh-pote-lay. The name used for jalapeño chillies once they've been dried and smoked. Having a deep, intensely smokey flavour, rather than a searing heat, chipotles are dark brown, almost black in colour and wrinkled in appearance.
flakes also sold as crushed chilli; dehydrated deep-red extremely fine slices and whole seeds.
green any unripened chilli; also some particular varieties that are ripe when green, such as jalapeño, habanero, poblano or serrano.
long red available both fresh and dried; a generic term used for any moderately hot, long, thin chilli (about 6cm to 8cm long).
powder the Asian variety is the hottest, made from dried ground thai chillies; can be used instead of fresh in the proportion of ½ teaspoon chilli powder to 1 medium chopped fresh red chilli.
thai (serrano) also known as "scuds"; tiny, very hot and bright red in colour.
CHINESE COOKING WINE also called shao hsing or chinese rice wine; made from fermented rice, wheat, sugar and salt with a 13.5 per cent alcohol content. Inexpensive and found in Asian food shops; if you can't find it, replace with mirin or sherry.
CHINESE SAUSAGE, DRIED also called lap cheong; highly spiced, bright red, thin pork sausages. The meat is preserved by the high spice content and can be kept at room temperature.
CHORIZO sausage of Spanish origin, made of coarsely ground pork and highly seasoned with garlic and chilli. They are deeply smoked, very spicy and dry-cured so that they do not need cooking.
CHOY SUM also known as pakaukeo or flowering cabbage, a member of the buk choy family; easy to identify with its long stems, light green leaves and yellow flowers. Stems and leaves are both edible, steamed or stir-fried.
CINNAMON available both in the piece (called sticks or quills) and ground into powder; one of the world's most common spices, used universally as a sweet, fragrant flavouring for both sweet and savoury foods.
CLOVES dried flower buds of a tropical tree; can be used whole or in ground form. They have a strong scent and taste so should be used sparingly.
COCONUT
desiccated concentrated, dried, unsweetened and finely shredded coconut flesh.
flaked dried flaked coconut flesh.
milk not the liquid found inside the fruit (coconut water), but the diluted liquid from the second pressing of the white flesh of a mature coconut (the first pressing produces coconut cream). Available in cans and cartons at most supermarkets.

water is the liquid from the centre of a young green coconut. It has fewer kilojoules than fruit juice, with no fat or protein. There are sugars present, but these are slowly absorbed giving coconut water a low GI.
CORIANDER (CILANTRO) also called pak chee or chinese parsley; bright-green-leafed herb with a pungent flavour. The leaves, stems and roots of coriander are also used. Also available ground or as seeds; these should not be substituted for fresh coriander as the tastes are completely different.
CORNFLOUR (CORNSTARCH) available made from corn or wheat (wheaten cornflour, gluten-free, gives a lighter texture in cakes); used as a thickening agent in cooking.
CREAM
pouring also called pure or fresh cream. It has no additives and contains a minimum fat content of 35 per cent.
thickened (heavy) a whipping cream containing thickener. Minimum fat content 35 per cent.
CRÈME FRAÎCHE a mature, naturally fermented cream (minimum fat content 35 per cent) having a velvety texture and slightly tangy, nutty flavour.
CUMIN also known as zeera or comino; resembling caraway in size, cumin is the dried seed of a plant related to the parsley family.
CURRY PASTES Some recipes in this book call for commercially prepared pastes of varying strengths and flavours. Use whichever one you feel best suits your spice-level tolerance.
massaman has a rich, spicy flavour reminiscent of Middle Eastern cooking; favoured by southern Thai cooks for use in hot and sour stew-like curries and satay sauces.
rogan josh a medium-hot blend that is a specialty of Kashmir in northern India. It contains tomatoes, fenugreek, coriander, paprika and cumin.
FENNEL also called finocchio or anise; a crunchy green vegetable slightly resembling celery that's eaten raw in salads; fried as an accompaniment; or used as an ingredient in soups and sauces. Also the name given to the dried seeds of the plant which have a stronger licorice flavour.
FIVE-SPICE POWDER (CHINESE FIVE-SPICE) a fragrant mixture of ground cinnamon, cloves, star anise, sichuan pepper and fennel seeds.
FLOUR
plain (all-purpose) unbleached wheat flour, the best for baking: the gluten content ensures a strong dough, for a light result.
self-raising all-purpose plain or wholemeal flour with baking powder and salt added; make at home in the proportion of 1 cup plain or wholemeal flour to 2 teaspoons baking powder.

GAI LAN also known as chinese broccoli, gai larn, kanah, gai lum and chinese kale; appreciated more for its stems than its coarse leaves.

GALANGAL a rhizome with a hot ginger-citrusy flavour; used similarly to ginger and garlic. Use fresh ginger if unavailable.

GARAM MASALA a blend of spices including cardamom, cinnamon, cloves, coriander, fennel and cumin, roasted and ground together.

GINGER

fresh also called green or root ginger; the thick gnarled root of a tropical plant.

ground also called powdered ginger; used as a flavouring in baking but cannot be substituted for fresh ginger.

KAFFIR LIME LEAVES also known as bai magrood and looks like two glossy dark green leaves joined end to end, forming a rounded hourglass shape. Used fresh or dried in many South-East Asian dishes, they are used like bay leaves or curry leaves, especially in Thai cooking. Sold fresh, dried or frozen, the dried leaves are less potent so double the number if using them as a substitute for fresh; a strip of fresh lime peel may be substituted for each kaffir lime leaf.

LEEK a member of the onion family, the leek resembles a green onion but is much larger and more subtle in flavour.

LEMON GRASS also known as takrai, serai or serah. A tall, clumping, lemon-smelling and tasting, sharp-edged aromatic tropical grass; the white lower part of the stem is used, finely chopped, in many South-East Asian dishes.

LENTILS (red, brown, yellow) dried pulses often identified by and named after their colour. Eaten by cultures all over the world, most famously perhaps in the dhals of India, lentils have high food value.

French-style green lentils related to the famous Fench lentils du puy; these green-blue, tiny lentils have a nutty, earthy flavour and a hardy nature that allows them to be rapidly cooked without disintegrating.

MAPLE SYRUP also called pure maple syrup; distilled from the sap of sugar maple trees found only in Canada and the USA. Maple-flavoured syrup or pancake syrup is not an adequate substitute for the real thing.

MAYONNAISE commercial mayonnaise of high quality made with whole eggs and labelled as such; some prepared mayonnaises substitute emulsifiers such as food starch, cellulose gel or other thickeners to mimic the same thick and creamy consistency but never achieve the same rich flavour. Must be refrigerated once opened.

MINT the most commonly used variety of mint is spearmint; it has pointed, bright-green leaves and a fresh flavour.

MUSHROOMS

button small, cultivated white mushrooms with a mild flavour.

portobello mature, fully opened swiss browns; large, dark brown mushrooms with full-bodied flavour; ideal for filling or barbecuing.

shiitake when fresh are also known as chinese black, forest or golden oak mushrooms. Large, meaty and, although cultivated, have the earthiness and taste of wild mushrooms.

swiss brown also known as roman or cremini. Light to dark brown mushrooms with full-bodied flavour; suited for use in casseroles or being stuffed and baked.

MUSLIN inexpensive, undyed, finely woven cotton fabric called for in cooking to strain stocks and sauces; if unavailable, use a clean chux or linen tea towel.

MUSTARD

dijon pale brown, distinctively flavoured, fairly mild-tasting french mustard.

wholegrain also known as seeded. A French-style coarse-grain mustard made from crushed mustard seeds and dijon-style french mustard.

MUSTARD SEEDS, BLACK also known as brown mustard seeds; more pungent than the white variety; used frequently in curries.

OIL

olive made from ripened olives. Extra virgin and virgin are the first and second press, respectively, of the olives and are therefore considered the best; 'light' refers to taste not fat levels.

peanut pressed from ground peanuts; most commonly used oil in Asian cooking because of its high smoke point (capacity to handle high heat without burning).

vegetable oils sourced from plant rather than animal fats.

ONIONS

baby also called pickling and cocktail onions; are baby brown onions but are larger than shallots.

brown and white interchangeable; white onions have a more pungent flesh.

green (scallions) also called, incorrectly, shallot; an immature onion picked before the bulb has formed, has a long, bright-green edible stalk.

red also known as spanish, red spanish or bermuda onion; a sweet-flavoured, large, purple-red onion.

PAPRIKA ground, dried, sweet red capsicum (bell pepper); there are many grades and types available, including sweet, hot, mild and smoked.

PASSATA sieved tomato puree. To substitute, puree and sieve canned tomatoes or use canned tomato puree which is similar, but slightly thicker.

PINE NUTS also known as pignoli; not a nut but a small, cream-coloured kernel from pine cones. They are best roasted before use to bring out the flavour.

POLENTA also known as cornmeal; a ground, flour-like cereal made of dried corn (maize) sold in several different textures. Also the name of the dish made from it.

POMEGRANATE dark-red, leathery-skinned fresh fruit about the size of an orange filled with hundreds of seeds, each wrapped in an edible lucent-crimson pulp having a unique tangy sweet-sour flavour.

molasses not to be confused with pomegranate syrup or grenadine; pomegranate molasses is thicker, browner, and more concentrated in flavour – tart and sharp, slightly sweet and fruity.

QUINCE yellow-skinned fruit with a hard texture and astringent, tart taste; eaten cooked or as a preserve. Long, slow cooking makes the flesh a deep rose pink.

SAFFRON stigma of a member of the crocus family, available ground or in strands; imparts a yellow-orange colour to food once infused. The quality can vary greatly; the best is the most expensive spice in the world. Should be stored in the freezer.

SAUCES

fish also called nam pla or nuoc nam; made from pulverised salted fermented fish, most often anchovies. Has a very pungent smell and strong taste, so use according to your taste level.

soy also known as sieu; made from fermented soya beans. Several variations are available in most supermarkets and Asian food stores. We use a mild Japanese variety in our recipes.

Tabasco brand name of an extremely fiery sauce made from vinegar, thai red chillies and salt.

worcestershire this dark-coloured condiment is made from garlic, lime, soy sauce, tamarind, onions, molasses, anchovies, vinegar and seasonings.

SESAME SEEDS black and white are the most common of this small oval seed, however there are also red and brown varieties. The seeds are used in cuisines the world over as an ingredient and as a condiment.

STAR ANISE dried star-shaped pod with an astringent aniseed flavour; used to flavour stocks and marinades. Available whole and ground, it is an essential ingredient in five-spice powder.

STERLISING JARS

It's important the jars be as clean as possible; make sure your hands, the preparation area, tea towels and cloths etc, are clean, too. The aim is to finish sterilising the jars and lids at the same time the preserve is ready to be bottled; the hot preserve should be bottled into hot, dry clean jars. Jars that aren't sterilised properly can cause deterioration of the preserves during storage. Always start with cleaned washed jars and lids, then follow one of these methods:

(1) Put jars and lids through the hottest cycle of a dishwasher without using any detergent.

(2) Lie jars down in a boiler with the lids, cover them with cold water then cover the boiler with a lid. Bring the water to the boil over a high heat and boil the jars for 20 minutes.

(3) Stand jars upright, without touching each other, on a wooden board on the lowest shelf in the oven. Turn the oven to the lowest possible temperature; leave jars to heat for 30 minutes. Remove the jars from the oven or dishwasher with a towel, or from the boiling water with tongs and rubber-gloved hands; the water will evaporate from hot wet jars quite quickly. Stand jars upright and not touching on a wooden board, or a bench covered with a towel to protect and insulate the bench. Fill the jars as directed in the recipe; secure the lids tightly, holding jars firmly with a towel or an oven mitt. Leave at room temperature to cool before storing.

SUGAR

caster (superfine) finely granulated table sugar.

brown a soft, finely granulated sugar retaining molasses for its characteristic colour and flavour.

palm also called nam tan pip, jaggery, jawa or gula melaka; made from the sap of the sugar palm tree. Light brown to black in colour and usually sold in rock-hard cakes; use light brown sugar if unavailable..

white (granulated) coarse, granulated table sugar, also known as crystal sugar.

TAMARIND PASTE the distillation of tamarind pulp into a condensed compacted paste with a sweet-sour, slightly astringent taste. Thick and purple-black, it requires no soaking. Found in Asian food stores.

VINEGAR

balsamic originally from Modena, Italy, there are now many balsamic vinegars on the market ranging in pungency and quality depending on how, and for how long, they have been aged. Made from the juice of Trebbiano grapes; it is a deep rich brown colour with a sweet and sour flavour. Quality can be determined up to a point by price; use the most expensive sparingly.

cider (apple cider) made from crushed fermented apples.

rice a colourless vinegar made from fermented rice and flavoured with sugar and salt. Sherry can be substituted.

white made from the spirit of cane sugar.

white wine made from a blend of white wines.

YOGHURT, GREEK-STYLE often made from sheep milk that is strained in a cloth (traditionally muslin) to remove the whey and to give it a thick, smooth, creamy consistency, almost like whipped cream.

CONVERSION CHART

MEASURES

One Australian metric measuring cup holds approximately 250ml; one Australian metric tablespoon holds 20ml; one Australian metric teaspoon holds 5ml.

The difference between one country's measuring cups and another's is within a two- or three-teaspoon variance, and will not affect your cooking results. North America, New Zealand and the United Kingdom use a 15ml tablespoon.

All cup and spoon measurements are level. The most accurate way of measuring dry ingredients is to weigh them. When measuring liquids, use a clear glass or plastic jug with the metric markings.

The imperial measurements used in these recipes are approximate only. Measurements for cake pans are approximate only. Using same-shaped cake pans of a similar size should not affect the outcome of your baking. We measure the inside top of the cake pan to determine sizes.

We use large eggs with an average weight of 60g.

DRY MEASURES

METRIC	IMPERIAL
15G	½OZ
30G	1OZ
60G	2OZ
90G	3OZ
125G	4OZ (¼LB)
155G	5OZ
185G	6OZ
220G	7OZ
250G	8OZ (½LB)
280G	9OZ
315G	10OZ
345G	11OZ
375G	12OZ (¾LB)
410G	13OZ
440G	14OZ
470G	15OZ
500G	16OZ (1LB)
750G	24OZ (1½LB)
1KG	32OZ (2LB)

LIQUID MEASURES

METRIC	IMPERIAL
30ML	1 FLUID OZ
60ML	2 FLUID OZ
100ML	3 FLUID OZ
125ML	4 FLUID OZ
150ML	5 FLUID OZ
190ML	6 FLUID OZ
250ML	8 FLUID OZ
300ML	10 FLUID OZ
500ML	16 FLUID OZ
600ML	20 FLUID OZ
1000ML (1 LITRE)	1¾ PINTS

LENGTH MEASURES

METRIC	IMPERIAL
3MM	⅛IN
6MM	¼IN
1CM	½IN
2CM	¾IN
2.5CM	1IN
5CM	2IN
6CM	2½IN
8CM	3IN
10CM	4IN
13CM	5IN
15CM	6IN
18CM	7IN
20CM	8IN
22CM	9IN
25CM	10IN
28CM	11IN
30CM	12IN (1FT)

OVEN TEMPERATURES

The oven temperatures in this book are for conventional ovens; if you have a fan-forced oven, decrease the temperature by 10-20 degrees.

	°C (CELSIUS)	°F (FAHRENHEIT)
VERY SLOW	120	250
SLOW	150	300
MODERATELY SLOW	160	325
MODERATE	180	350
MODERATELY HOT	200	400
HOT	220	425
VERY HOT	240	475

INDEX